WON TON SOUP 2

BY
JAMES STOKOE

Story & Art James Stokoe

Edited by James Lucas Jones & Douglas Sherwood

Digital Production by Steven Birch @ Servo

Published by Oni Press, Inc.

Publisher Joe Nozemack

Editor in chief James Lucas Jones

Managing editor Randal C. Jarrell

Marketing Director Cory Casoni

Art Director Keith Wood

Assistant Editor Jill Beaton

Production Assistant Douglas E. Sherwood

Oni Press, Inc.
1305 SE Martin Luther King Blvd.
Suite A
Portland, OR 97214

Wonton Soup Volume 2
First Edition: May 2009
ISBN 978-1-934964-20-0

www.onipress.com

1 3 5 7 9 10 8 6 4 2
PRINTED IN CANADA

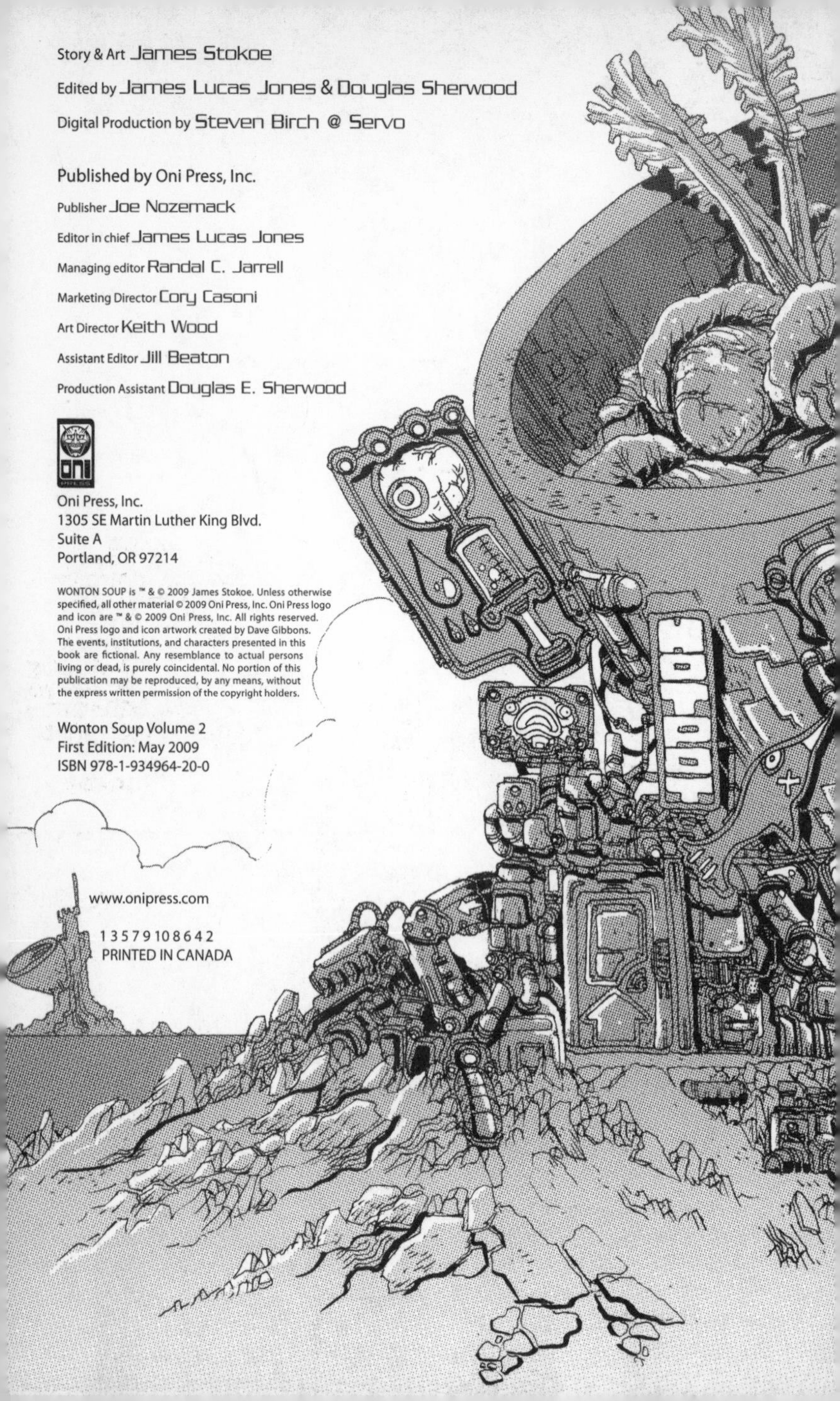
HOTPOT

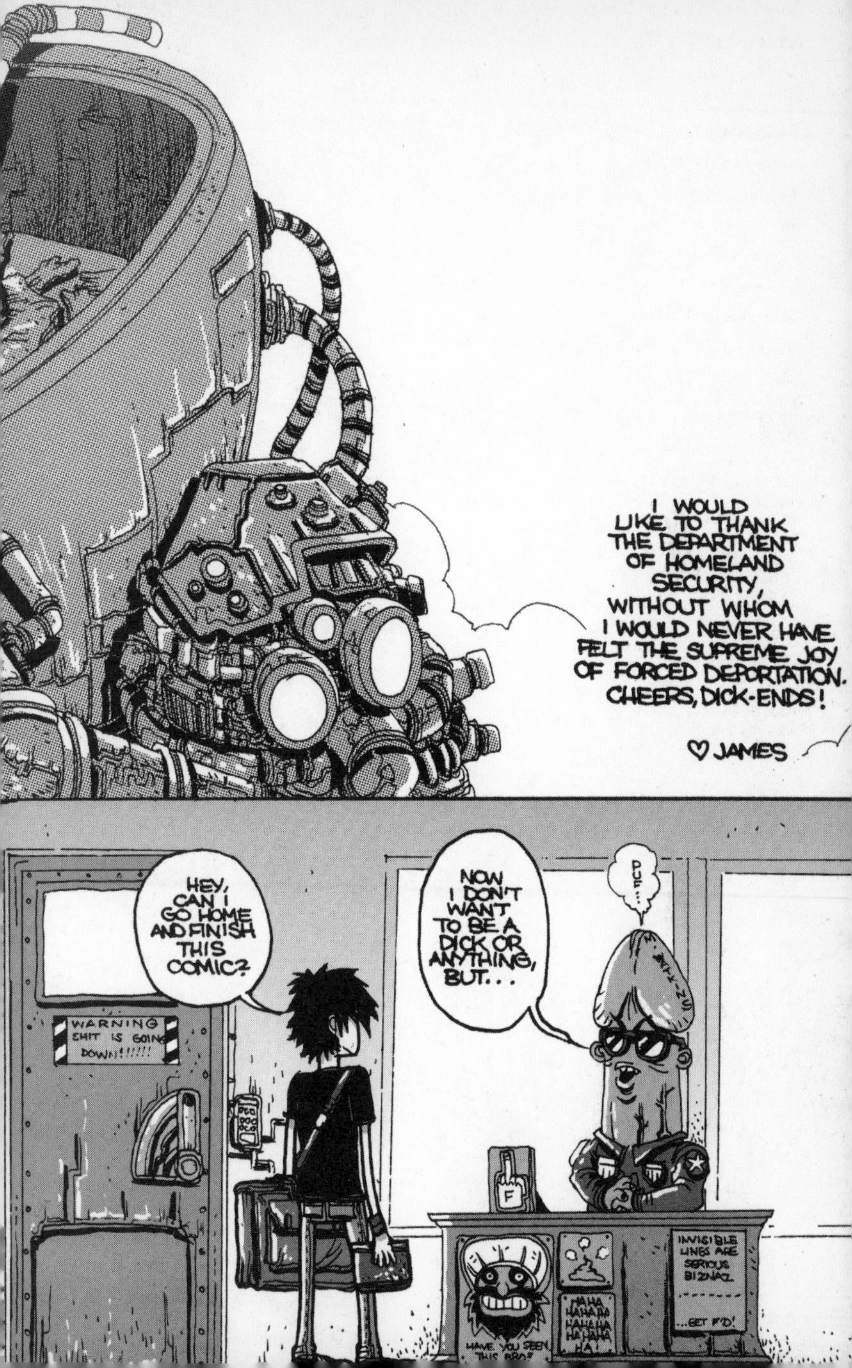
I WOULD LIKE TO THANK THE DEPARTMENT OF HOMELAND SECURITY, WITHOUT WHOM I WOULD NEVER HAVE FELT THE SUPREME JOY OF FORCED DEPORTATION. CHEERS, DICK-ENDS!
♡ JAMES
HEY, CAN I GO HOME AND FINISH THIS COMIC?
NOW I DON'T WANT TO BE A DICK OR ANYTHING, BUT...
PUF...
WARNING
SHIT IS GOING DOWN!!!!!!
F
INVISIBLE LINES ARE SERIOUS BIZNAZ
...GET F'D!
HAHA HAHAHA HAHAHA HAHAHA HA!
HAVE YOU SEEN THIS BRO?

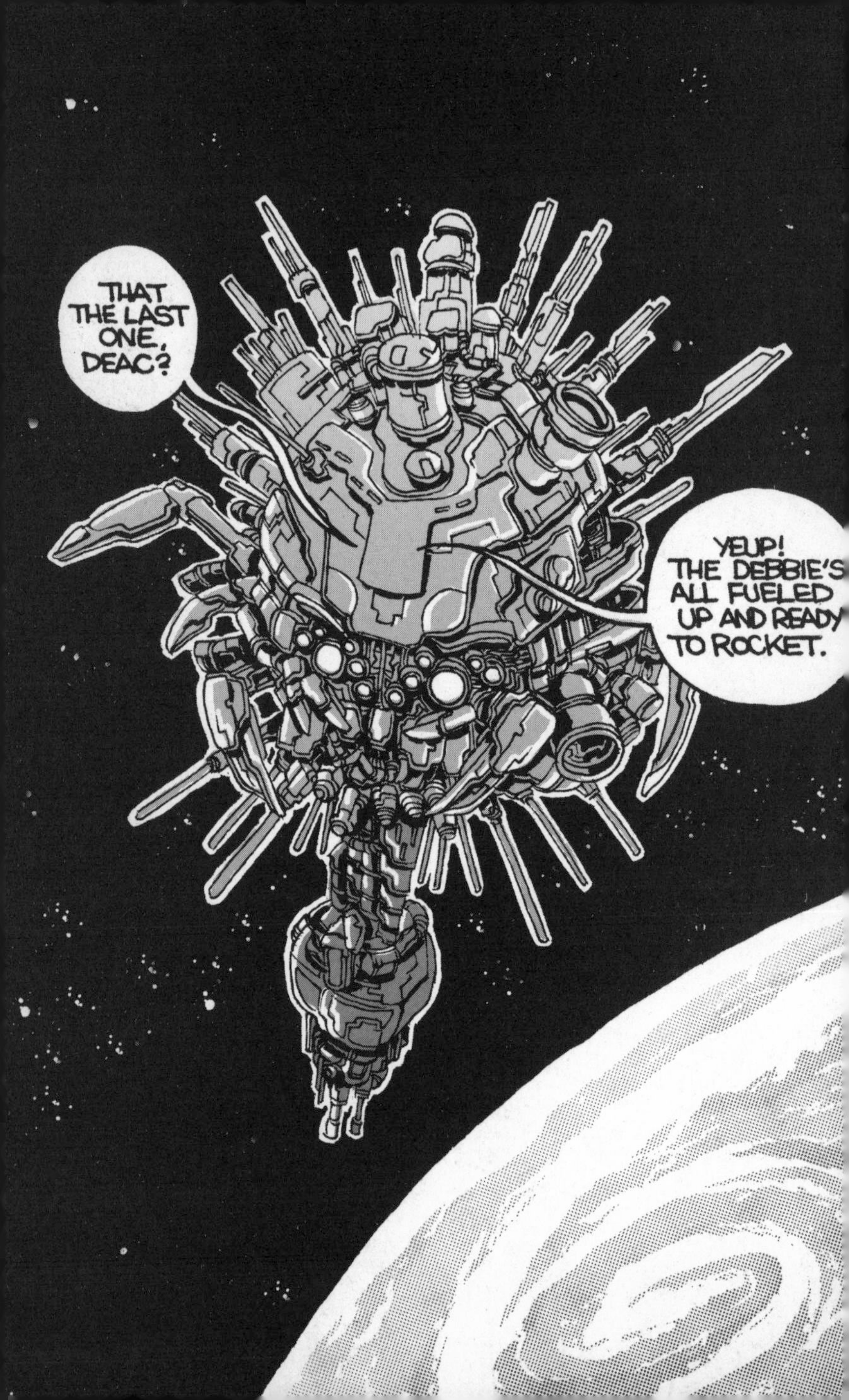
THAT THE LAST ONE, DEAC?
YEUP! THE DEBBIE'S ALL FUELED UP AND READY TO ROCKET.

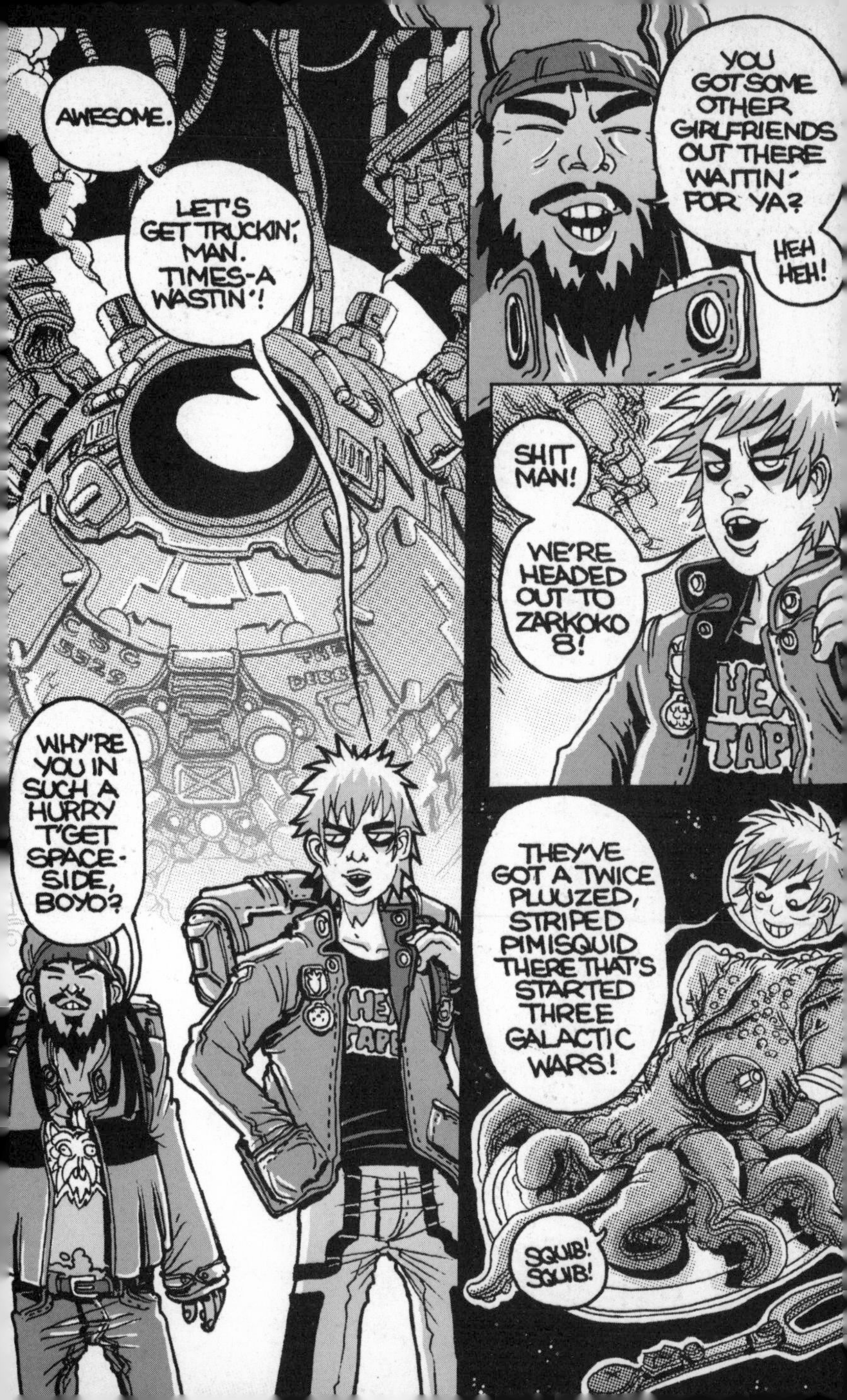
AWESOME.
LET'S GET TRUCKIN', MAN. TIMES-A WASTIN'!
WHY'RE YOU IN SUCH A HURRY T'GET SPACE-SIDE, BOYO?
YOU GOT SOME OTHER GIRLFRIENDS OUT THERE WAITIN' FOR YA?
HEH HEH!
SHIT MAN!
WE'RE HEADED OUT TO ZARKOKO 8!
THEY'VE GOT A TWICE PLUUZED, STRIPED PIMISQUID THERE THAT'S STARTED THREE GALACTIC WARS!
SQUIB! SQUIB!

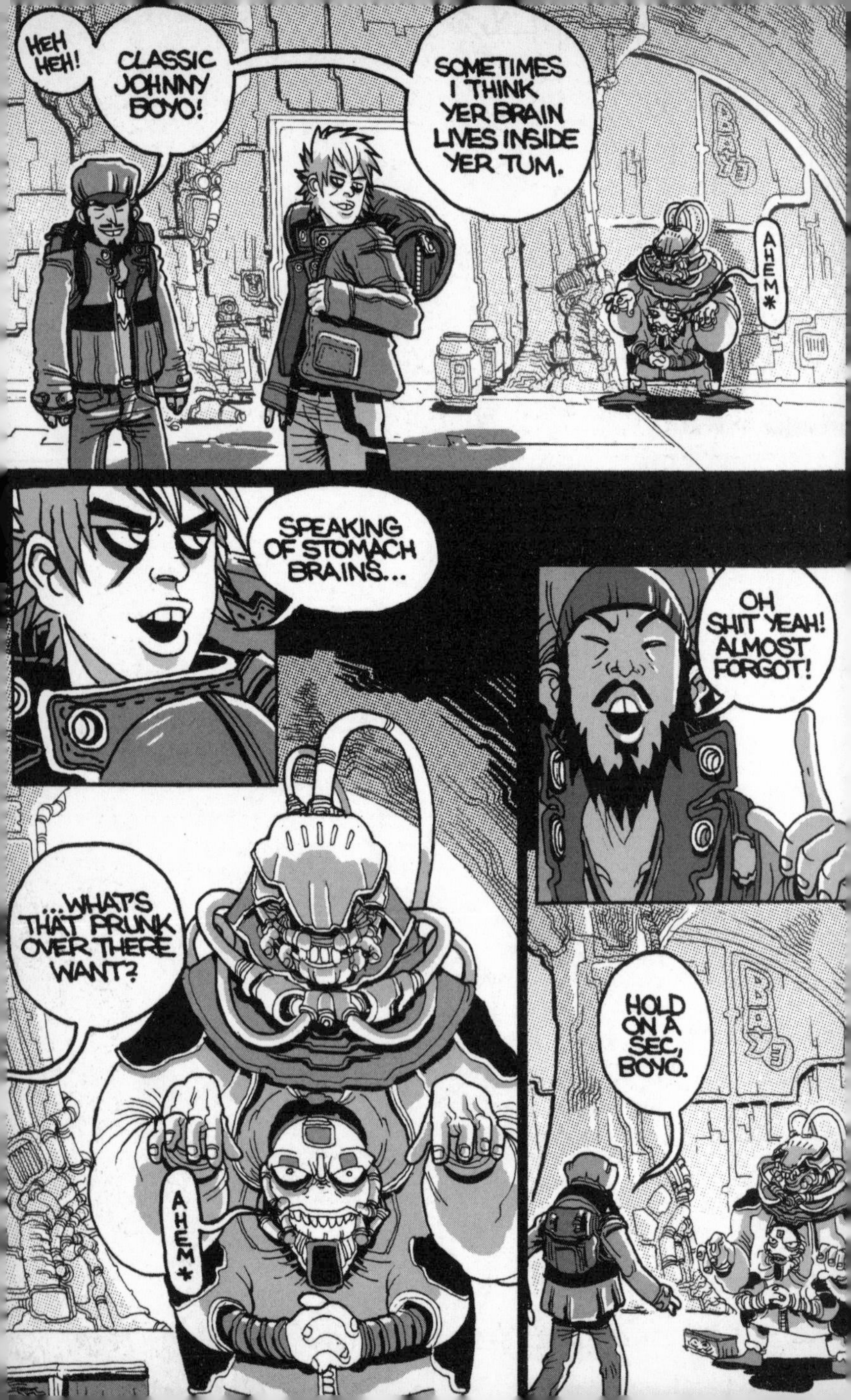
HEH HEH!
CLASSIC JOHNNY BOYO!
SOMETIMES I THINK YER BRAIN LIVES INSIDE YER TUM.
AHEM*
SPEAKING OF STOMACH BRAINS...
OH SHIT YEAH! ALMOST FORGOT!
...WHAT'S THAT PRUNK OVER THERE WANT?
AHEM*
HOLD ON A SEC, BOYO.

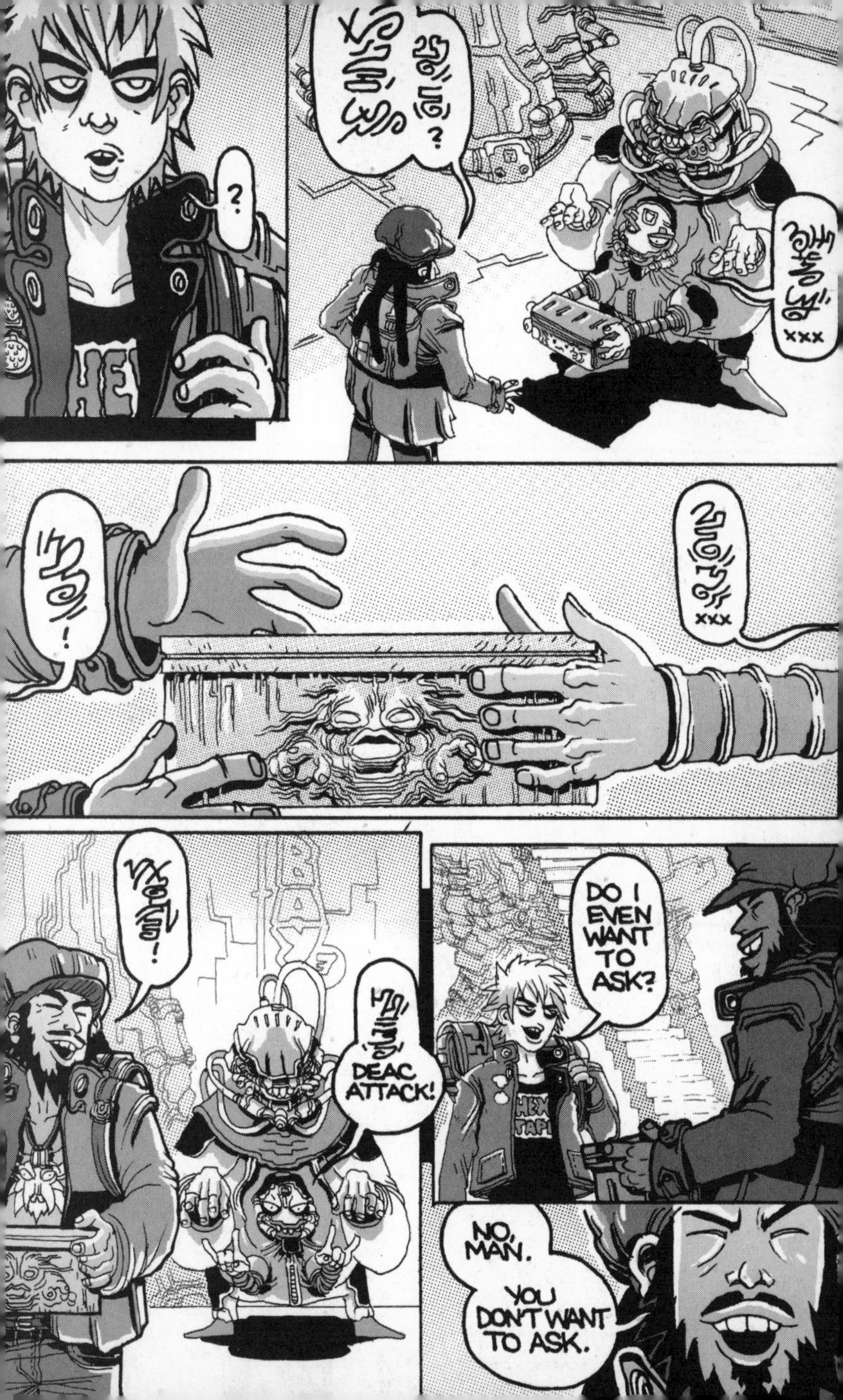
?
XXX
XXX
DEAC ATTACK!
DO I EVEN WANT TO ASK?
NO, MAN.
YOU DON'T WANT TO ASK.

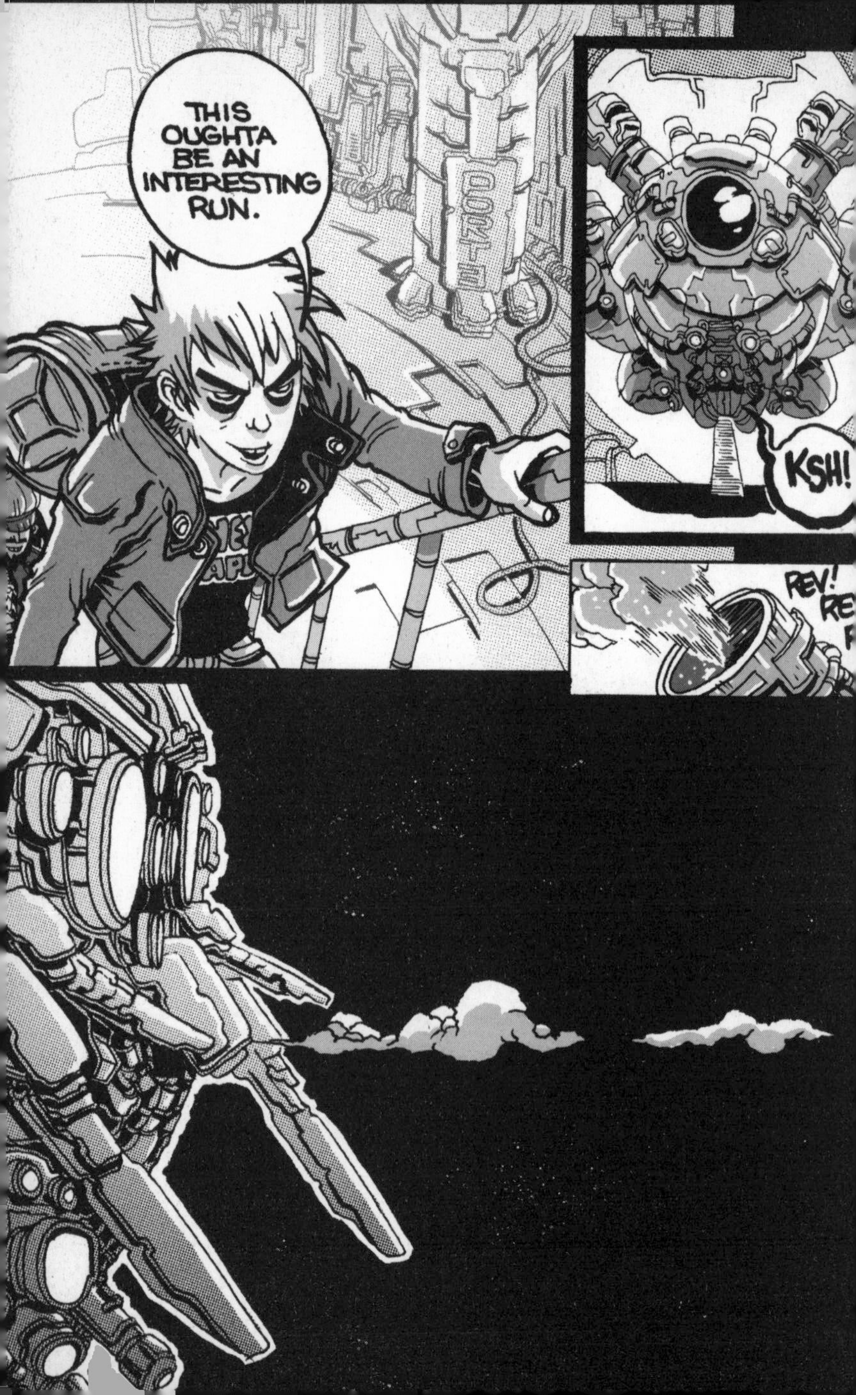
THIS OUGHTA BE AN INTERESTING RUN.
KSH!
REV!

KSH!
KSH!

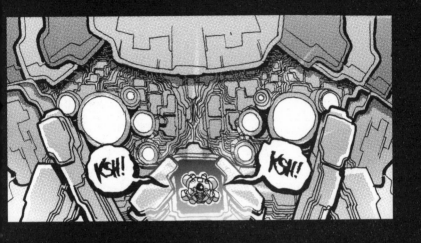

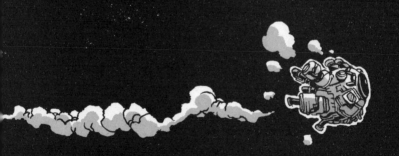

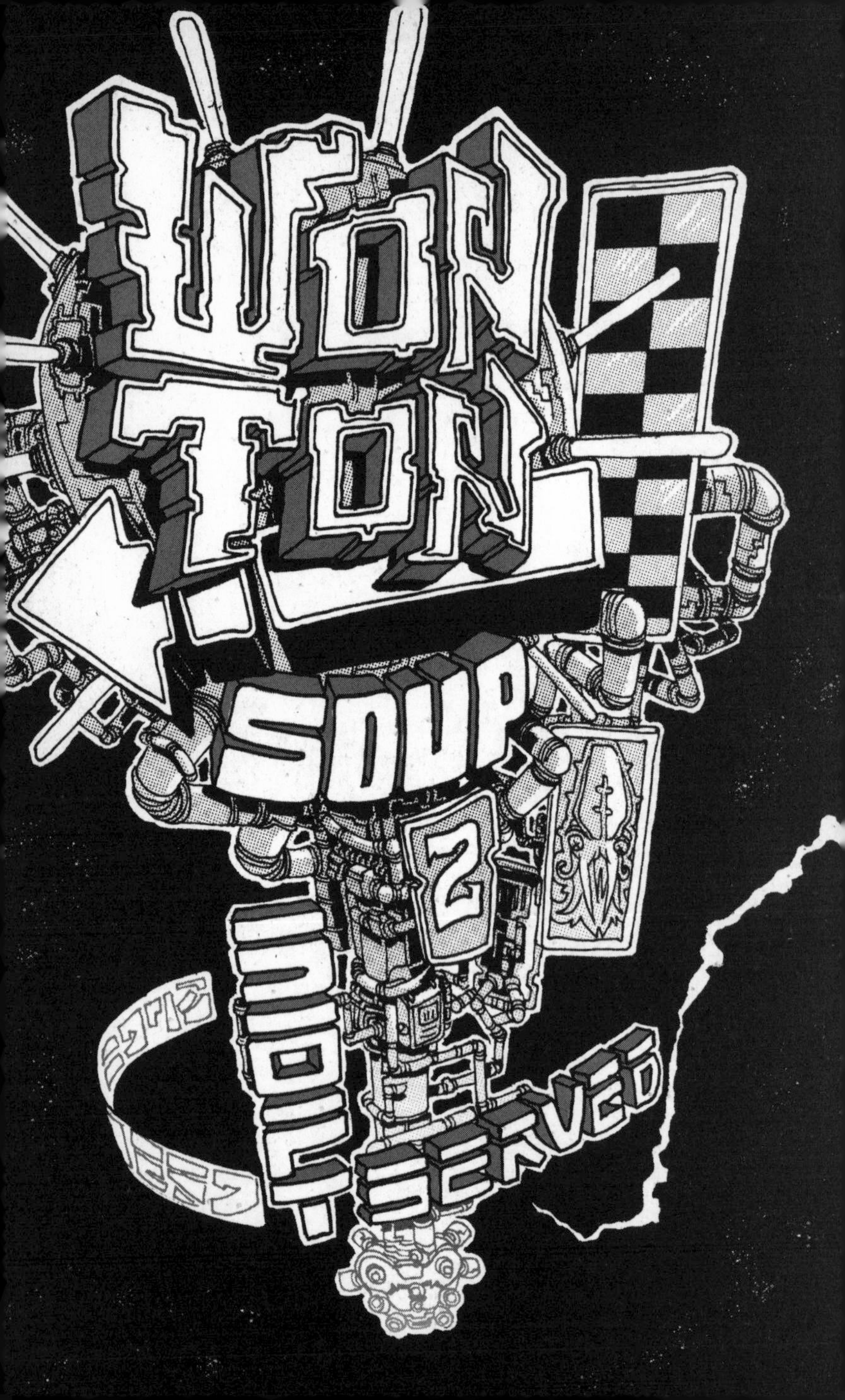
WON TON
SOUP
2
SERVED

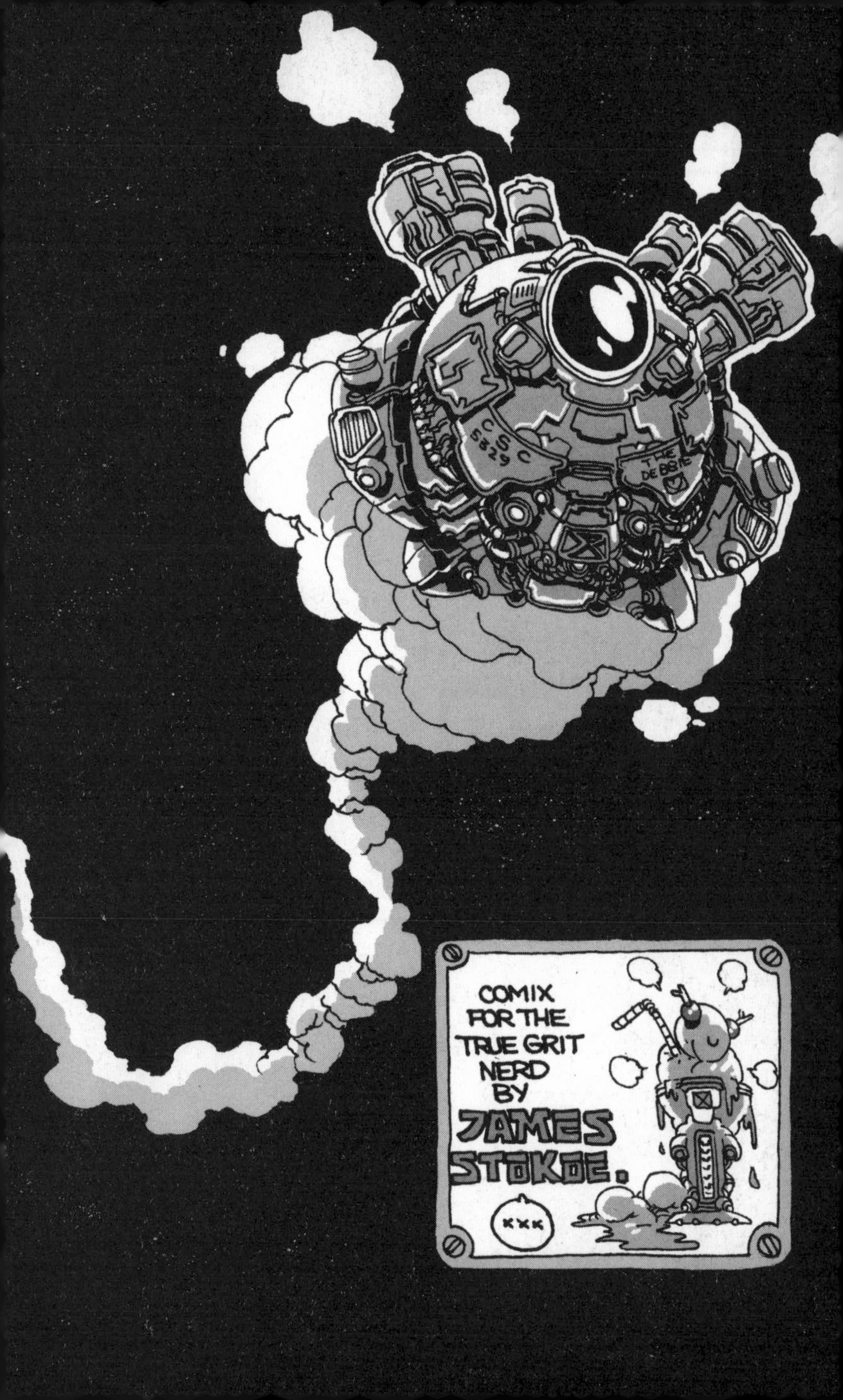
CSC
S829
THE DEBBIE
COMIX
FOR THE
TRUE GRIT
NERD
BY
JAMES
STOKOE.

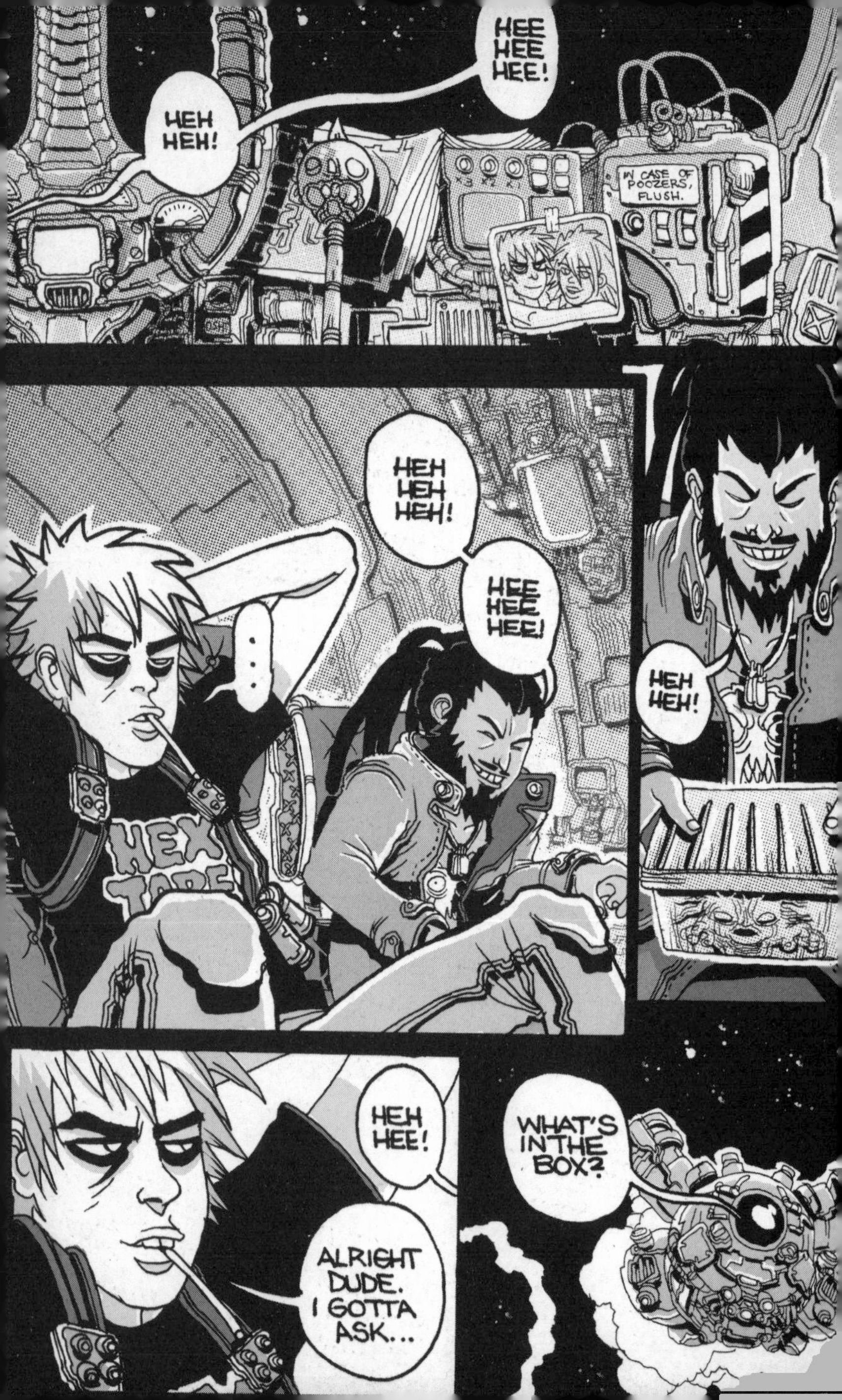
HEH HEH!
HEE HEE HEE!
IN CASE OF POOZERS, FLUSH.
HEH HEH HEH!
HEE HEE HEE!
...
HEH HEH!
HEX TAPE
HEH HEE!
ALRIGHT DUDE. I GOTTA ASK...
WHAT'S IN THE BOX?

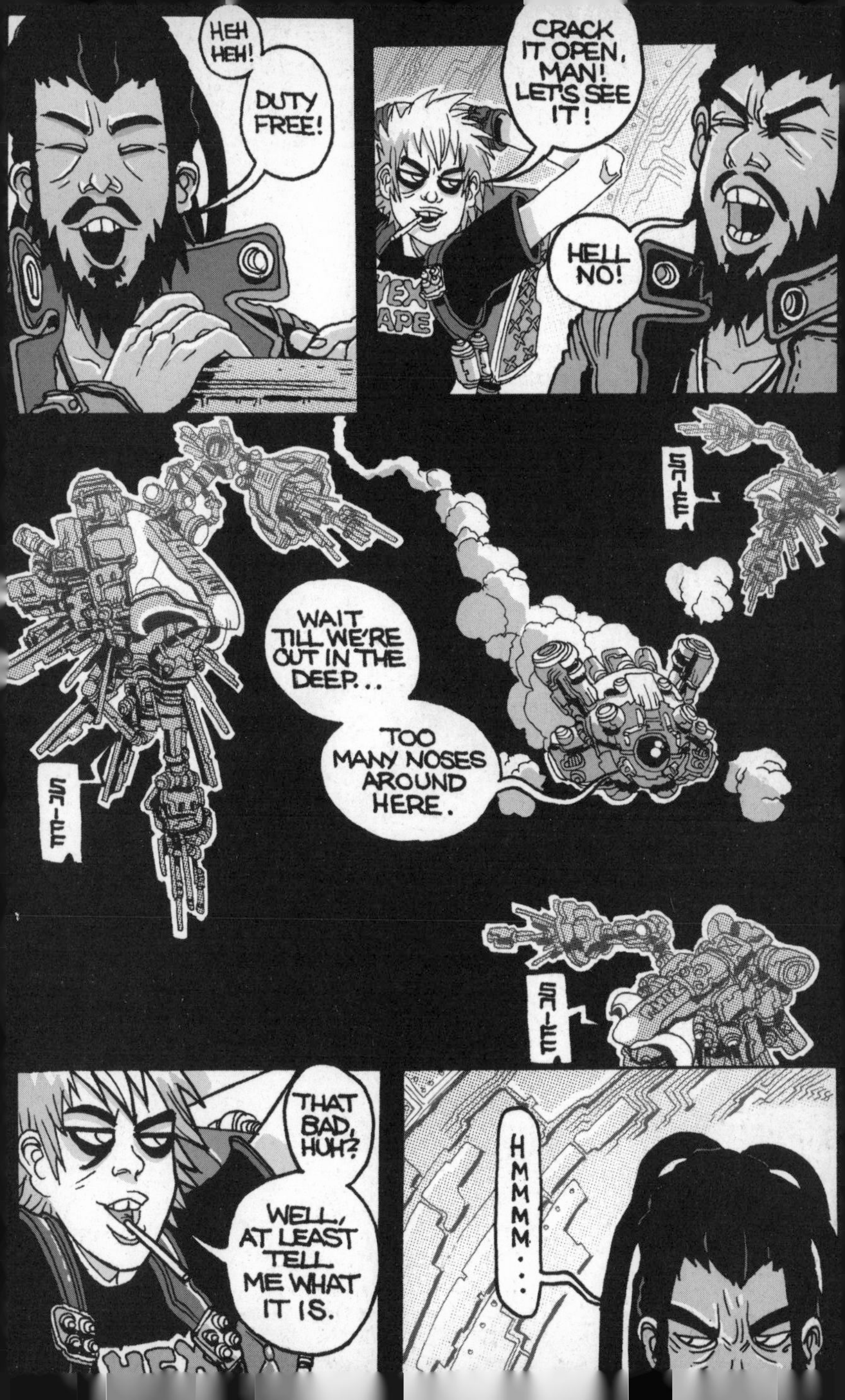
HEH HEH!
DUTY FREE!
CRACK IT OPEN, MAN! LET'S SEE IT!
HELL NO!
TEX APE
SNIEE
WAIT TILL WE'RE OUT IN THE DEEP...
TOO MANY NOSES AROUND HERE.
SNIEE
SNIEE
THAT BAD, HUH?
WELL, AT LEAST TELL ME WHAT IT IS.
HMMMM...

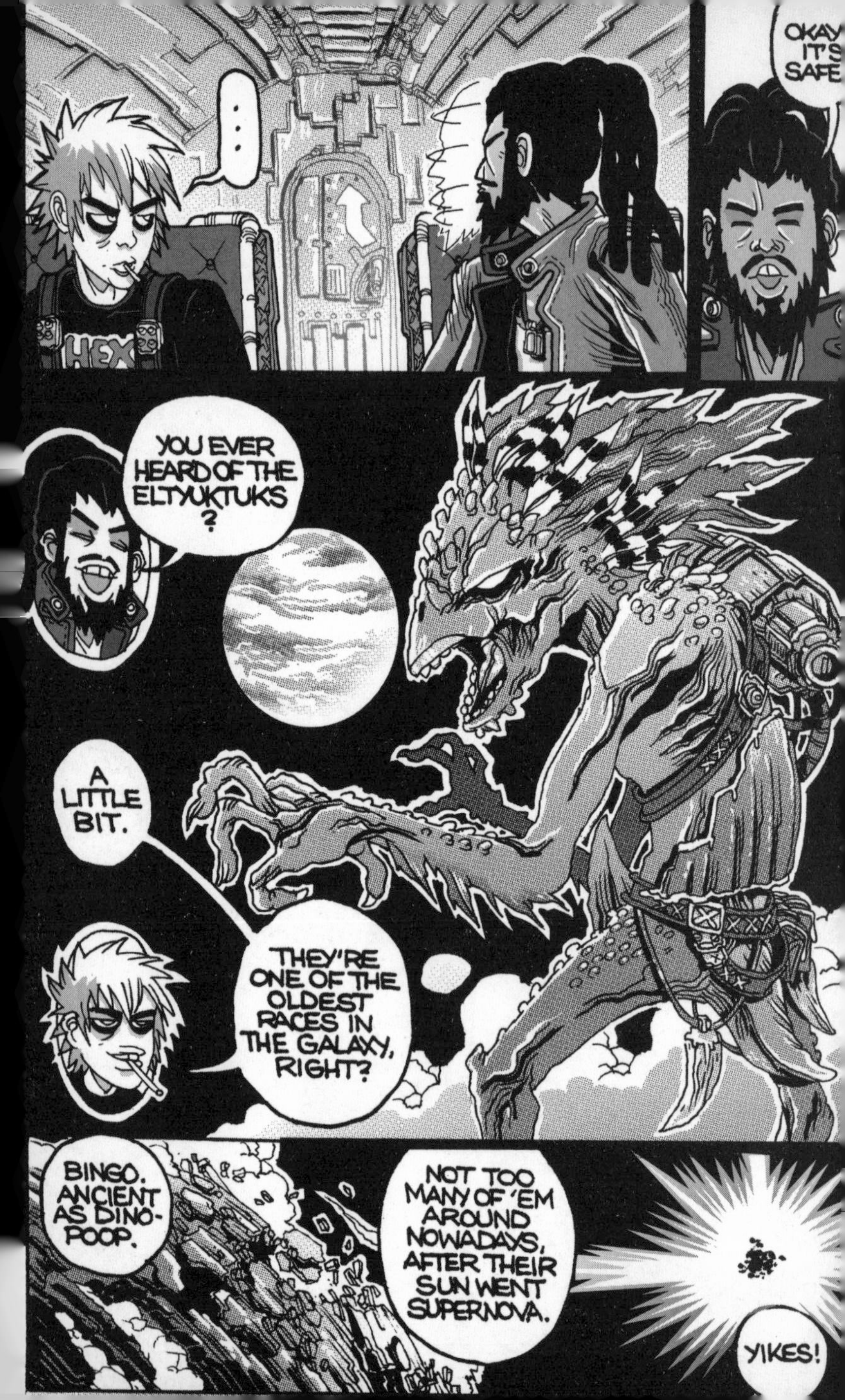
...
OKAY IT'S SAFE
YOU EVER HEARD OF THE ELTYUKTUKS ?
A LITTLE BIT.
THEY'RE ONE OF THE OLDEST RACES IN THE GALAXY, RIGHT?
BINGO. ANCIENT AS DINO-POOP.
NOT TOO MANY OF 'EM AROUND NOWADAYS, AFTER THEIR SUN WENT SUPERNOVA.
YIKES!

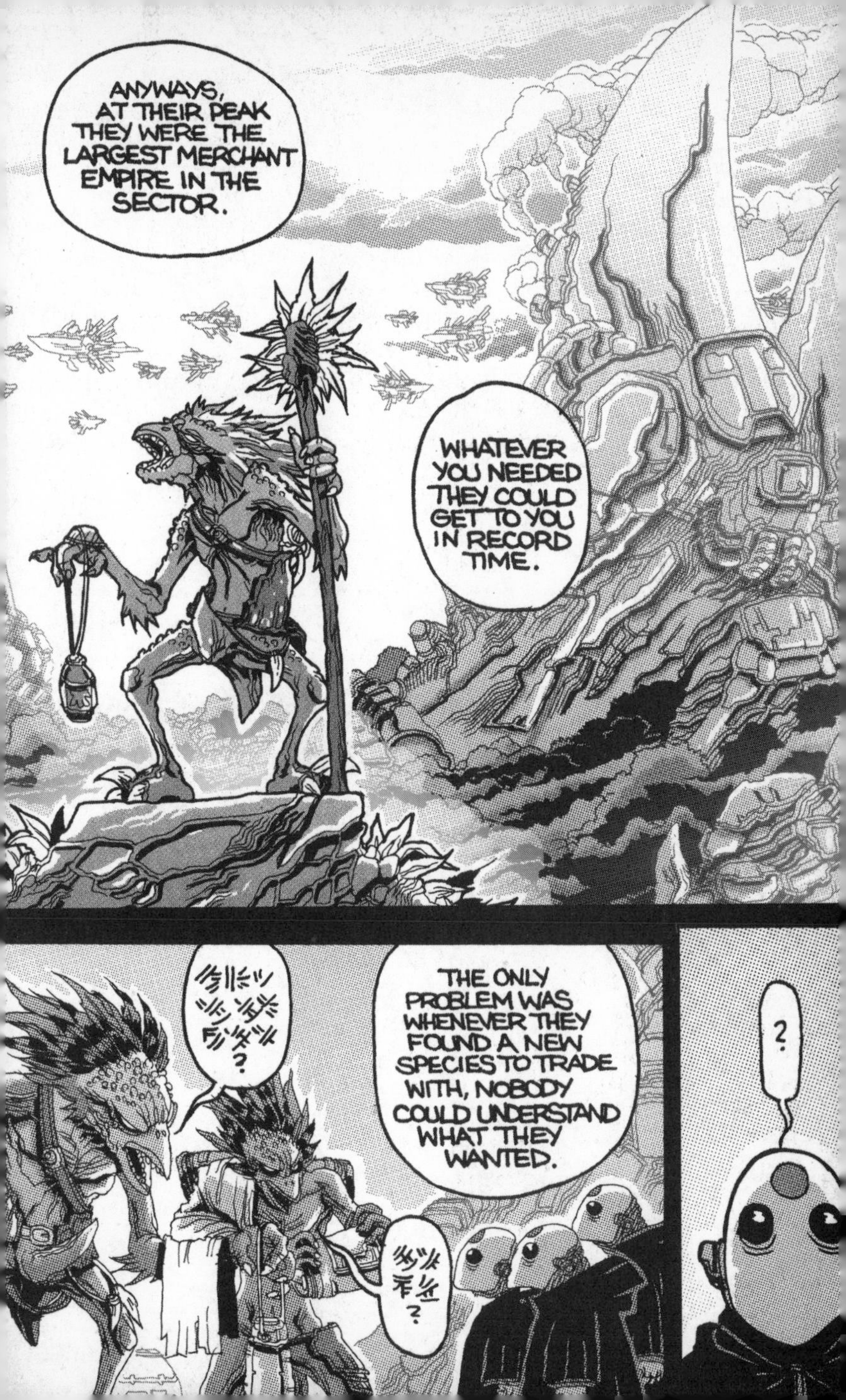
ANYWAYS, AT THEIR PEAK THEY WERE THE LARGEST MERCHANT EMPIRE IN THE SECTOR.
WHATEVER YOU NEEDED THEY COULD GET TO YOU IN RECORD TIME.
THE ONLY PROBLEM WAS WHENEVER THEY FOUND A NEW SPECIES TO TRADE WITH, NOBODY COULD UNDERSTAND WHAT THEY WANTED.
?

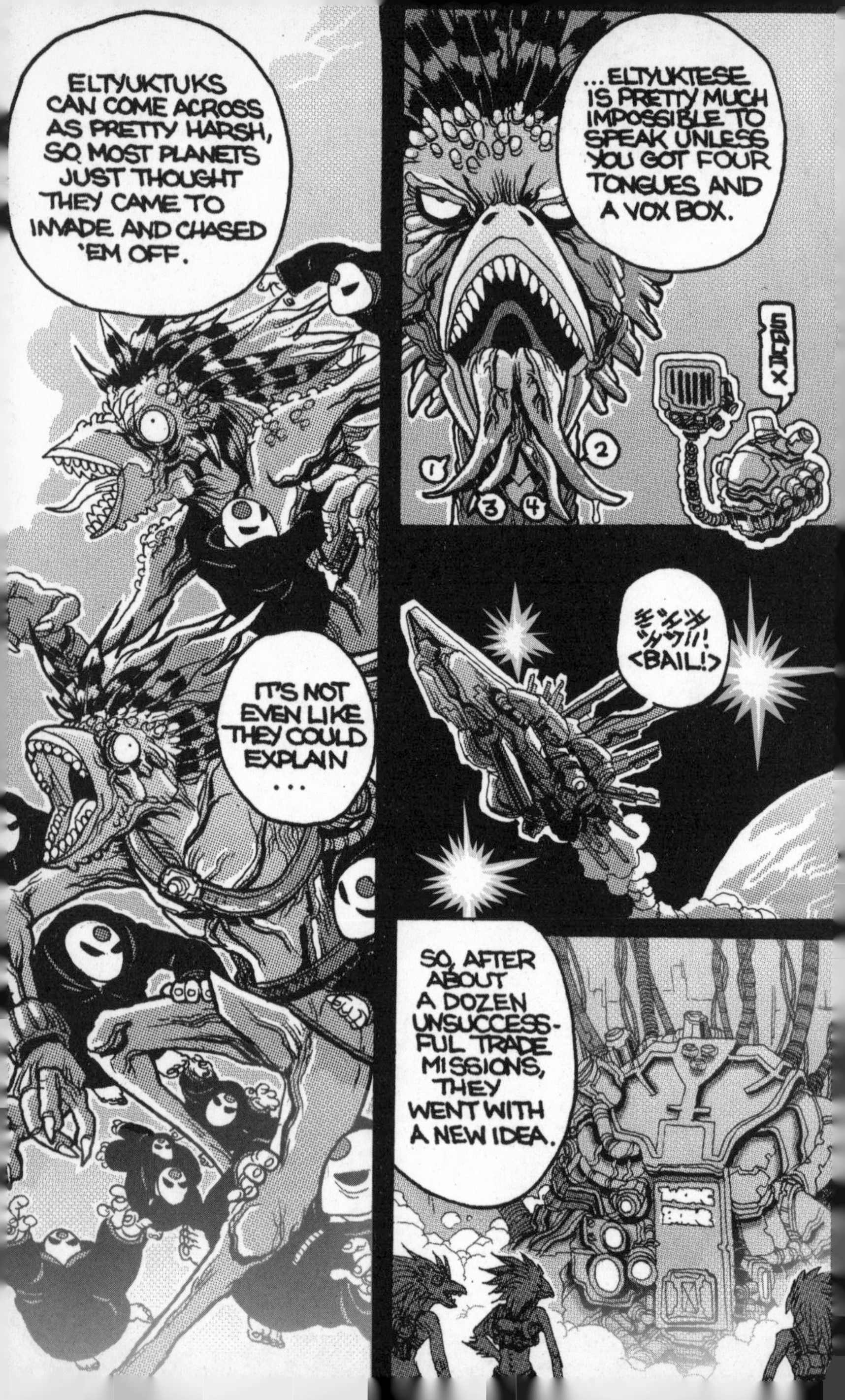
ELTYUKTUKS CAN COME ACROSS AS PRETTY HARSH, SO MOST PLANETS JUST THOUGHT THEY CAME TO INVADE AND CHASED 'EM OFF.
IT'S NOT EVEN LIKE THEY COULD EXPLAIN ...
...ELTYUKTESE IS PRETTY MUCH IMPOSSIBLE TO SPEAK UNLESS YOU GOT FOUR TONGUES AND A VOX BOX.
1
2
3
4
<BAIL!>
SO, AFTER ABOUT A DOZEN UNSUCCESS-FUL TRADE MISSIONS, THEY WENT WITH A NEW IDEA.

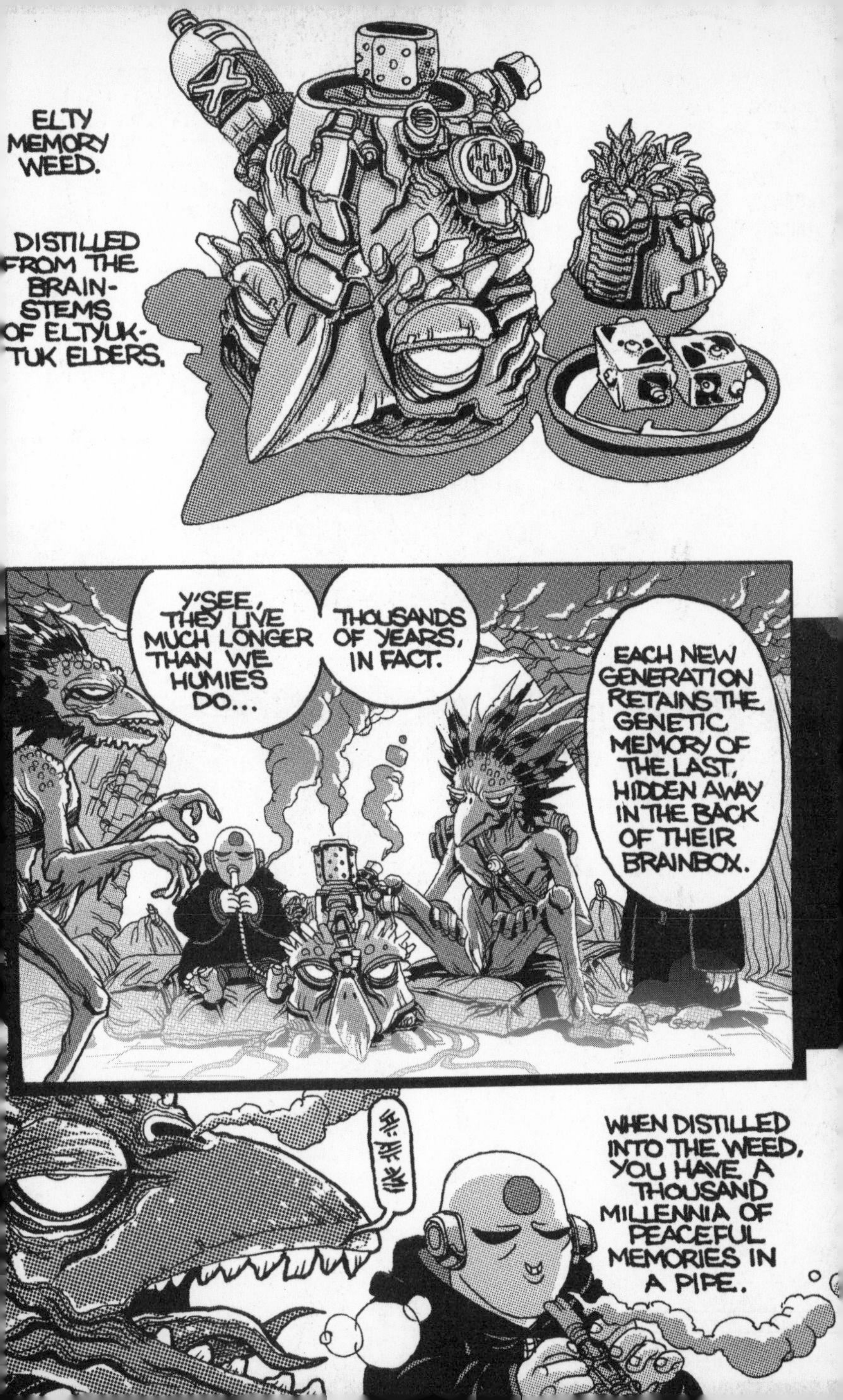
ELTY MEMORY WEED.
DISTILLED FROM THE BRAIN-STEMS OF ELTYUK-TUK ELDERS.
Y'SEE, THEY LIVE MUCH LONGER THAN WE HUMIES DO...
THOUSANDS OF YEARS, IN FACT.
EACH NEW GENERATION RETAINS THE GENETIC MEMORY OF THE LAST, HIDDEN AWAY IN THE BACK OF THEIR BRAINBOX.
WHEN DISTILLED INTO THE WEED, YOU HAVE A THOUSAND MILLENNIA OF PEACEFUL MEMORIES IN A PIPE.

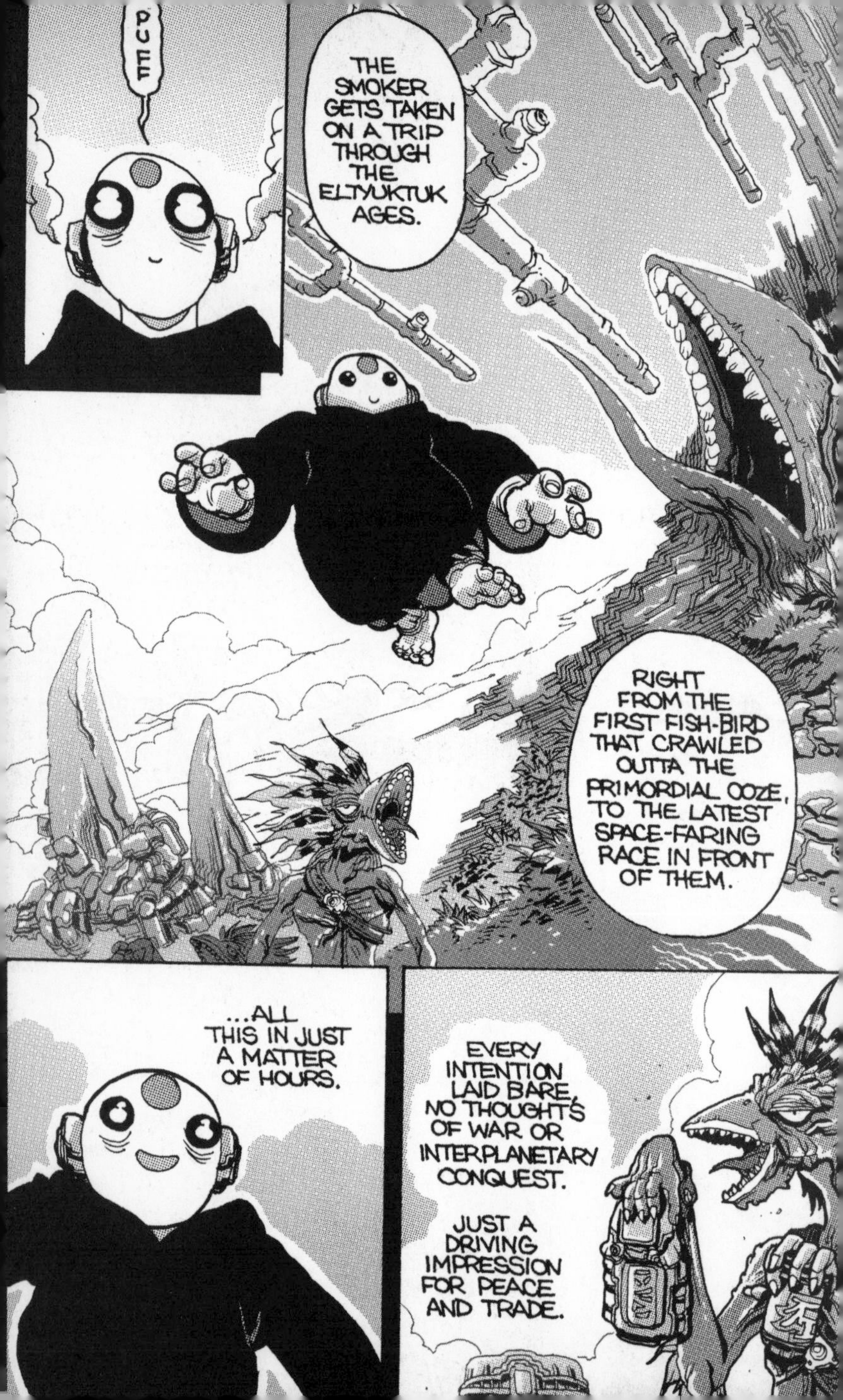
PUFF
THE SMOKER GETS TAKEN ON A TRIP THROUGH THE ELTYUKTUK AGES.
RIGHT FROM THE FIRST FISH-BIRD THAT CRAWLED OUTTA THE PRIMORDIAL OOZE, TO THE LATEST SPACE-FARING RACE IN FRONT OF THEM.
...ALL THIS IN JUST A MATTER OF HOURS.
EVERY INTENTION LAID BARE, NO THOUGHTS OF WAR OR INTERPLANETARY CONQUEST.
JUST A DRIVING IMPRESSION FOR PEACE AND TRADE.

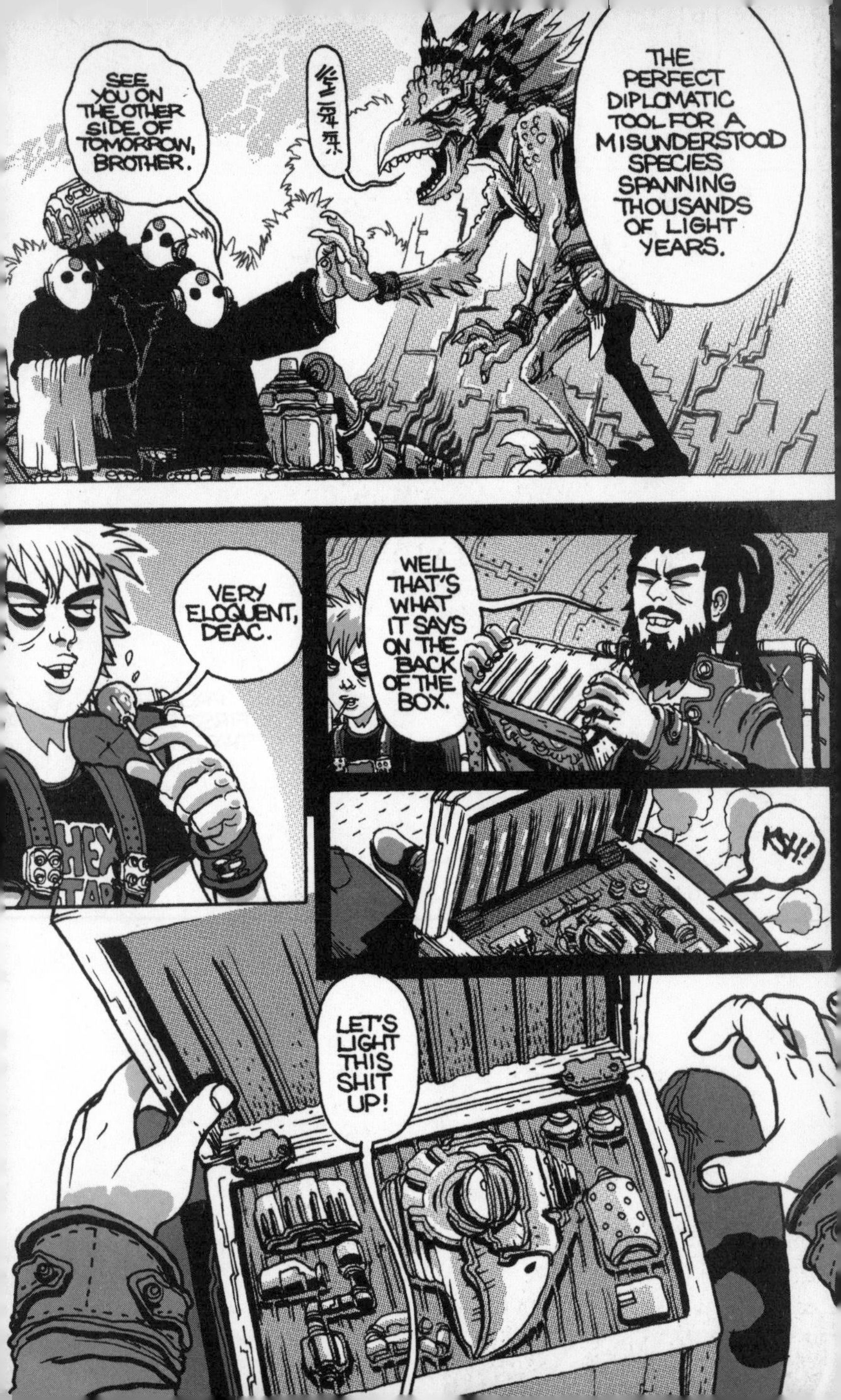
SEE YOU ON THE OTHER SIDE OF TOMORROW, BROTHER.
THE PERFECT DIPLOMATIC TOOL FOR A MISUNDERSTOOD SPECIES SPANNING THOUSANDS OF LIGHT YEARS.
VERY ELOQUENT, DEAC.
WELL THAT'S WHAT IT SAYS ON THE BACK OF THE BOX.
KSH!!
LET'S LIGHT THIS SHIT UP!

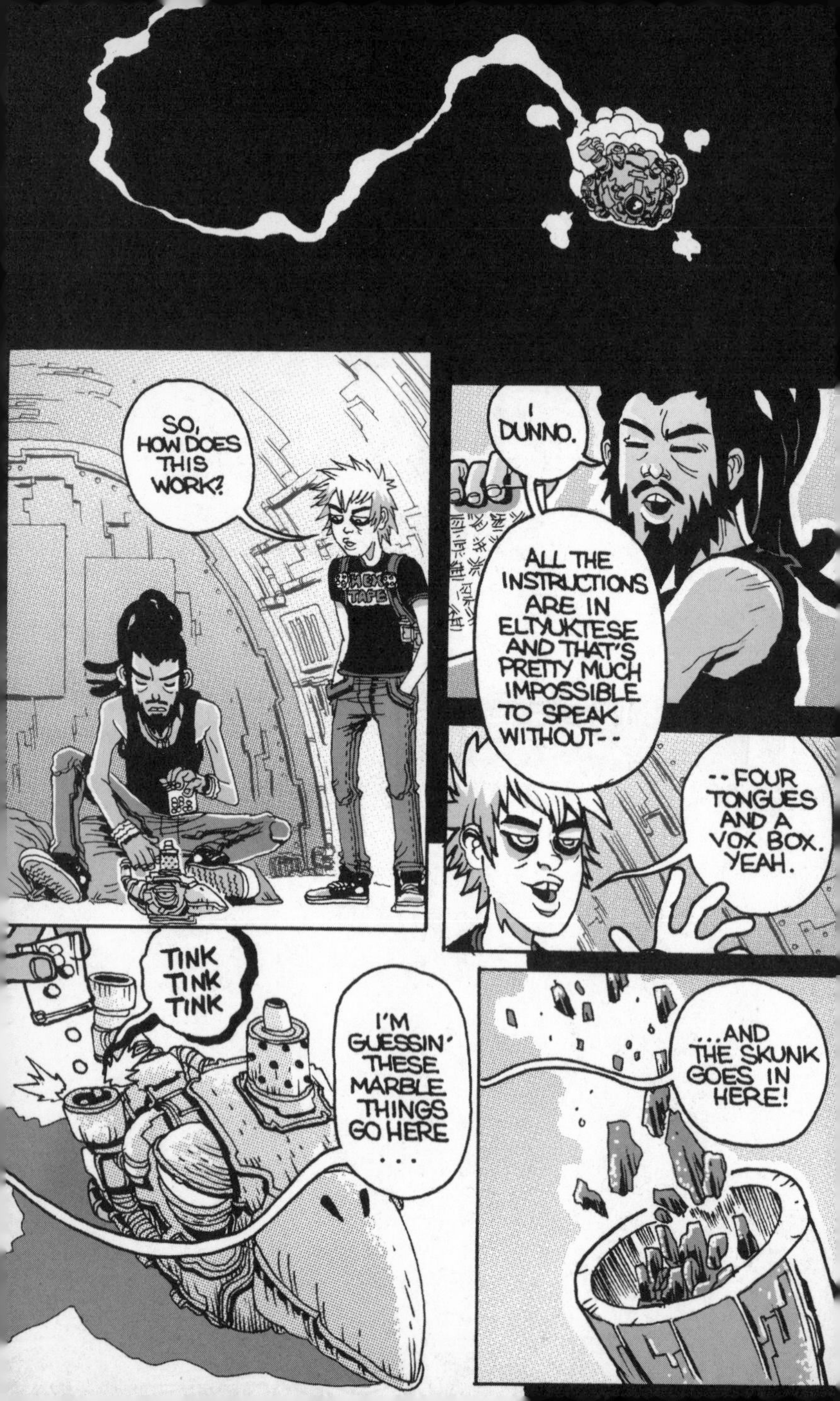

SO, HOW DOES THIS WORK?
I DUNNO.
ALL THE INSTRUCTIONS ARE IN ELTYUKTESE AND THAT'S PRETTY MUCH IMPOSSIBLE TO SPEAK WITHOUT--
--FOUR TONGUES AND A VOX BOX. YEAH.
TINK TINK TINK
I'M GUESSIN' THESE MARBLE THINGS GO HERE...
...AND THE SKUNK GOES IN HERE!

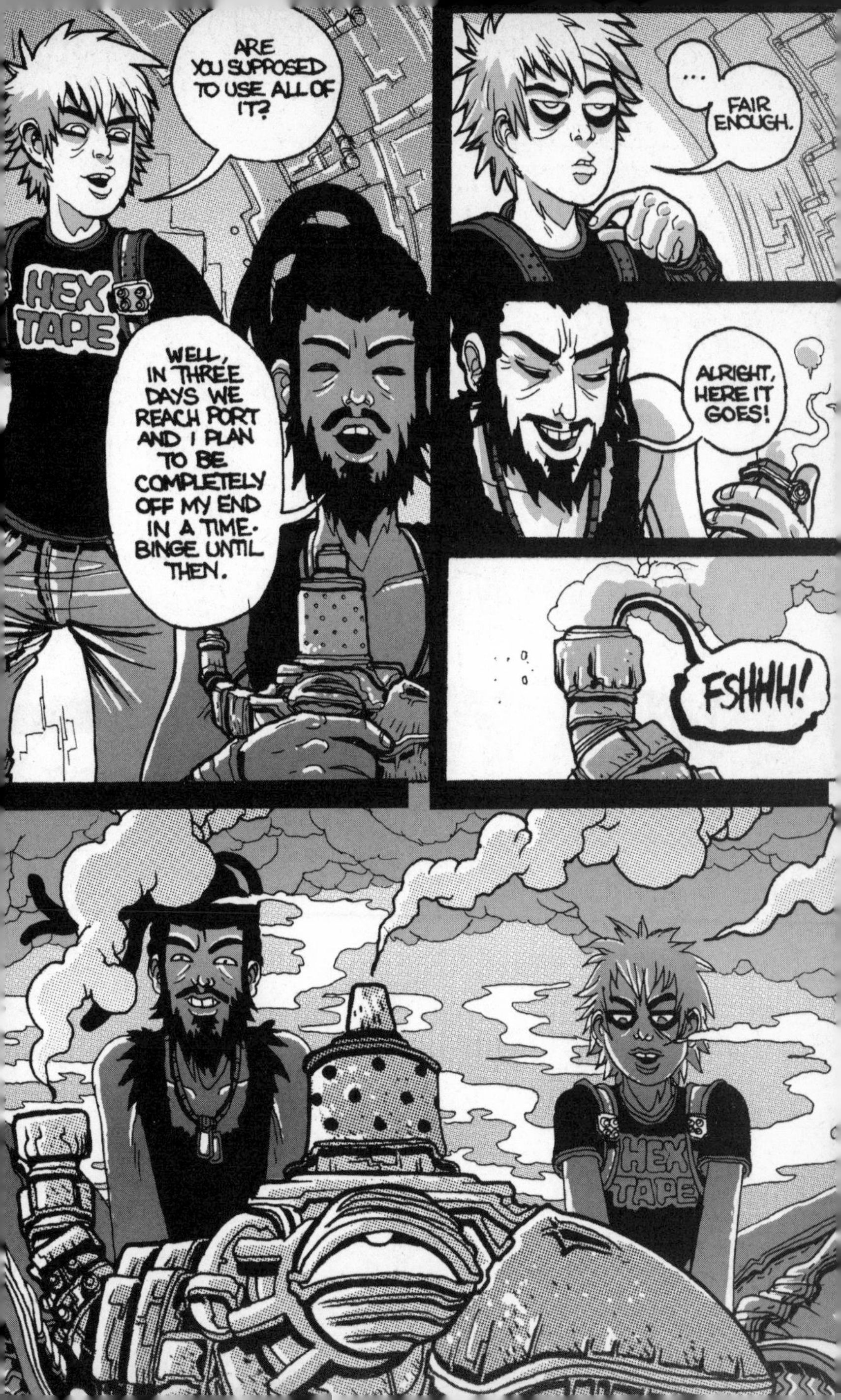

ARE YOU SUPPOSED TO USE ALL OF IT?
WELL, IN THREE DAYS WE REACH PORT AND I PLAN TO BE COMPLETELY OFF MY END IN A TIME-BINGE UNTIL THEN.
... FAIR ENOUGH.
ALRIGHT, HERE IT GOES!
FSHHH!
HEX TAPE

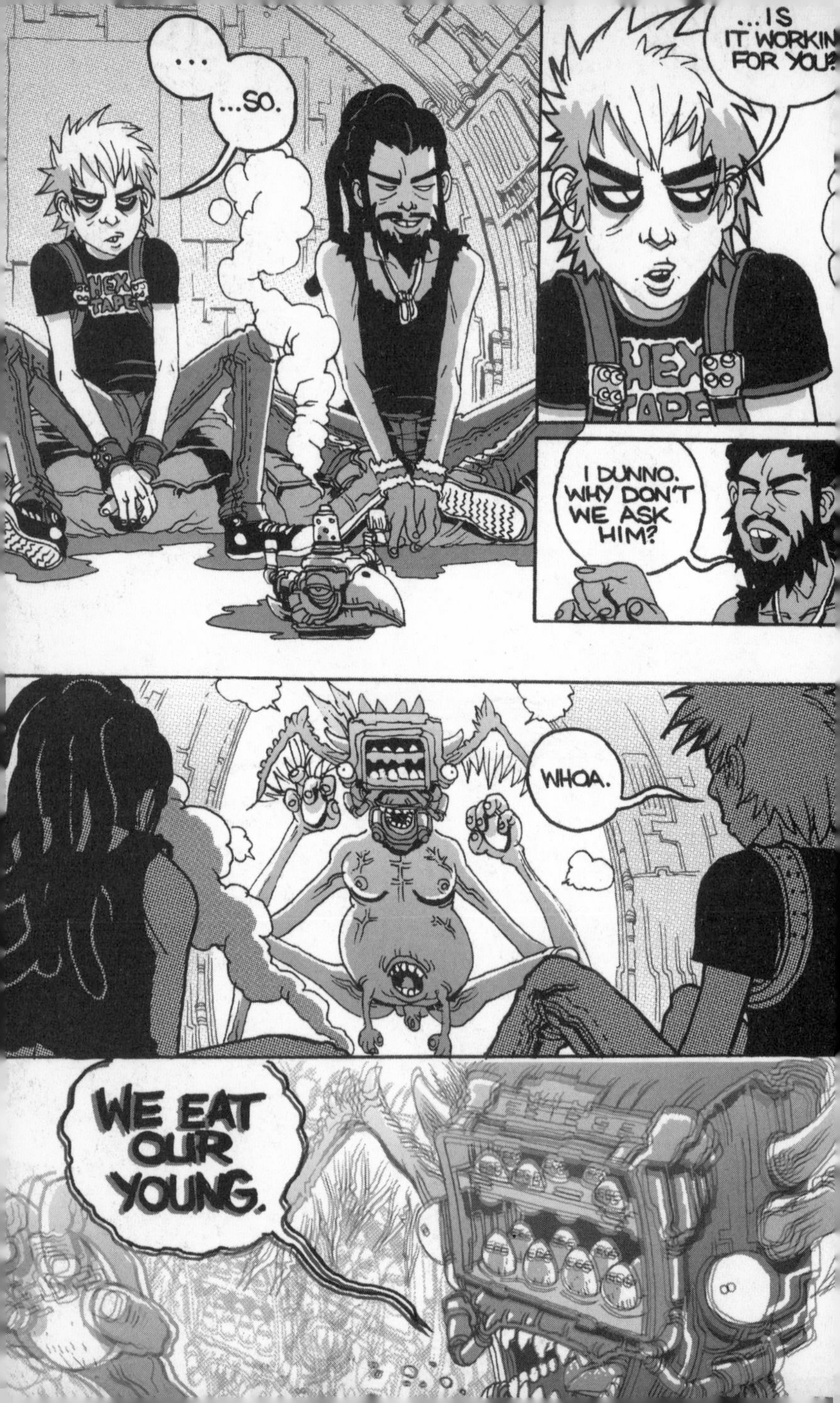
...
...SO.
...IS IT WORKIN FOR YOU?
I DUNNO. WHY DON'T WE ASK HIM?
WHOA.
WE EAT OUR YOUNG.

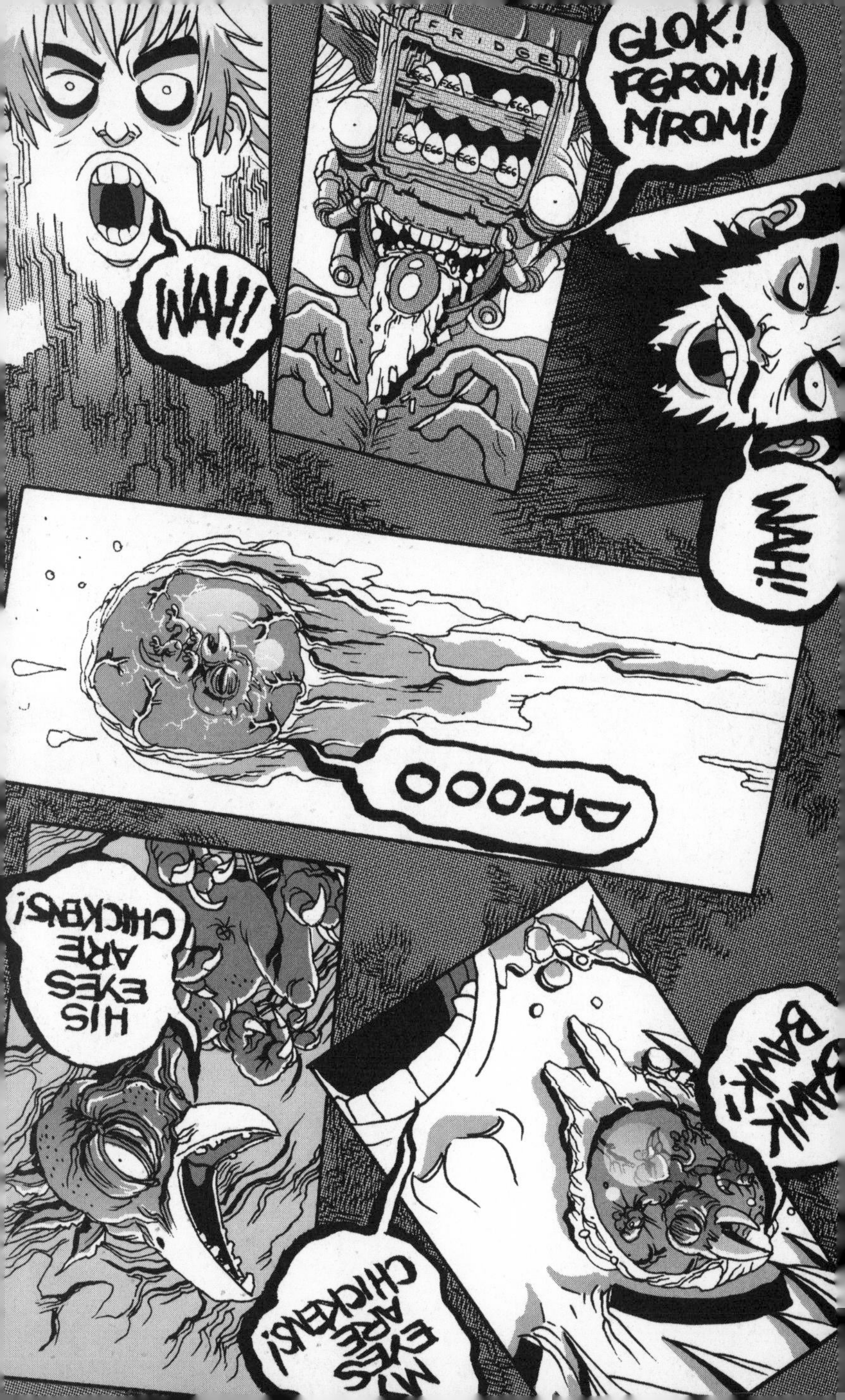
WAH!
FRIDGE
GLOK! FGROM! MROM!
WAH!
DROOO
HIS EYES ARE CHICKENS!
BAWK!
MY EYES ARE CHICKENS!

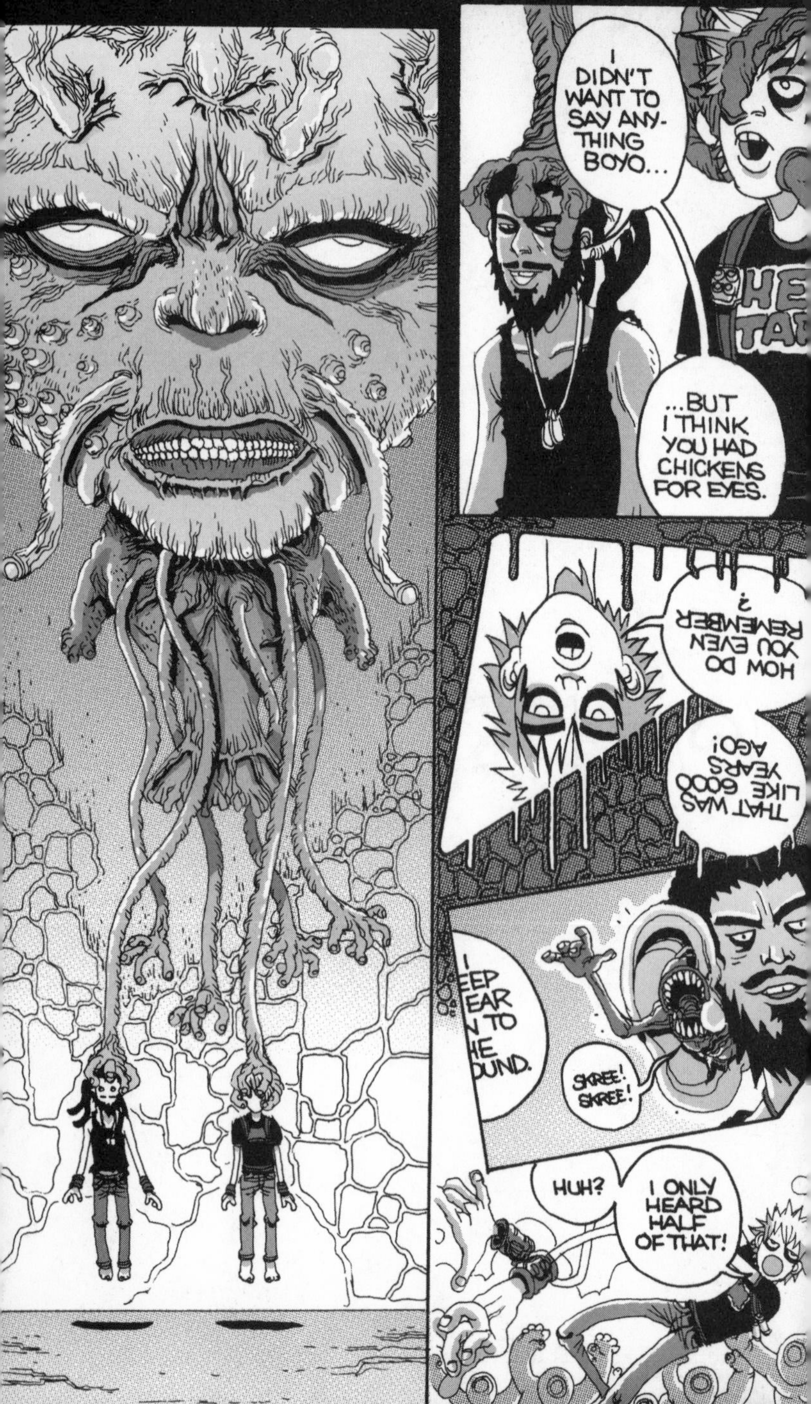
I DIDN'T WANT TO SAY ANY-THING BOYO...
...BUT I THINK YOU HAD CHICKENS FOR EYES.
HOW DO YOU EVEN REMEMBER ?
THAT WAS LIKE 6000 YEARS AGO!
SKREE! SKREE!
HUH?
I ONLY HEARD HALF OF THAT!

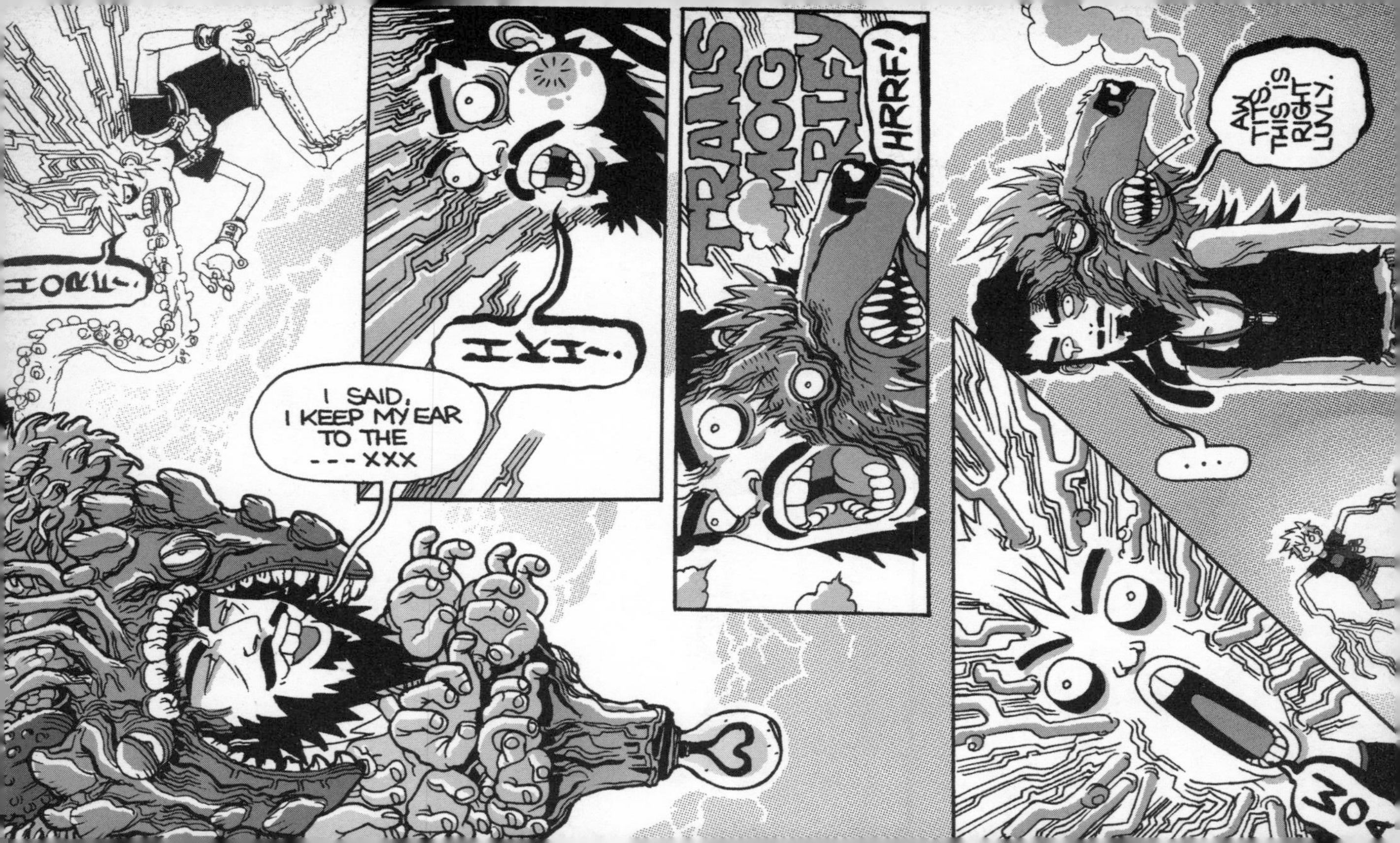
HORF!
I SAID, I KEEP MY EAR TO THE ---XXX
HKH!
TRANS MOG RIFY
HRRF!
...
AW TITS. THIS IS RIGHT LUVLY.
WOA

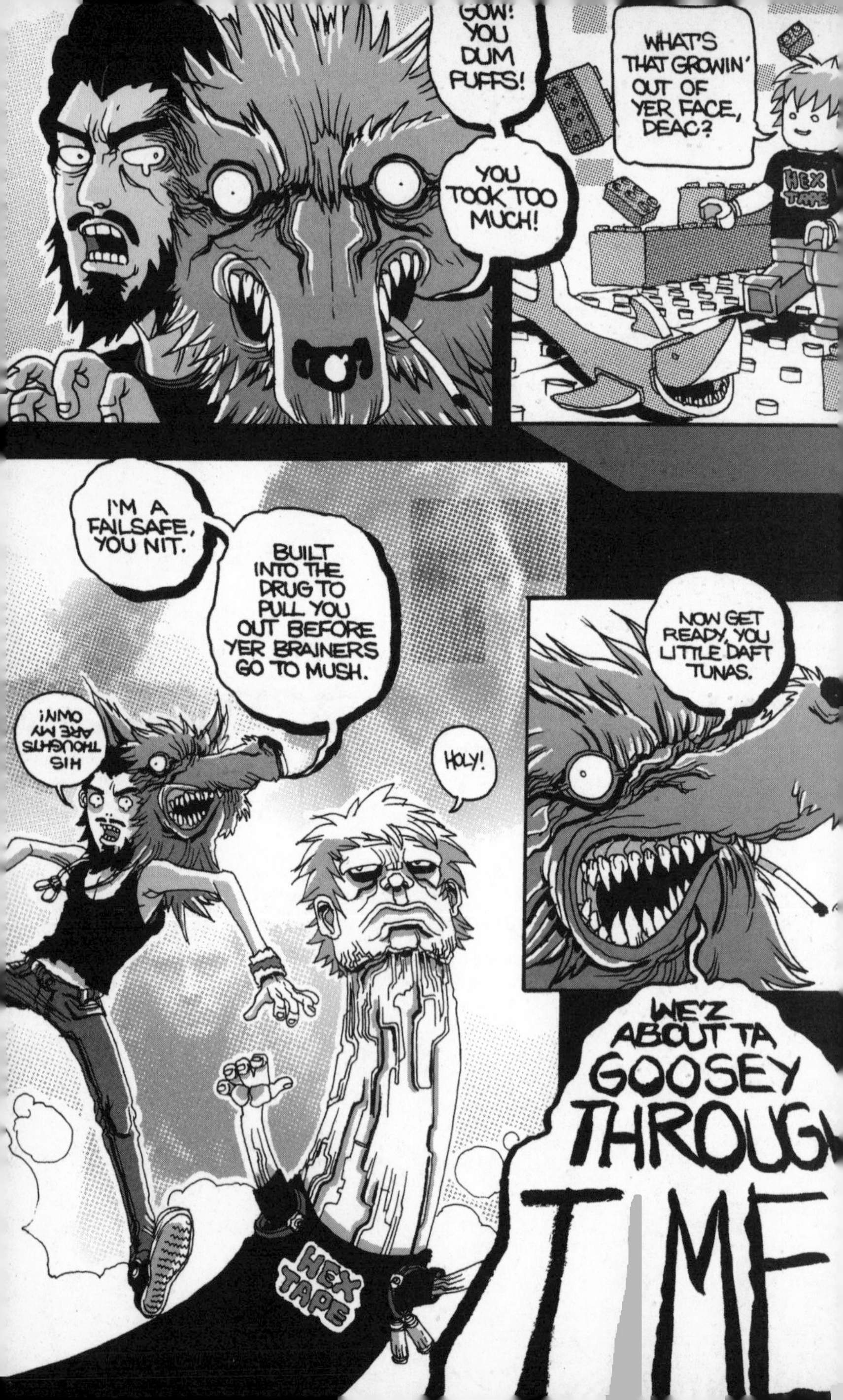

GOW! YOU DUM PUFFS!
YOU TOOK TOO MUCH!
WHAT'S THAT GROWIN' OUT OF YER FACE, DEAC?
HEX TAPE
I'M A FAILSAFE, YOU NIT.
BUILT INTO THE DRUG TO PULL YOU OUT BEFORE YER BRAINERS GO TO MUSH.
HIS THOUGHTS ARE MY OWN!
HOLY!
NOW GET READY, YOU LITTLE DAFT TUNAS.
WE'Z ABOUT TA GOOSEY
HEX TAPE

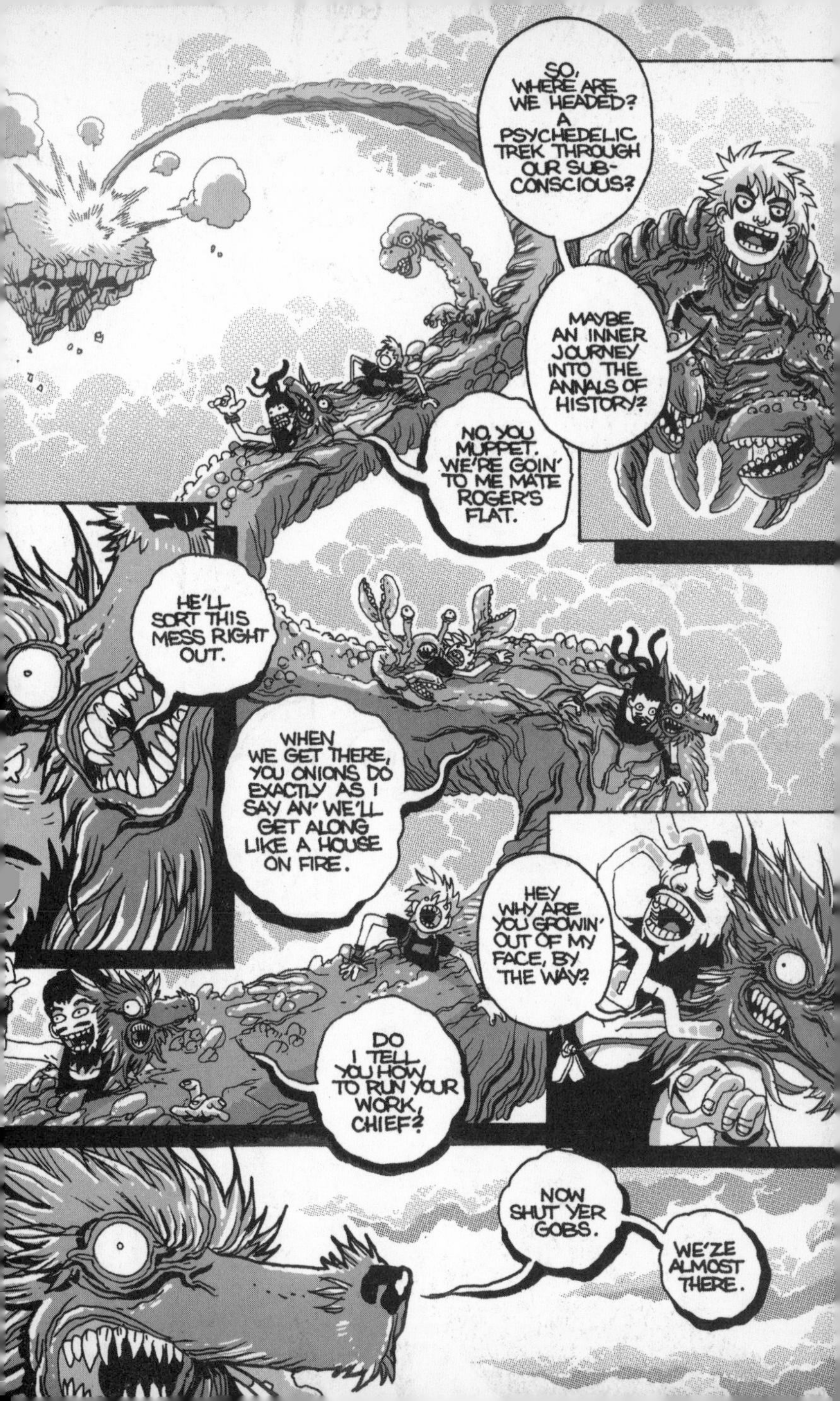
SO, WHERE ARE WE HEADED? A PSYCHEDELIC TREK THROUGH OUR SUB-CONSCIOUS?
MAYBE AN INNER JOURNEY INTO THE ANNALS OF HISTORY?
NO, YOU MUPPET. WE'RE GOIN' TO ME MATE ROGER'S FLAT.
HE'LL SORT THIS MESS RIGHT OUT.
WHEN WE GET THERE, YOU ONIONS DO EXACTLY AS I SAY AN' WE'LL GET ALONG LIKE A HOUSE ON FIRE.
HEY WHY ARE YOU GROWIN' OUT OF MY FACE, BY THE WAY?
DO I TELL YOU HOW TO RUN YOUR WORK, CHIEF?
NOW SHUT YER GOBS.
WE'ZE ALMOST THERE.

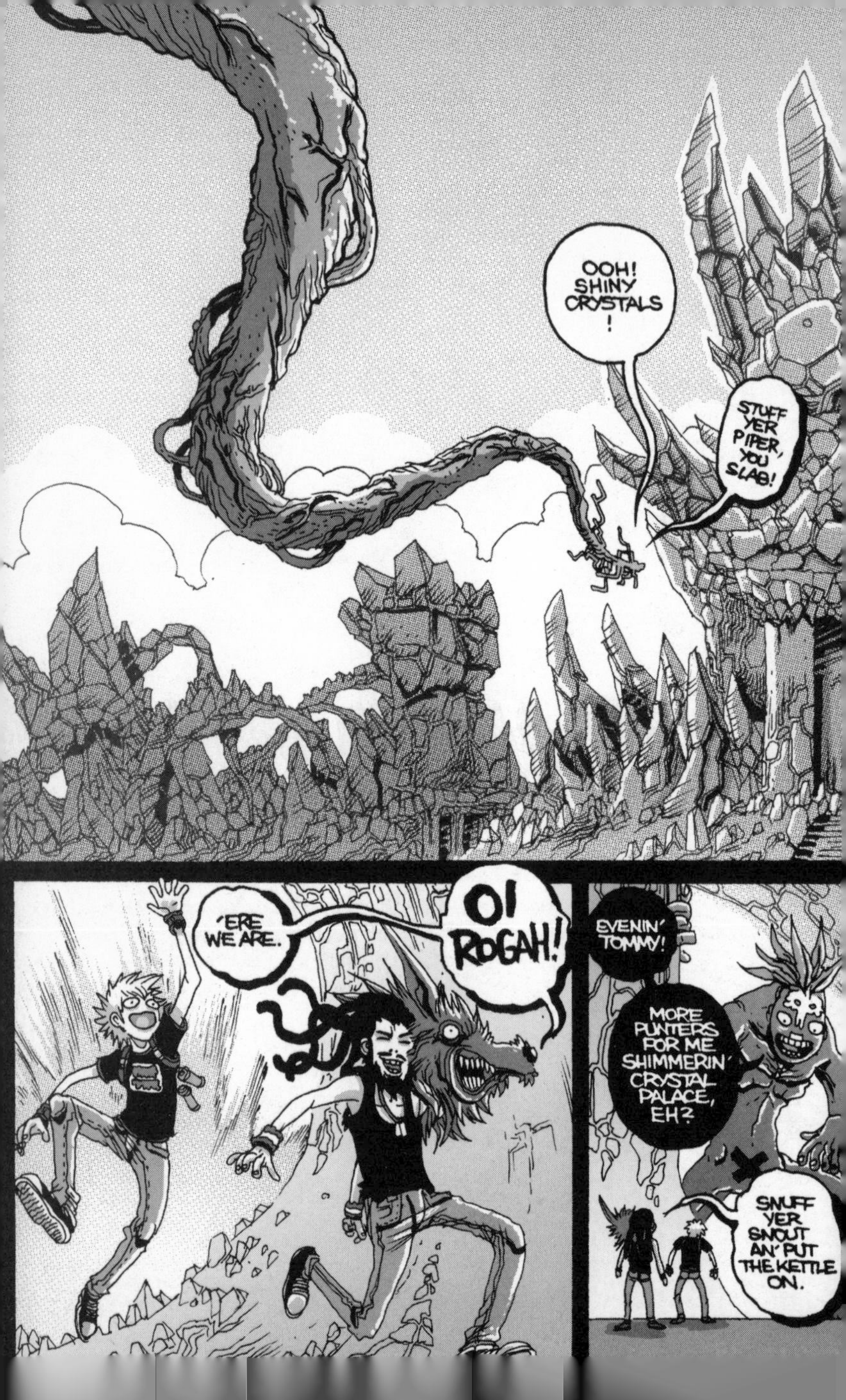
OOH! SHINY CRYSTALS !
STUFF YER PIPER, YOU SLAB!
'ERE WE ARE.
OI ROGAH!
EVENIN' TOMMY!
MORE PUNTERS FOR ME SHIMMERIN' CRYSTAL PALACE, EH?
SNUFF YER SNOUT AN' PUT THE KETTLE ON.

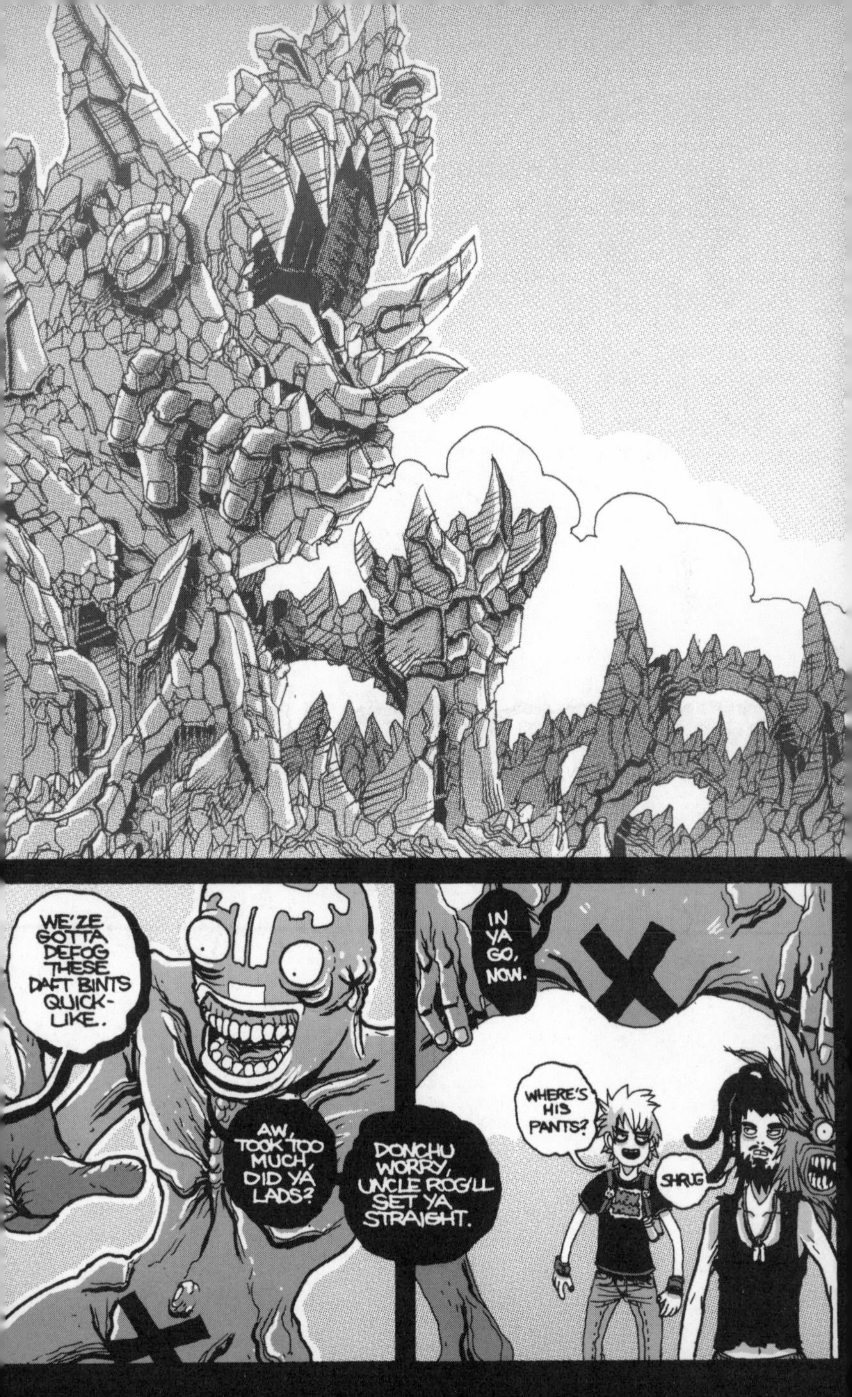

WE'ZE GOTTA DEFOG THESE DAFT BINTS QUICK-LIKE.
AW, TOOK TOO MUCH, DID YA LADS?
DONCHU WORRY, UNCLE ROG'LL SET YA STRAIGHT.
IN YA GO, NOW.
WHERE'S HIS PANTS?
SHRUG

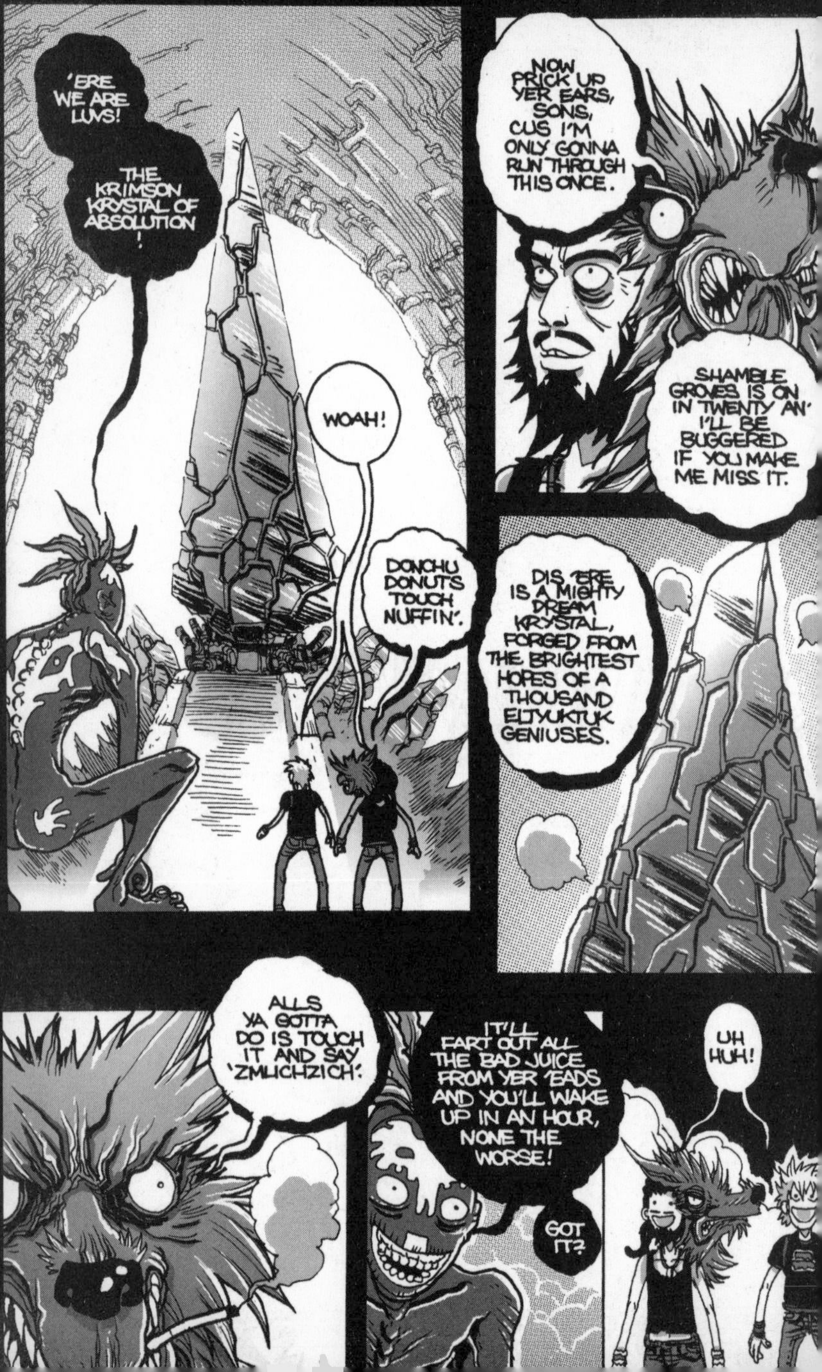

'ERE WE ARE LUVS!
THE KRIMSON KRYSTAL OF ABSOLUTION!
WOAH!
DONCHU DONUTS TOUCH NUFFIN'.
NOW PRICK UP YER EARS, SONS, CUS I'M ONLY GONNA RUN THROUGH THIS ONCE.
SHAMBLE GROVES IS ON IN TWENTY AN' I'LL BE BUGGERED IF YOU MAKE ME MISS IT.
DIS 'ERE IS A MIGHTY DREAM KRYSTAL, FORGED FROM THE BRIGHTEST HOPES OF A THOUSAND ELTYUKTUK GENIUSES.
ALLS YA GOTTA DO IS TOUCH IT AND SAY 'ZMLICHZICH'.
IT'LL FART OUT ALL THE BAD JUICE FROM YER 'EADS AND YOU'LL WAKE UP IN AN HOUR, NONE THE WORSE!
GOT IT?
UH HUH!

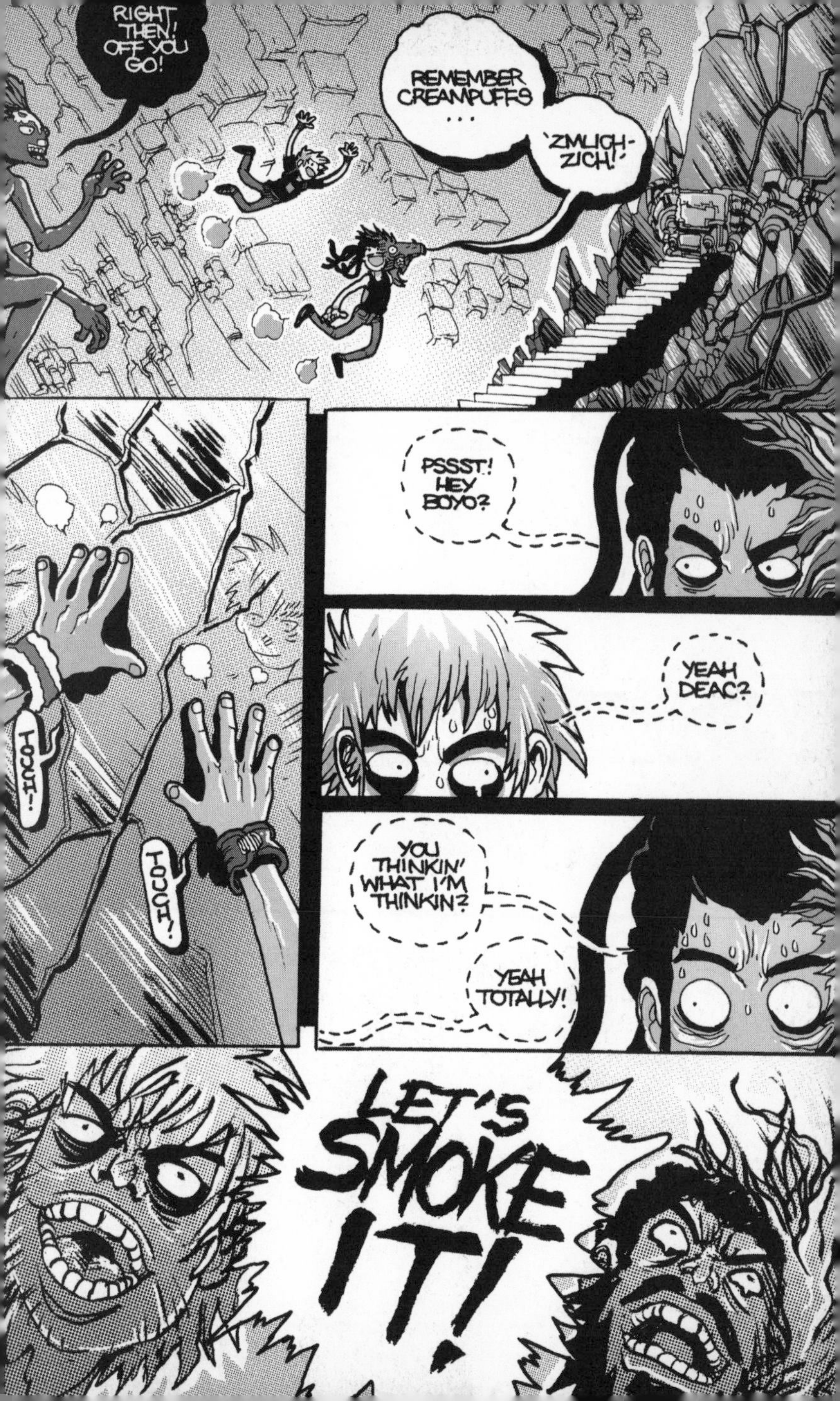
RIGHT THEN! OFF YOU GO!
REMEMBER CREAMPUFFS ...
'ZMUGH-ZICH!'
TOUCH!
TOUCH!
PSSST! HEY BOYO?
YEAH DEAC?
YOU THINKIN' WHAT I'M THINKIN?
YEAH TOTALLY!
LET'S SMOKE IT!

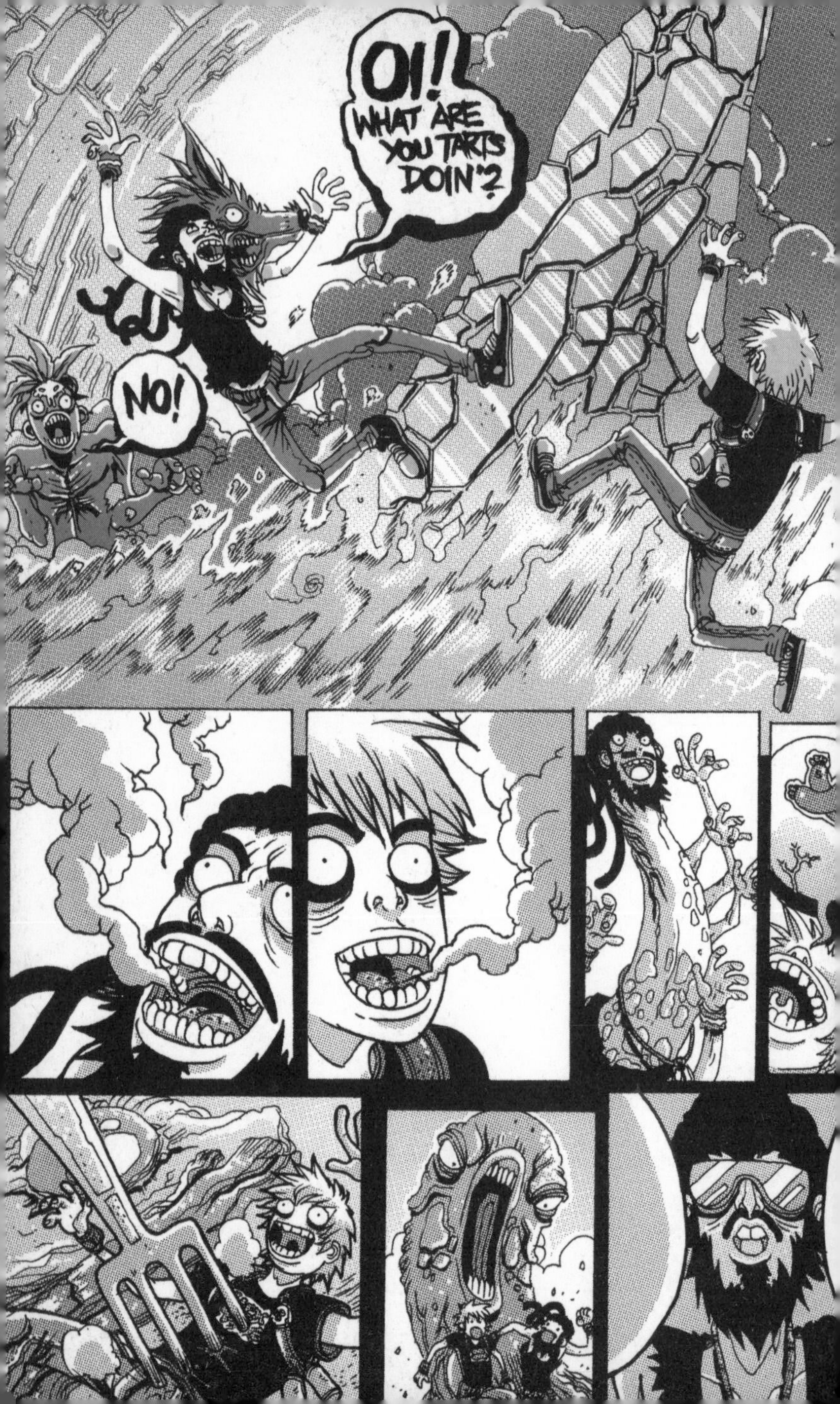
OI! WHAT ARE YOU TARTS DOIN'?
NO!

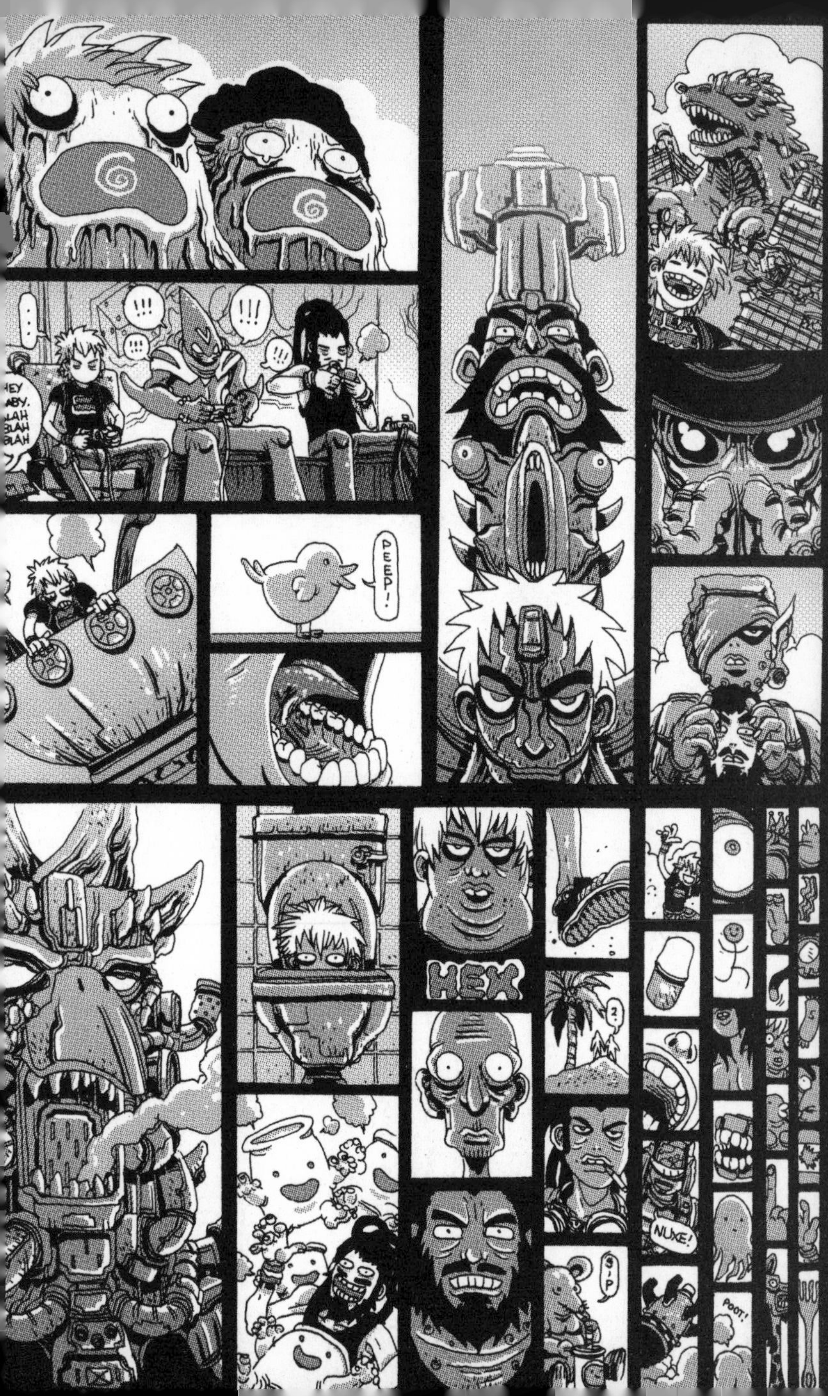
!!!
!!!
!!!
!!!
HEY
BLAH
BLAH
PEEP!
HEX
?
NUXE!
SIP
POOT!

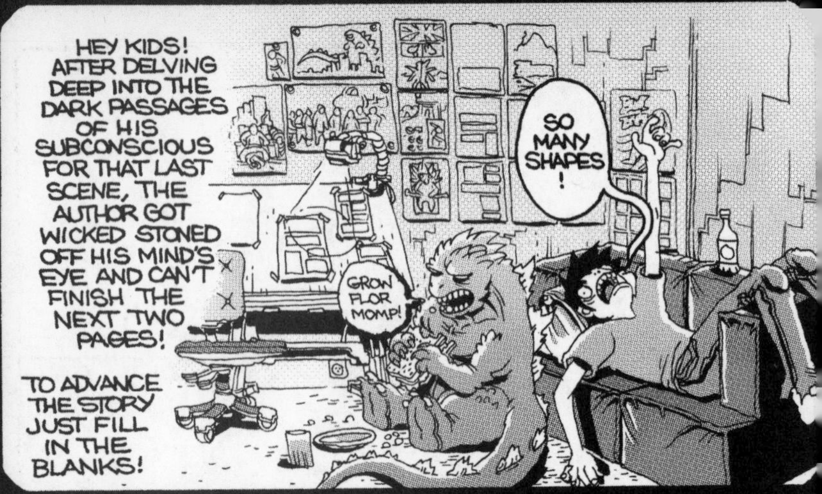
HEY KIDS! AFTER DELVING DEEP INTO THE DARK PASSAGES OF HIS SUBCONSCIOUS FOR THAT LAST SCENE, THE AUTHOR GOT WICKED STONED OFF HIS MIND'S EYE AND CAN'T FINISH THE NEXT TWO PAGES!
TO ADVANCE THE STORY JUST FILL IN THE BLANKS!
SO MANY SHAPES!
GROW FLOR MOMP!

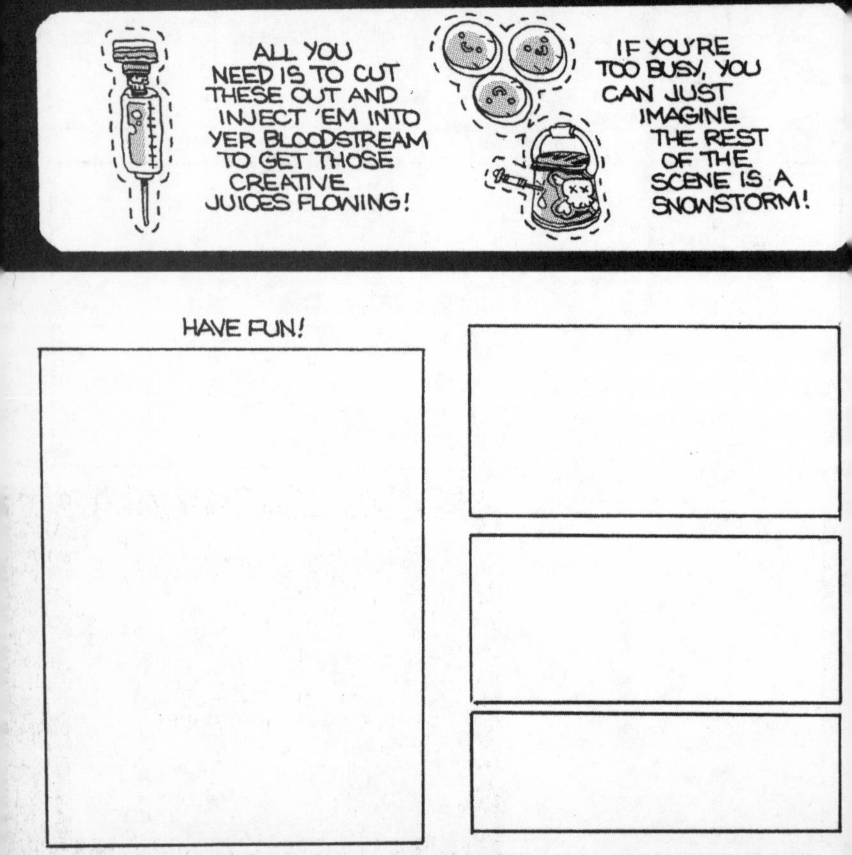
ALL YOU NEED IS TO CUT THESE OUT AND INJECT 'EM INTO YER BLOODSTREAM TO GET THOSE CREATIVE JUICES FLOWING!
IF YOU'RE TOO BUSY, YOU CAN JUST IMAGINE THE REST OF THE SCENE IS A SNOWSTORM!

HAVE FUN!

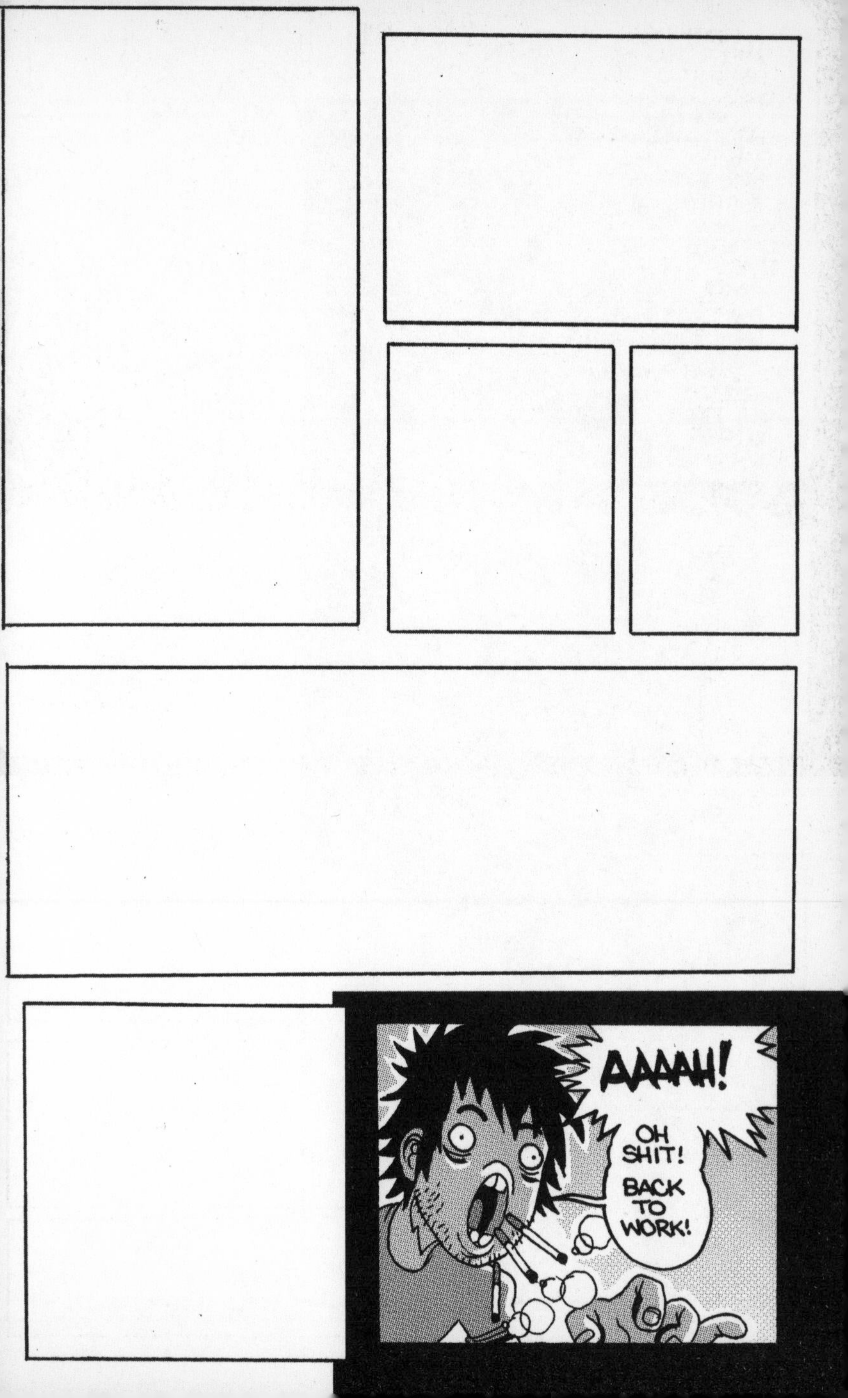
AAAAH!
OH SHIT! BACK TO WORK!

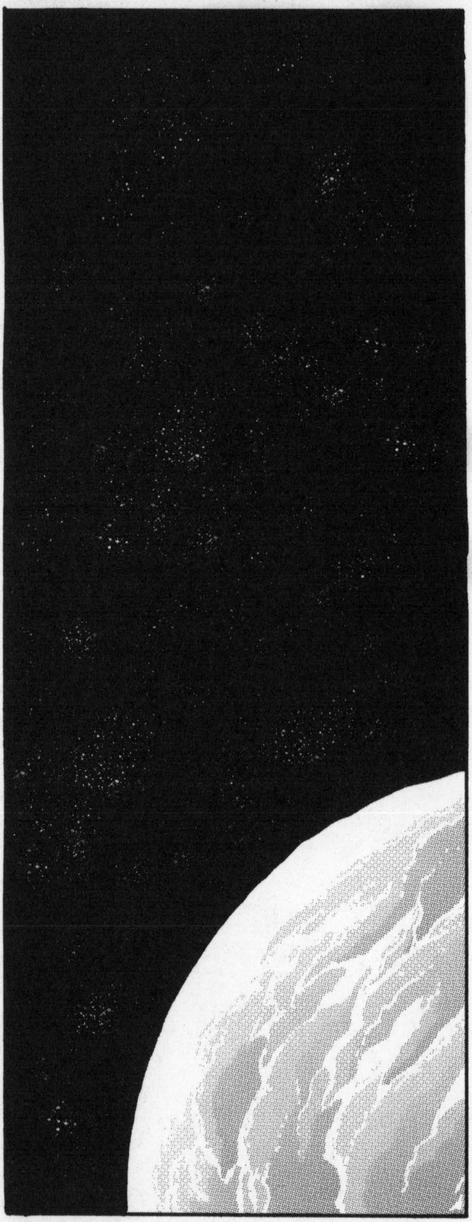

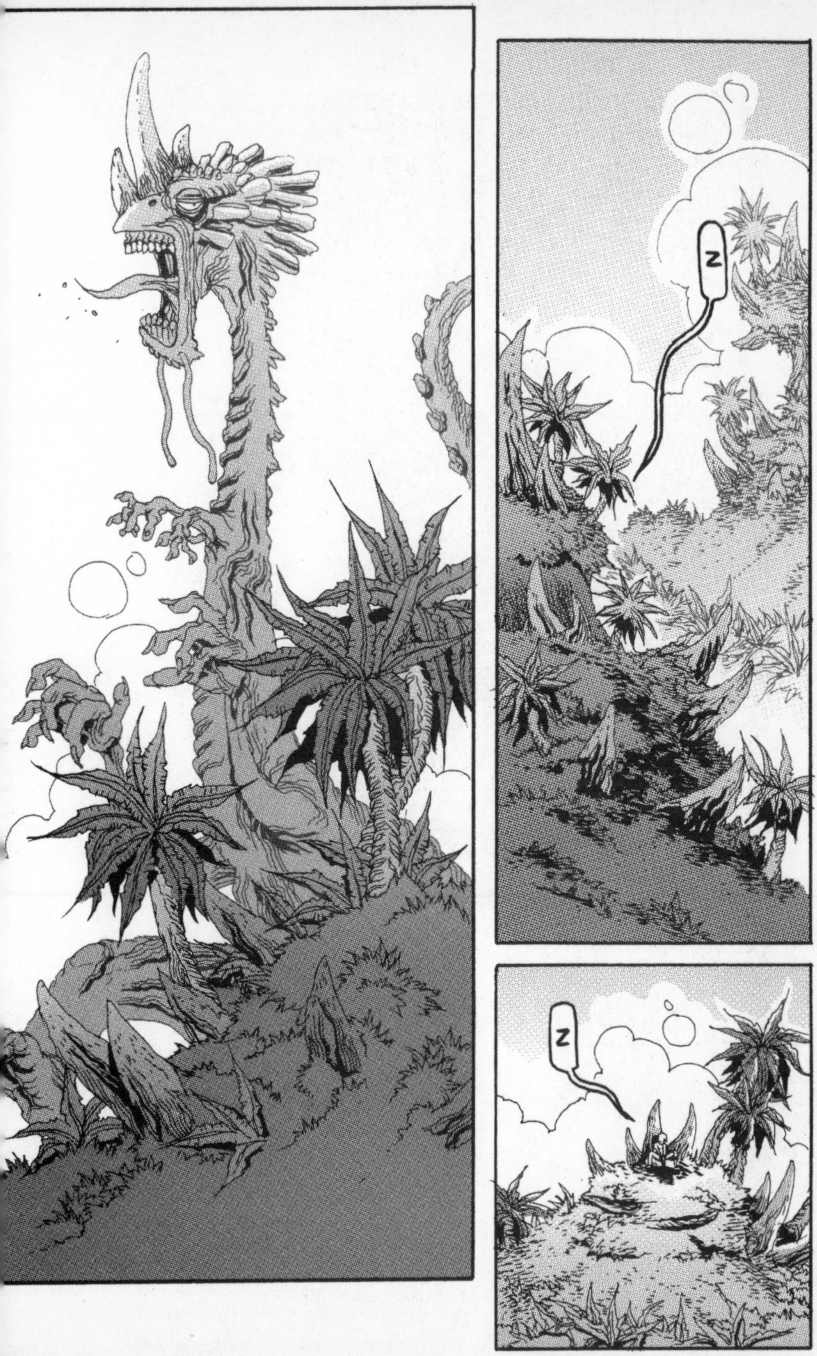
Z
Z

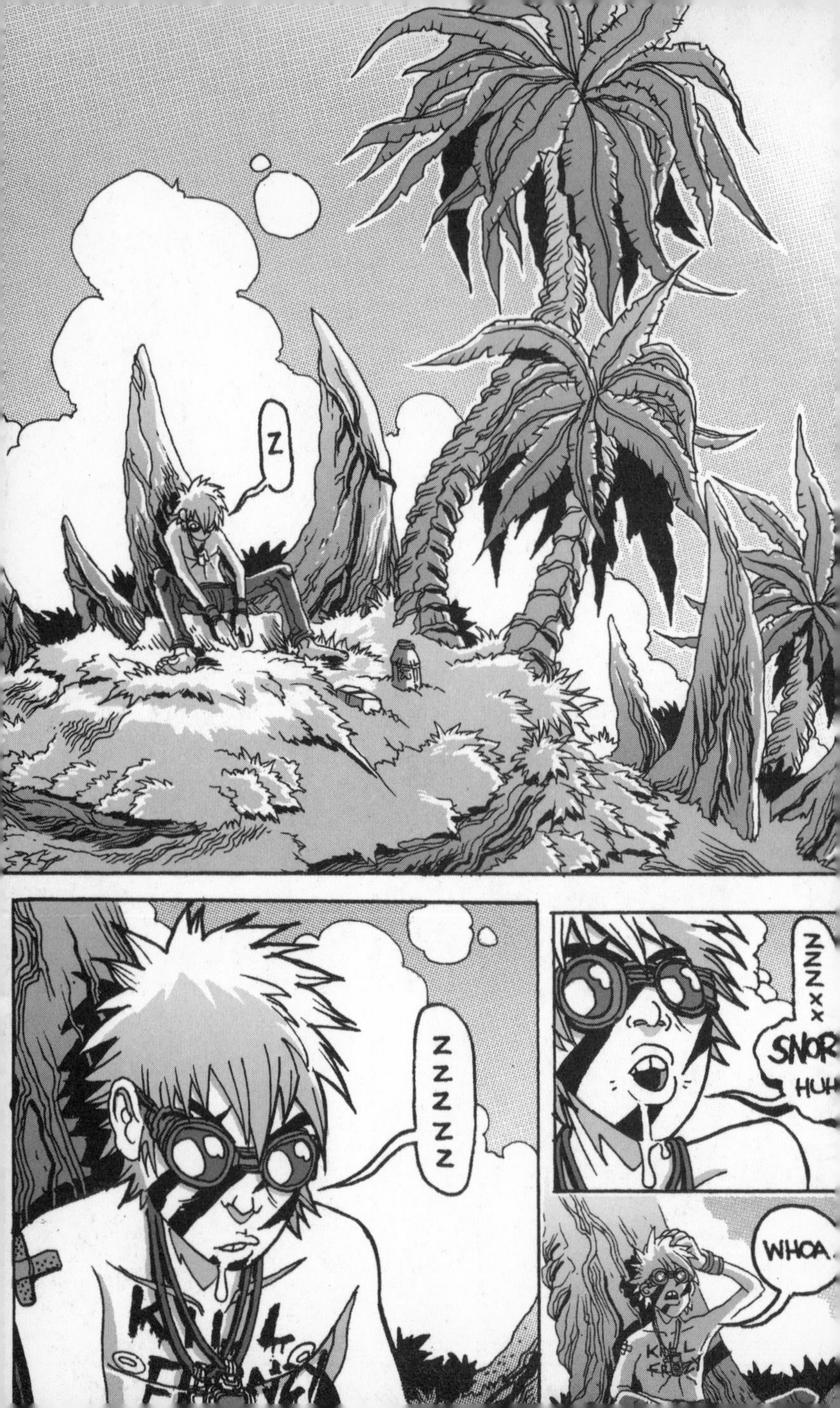
Z
ZZZZZ
ZZZxx
SNOR
HUH
WHOA.

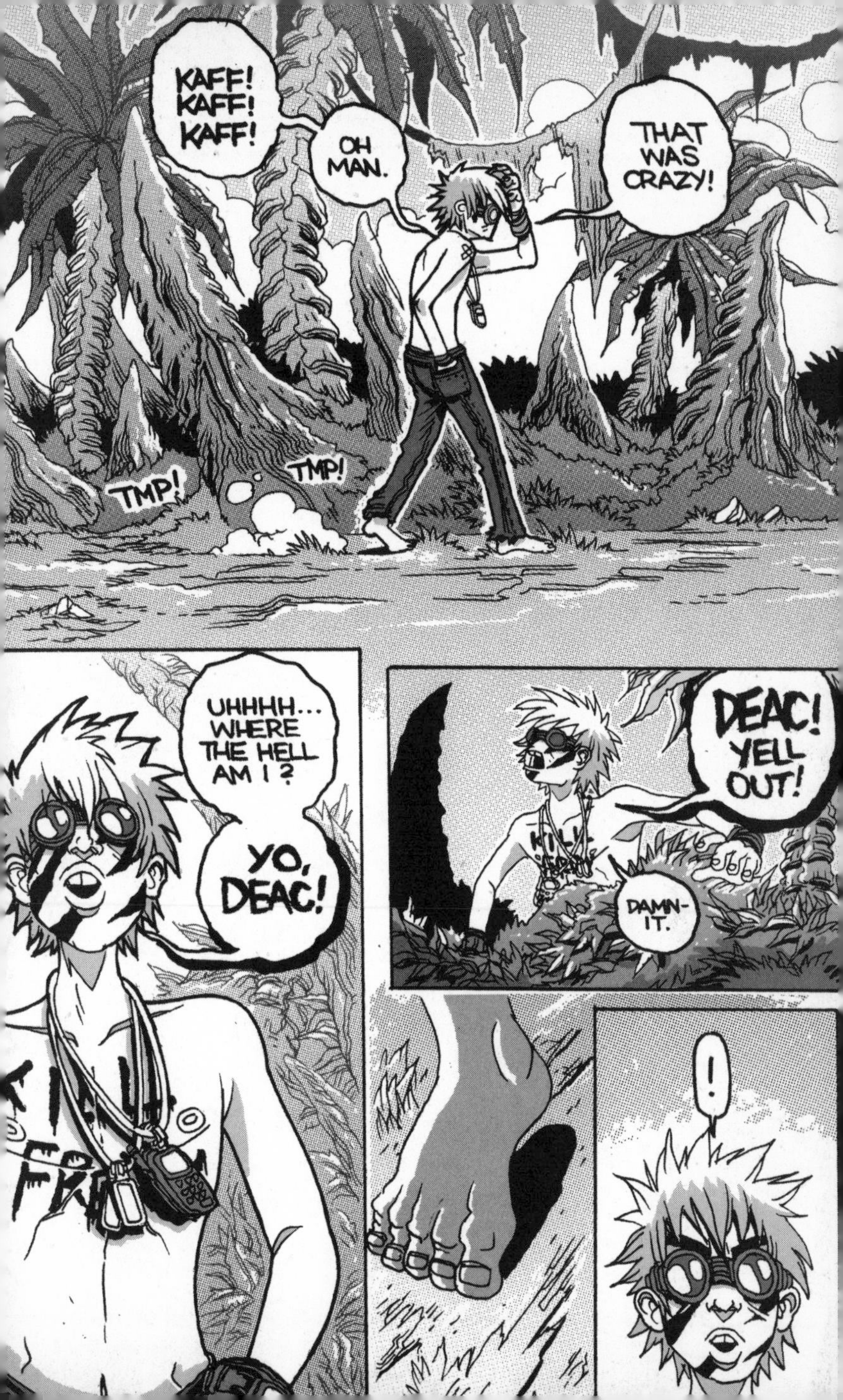
KAFF! KAFF! KAFF!
OH MAN.
THAT WAS CRAZY!
TMP!
TMP!
UHHHH... WHERE THE HELL AM I ?
YO, DEAC!
DEAC! YELL OUT!
DAMN-IT.
!

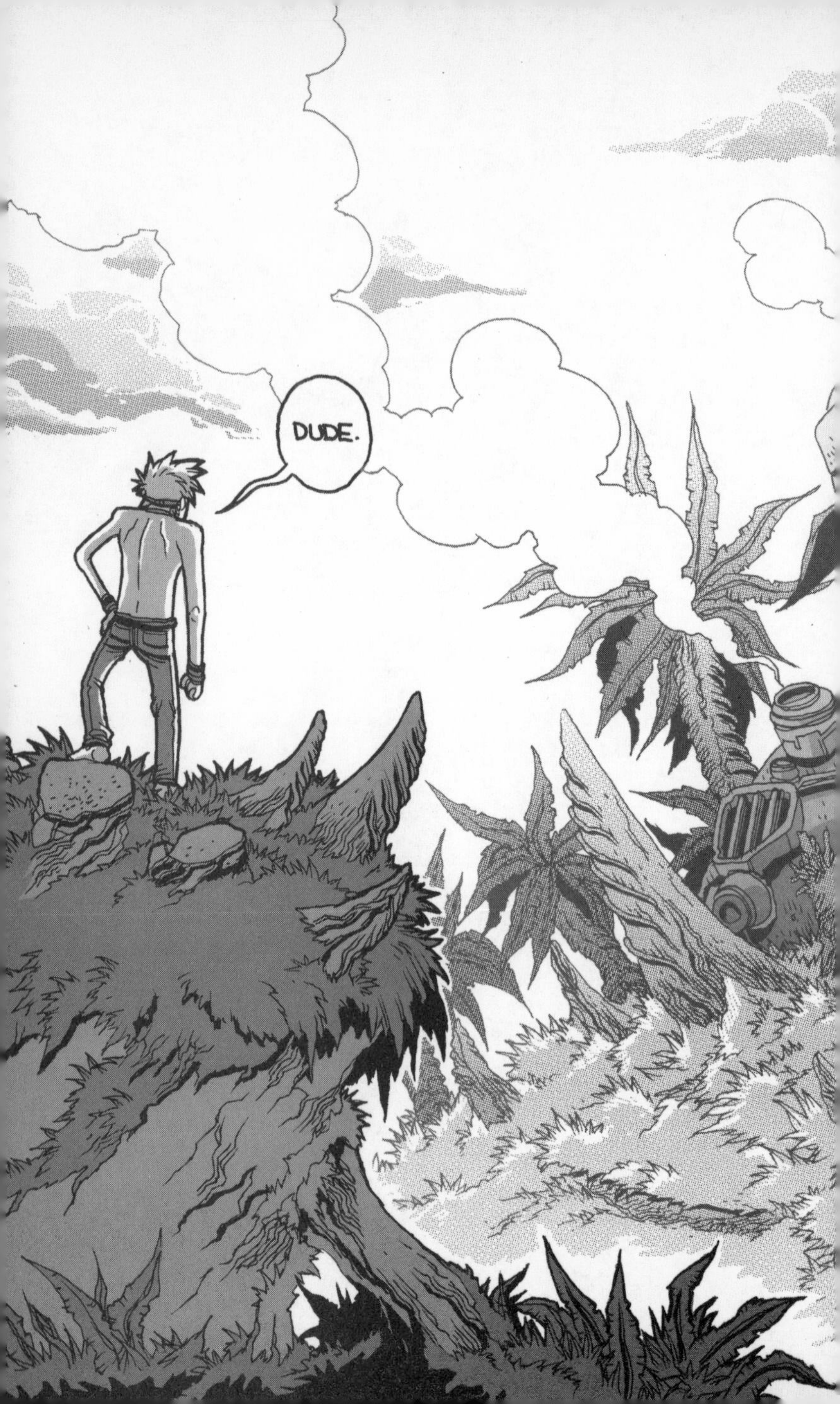
DUDE.

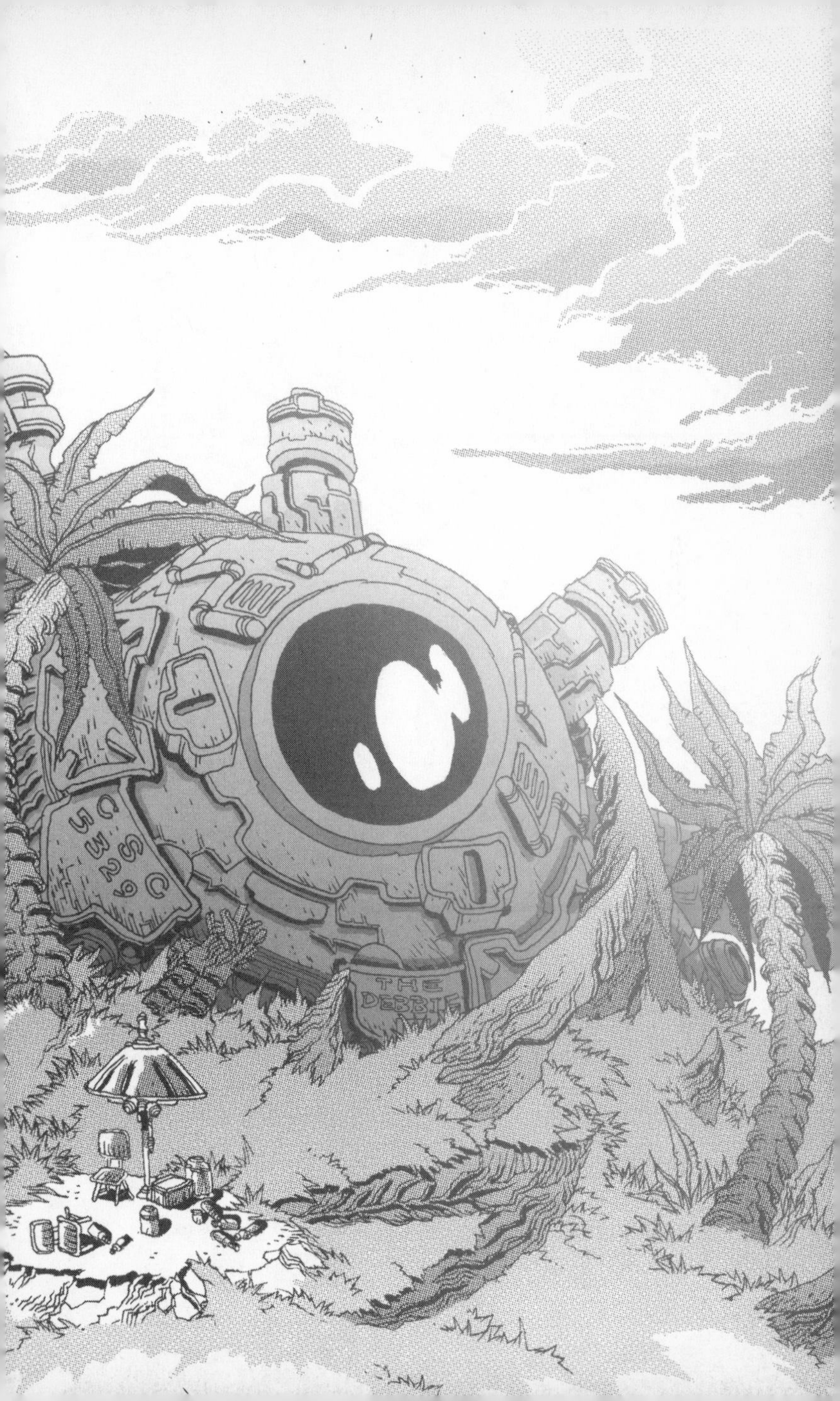
THE DEBBIE

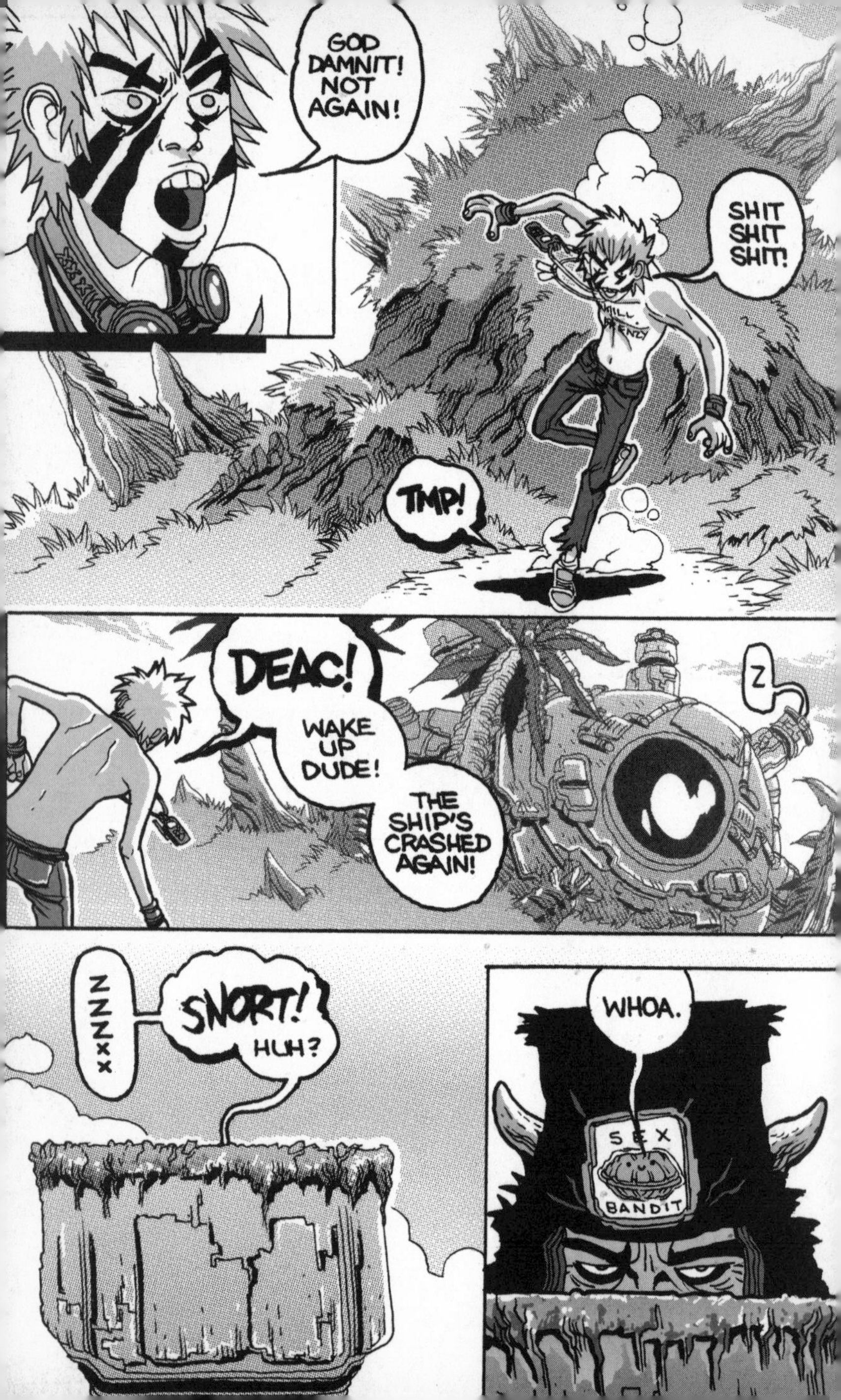

GOD DAMNIT! NOT AGAIN!
SHIT SHIT SHIT!
TMP!
DEAC!
WAKE UP DUDE!
THE SHIP'S CRASHED AGAIN!
Z
ZZZxx
SNORT!
HUH?
WHOA.
SEX BANDIT

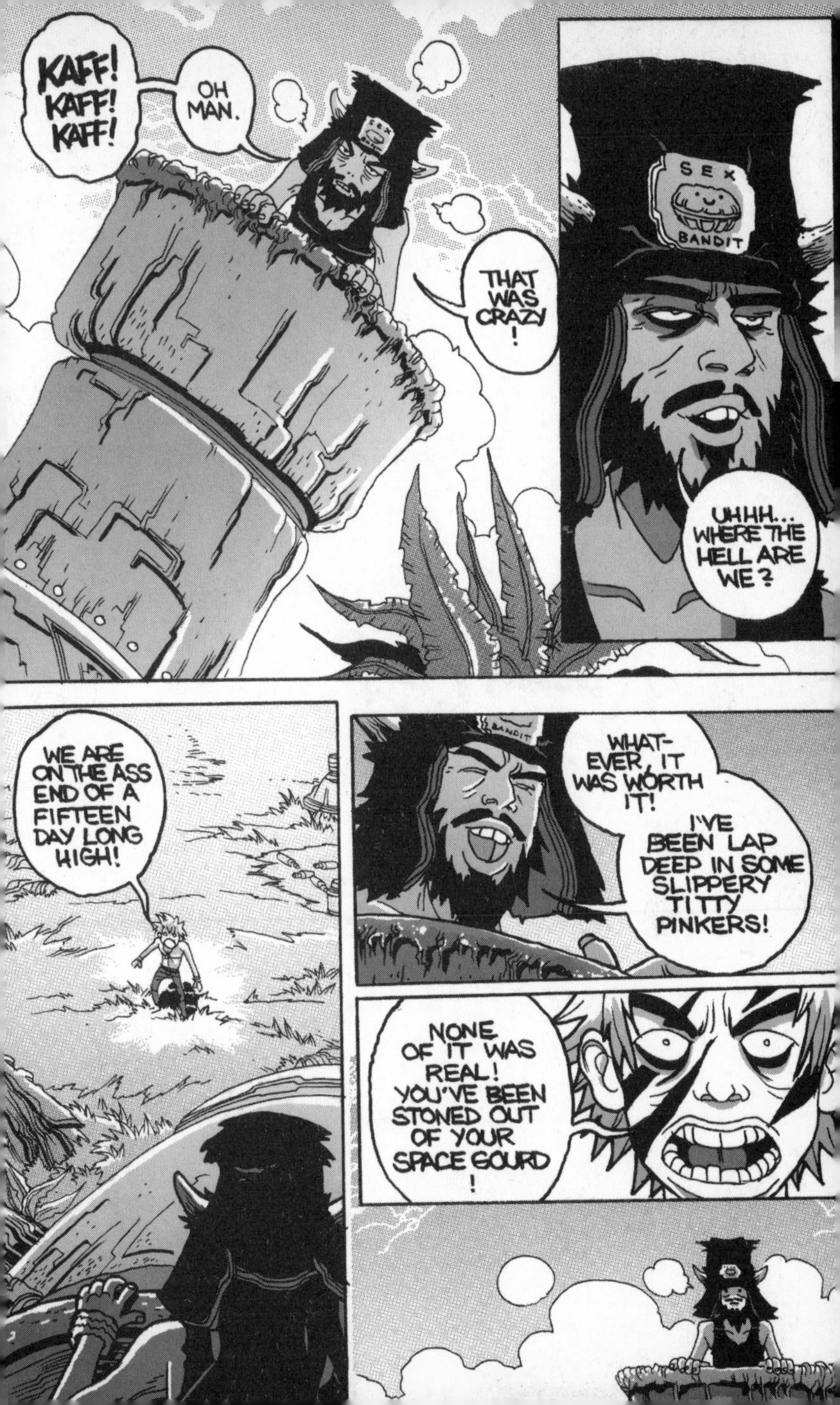
KAFF! KAFF! KAFF!
OH MAN.
THAT WAS CRAZY!
SEX BANDIT
UHHH... WHERE THE HELL ARE WE?
WE ARE ON THE ASS END OF A FIFTEEN DAY LONG HIGH!
WHAT-EVER, IT WAS WORTH IT!
I'VE BEEN LAP DEEP IN SOME SLIPPERY TITTY PINKERS!
NONE OF IT WAS REAL! YOU'VE BEEN STONED OUT OF YOUR SPACE GOURD!

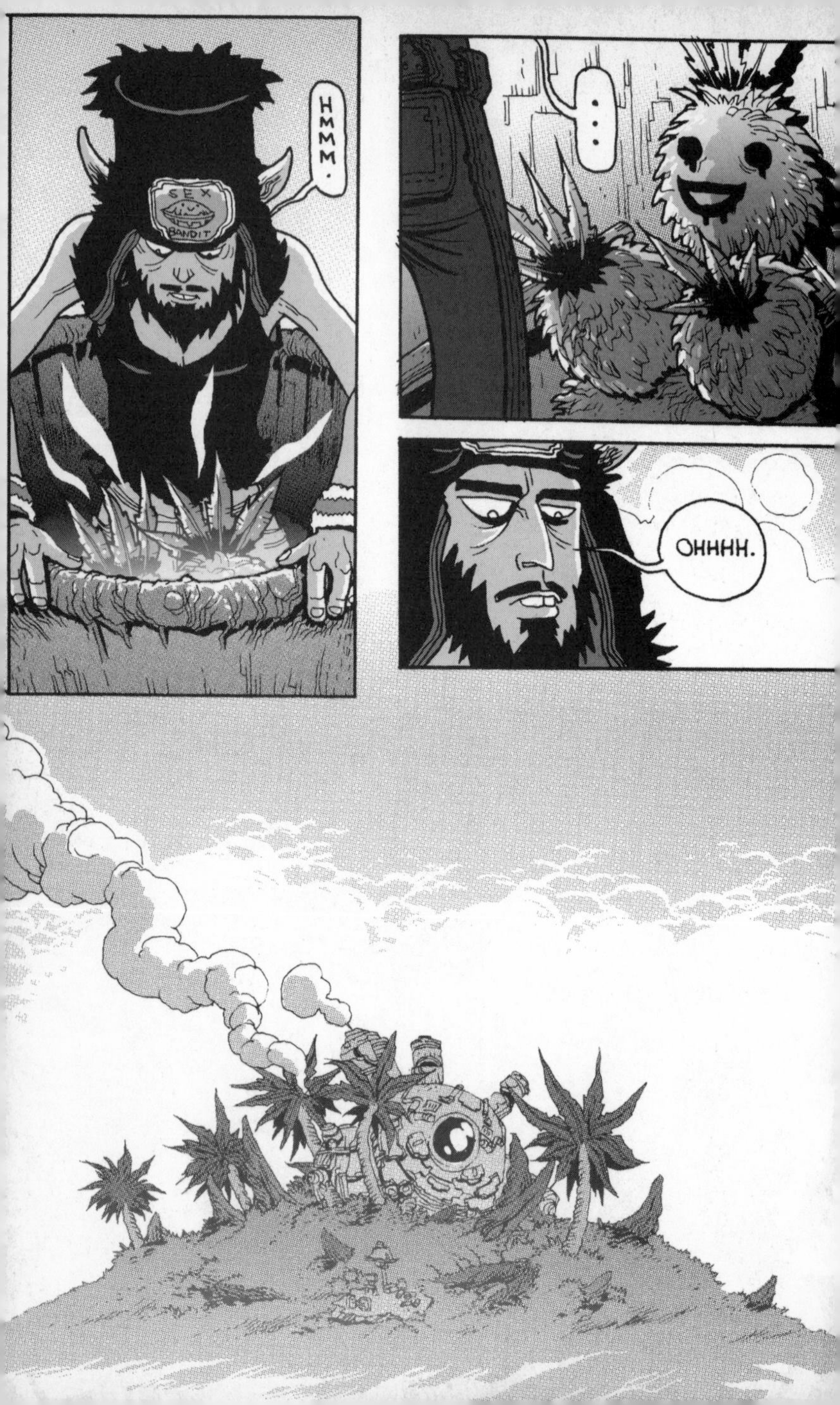
HMMM.
...
OHHHH.

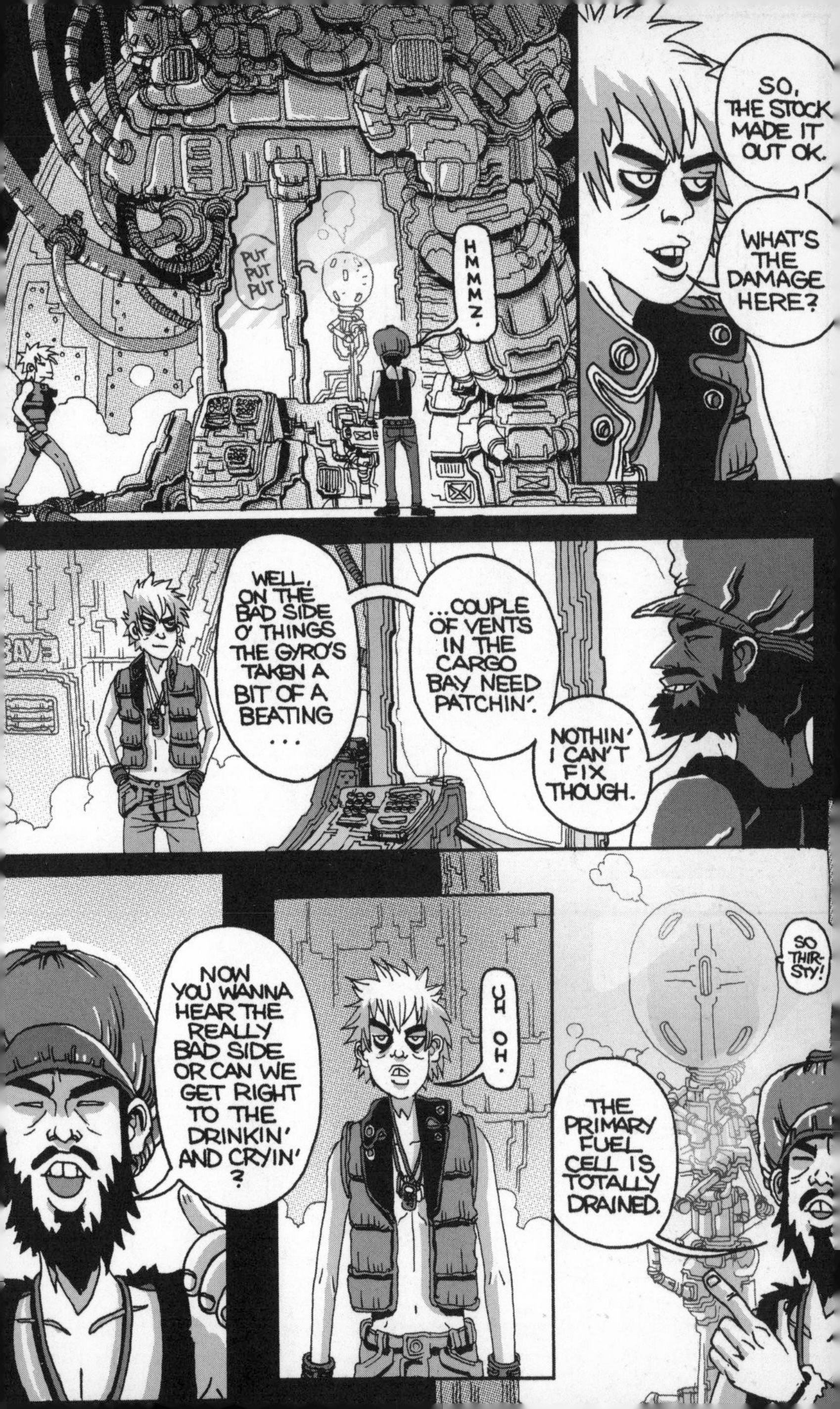
PUT PUT PUT
HMMMZ.
SO, THE STOCK MADE IT OUT OK.
WHAT'S THE DAMAGE HERE?
BAYS
WELL, ON THE BAD SIDE O' THINGS THE GYRO'S TAKEN A BIT OF A BEATING . . .
...COUPLE OF VENTS IN THE CARGO BAY NEED PATCHIN'.
NOTHIN' I CAN'T FIX THOUGH.
NOW YOU WANNA HEAR THE REALLY BAD SIDE OR CAN WE GET RIGHT TO THE DRINKIN' AND CRYIN'?
UH OH.
SO THIR-STY!
THE PRIMARY FUEL CELL IS TOTALLY DRAINED.

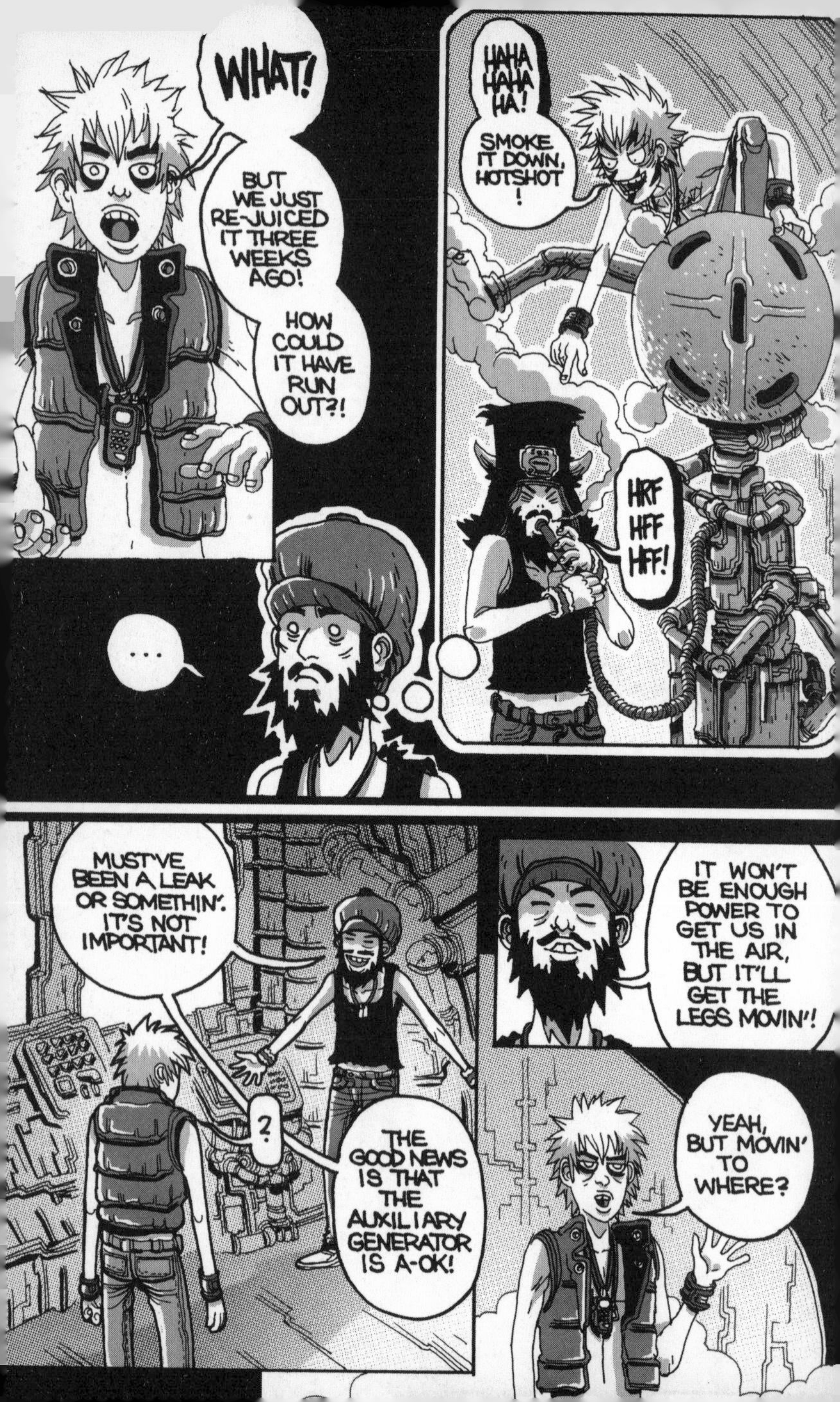
WHAT!
BUT WE JUST RE-JUICED IT THREE WEEKS AGO!
HOW COULD IT HAVE RUN OUT?!
...
HAHA HAHA HA!
SMOKE IT DOWN, HOTSHOT!
HRF HFF HFF!
MUST'VE BEEN A LEAK OR SOMETHIN'. IT'S NOT IMPORTANT!
?
THE GOOD NEWS IS THAT THE AUXILIARY GENERATOR IS A-OK!
IT WON'T BE ENOUGH POWER TO GET US IN THE AIR, BUT IT'LL GET THE LEGS MOVIN'!
YEAH, BUT MOVIN' TO WHERE?

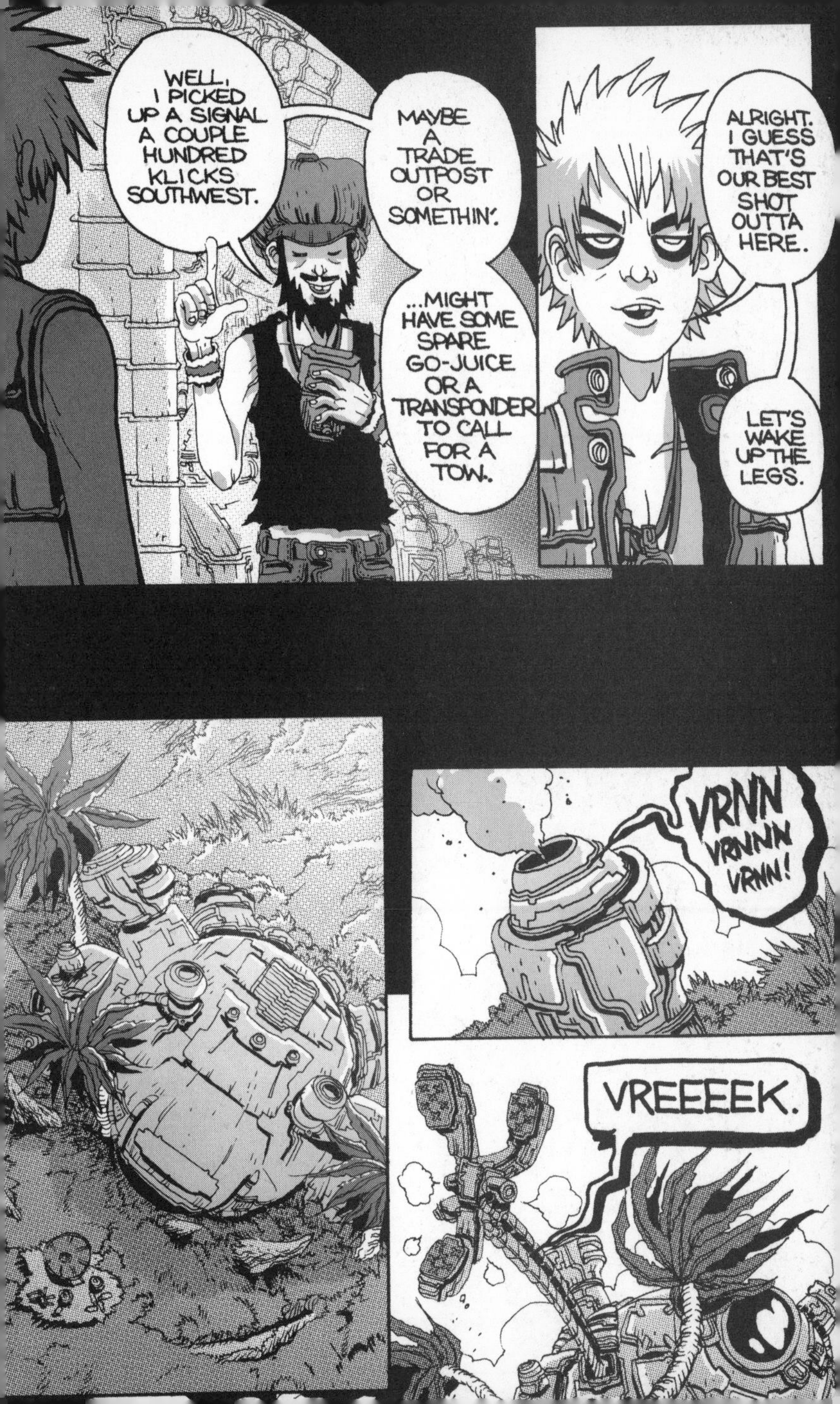
WELL, I PICKED UP A SIGNAL A COUPLE HUNDRED KLICKS SOUTHWEST.
MAYBE A TRADE OUTPOST OR SOMETHIN'.
...MIGHT HAVE SOME SPARE GO-JUICE OR A TRANSPONDER TO CALL FOR A TOW.
ALRIGHT. I GUESS THAT'S OUR BEST SHOT OUTTA HERE.
LET'S WAKE UP THE LEGS.
VRNN VRNNN VRNN!
VREEEEK.

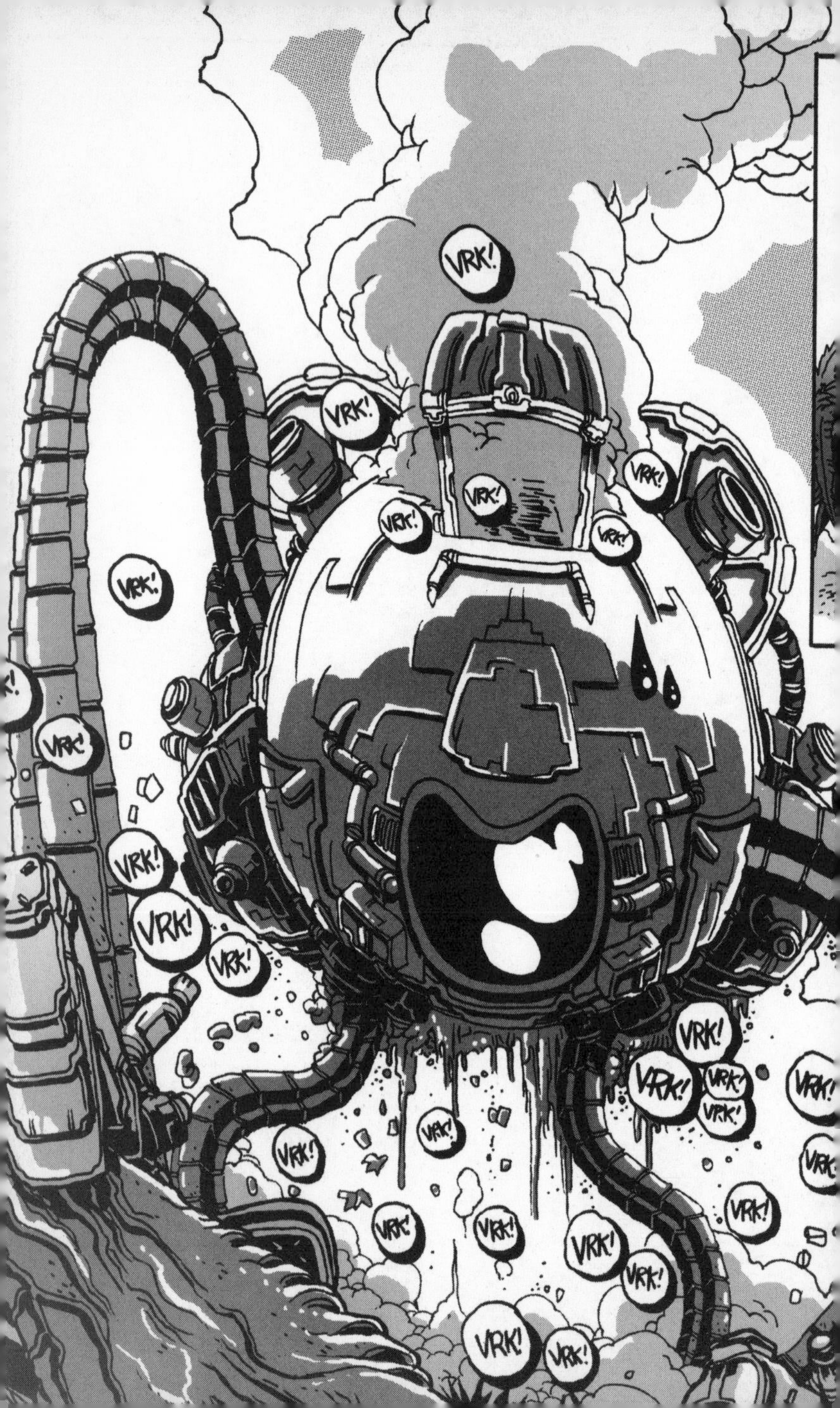
VRK!
VRK!
VRK!
VRK!
VRK!
VRK!
VRK!
VRK!
VRK!
VRK!
VRK!
VRK!
VRK!
VRK!
VRK!
VRK!
VRK!
VRK!
VRK!
VRK!
VRK!
VRK!
VRK!
VRK!
VRK!
VRK!

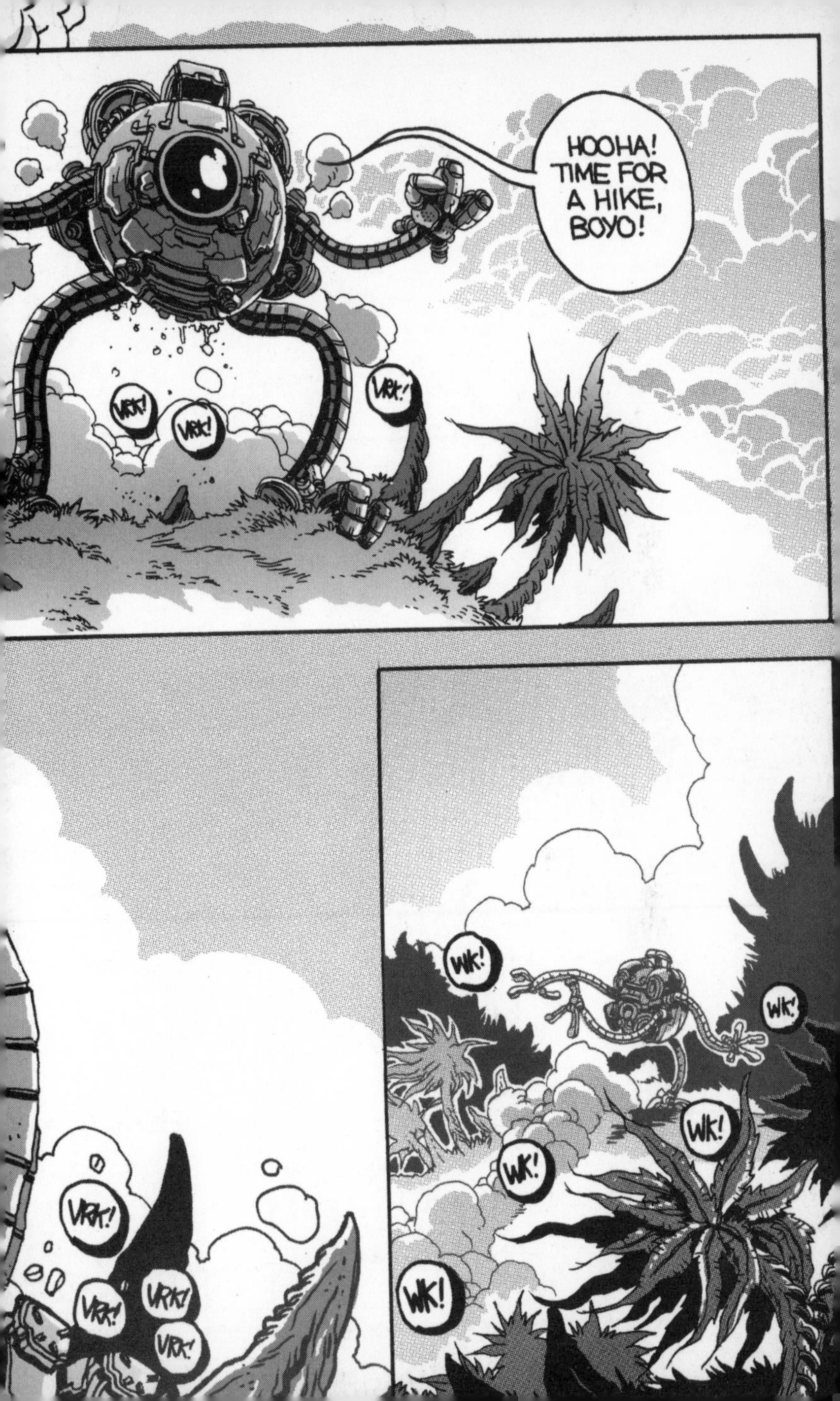
HOOHA! TIME FOR A HIKE, BOYO!
VRK!
VRK!
VRK!
VRK!
VRK!
VRK!
VRK!
WK!
WK!
WK!
WK!
WK!

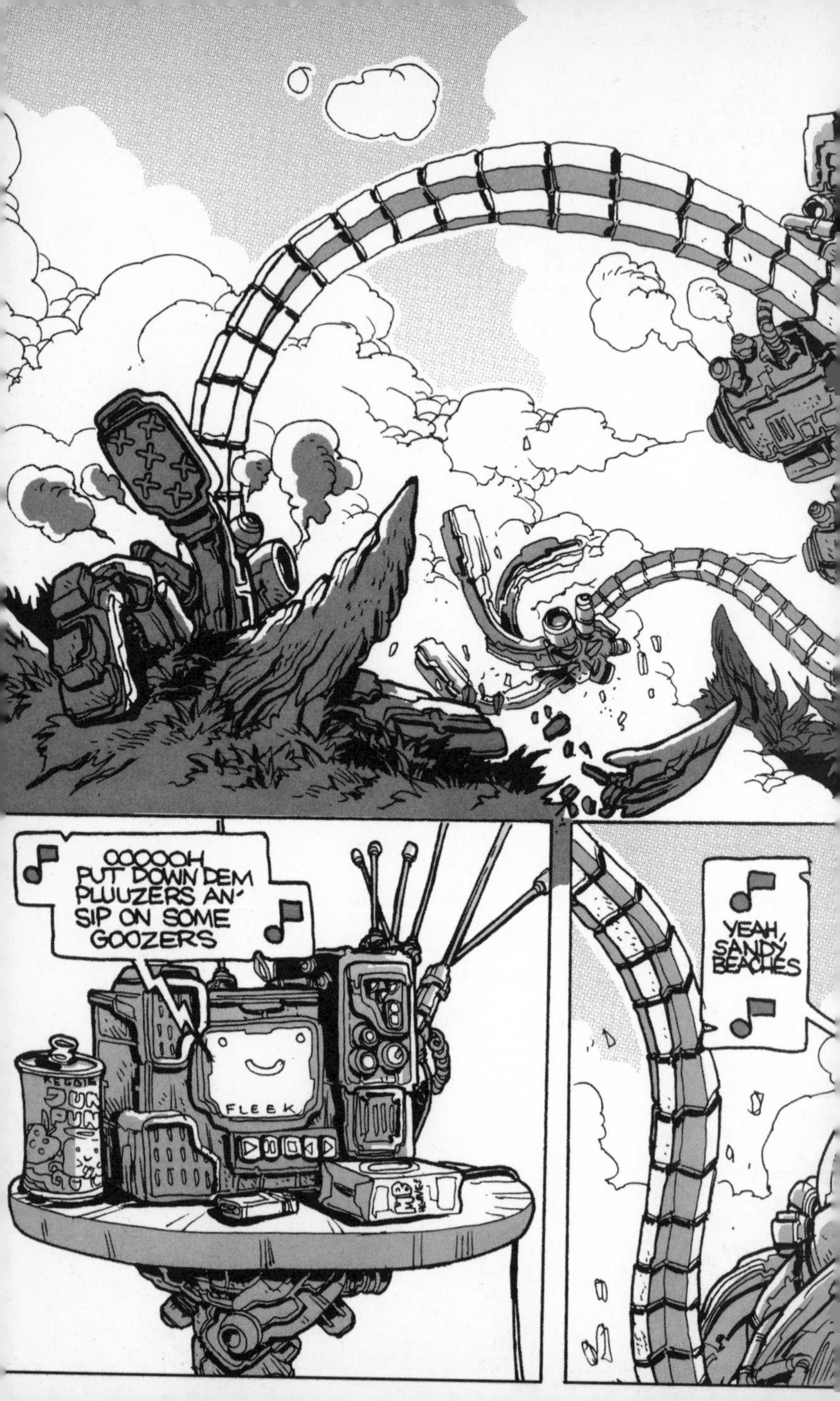
OOOOOH PUT DOWN DEM PLUUZERS AN' SIP ON SOME GOOZERS
FLEEK
YEAH, SANDY BEACHES

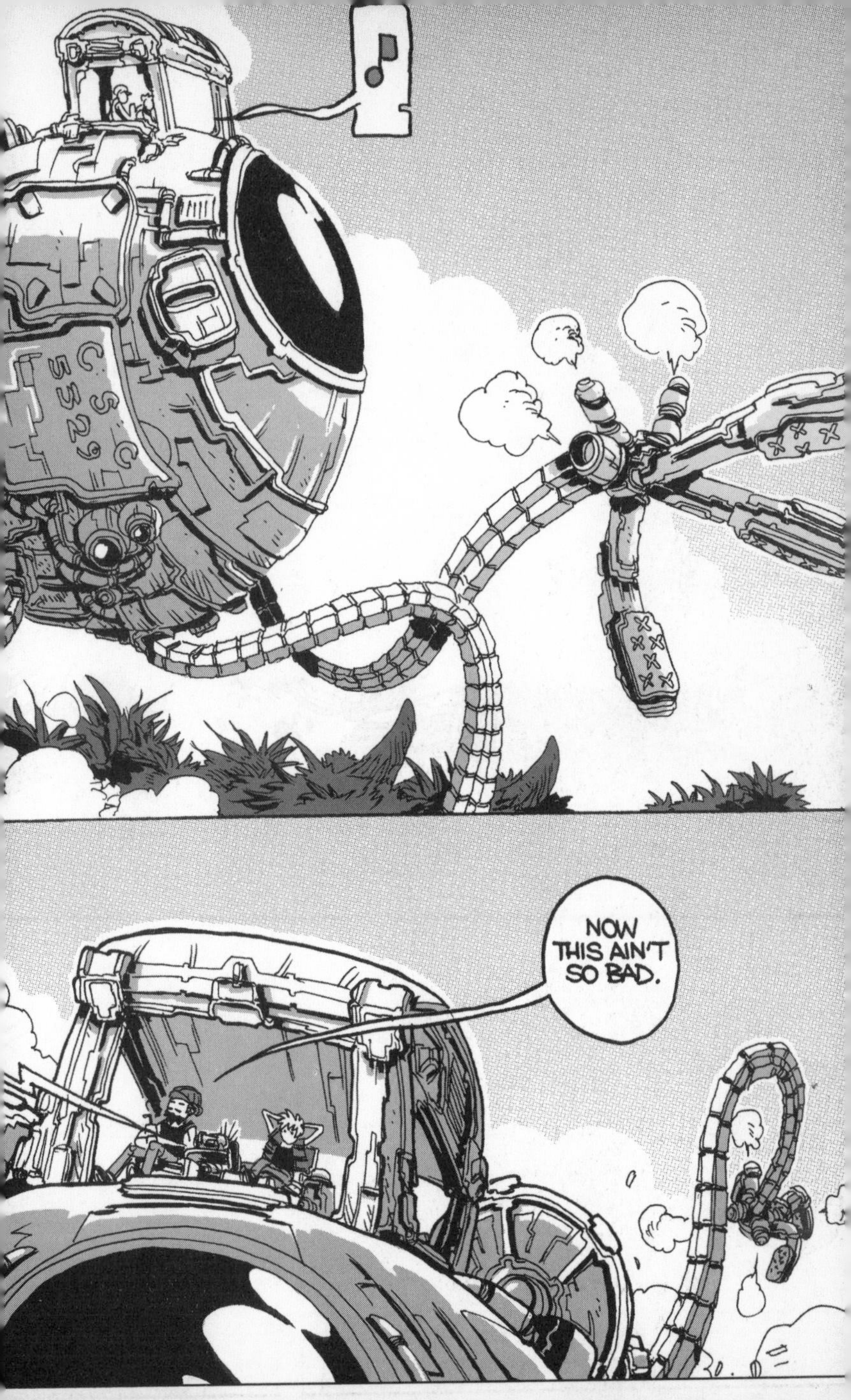
NOW THIS AIN'T SO BAD.

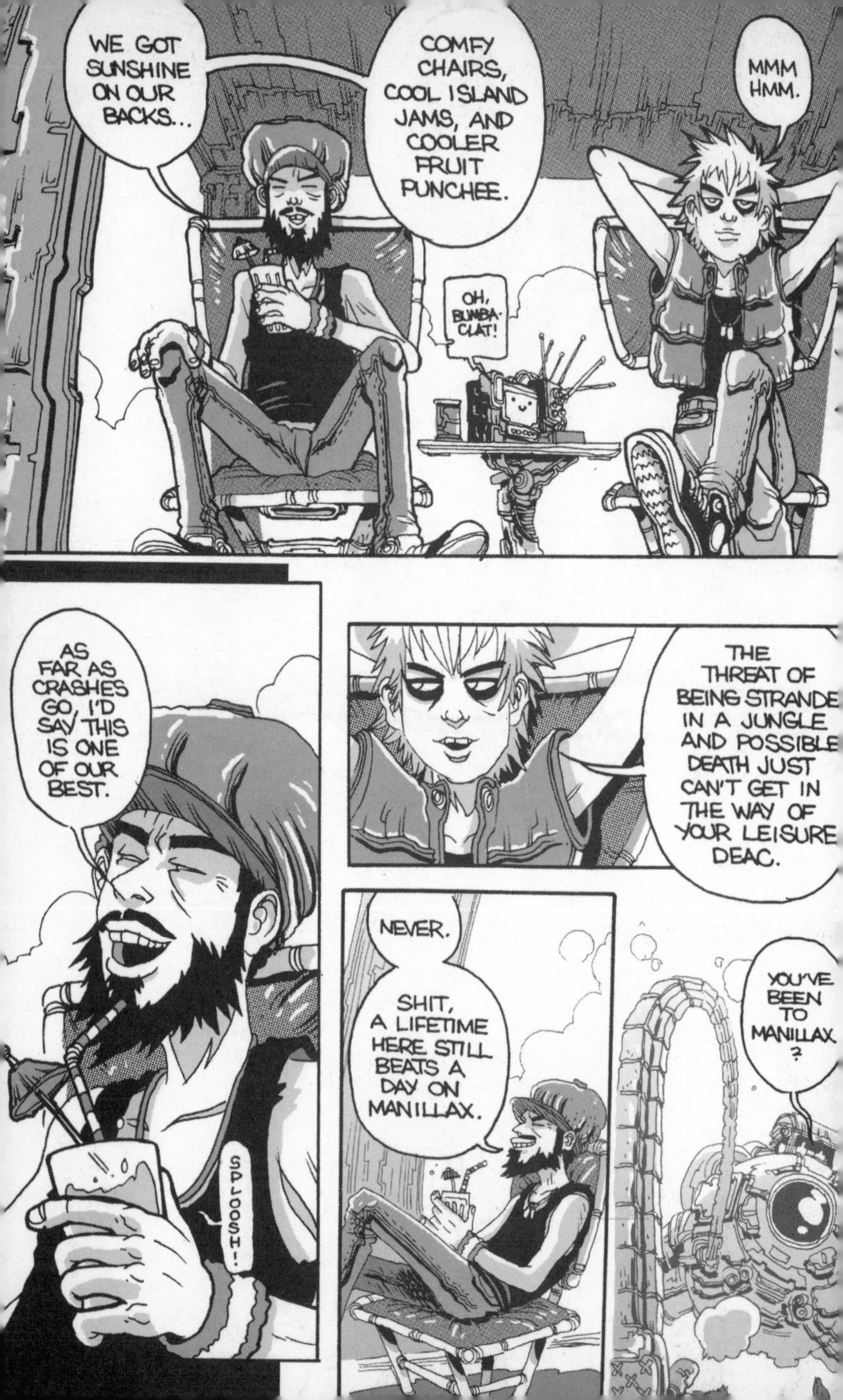
WE GOT SUNSHINE ON OUR BACKS...
COMFY CHAIRS, COOL ISLAND JAMS, AND COOLER FRUIT PUNCHEE.
MMM HMM.
OH, BUMBA-CLAT!
AS FAR AS CRASHES GO, I'D SAY THIS IS ONE OF OUR BEST.
THE THREAT OF BEING STRANDE IN A JUNGLE AND POSSIBLE DEATH JUST CAN'T GET IN THE WAY OF YOUR LEISURE DEAC.
SPLOOSH!
NEVER.
SHIT, A LIFETIME HERE STILL BEATS A DAY ON MANILLAX.
YOU'VE BEEN TO MANILLAX ?

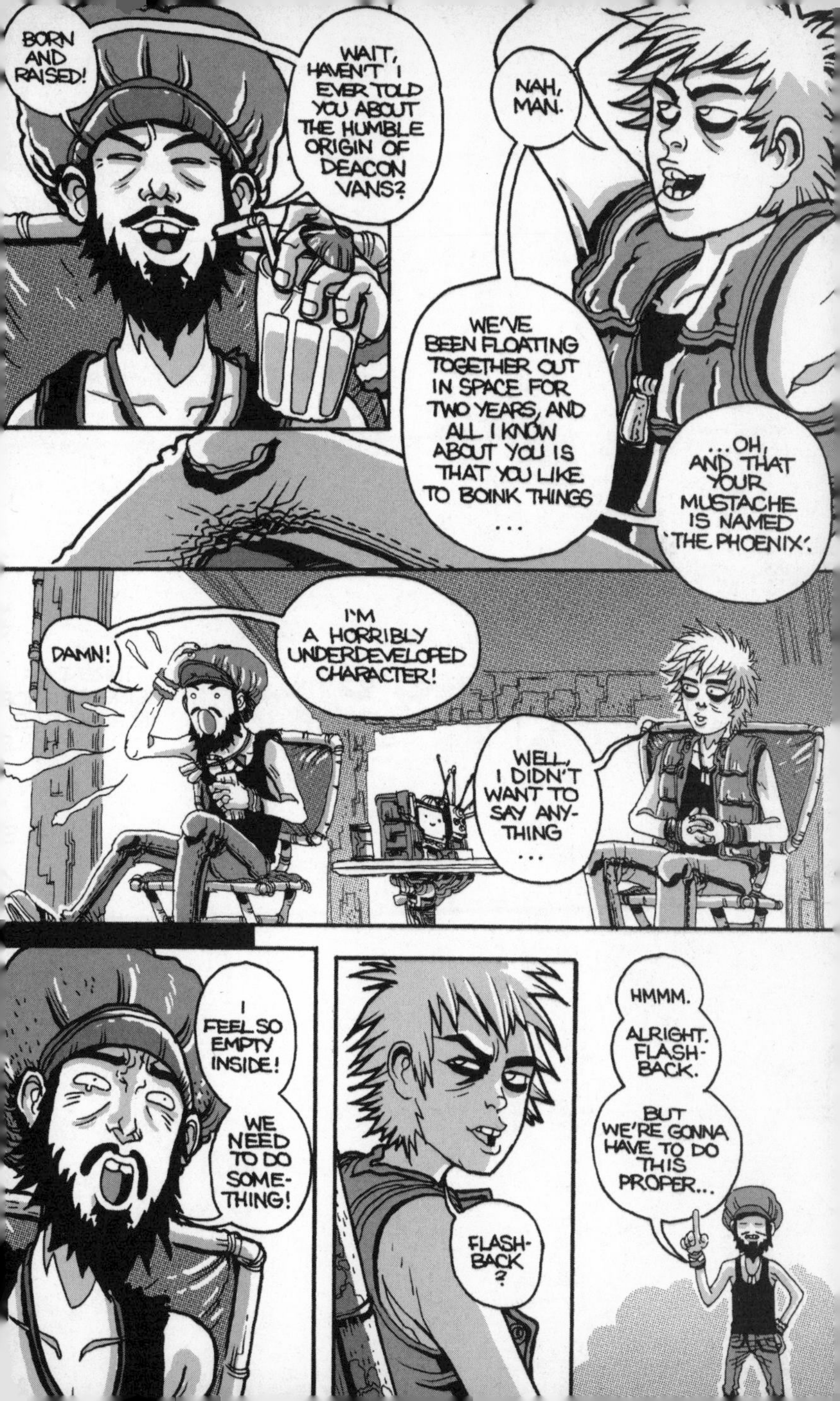
BORN AND RAISED!
WAIT, HAVEN'T I EVER TOLD YOU ABOUT THE HUMBLE ORIGIN OF DEACON VANS?
NAH, MAN.
WE'VE BEEN FLOATING TOGETHER OUT IN SPACE FOR TWO YEARS, AND ALL I KNOW ABOUT YOU IS THAT YOU LIKE TO BOINK THINGS ...
...OH, AND THAT YOUR MUSTACHE IS NAMED 'THE PHOENIX'.
DAMN!
I'M A HORRIBLY UNDERDEVELOPED CHARACTER!
WELL, I DIDN'T WANT TO SAY ANY-THING ...
I FEEL SO EMPTY INSIDE!
WE NEED TO DO SOME-THING!
FLASH-BACK?
HMMM.
ALRIGHT. FLASH-BACK.
BUT WE'RE GONNA HAVE TO DO THIS PROPER...

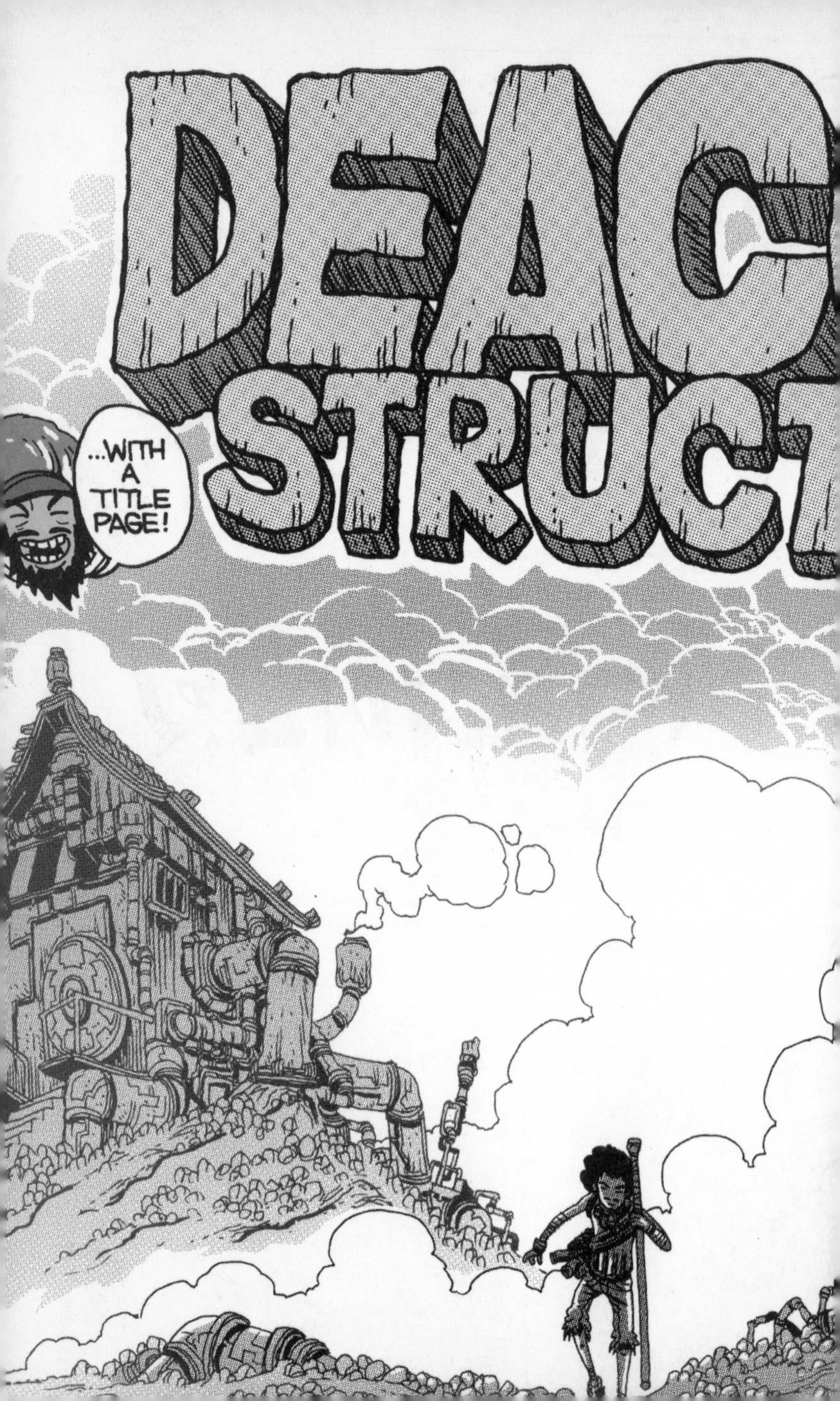
DEAC
STRUCT
...WITH A TITLE PAGE!

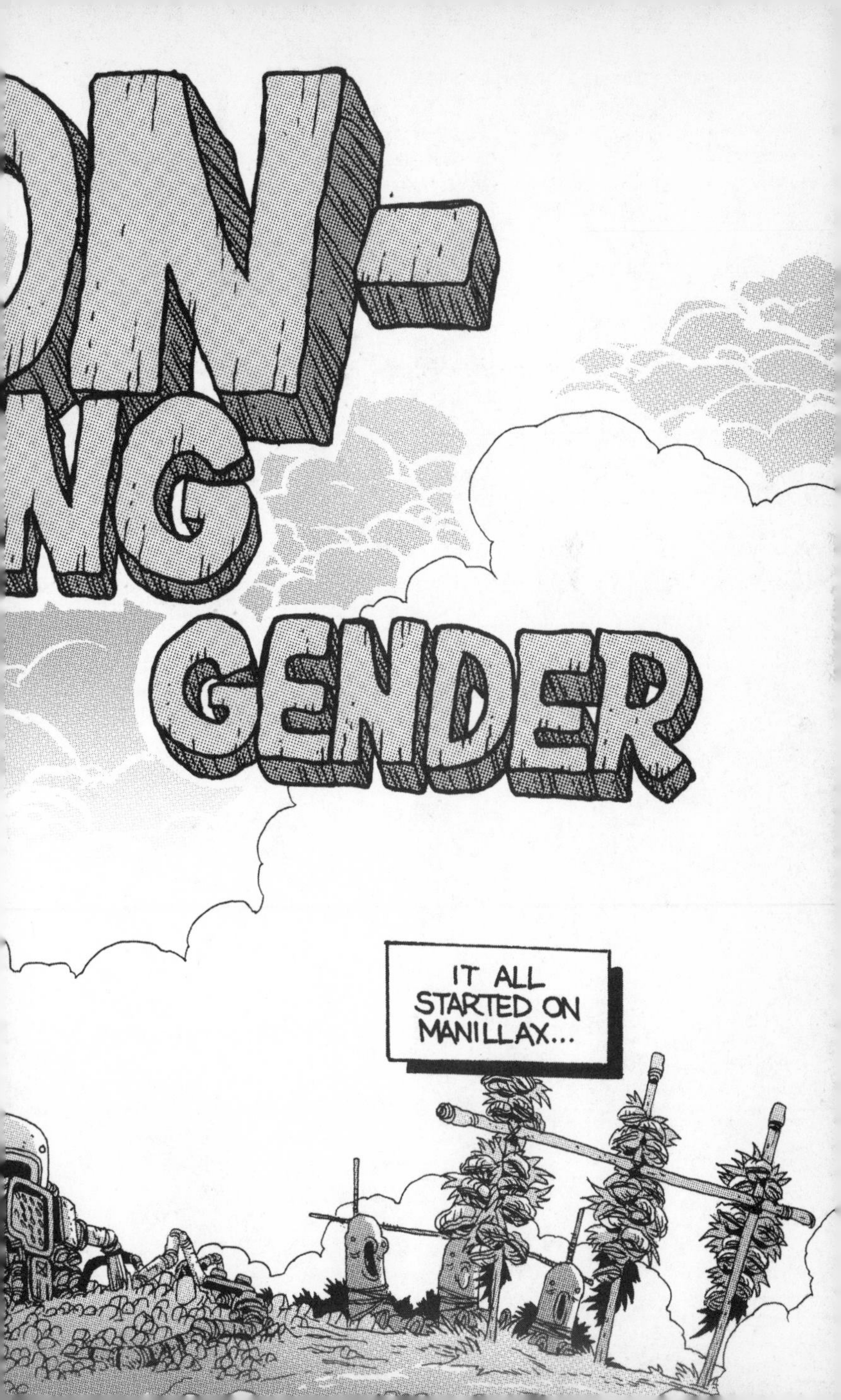

ON-
NG
GENDER
IT ALL STARTED ON MANILLAX...

DEAD, DRY-FART OF A BACKWATER WORLD. THE ONLY NOTABLE FEATURE IS ITS HOT PRODUCTION OF BLACK MARKET GOODS.

I HAD JUST INHERITED A SMALL SEX FARM FROM MY LATE UNCLE SEBASTIAN.

SMALL CROPS OF ILLEGAL AG ASSCLAM, TITT TOTS, AND HOL IN HOLES... NOTHIN' TOO HEAVY.

COCK BANDITS!

ONE DAY AFTER FINISHING MY ROUNDS, I HEARD A MANIC WHINING COMIN' FROM THE ABANDONED SILO AT THE END OF MY LOT...

BRAAW

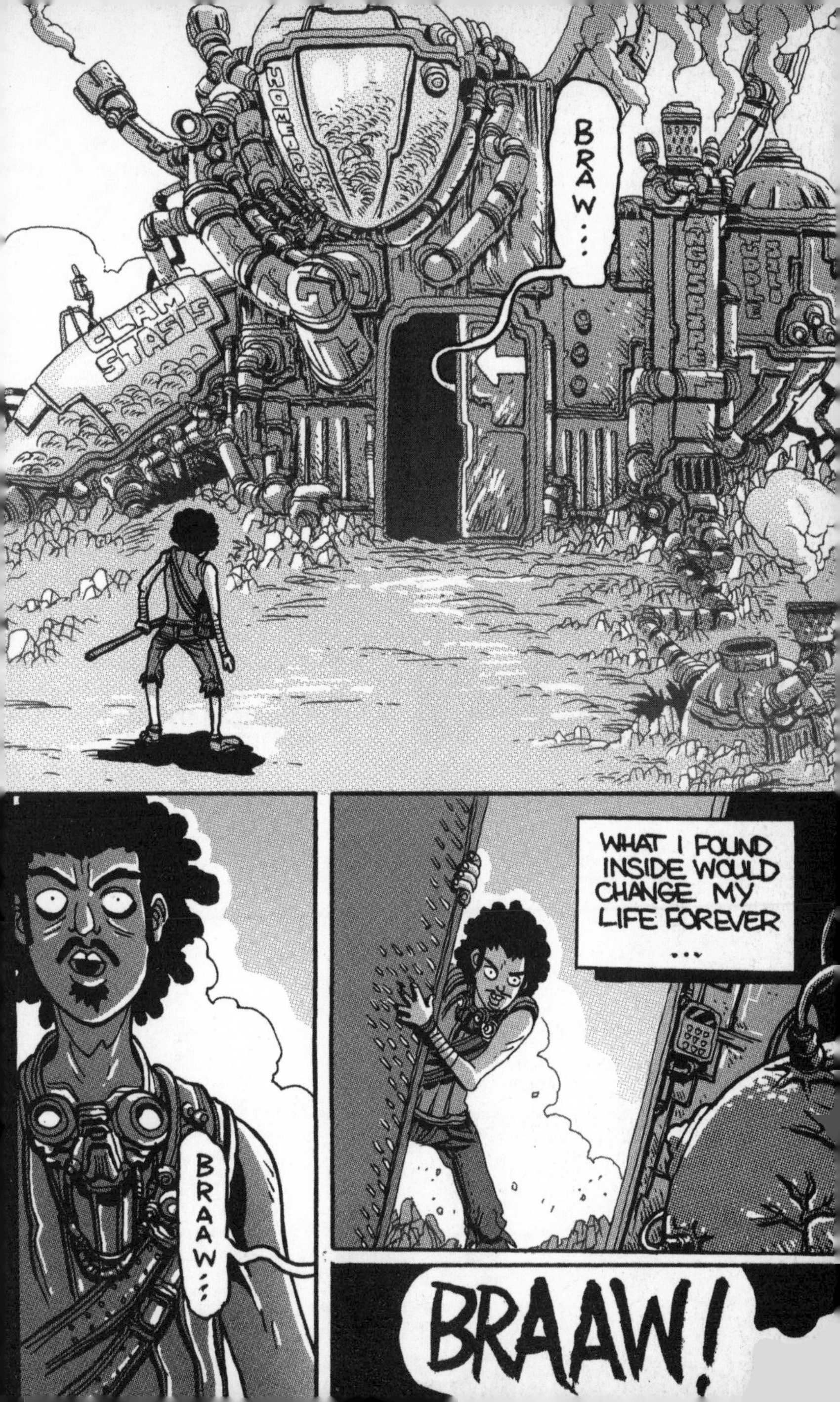
CLAM STASIS
BRAW...
BRAAW...
WHAT I FOUND INSIDE WOULD CHANGE MY LIFE FOREVER ...
BRAAW!

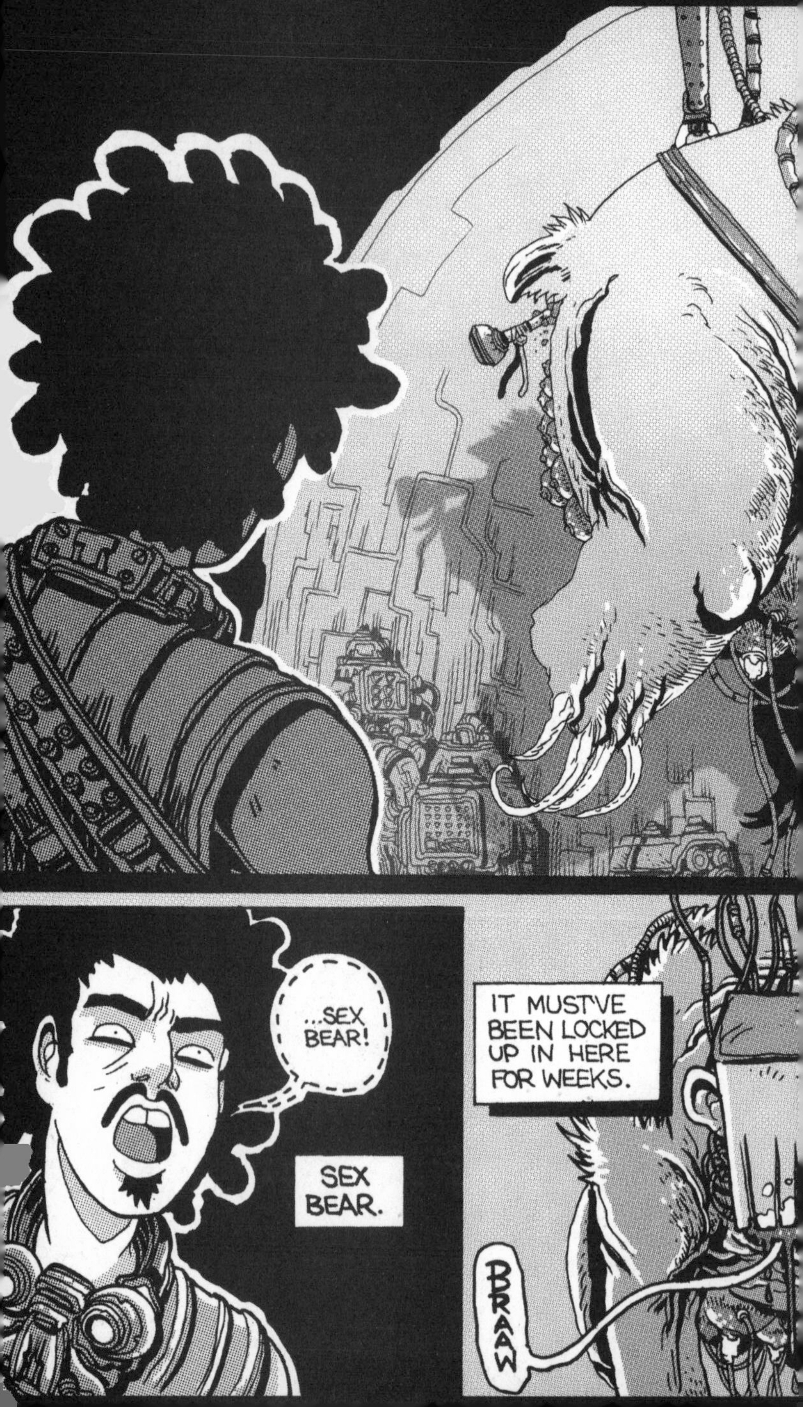

...SEX BEAR!
SEX BEAR.
IT MUST'VE BEEN LOCKED UP IN HERE FOR WEEKS.
DBRAAW

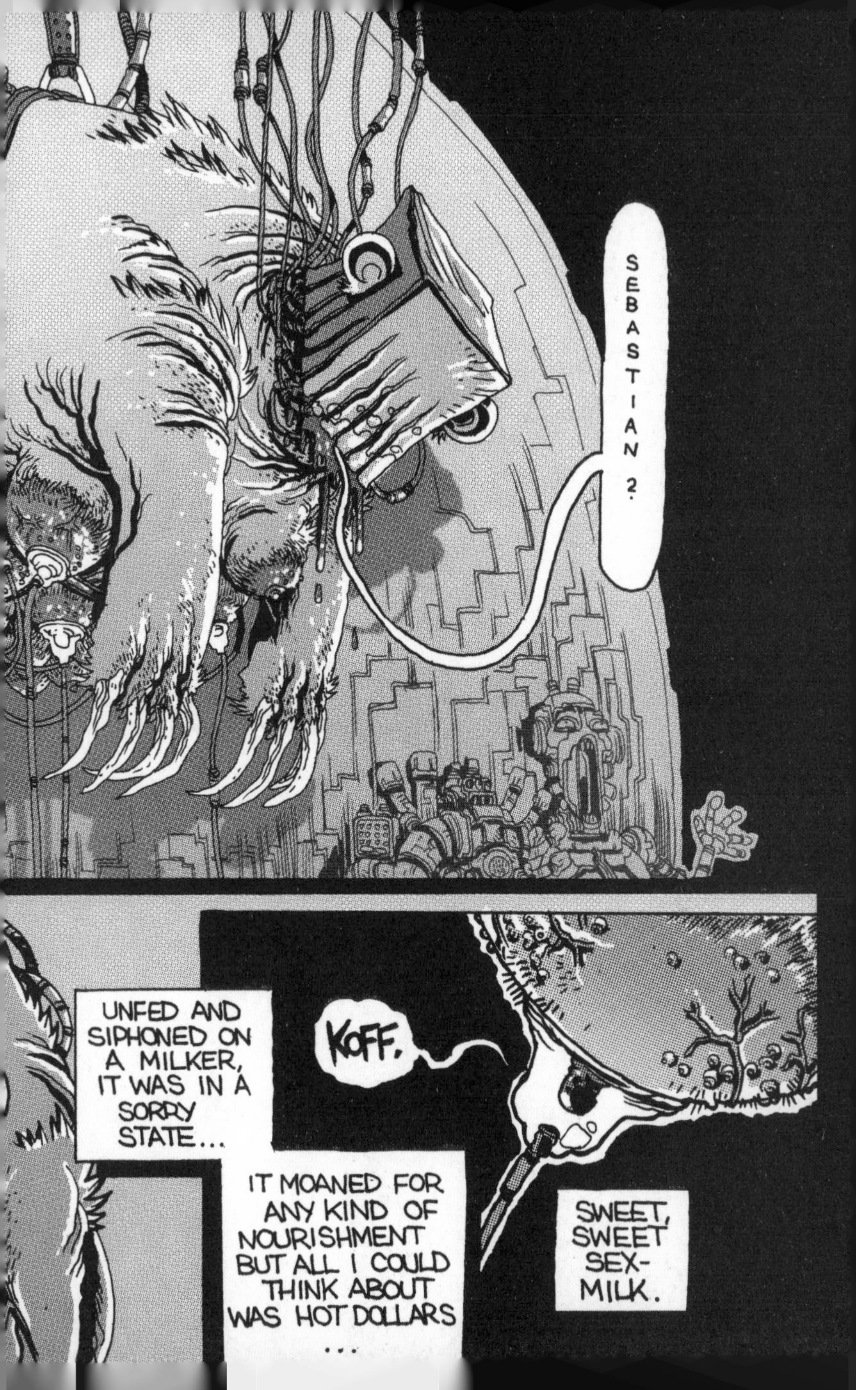
SEBASTIAN?
UNFED AND SIPHONED ON A MILKER, IT WAS IN A SORRY STATE...
KOFF.
IT MOANED FOR ANY KIND OF NOURISHMENT BUT ALL I COULD THINK ABOUT WAS HOT DOLLARS ...
SWEET, SWEET SEX-MILK.

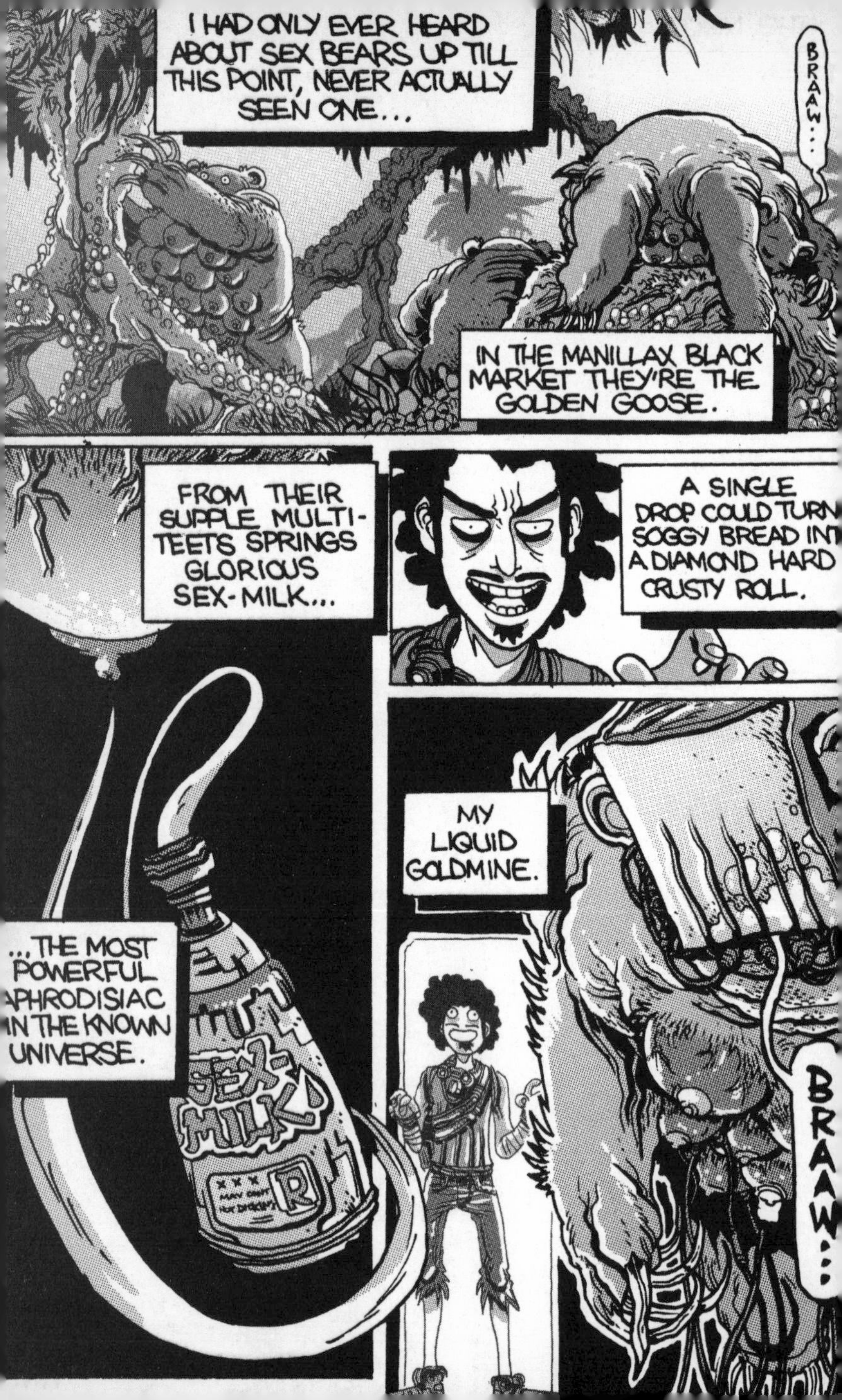
I HAD ONLY EVER HEARD ABOUT SEX BEARS UP TILL THIS POINT, NEVER ACTUALLY SEEN ONE...
BRAAW...
IN THE MANILLAX BLACK MARKET THEY'RE THE GOLDEN GOOSE.
FROM THEIR SUPPLE MULTI-TEETS SPRINGS GLORIOUS SEX-MILK...
A SINGLE DROP COULD TURN SOGGY BREAD INT A DIAMOND HARD CRUSTY ROLL.
...THE MOST POWERFUL APHRODISIAC IN THE KNOWN UNIVERSE.
SEX-MILK
R
MY LIQUID GOLDMINE.
BRAAW...

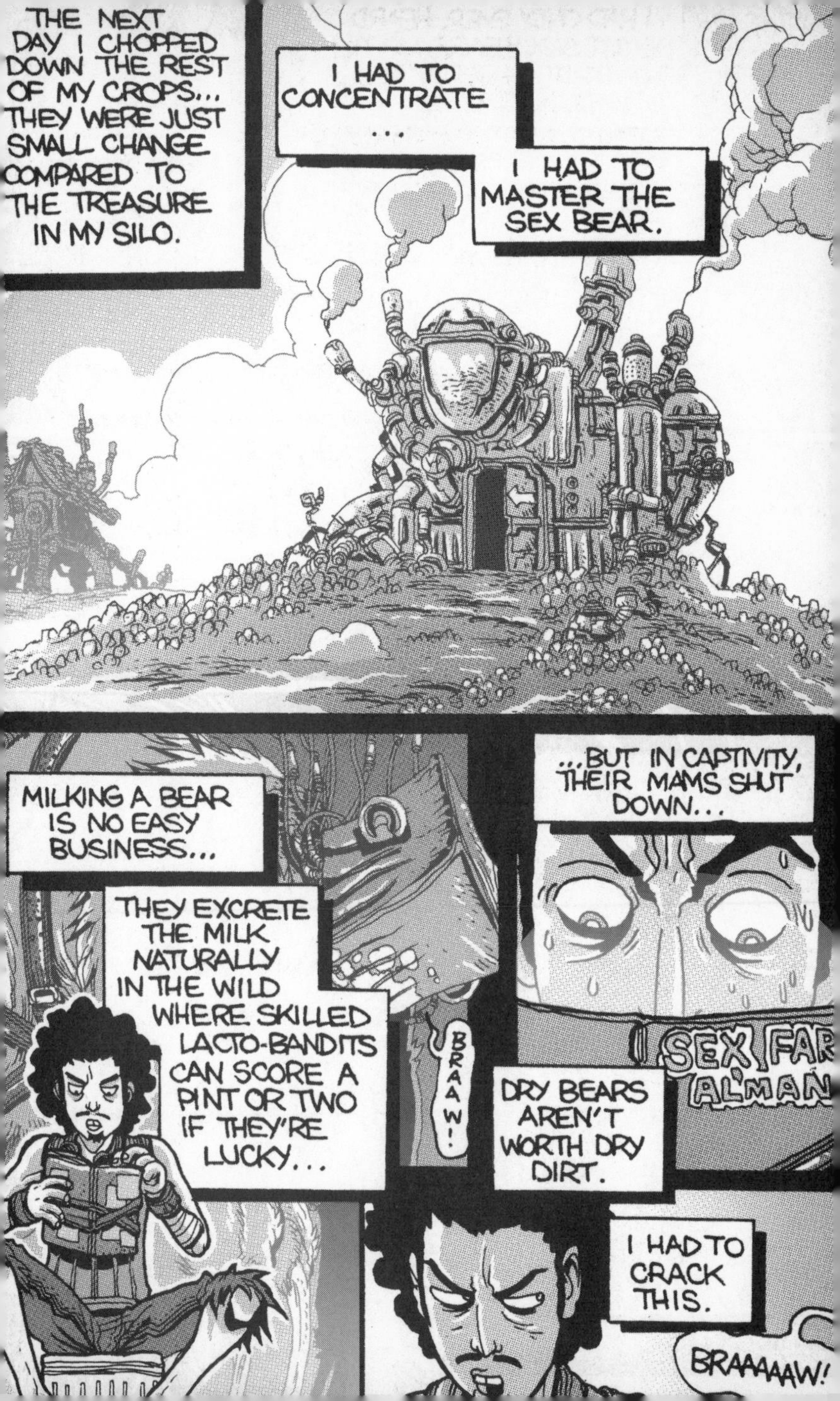
THE NEXT DAY I CHOPPED DOWN THE REST OF MY CROPS... THEY WERE JUST SMALL CHANGE COMPARED TO THE TREASURE IN MY SILO.
I HAD TO CONCENTRATE ...
I HAD TO MASTER THE SEX BEAR.
MILKING A BEAR IS NO EASY BUSINESS...
THEY EXCRETE THE MILK NATURALLY IN THE WILD WHERE SKILLED LACTO-BANDITS CAN SCORE A PINT OR TWO IF THEY'RE LUCKY...
BRAAW!
...BUT IN CAPTIVITY, THEIR MAMS SHUT DOWN...
SEX FAR
AL'MAN
DRY BEARS AREN'T WORTH DRY DIRT.
I HAD TO CRACK THIS.
BRAAAAAW!

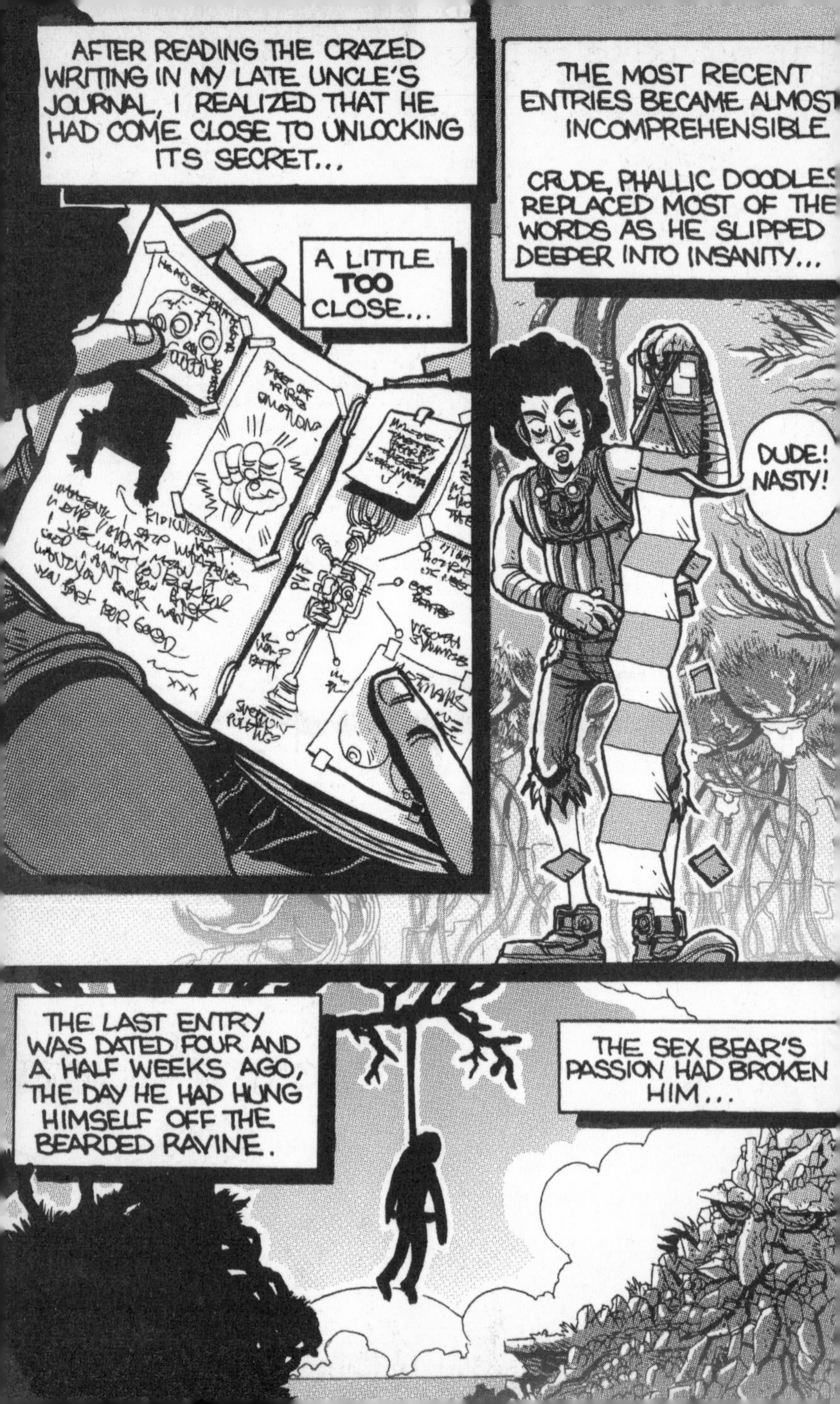

AFTER READING THE CRAZED WRITING IN MY LATE UNCLE'S JOURNAL, I REALIZED THAT HE HAD COME CLOSE TO UNLOCKING ITS SECRET...
A LITTLE TOO CLOSE...
THE MOST RECENT ENTRIES BECAME ALMOST INCOMPREHENSIBLE
CRUDE, PHALLIC DOODLES REPLACED MOST OF THE WORDS AS HE SLIPPED DEEPER INTO INSANITY...
DUDE! NASTY!
THE LAST ENTRY WAS DATED FOUR AND A HALF WEEKS AGO, THE DAY HE HAD HUNG HIMSELF OFF THE BEARDED RAVINE.
THE SEX BEAR'S PASSION HAD BROKEN HIM...

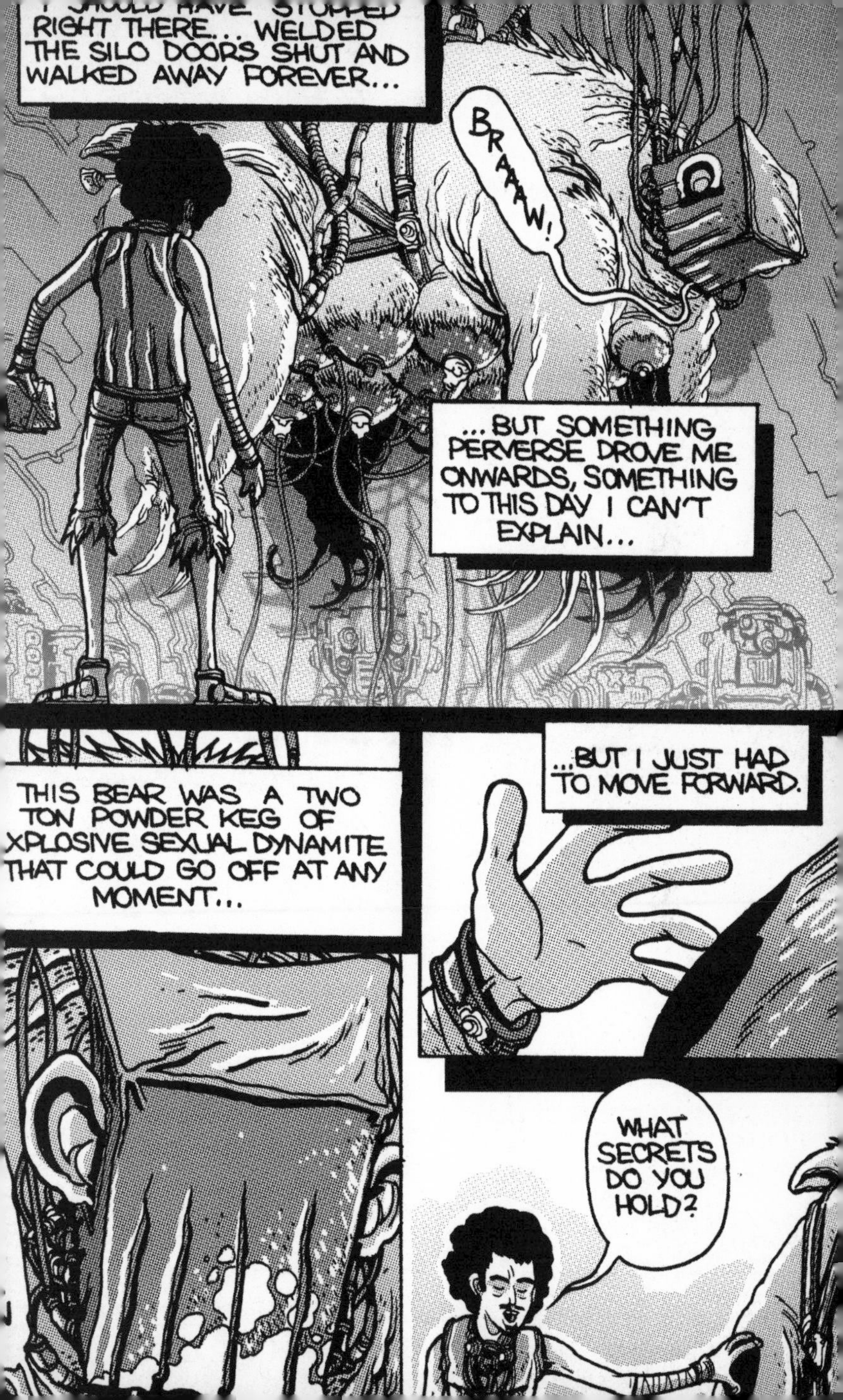
RIGHT THERE... WELDED THE SILO DOORS SHUT AND WALKED AWAY FOREVER...
BRAAAAW!
...BUT SOMETHING PERVERSE DROVE ME ONWARDS, SOMETHING TO THIS DAY I CAN'T EXPLAIN...
THIS BEAR WAS A TWO TON POWDER KEG OF XPLOSIVE SEXUAL DYNAMITE THAT COULD GO OFF AT ANY MOMENT...
...BUT I JUST HAD TO MOVE FORWARD.
WHAT SECRETS DO YOU HOLD?

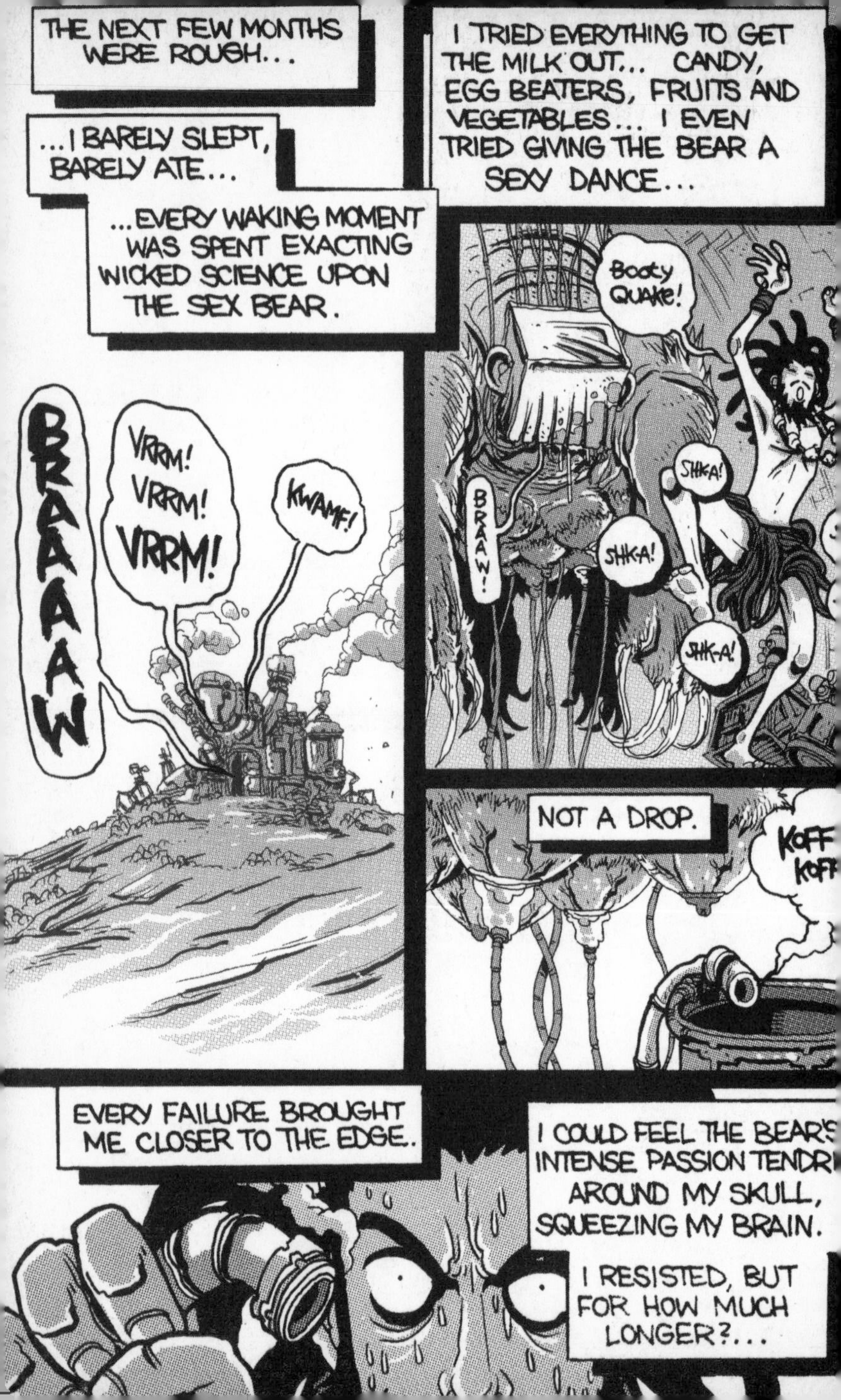
THE NEXT FEW MONTHS WERE ROUGH...
...I BARELY SLEPT, BARELY ATE...
...EVERY WAKING MOMENT WAS SPENT EXACTING WICKED SCIENCE UPON THE SEX BEAR.
BRAAAAW
VRRM! VRRM! VRRM!
KWAMF!
I TRIED EVERYTHING TO GET THE MILK OUT... CANDY, EGG BEATERS, FRUITS AND VEGETABLES... I EVEN TRIED GIVING THE BEAR A SEXY DANCE...
Booty QUAKE!
BRAAAW!
SHKA!
SHKA!
SHK-A!
NOT A DROP.
KOFF KOFF
EVERY FAILURE BROUGHT ME CLOSER TO THE EDGE.
I COULD FEEL THE BEAR'S INTENSE PASSION TENDRI AROUND MY SKULL, SQUEEZING MY BRAIN.
I RESISTED, BUT FOR HOW MUCH LONGER?...

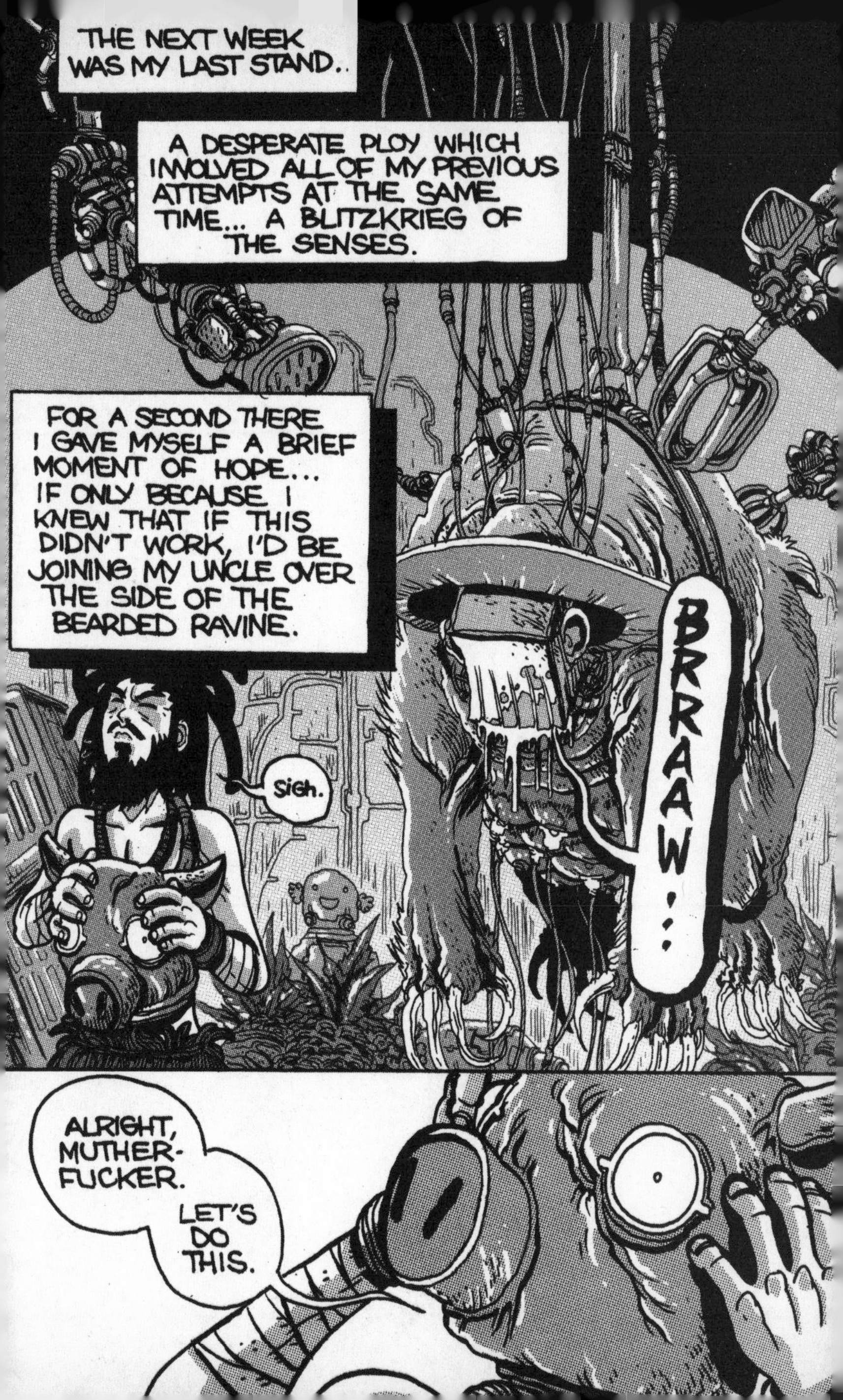
THE NEXT WEEK WAS MY LAST STAND..
A DESPERATE PLOY WHICH INVOLVED ALL OF MY PREVIOUS ATTEMPTS AT THE SAME TIME... A BLITZKRIEG OF THE SENSES.
FOR A SECOND THERE I GAVE MYSELF A BRIEF MOMENT OF HOPE... IF ONLY BECAUSE I KNEW THAT IF THIS DIDN'T WORK, I'D BE JOINING MY UNCLE OVER THE SIDE OF THE BEARDED RAVINE.
BRRAAW...
Sigh.
ALRIGHT, MUTHER-FUCKER.
LET'S DO THIS.

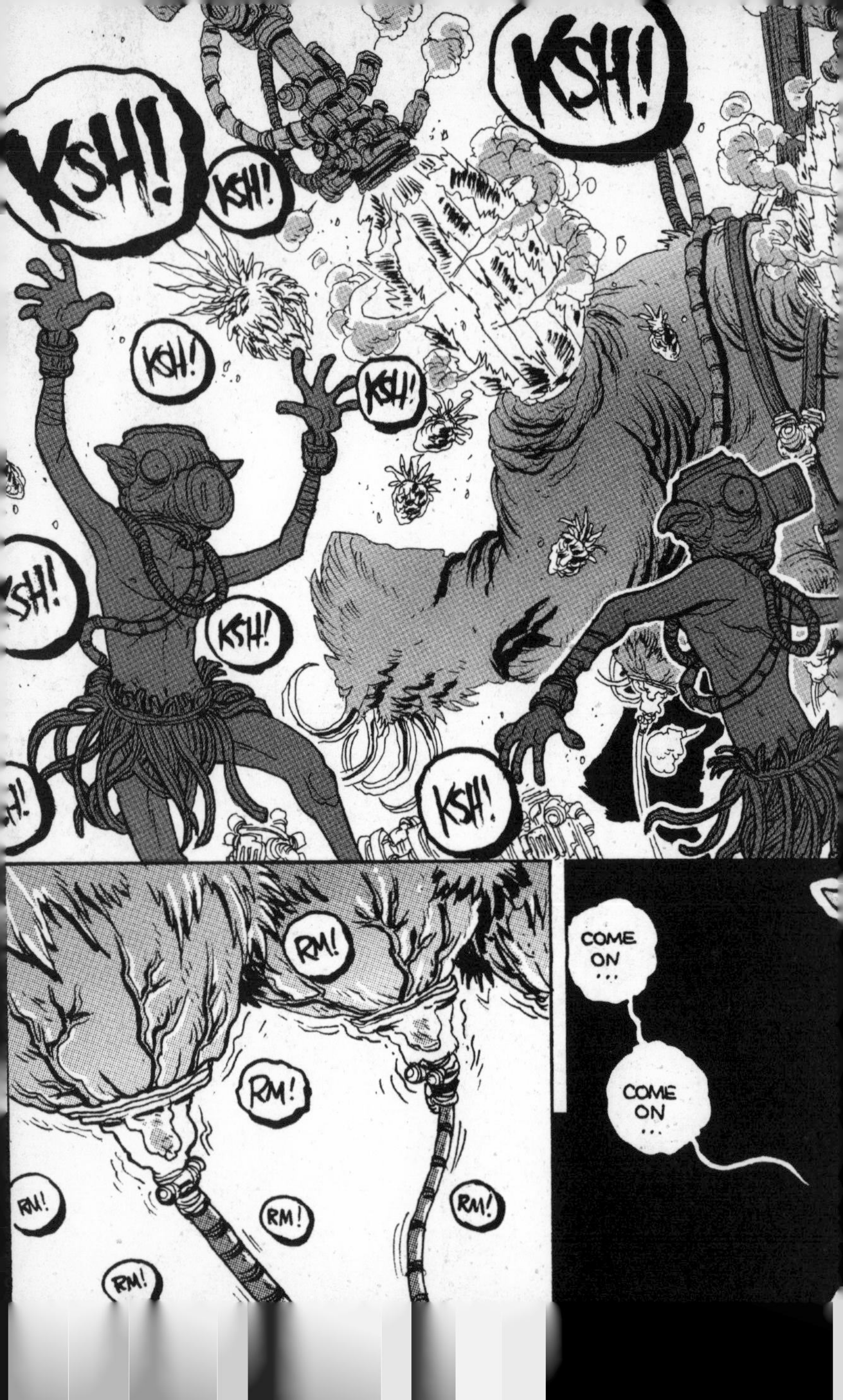
KSH!
KSH!
KSH!
KSH!
KSH!
KSH!
KSH!
RM!
RM!
RM!
RM!
RM!
RM!
COME ON ...
COME ON ...

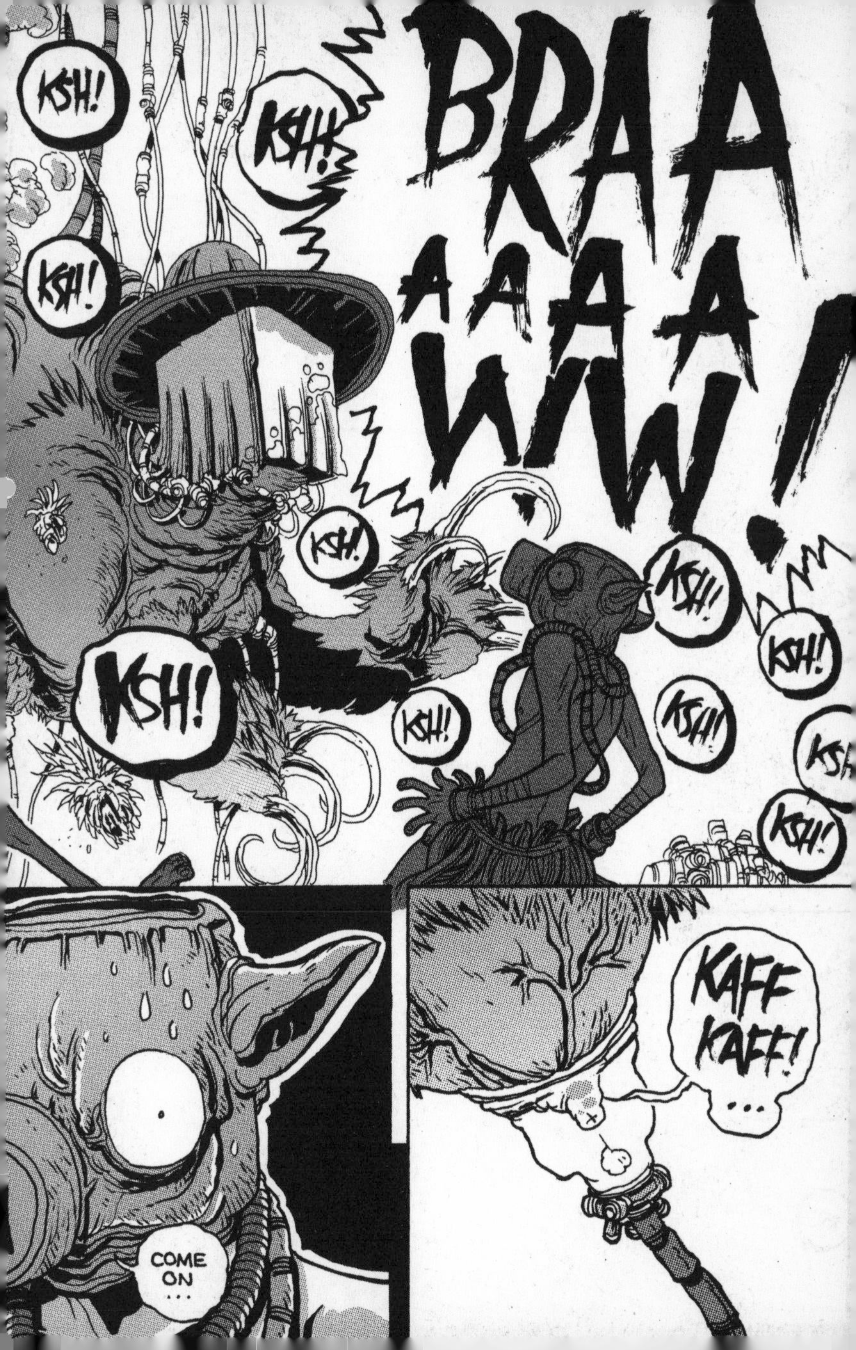
KSH!
KSH!
KSH!
BRAAAAAWW!
KSH!
KSH!
KSH!
KSH!
KSH!
KSH!
KSH!
COME ON...
KAFF KAFF!
...

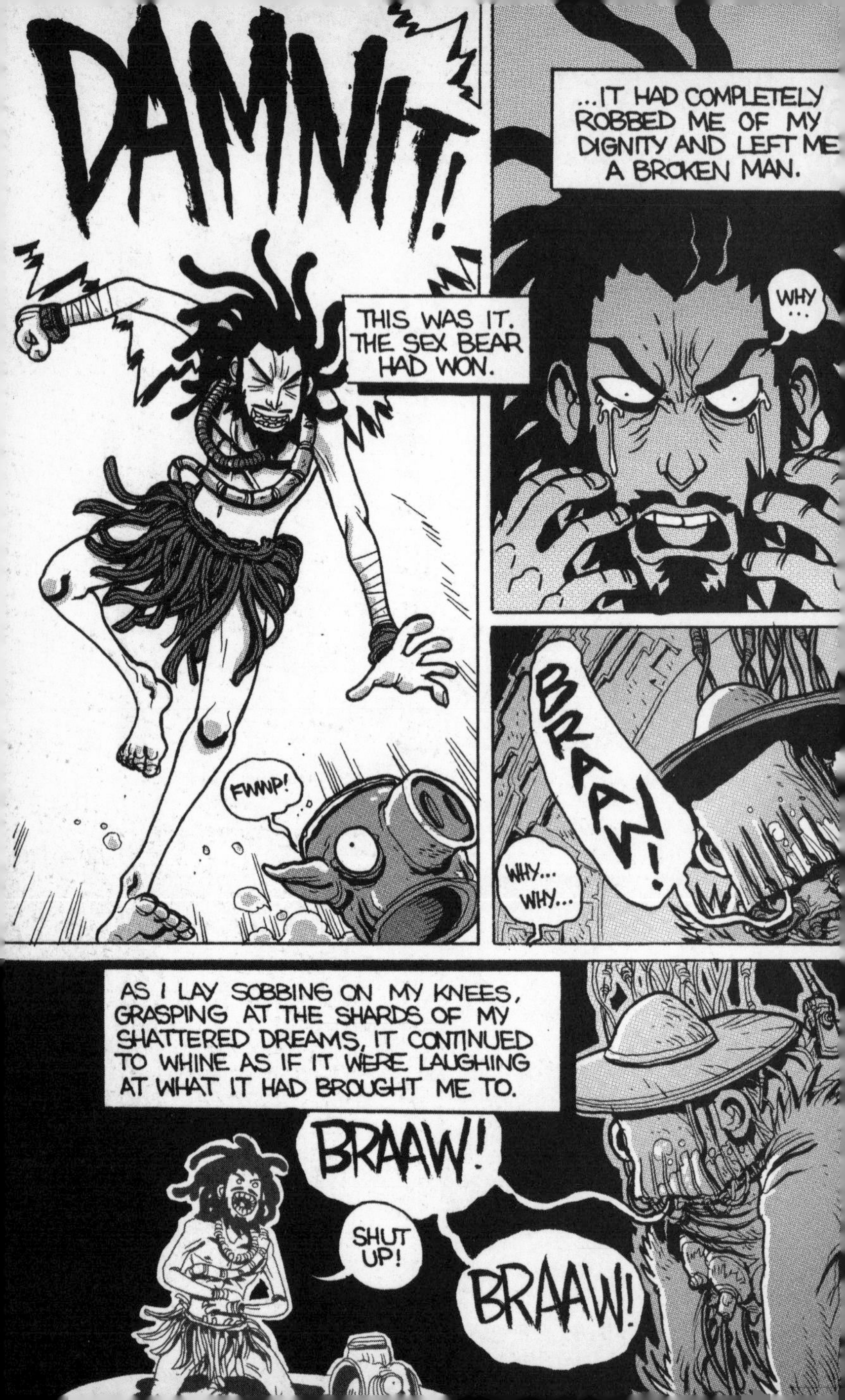
DAMNIT!
THIS WAS IT. THE SEX BEAR HAD WON.
FWMP!
...IT HAD COMPLETELY ROBBED ME OF MY DIGNITY AND LEFT ME A BROKEN MAN.
WHY...
BRAAW!
WHY... WHY...
AS I LAY SOBBING ON MY KNEES, GRASPING AT THE SHARDS OF MY SHATTERED DREAMS, IT CONTINUED TO WHINE AS IF IT WERE LAUGHING AT WHAT IT HAD BROUGHT ME TO.
BRAAW!
SHUT UP!
BRAAW!

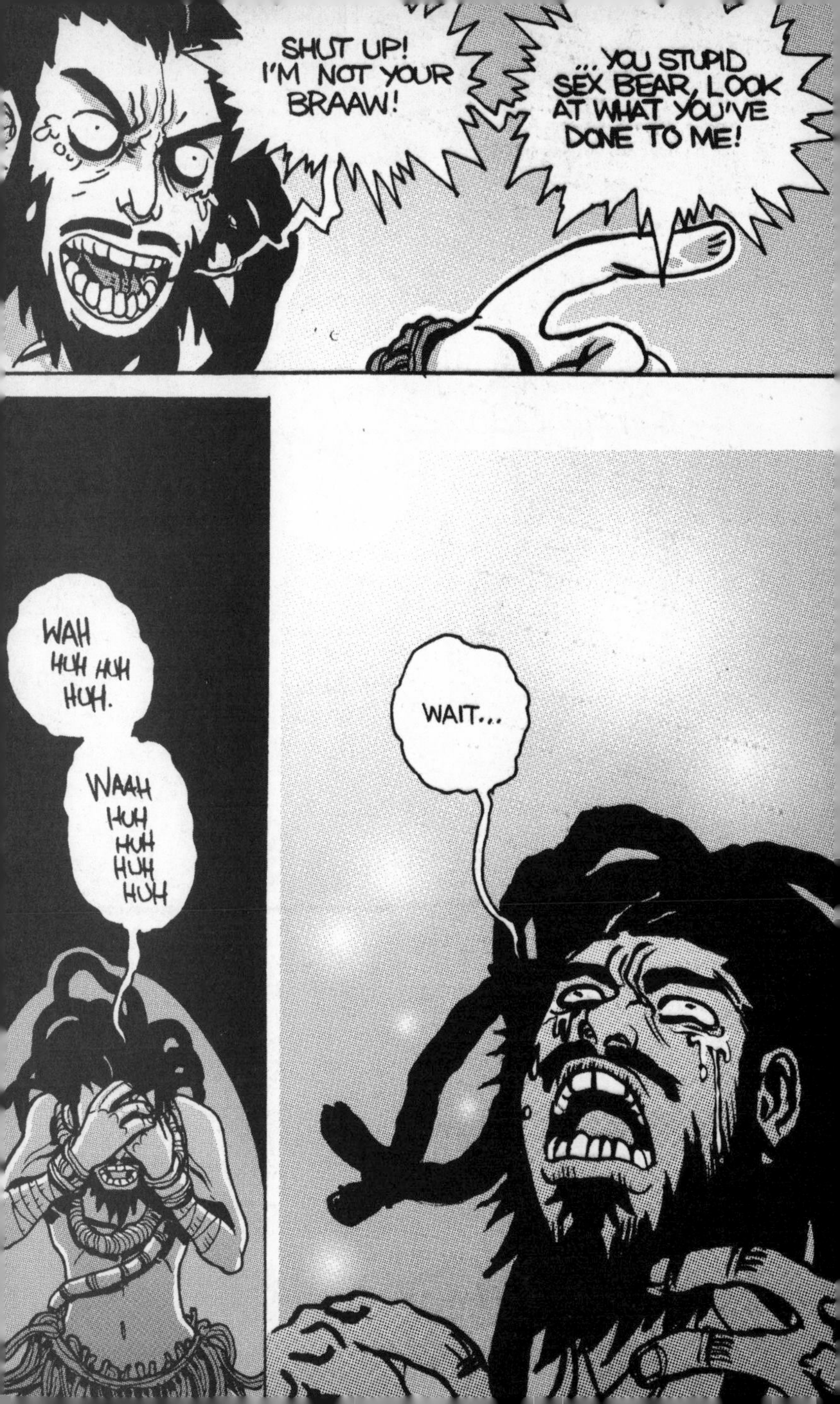
SHUT UP! I'M NOT YOUR BRAAW!
...YOU STUPID SEX BEAR, LOOK AT WHAT YOU'VE DONE TO ME!
WAH HUH HUH HUH.
WAAH HUH HUH HUH HUH
WAIT...

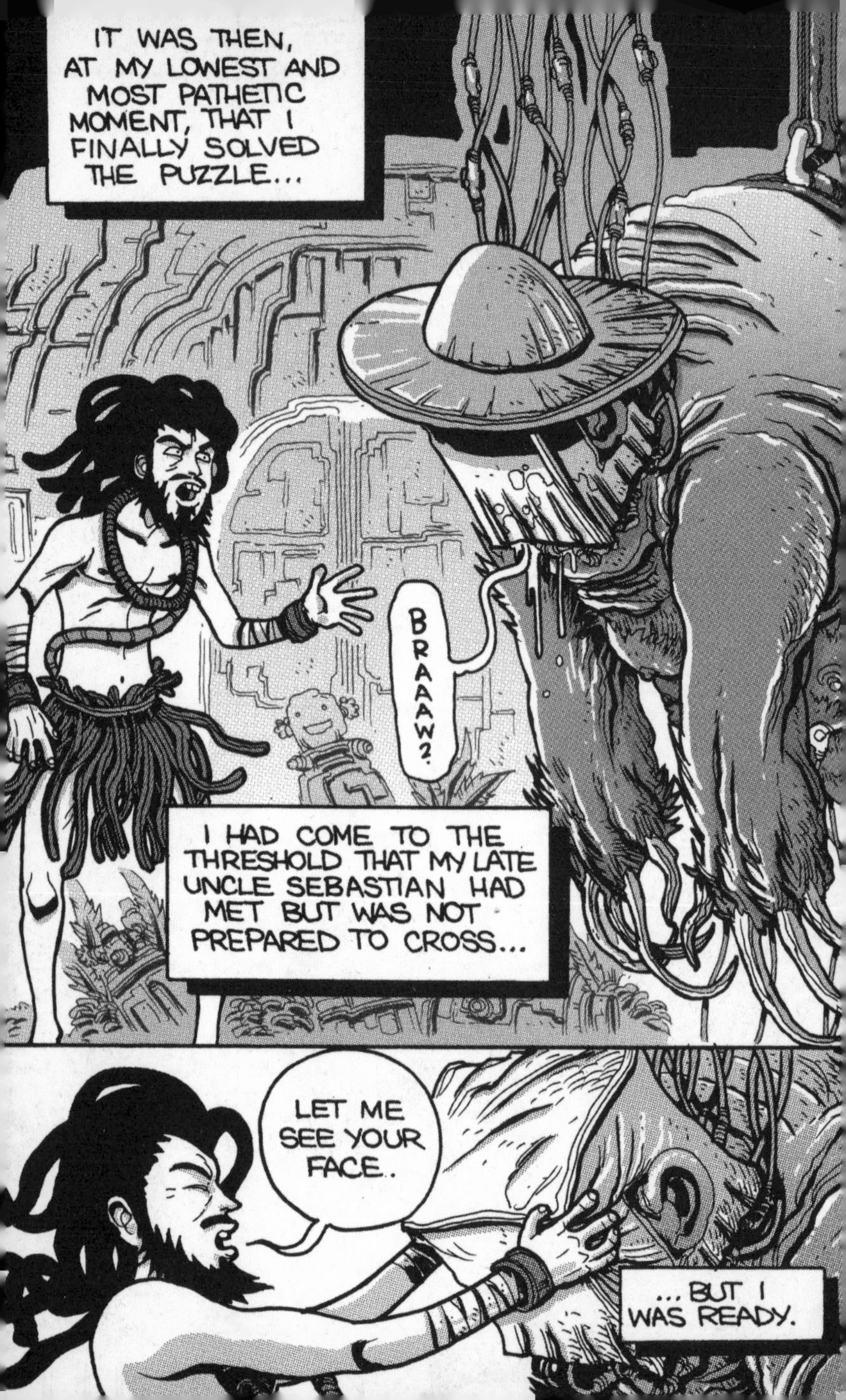
IT WAS THEN, AT MY LOWEST AND MOST PATHETIC MOMENT, THAT I FINALLY SOLVED THE PUZZLE...
BRAAAW?
I HAD COME TO THE THRESHOLD THAT MY LATE UNCLE SEBASTIAN HAD MET BUT WAS NOT PREPARED TO CROSS...
LET ME SEE YOUR FACE..
...BUT I WAS READY.

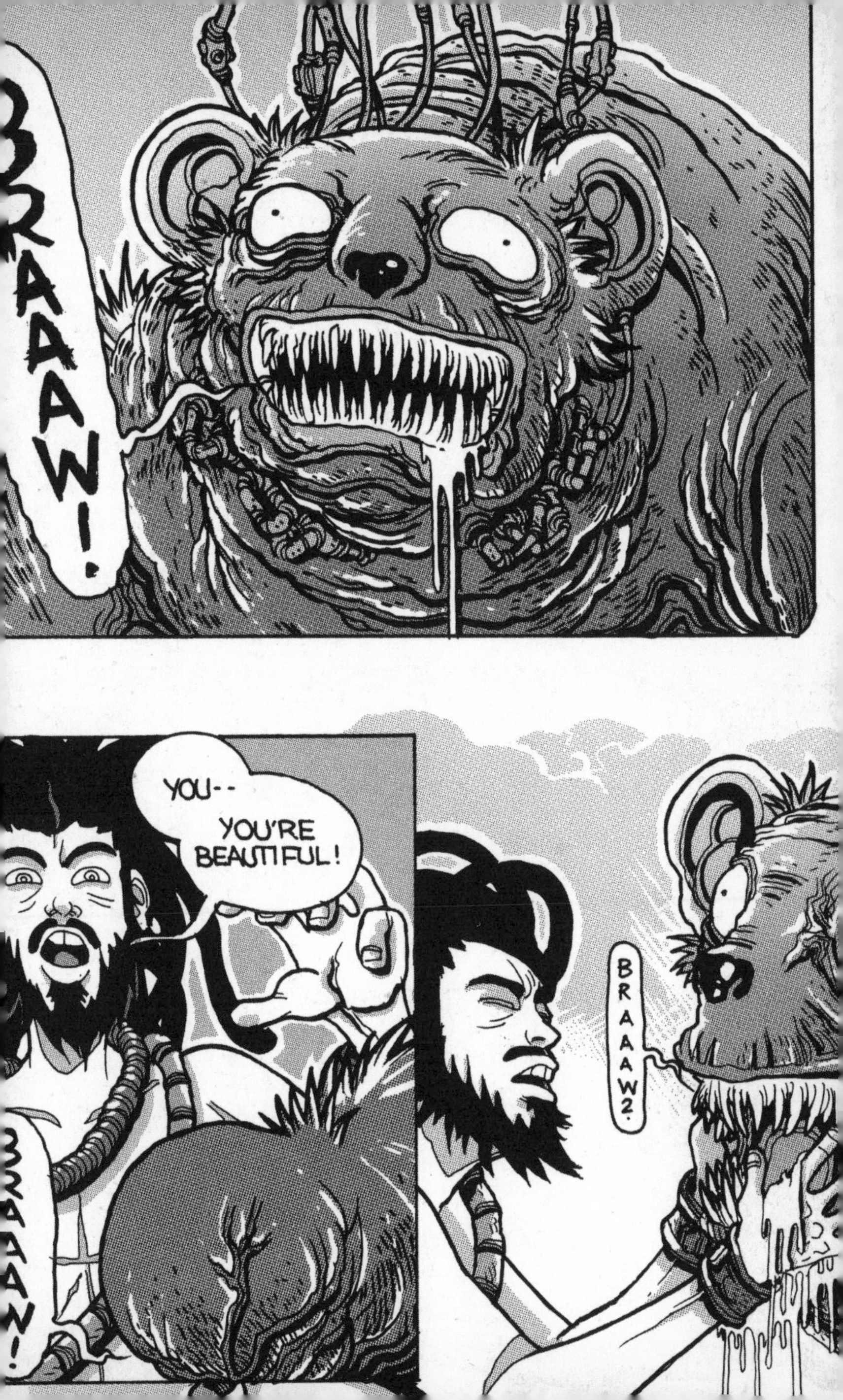
BRAAAW!
YOU-- YOU'RE BEAUTIFUL!
BRAAAN!
BRAAAW?

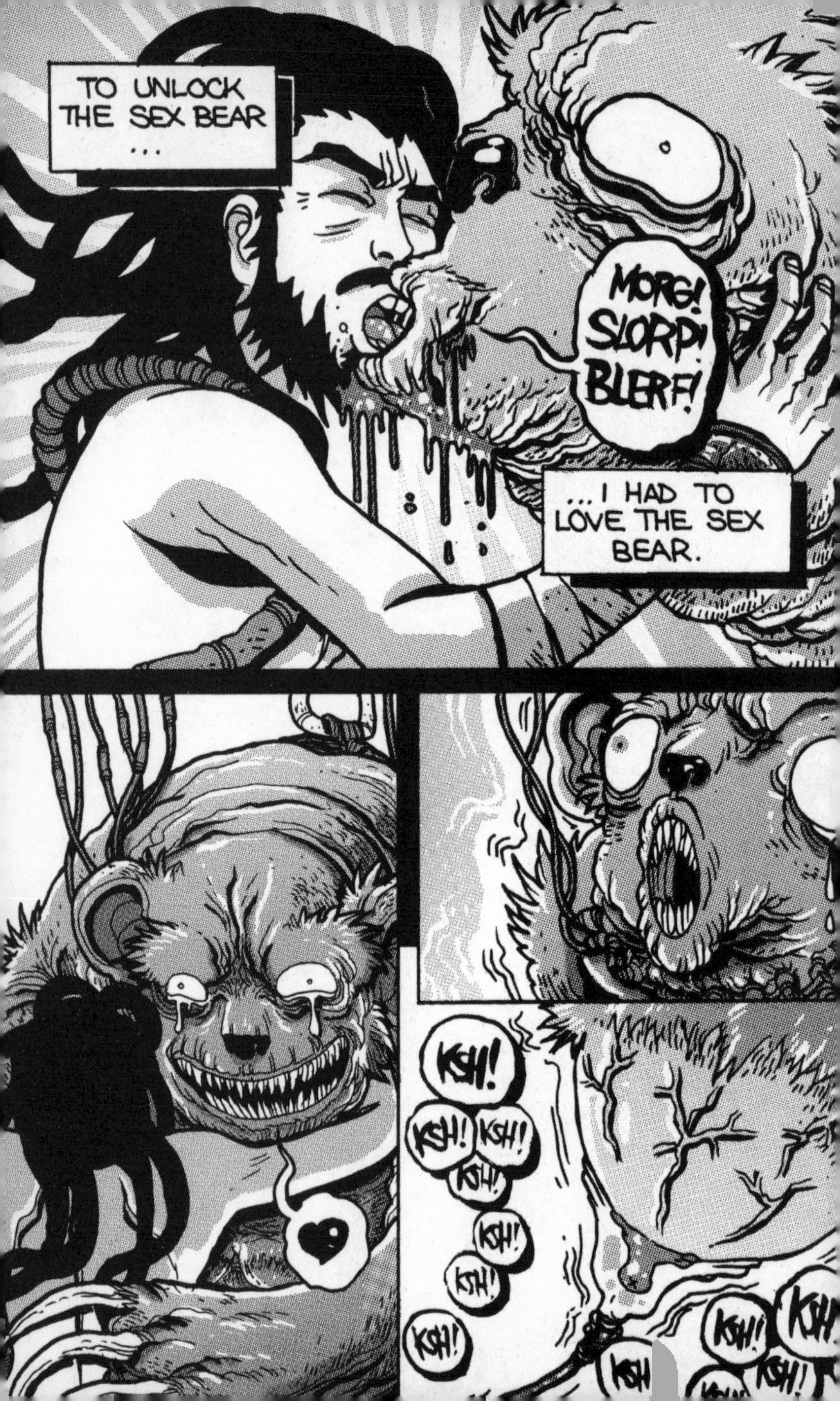

TO UNLOCK THE SEX BEAR ...
MORG! SLORP! BLERF!
... I HAD TO LOVE THE SEX BEAR.
KSH!
KSH! KSH!
KSH!
KSH!
KSH!
KSH!
KSH!
KSH!
KSH!
KSH!

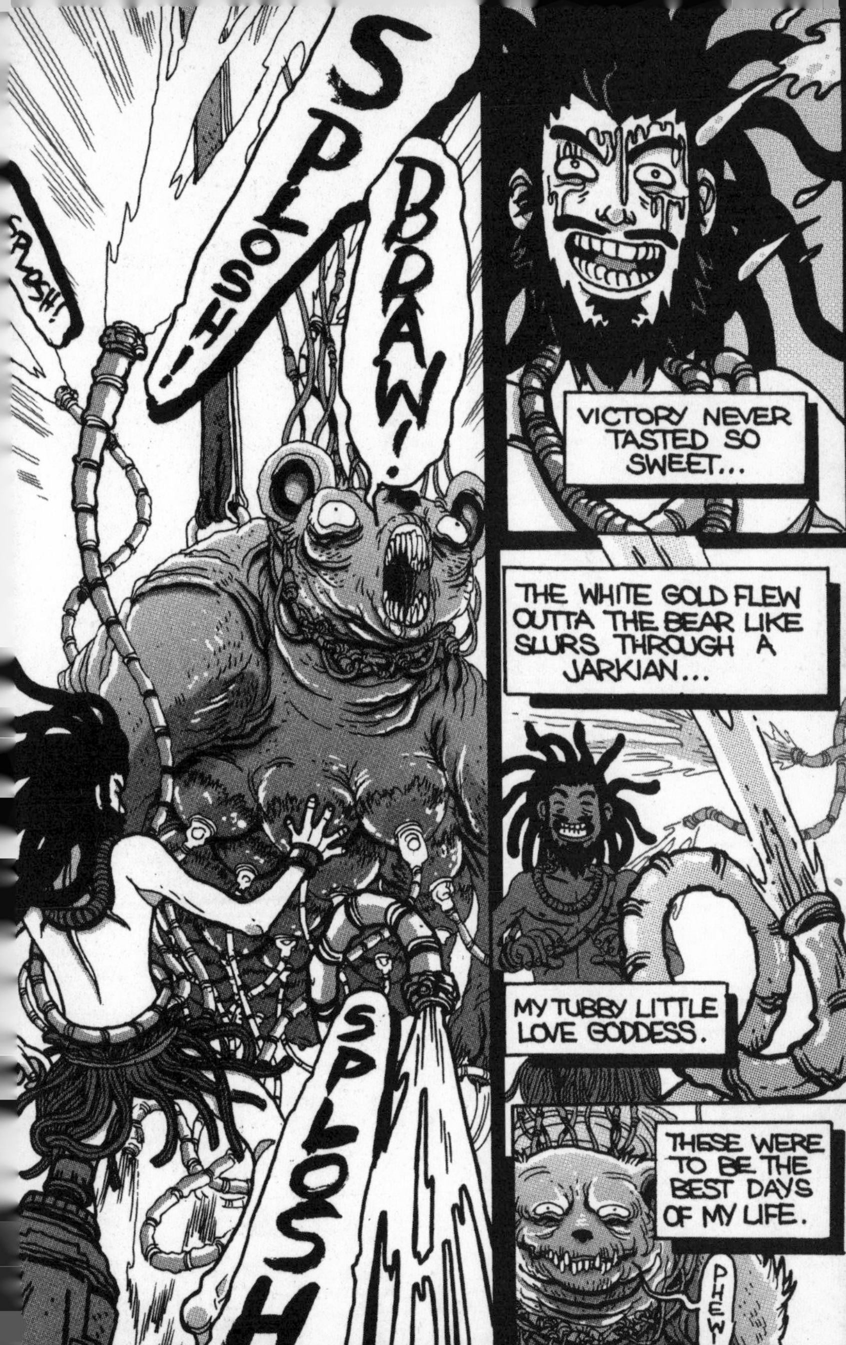
SPLOSH!
SPLOSH!
BDAW!
VICTORY NEVER TASTED SO SWEET...
THE WHITE GOLD FLEW OUTTA THE BEAR LIKE SLURS THROUGH A JARKIAN...
MY TUBBY LITTLE LOVE GODDESS.
SPLOSH
THESE WERE TO BE THE BEST DAYS OF MY LIFE.
PHEW!

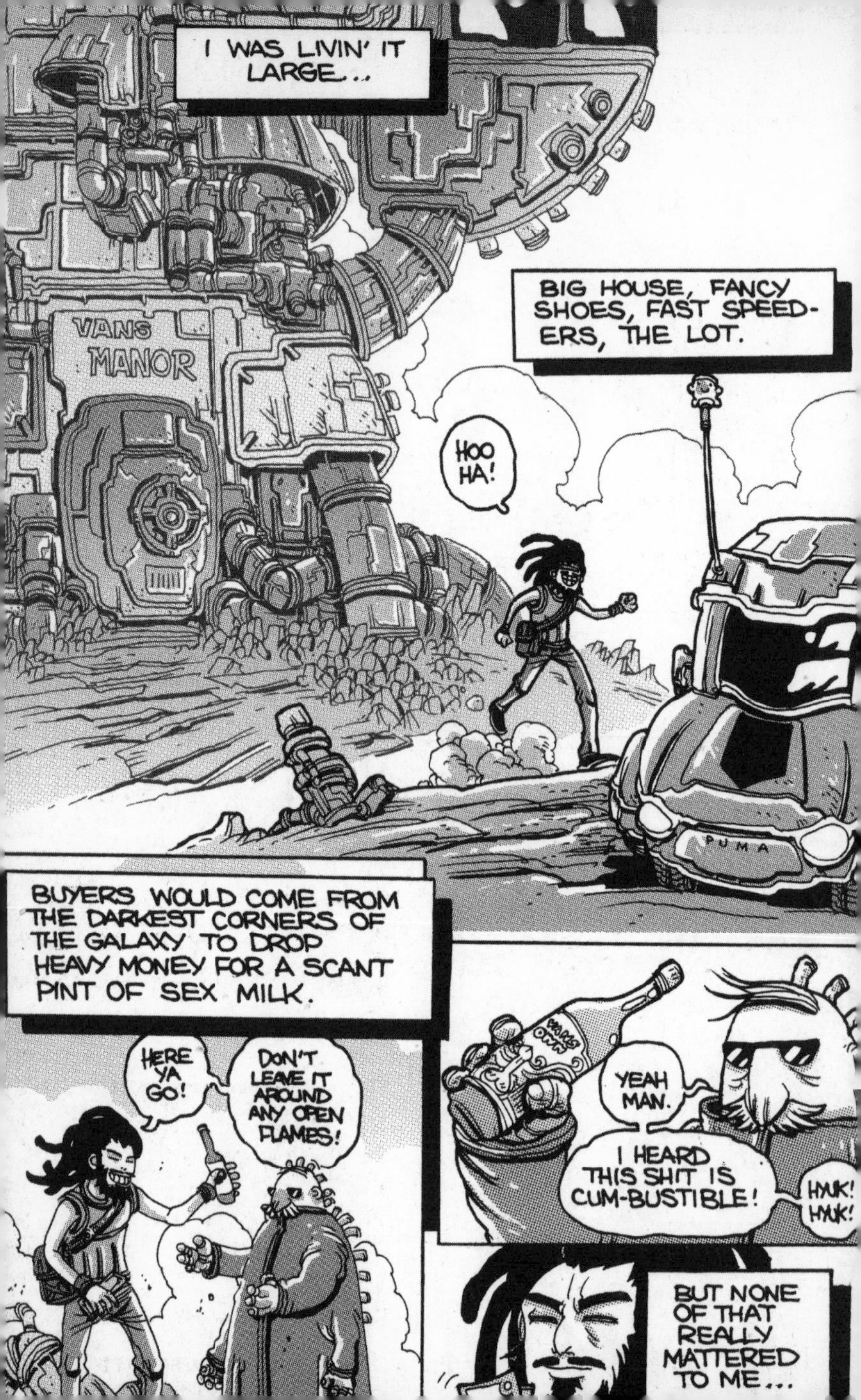
I WAS LIVIN' IT LARGE...
VANS MANOR
BIG HOUSE, FANCY SHOES, FAST SPEEDERS, THE LOT.
HOO HA!
PUMA
BUYERS WOULD COME FROM THE DARKEST CORNERS OF THE GALAXY TO DROP HEAVY MONEY FOR A SCANT PINT OF SEX MILK.
HERE YA GO!
DON'T LEAVE IT AROUND ANY OPEN FLAMES!
VANS OWN
YEAH MAN.
I HEARD THIS SHIT IS CUM-BUSTIBLE!
HYUK! HYUK!
BUT NONE OF THAT REALLY MATTERED TO ME...

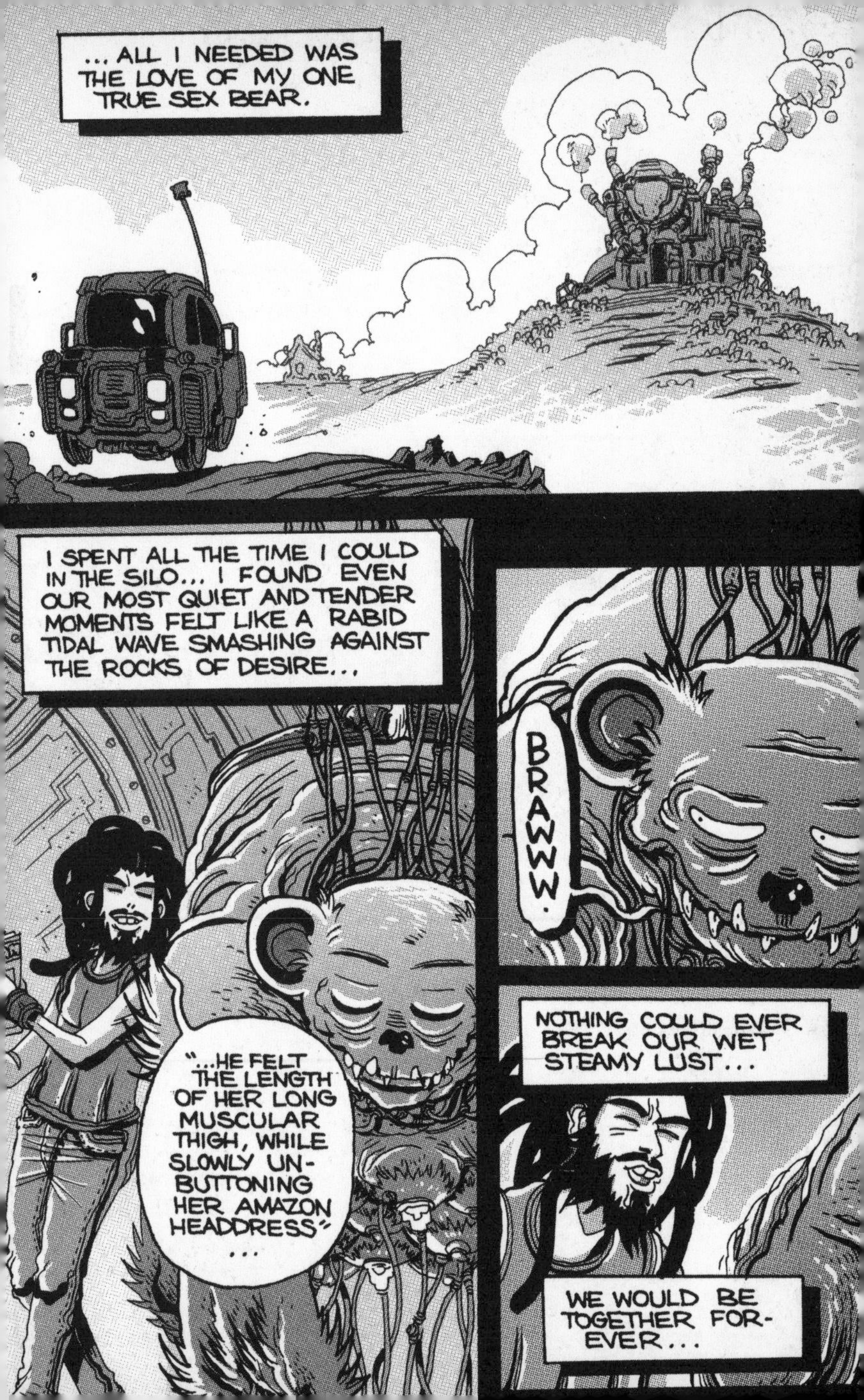

... ALL I NEEDED WAS THE LOVE OF MY ONE TRUE SEX BEAR.
I SPENT ALL THE TIME I COULD IN THE SILO... I FOUND EVEN OUR MOST QUIET AND TENDER MOMENTS FELT LIKE A RABID TIDAL WAVE SMASHING AGAINST THE ROCKS OF DESIRE...
"...HE FELT THE LENGTH OF HER LONG MUSCULAR THIGH, WHILE SLOWLY UN-BUTTONING HER AMAZON HEADDRESS" ...
BRAWWW.
NOTHING COULD EVER BREAK OUR WET STEAMY LUST...
WE WOULD BE TOGETHER FOR-EVER...

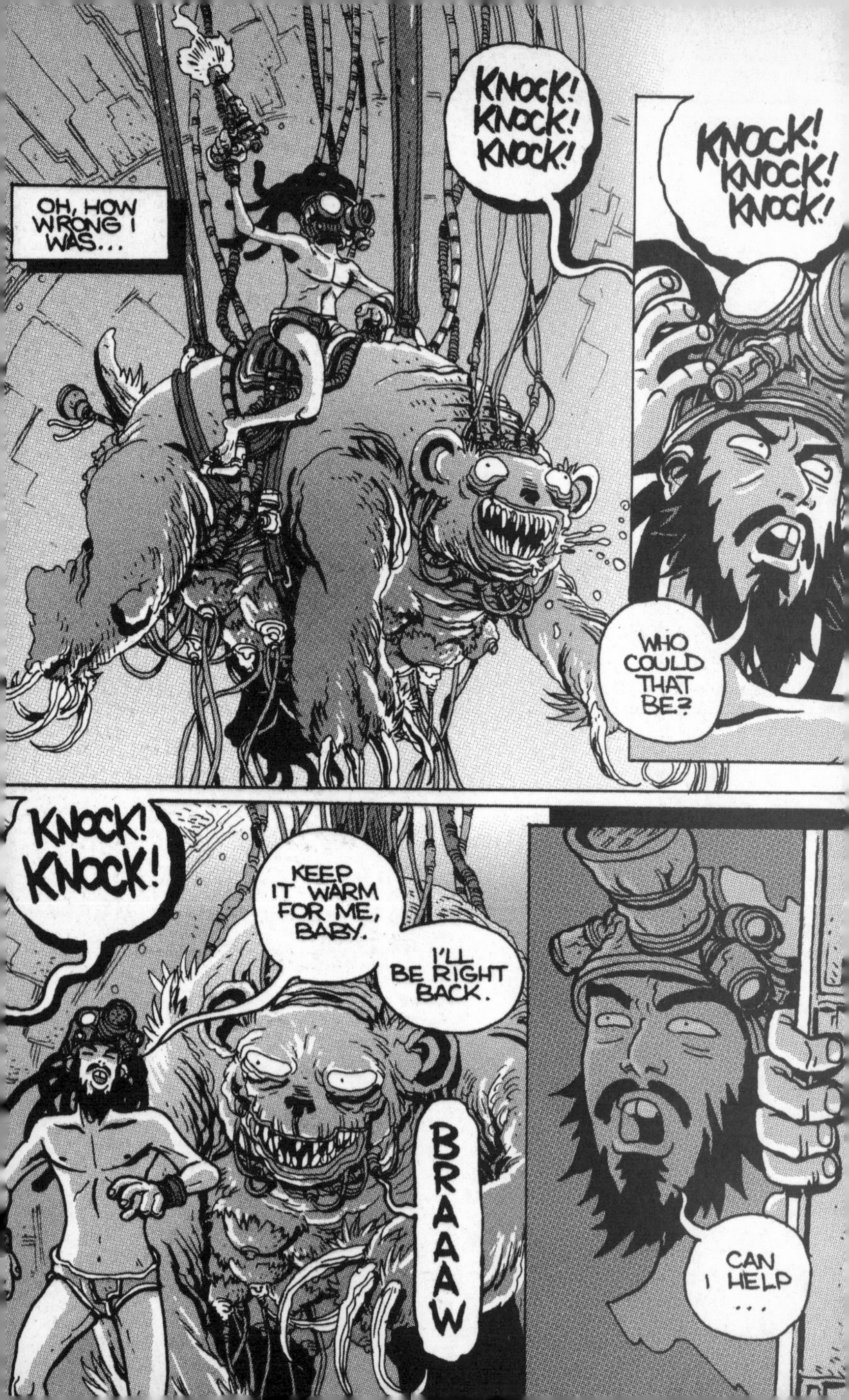
OH, HOW WRONG I WAS...
KNOCK! KNOCK! KNOCK!
KNOCK! KNOCK! KNOCK!
WHO COULD THAT BE?
KNOCK! KNOCK!
KEEP IT WARM FOR ME, BABY.
I'LL BE RIGHT BACK.
BRAAAW
CAN I HELP ...

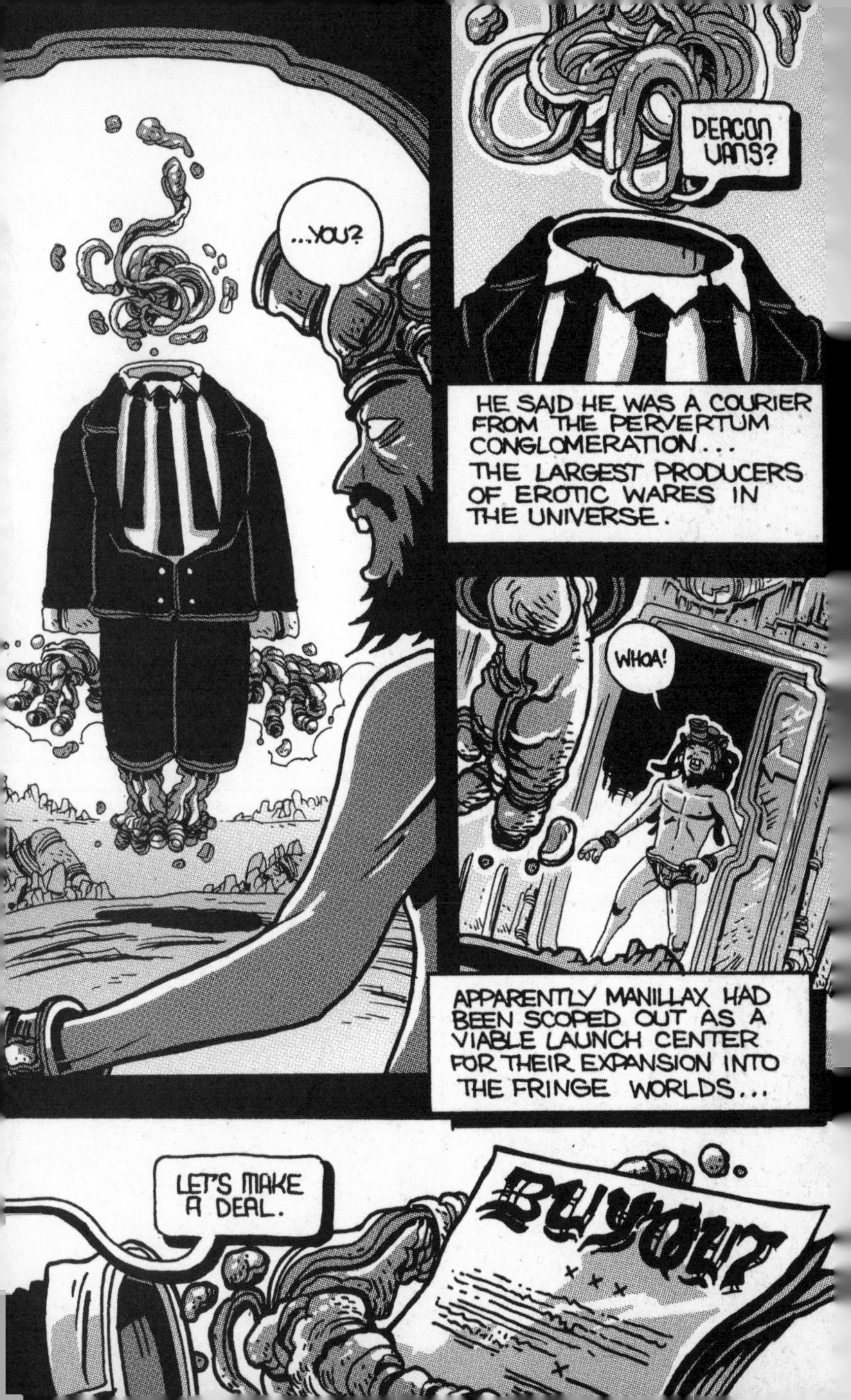
...YOU?
DEACON VANS?
HE SAID HE WAS A COURIER FROM THE PERVERTUM CONGLOMERATION...
THE LARGEST PRODUCERS OF EROTIC WARES IN THE UNIVERSE.
WHOA!
APPARENTLY MANILLAX HAD BEEN SCOPED OUT AS A VIABLE LAUNCH CENTER FOR THEIR EXPANSION INTO THE FRINGE WORLDS...
LET'S MAKE A DEAL.
BUYOUT

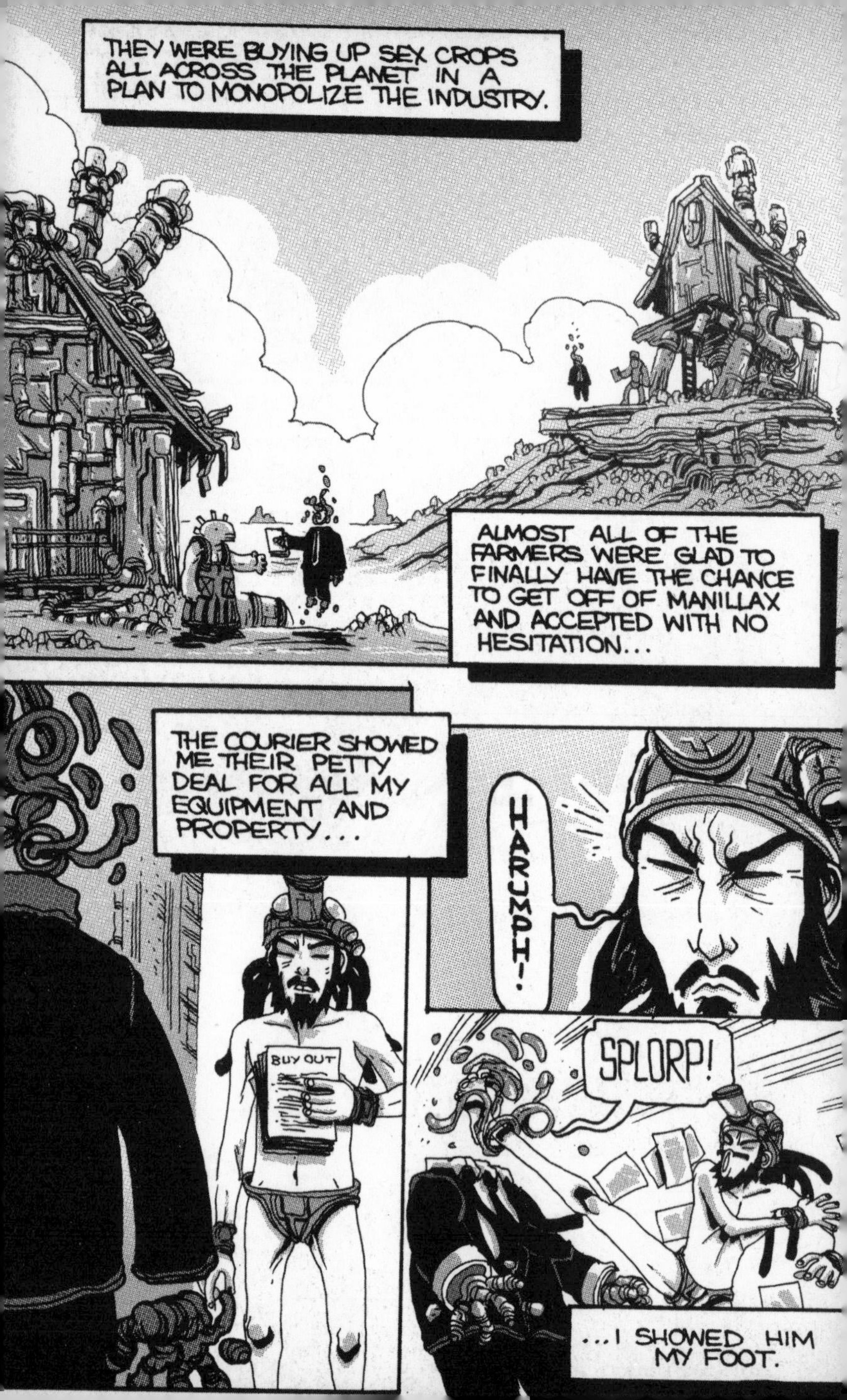
THEY WERE BUYING UP SEX CROPS ALL ACROSS THE PLANET IN A PLAN TO MONOPOLIZE THE INDUSTRY.
ALMOST ALL OF THE FARMERS WERE GLAD TO FINALLY HAVE THE CHANCE TO GET OFF OF MANILLAX AND ACCEPTED WITH NO HESITATION...
THE COURIER SHOWED ME THEIR PETTY DEAL FOR ALL MY EQUIPMENT AND PROPERTY...
BUY OUT
HARUMPH!
SPLORP!
...I SHOWED HIM MY FOOT.

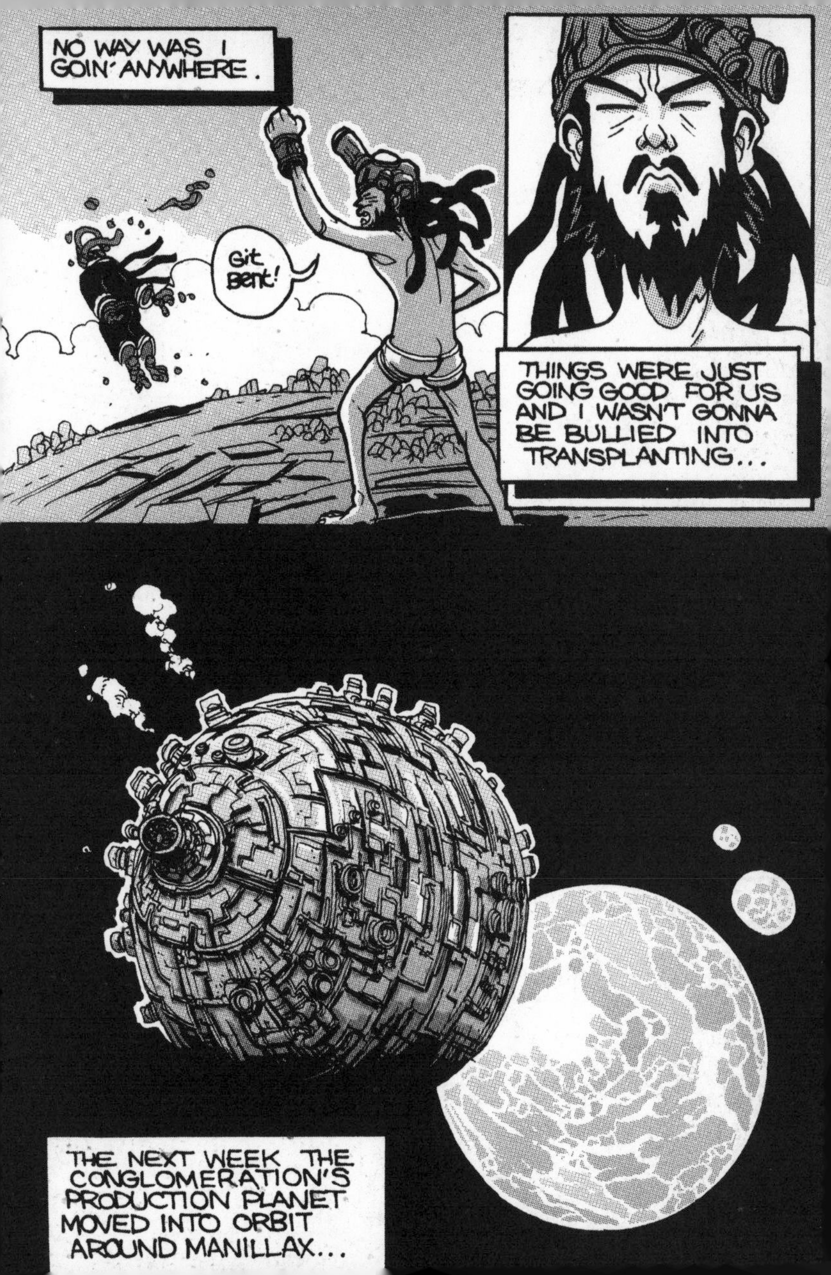
NO WAY WAS I GOIN' ANYWHERE.
Git Bent!
THINGS WERE JUST GOING GOOD FOR US AND I WASN'T GONNA BE BULLIED INTO TRANSPLANTING...
THE NEXT WEEK THE CONGLOMERATION'S PRODUCTION PLANET MOVED INTO ORBIT AROUND MANILLAX...

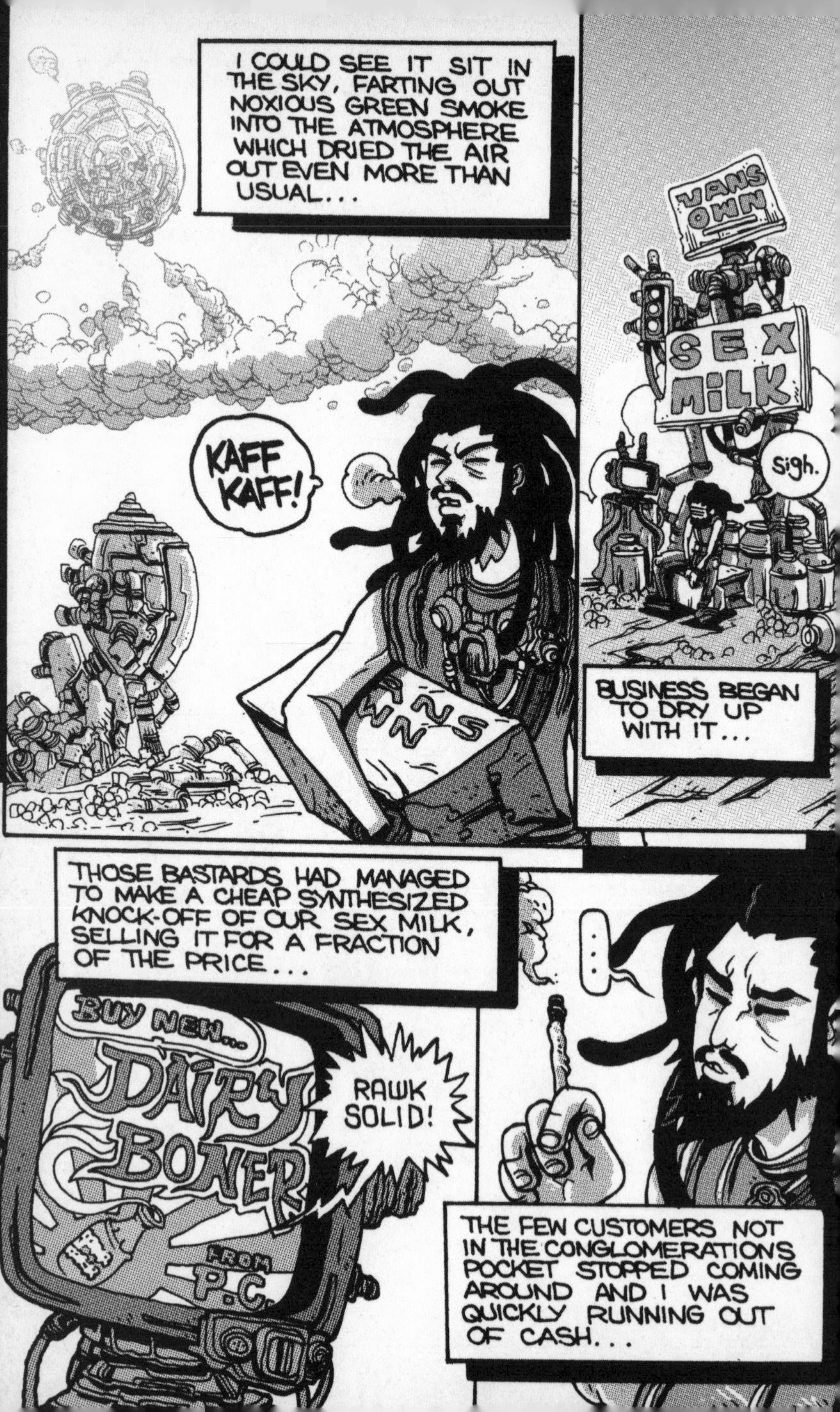
I COULD SEE IT SIT IN THE SKY, FARTING OUT NOXIOUS GREEN SMOKE INTO THE ATMOSPHERE WHICH DRIED THE AIR OUT EVEN MORE THAN USUAL...
KAFF KAFF!
VANS OWN
SEX MILK
sigh.
BUSINESS BEGAN TO DRY UP WITH IT...
THOSE BASTARDS HAD MANAGED TO MAKE A CHEAP SYNTHESIZED KNOCK-OFF OF OUR SEX MILK, SELLING IT FOR A FRACTION OF THE PRICE...
...
BUY NEW...
DAIRY BONER
RAWK SOLID!
FROM P.C.
THE FEW CUSTOMERS NOT IN THE CONGLOMERATIONS POCKET STOPPED COMING AROUND AND I WAS QUICKLY RUNNING OUT OF CASH...

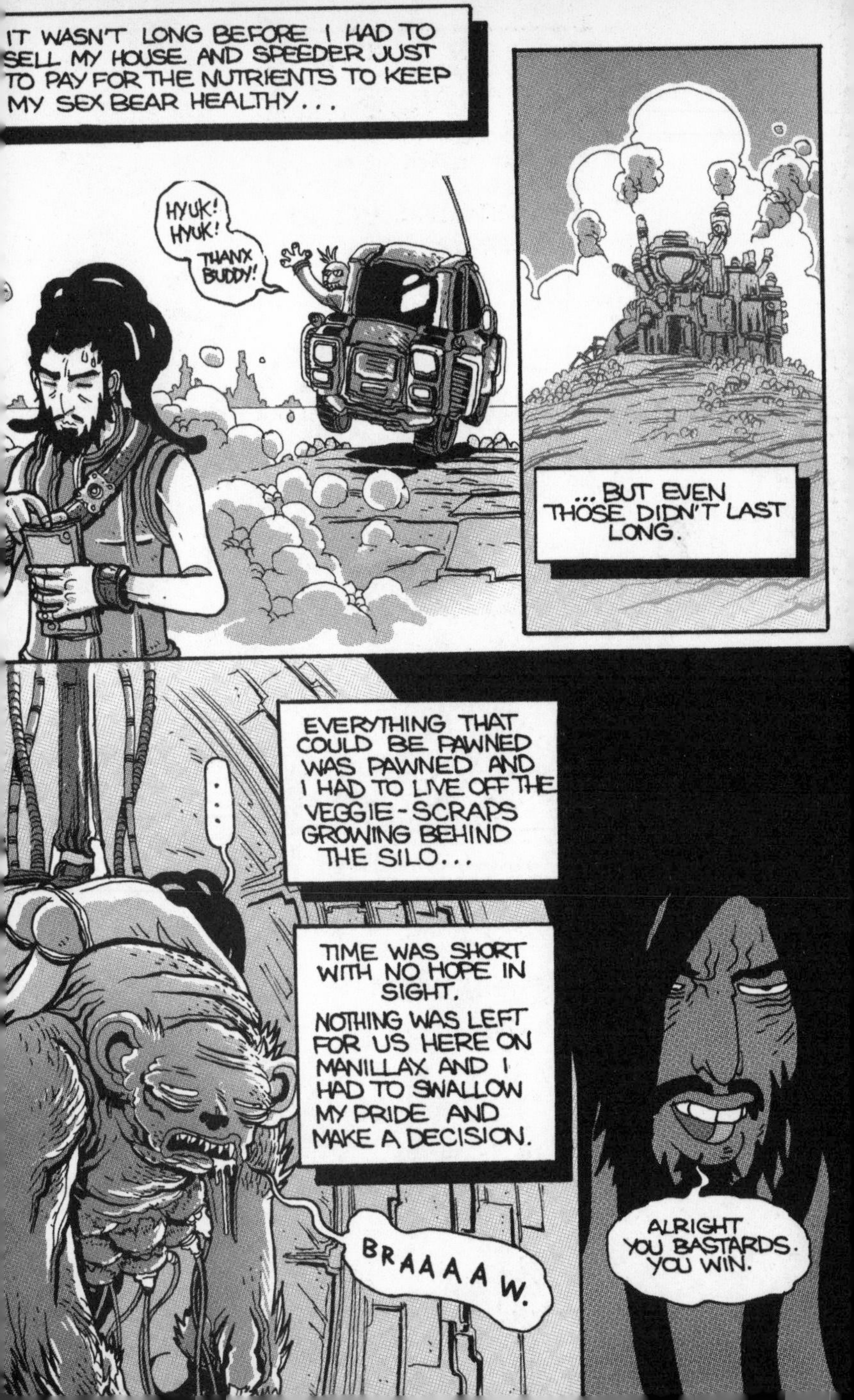
IT WASN'T LONG BEFORE I HAD TO SELL MY HOUSE AND SPEEDER JUST TO PAY FOR THE NUTRIENTS TO KEEP MY SEX BEAR HEALTHY...
HYUK! HYUK!
THANX BUDDY!
...BUT EVEN THOSE DIDN'T LAST LONG.
EVERYTHING THAT COULD BE PAWNED WAS PAWNED AND I HAD TO LIVE OFF THE VEGGIE-SCRAPS GROWING BEHIND THE SILO...
...
TIME WAS SHORT WITH NO HOPE IN SIGHT.
NOTHING WAS LEFT FOR US HERE ON MANILLAX AND I HAD TO SWALLOW MY PRIDE AND MAKE A DECISION.
BRAAAAAW.
ALRIGHT YOU BASTARDS. YOU WIN.

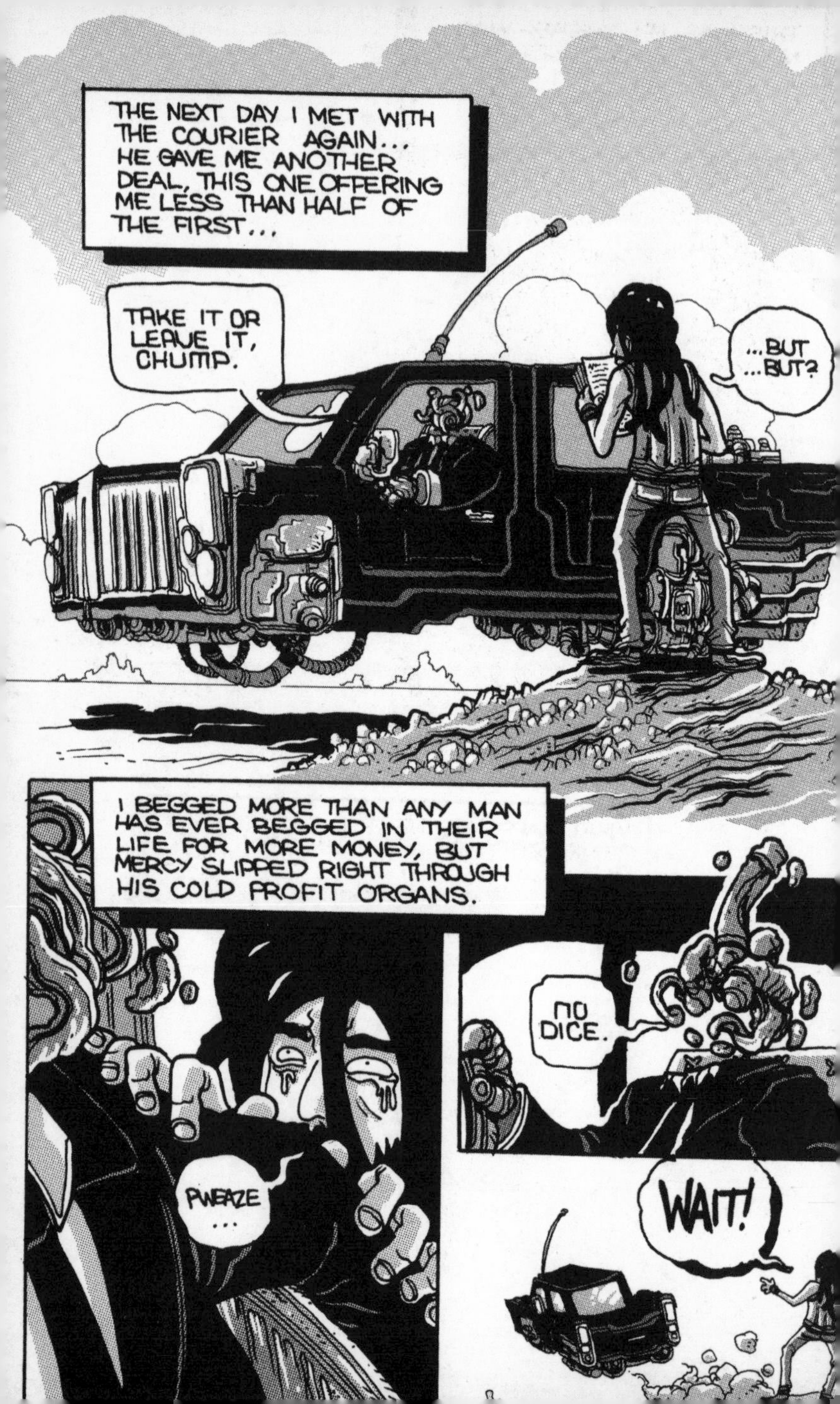
THE NEXT DAY I MET WITH THE COURIER AGAIN... HE GAVE ME ANOTHER DEAL, THIS ONE OFFERING ME LESS THAN HALF OF THE FIRST...
TAKE IT OR LEAVE IT, CHUMP.
...BUT ...BUT?
I BEGGED MORE THAN ANY MAN HAS EVER BEGGED IN THEIR LIFE FOR MORE MONEY, BUT MERCY SLIPPED RIGHT THROUGH HIS COLD PROFIT ORGANS.
PWEAZE ...
NO DICE.
WAIT!

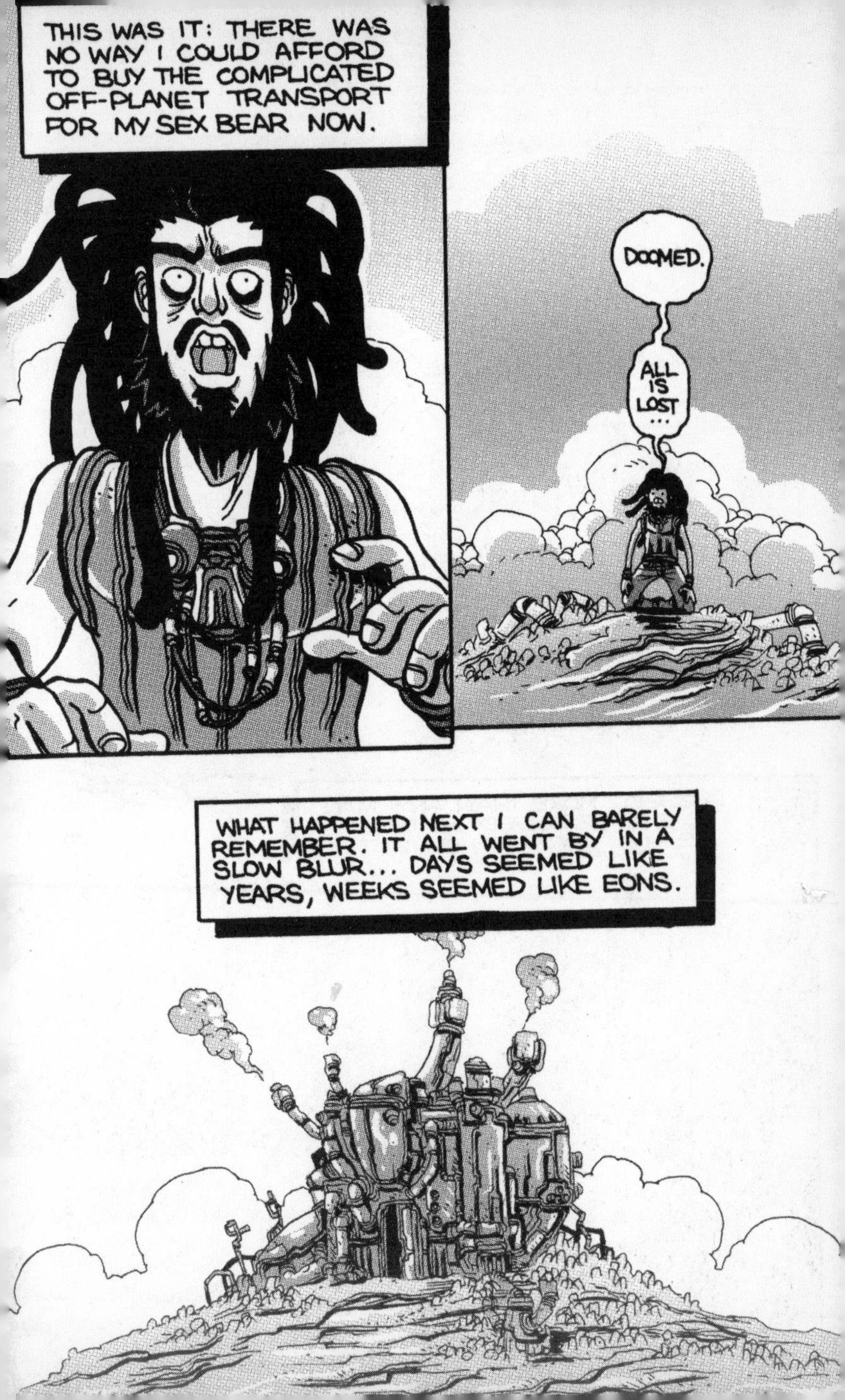
THIS WAS IT: THERE WAS NO WAY I COULD AFFORD TO BUY THE COMPLICATED OFF-PLANET TRANSPORT FOR MY SEX BEAR NOW.
DOOMED.
ALL IS LOST...
WHAT HAPPENED NEXT I CAN BARELY REMEMBER. IT ALL WENT BY IN A SLOW BLUR... DAYS SEEMED LIKE YEARS, WEEKS SEEMED LIKE EONS.

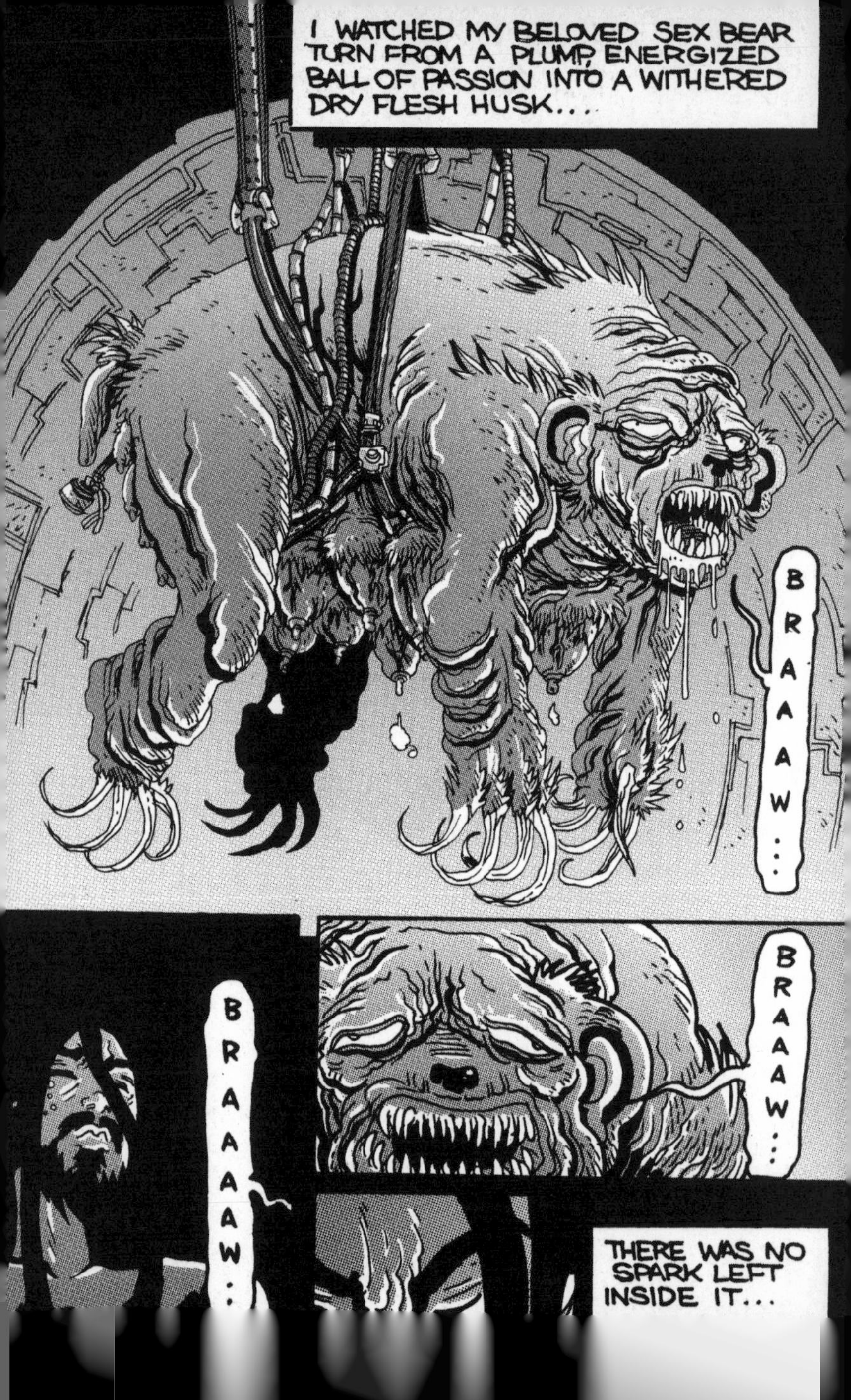
I WATCHED MY BELOVED SEX BEAR TURN FROM A PLUMP, ENERGIZED BALL OF PASSION INTO A WITHERED DRY FLESH HUSK...
BRAAAW...
BRAAAW...
BRAAAAW...
THERE WAS NO SPARK LEFT INSIDE IT...

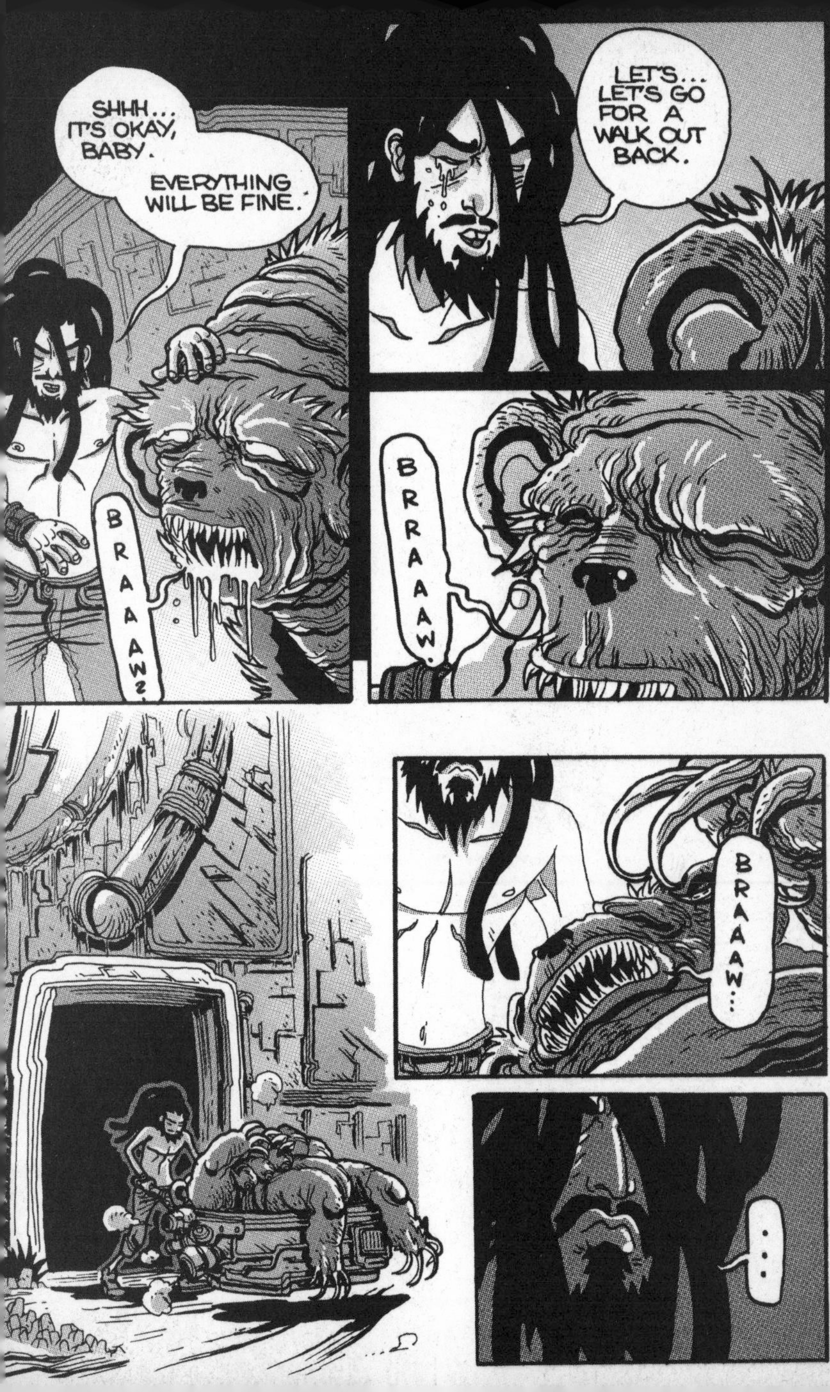
SHHH... IT'S OKAY, BABY.
EVERYTHING WILL BE FINE.
BRAAAW?
LET'S... LET'S GO FOR A WALK OUT BACK.
BRRAAAAW.
BRAAAW...
...

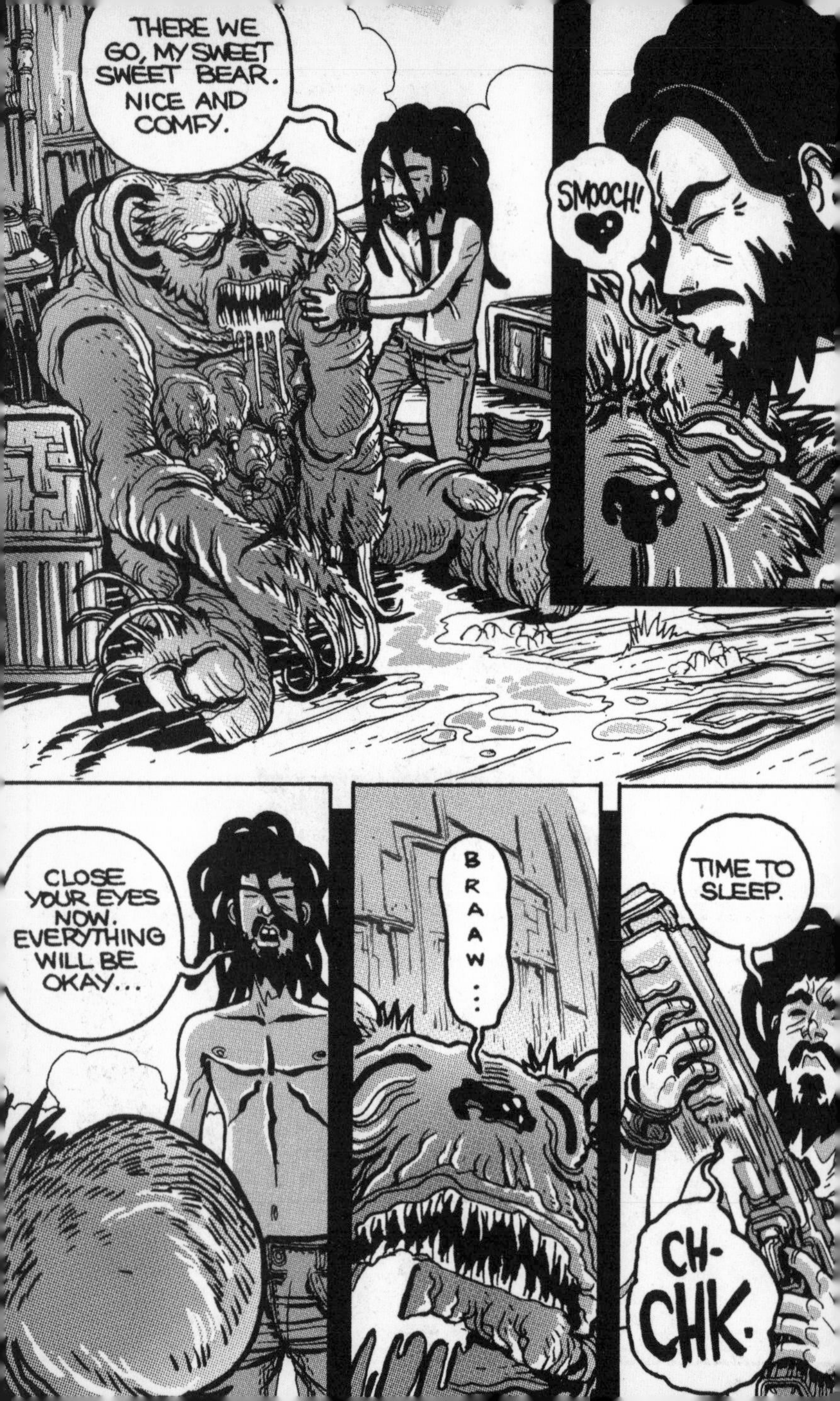
THERE WE GO, MY SWEET SWEET BEAR. NICE AND COMFY.
SMOOCH!
CLOSE YOUR EYES NOW. EVERYTHING WILL BE OKAY...
BRAAW...
TIME TO SLEEP.
CH-CHK.

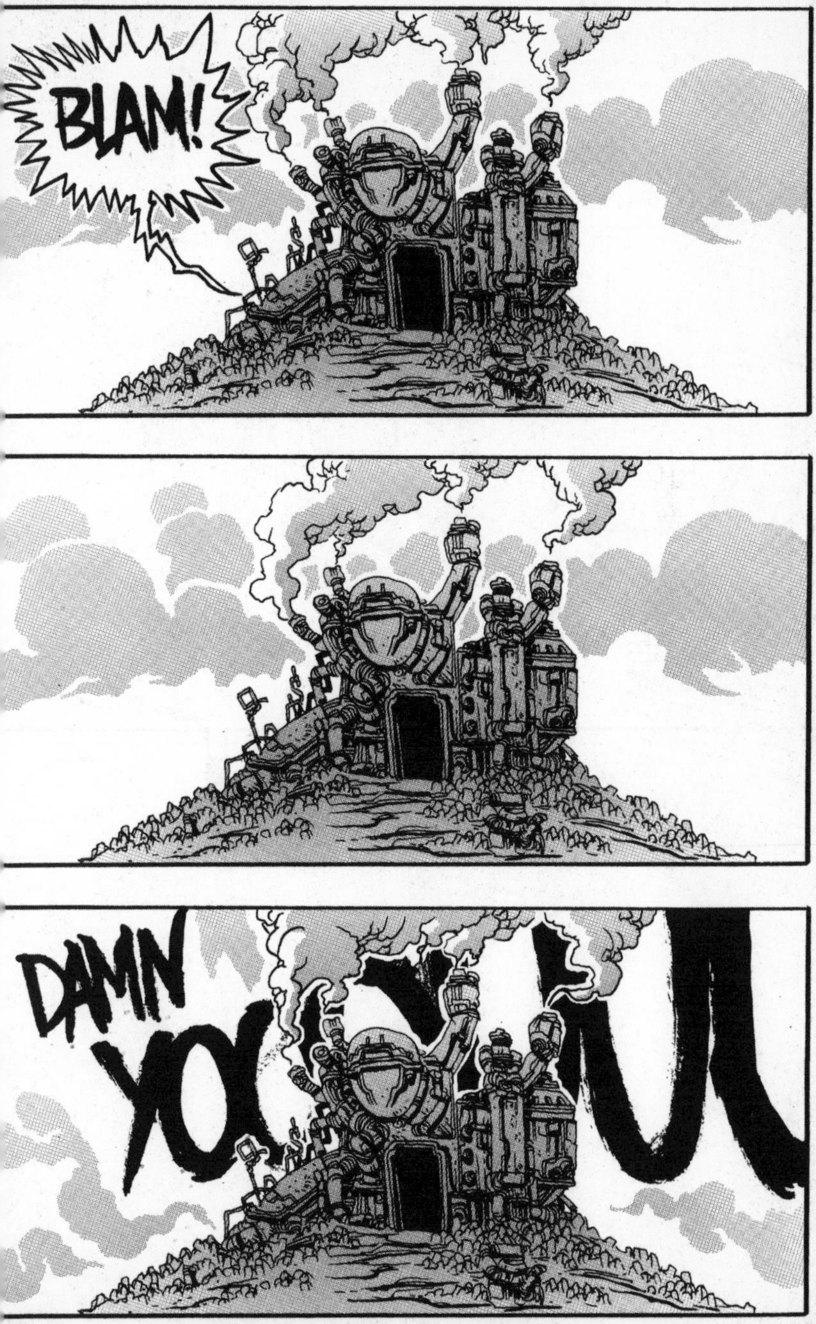
BLAM!
DAMN
YOOOUU

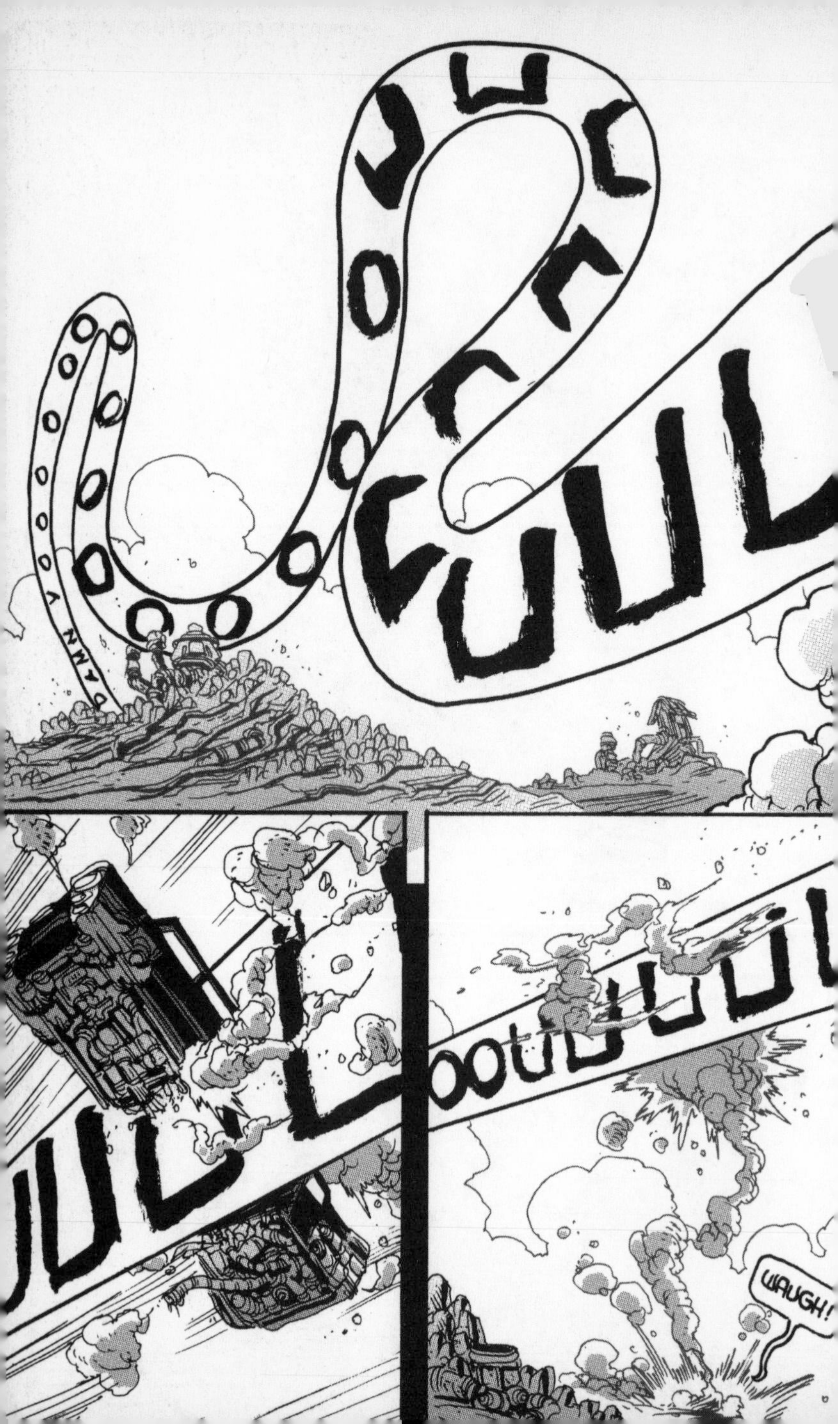
DAMN
WAUGH!

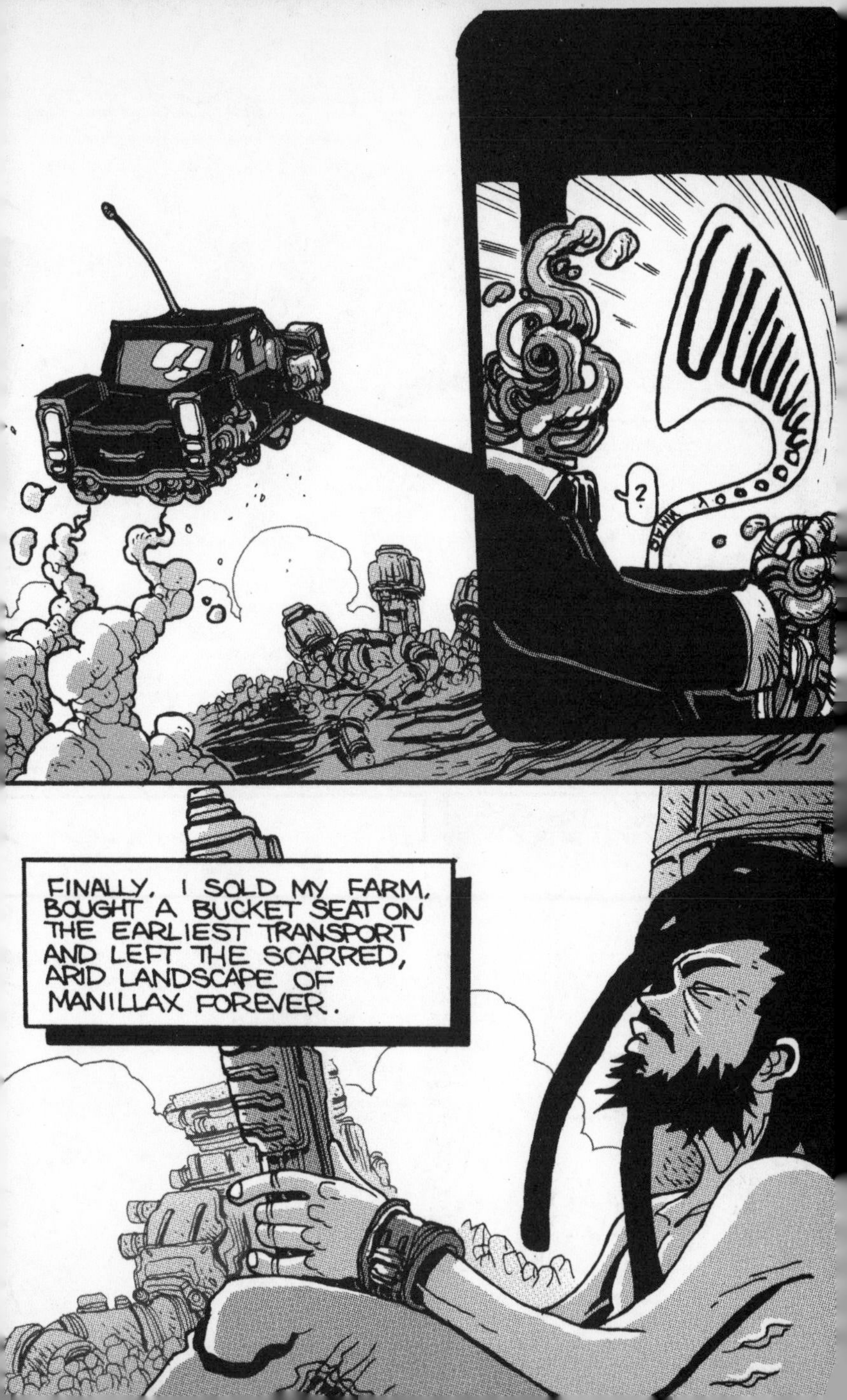
?
FINALLY, I SOLD MY FARM, BOUGHT A BUCKET SEAT ON THE EARLIEST TRANSPORT AND LEFT THE SCARRED, ARID LANDSCAPE OF MANILLAX FOREVER.

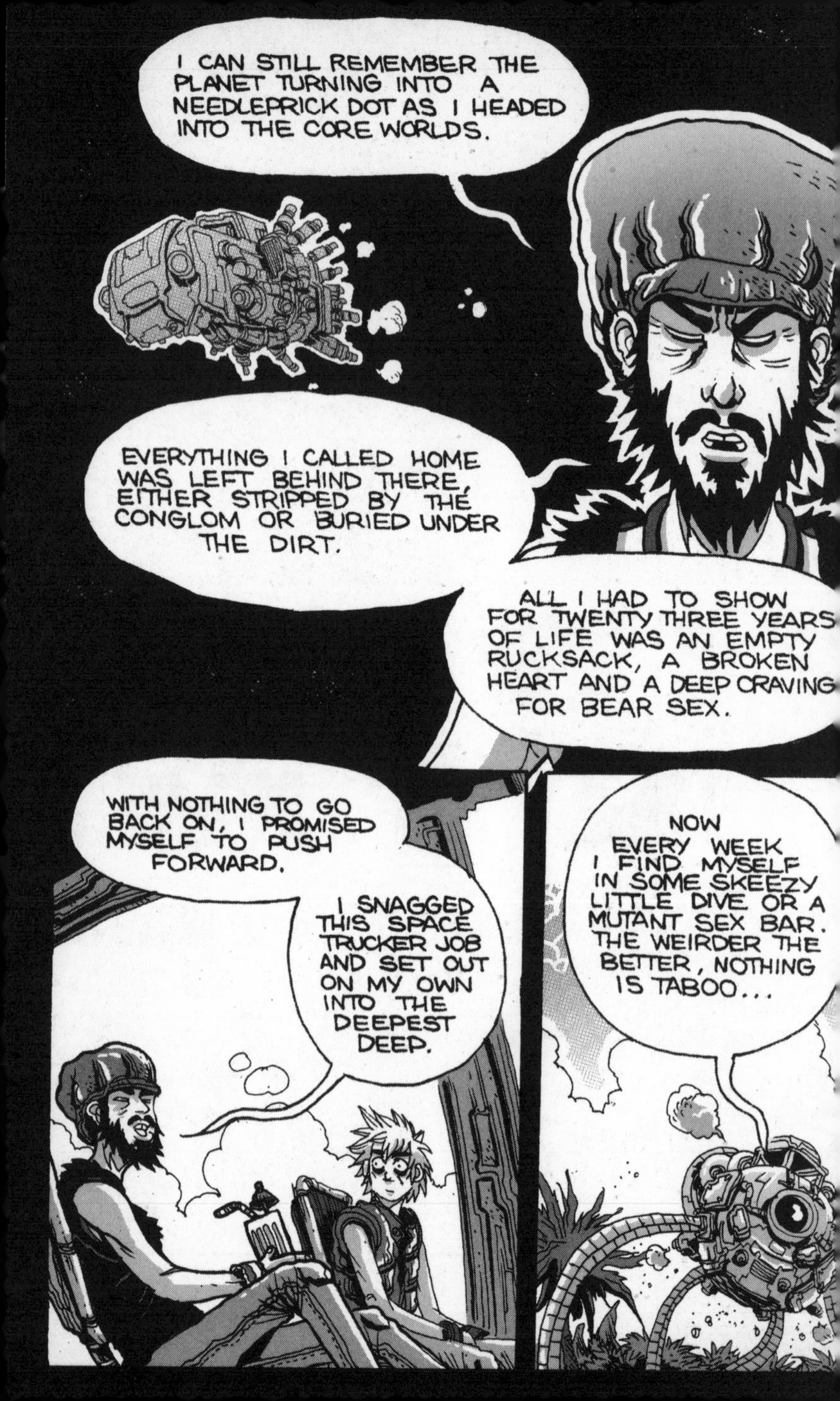

I CAN STILL REMEMBER THE PLANET TURNING INTO A NEEDLEPRICK DOT AS I HEADED INTO THE CORE WORLDS.
EVERYTHING I CALLED HOME WAS LEFT BEHIND THERE, EITHER STRIPPED BY THE CONGLOM OR BURIED UNDER THE DIRT.
ALL I HAD TO SHOW FOR TWENTY THREE YEARS OF LIFE WAS AN EMPTY RUCKSACK, A BROKEN HEART AND A DEEP CRAVING FOR BEAR SEX.
WITH NOTHING TO GO BACK ON, I PROMISED MYSELF TO PUSH FORWARD.
I SNAGGED THIS SPACE TRUCKER JOB AND SET OUT ON MY OWN INTO THE DEEPEST DEEP.
NOW EVERY WEEK I FIND MYSELF IN SOME SKEEZY LITTLE DIVE OR A MUTANT SEX BAR. THE WEIRDER THE BETTER, NOTHING IS TABOO...

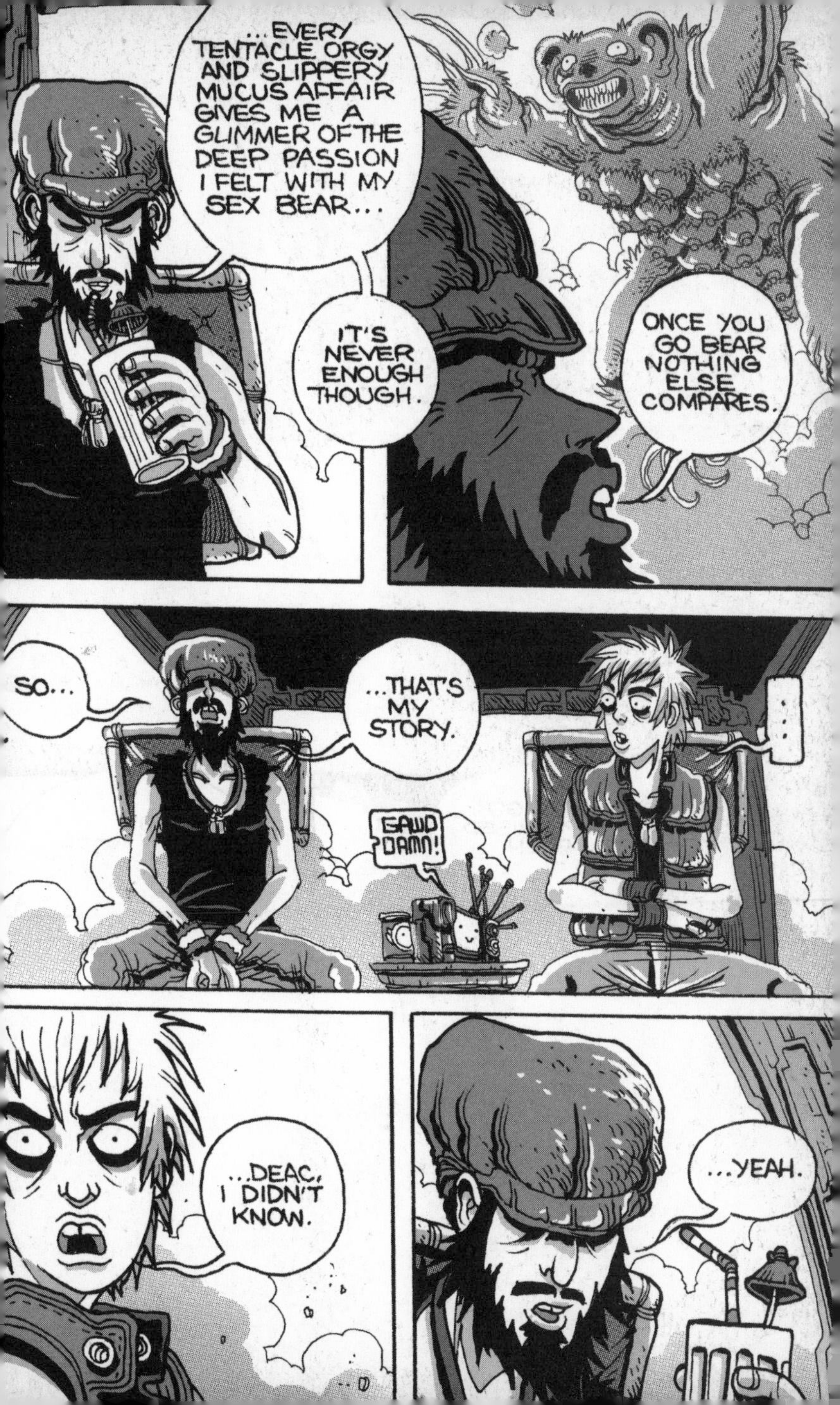
...EVERY TENTACLE ORGY AND SLIPPERY MUCUS AFFAIR GIVES ME A GLIMMER OF THE DEEP PASSION I FELT WITH MY SEX BEAR...
IT'S NEVER ENOUGH THOUGH.
ONCE YOU GO BEAR NOTHING ELSE COMPARES.
SO...
...THAT'S MY STORY.
...
GAWD DAMN!
...DEAC, I DIDN'T KNOW.
...YEAH.

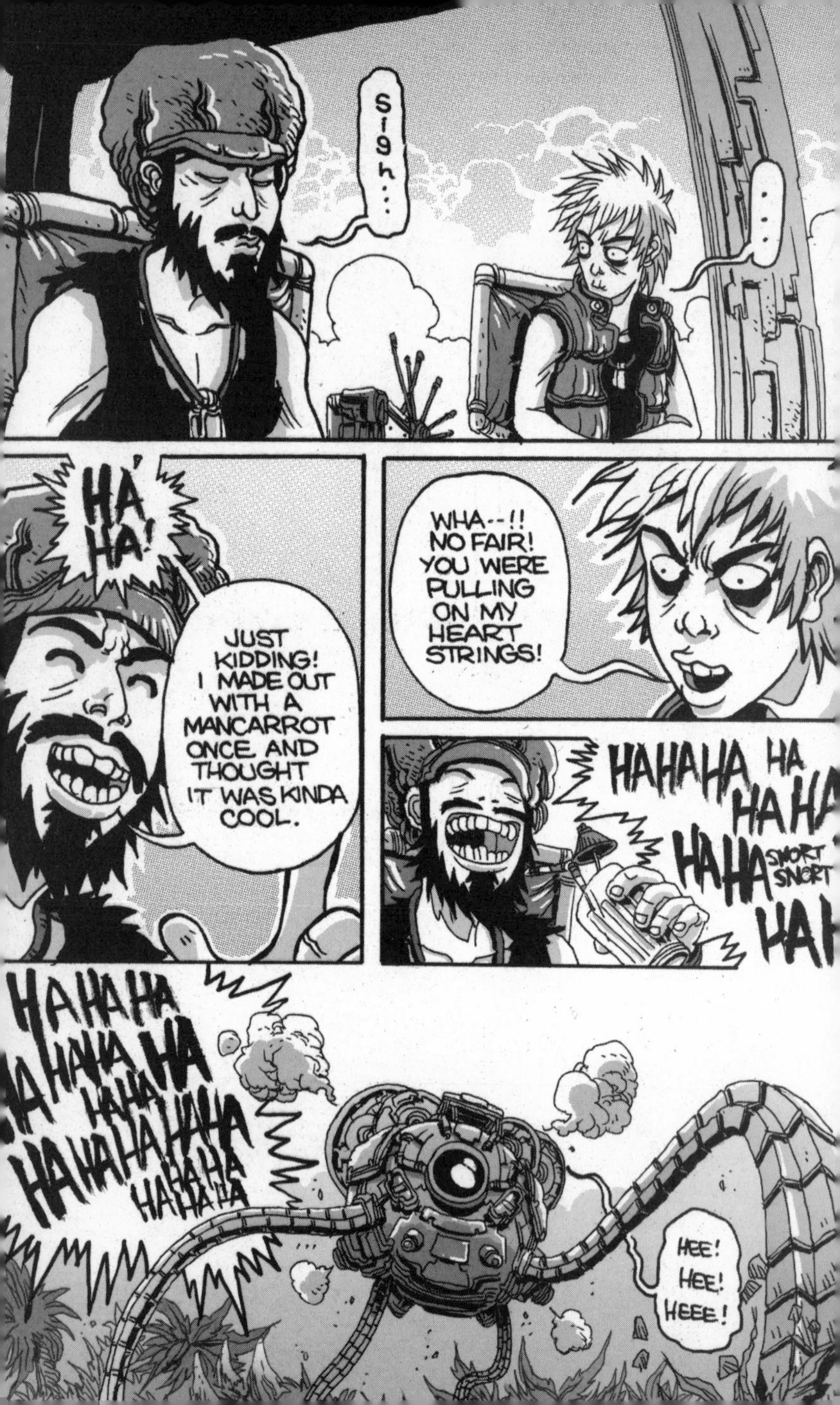
Sigh...
...
HA HA!
JUST KIDDING! I MADE OUT WITH A MANCARROT ONCE AND THOUGHT IT WAS KINDA COOL.
WHA--!! NO FAIR! YOU WERE PULLING ON MY HEART STRINGS!
HAHAHA HA HAHA HAHA SNORT SNORT HA
HAHAHA HAHAHAHA HAHA HAHAHAHA HAHAHAHA HAHAHA
HEE! HEE! HEEE!

OH, DEAC, YOU'RE SUCH A CARD.

HEE HEE HEEE!

I SURE AM!

Sigh...

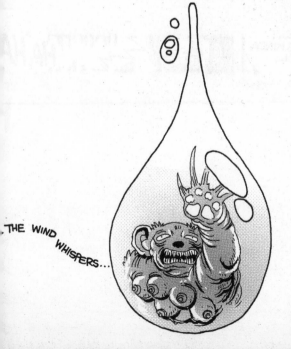

...THE WIND WHISPERS...

...SEX BEAR...

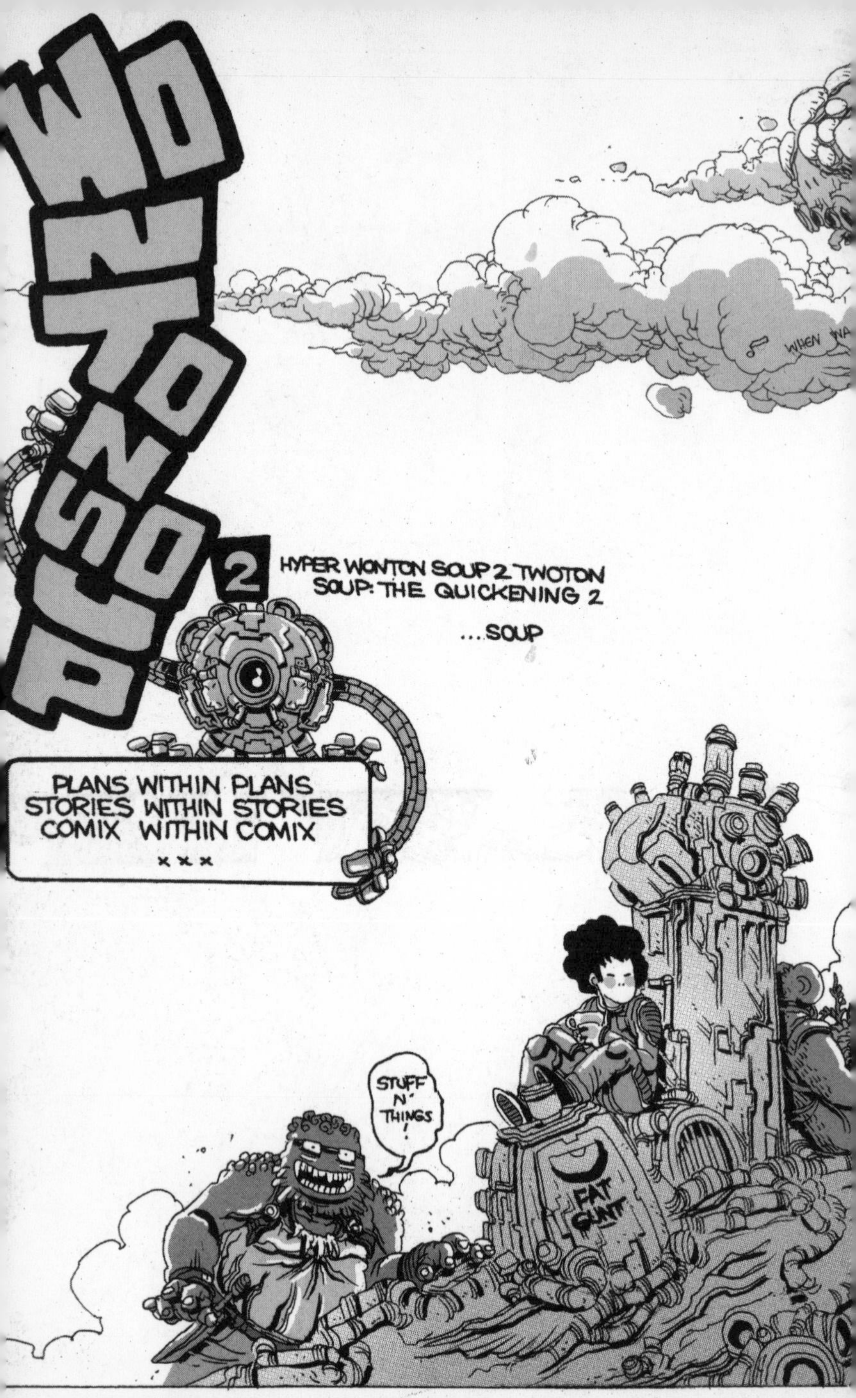

WONTON SOUP 2
HYPER WONTON SOUP 2 TWOTON SOUP: THE QUICKENING 2
...SOUP
PLANS WITHIN PLANS
STORIES WITHIN STORIES
COMIX WITHIN COMIX
x x x
STUFF N' THINGS!
FAT GUNT

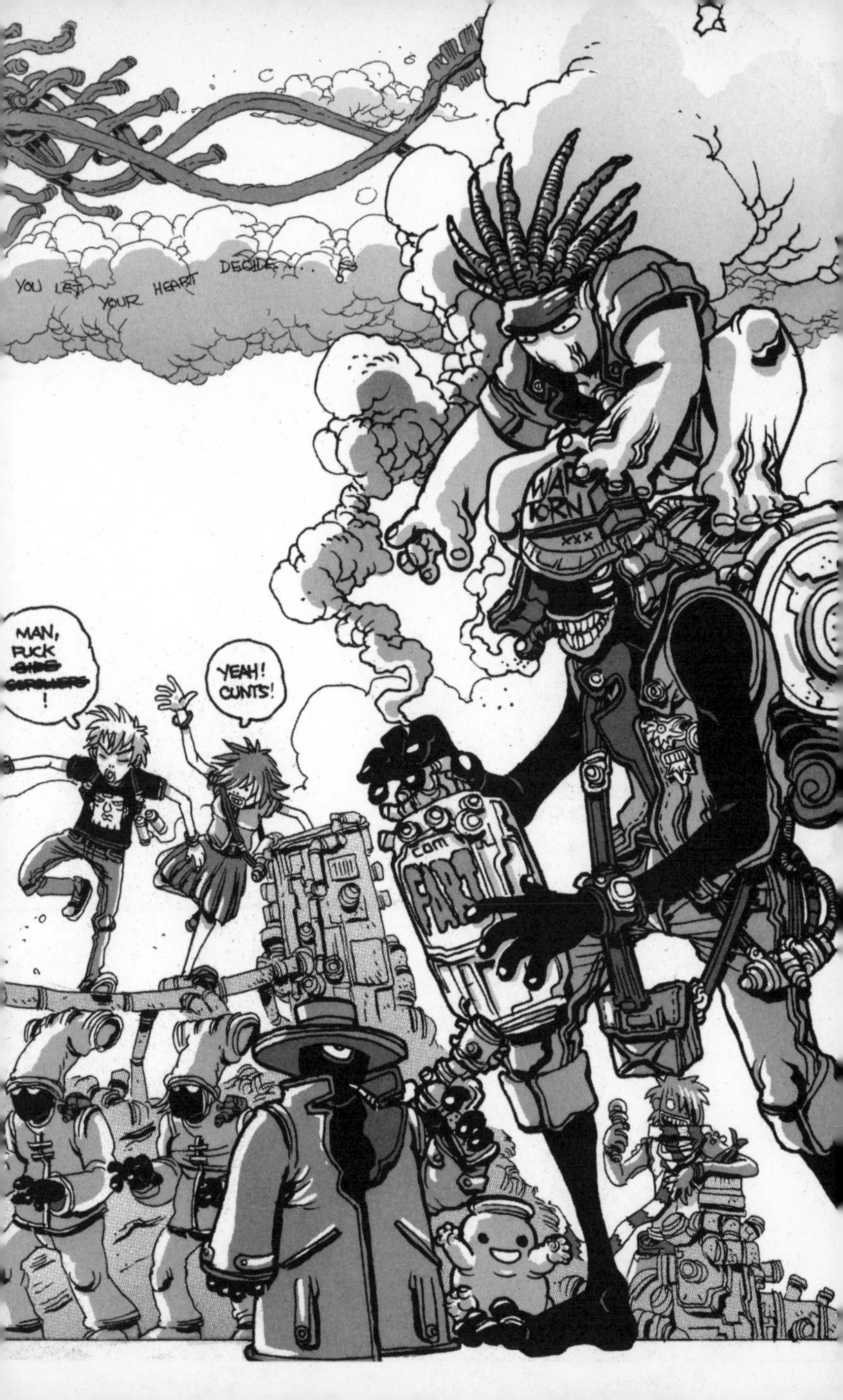
YOU LET YOUR HEART DECIDE...
MAN, FUCK !
YEAH! CUNTS!

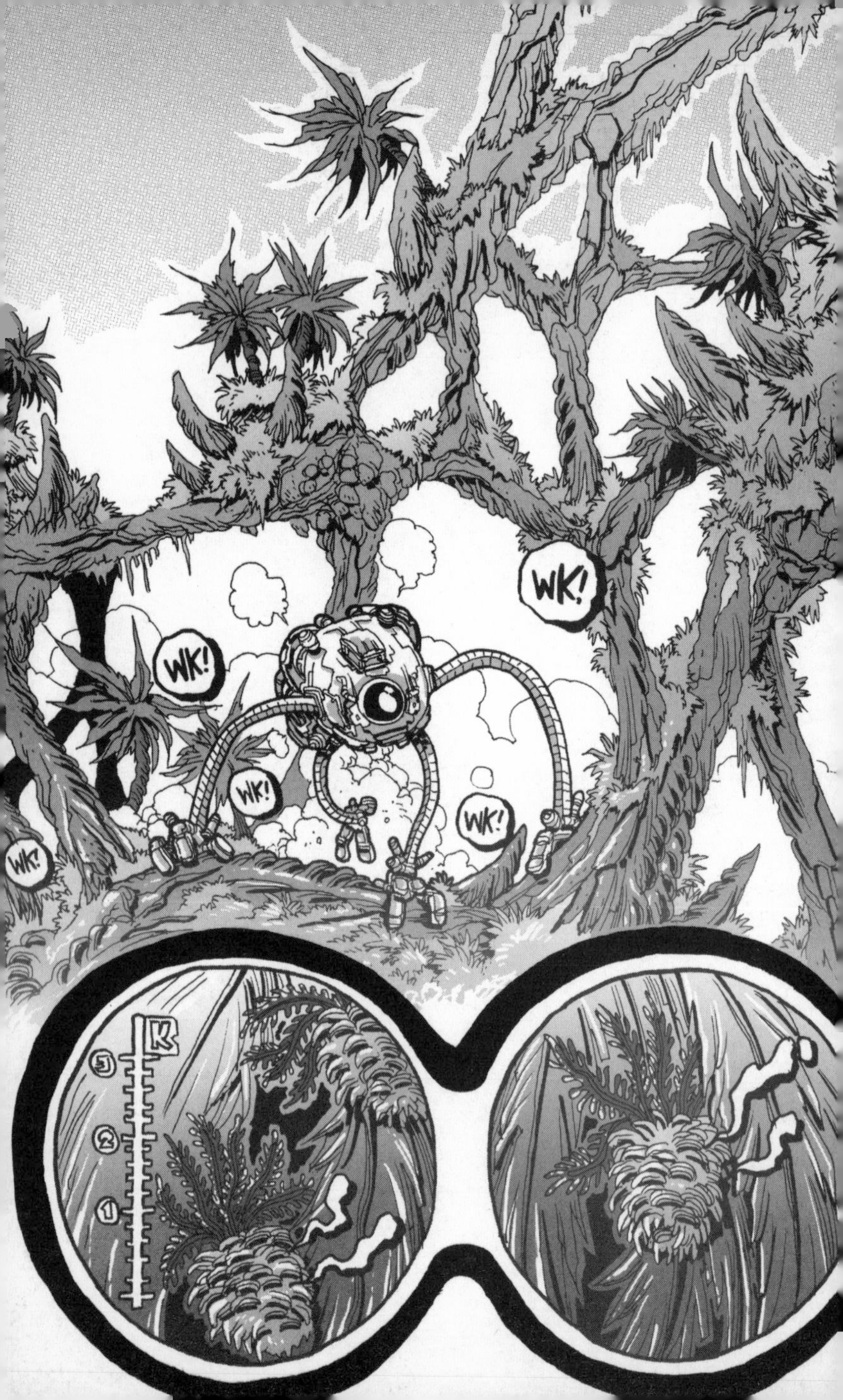
WK!
WK!
WK!
WK!
WK!
K
3
2
1

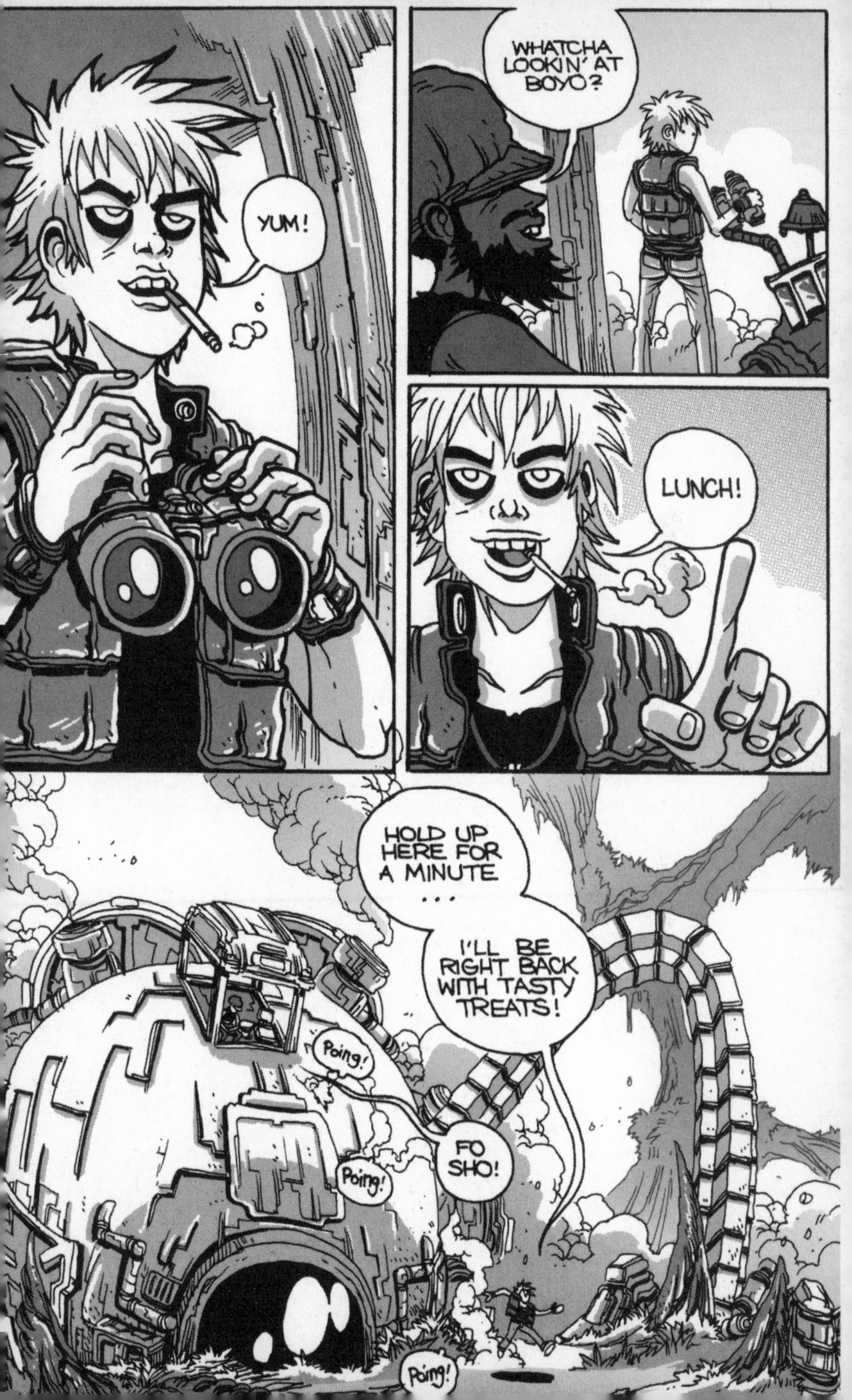
YUM!
WHATCHA LOOKIN' AT BOYO?
LUNCH!
HOLD UP HERE FOR A MINUTE ...
I'LL BE RIGHT BACK WITH TASTY TREATS!
Poing!
FO SHO!
Poing!
Poing!

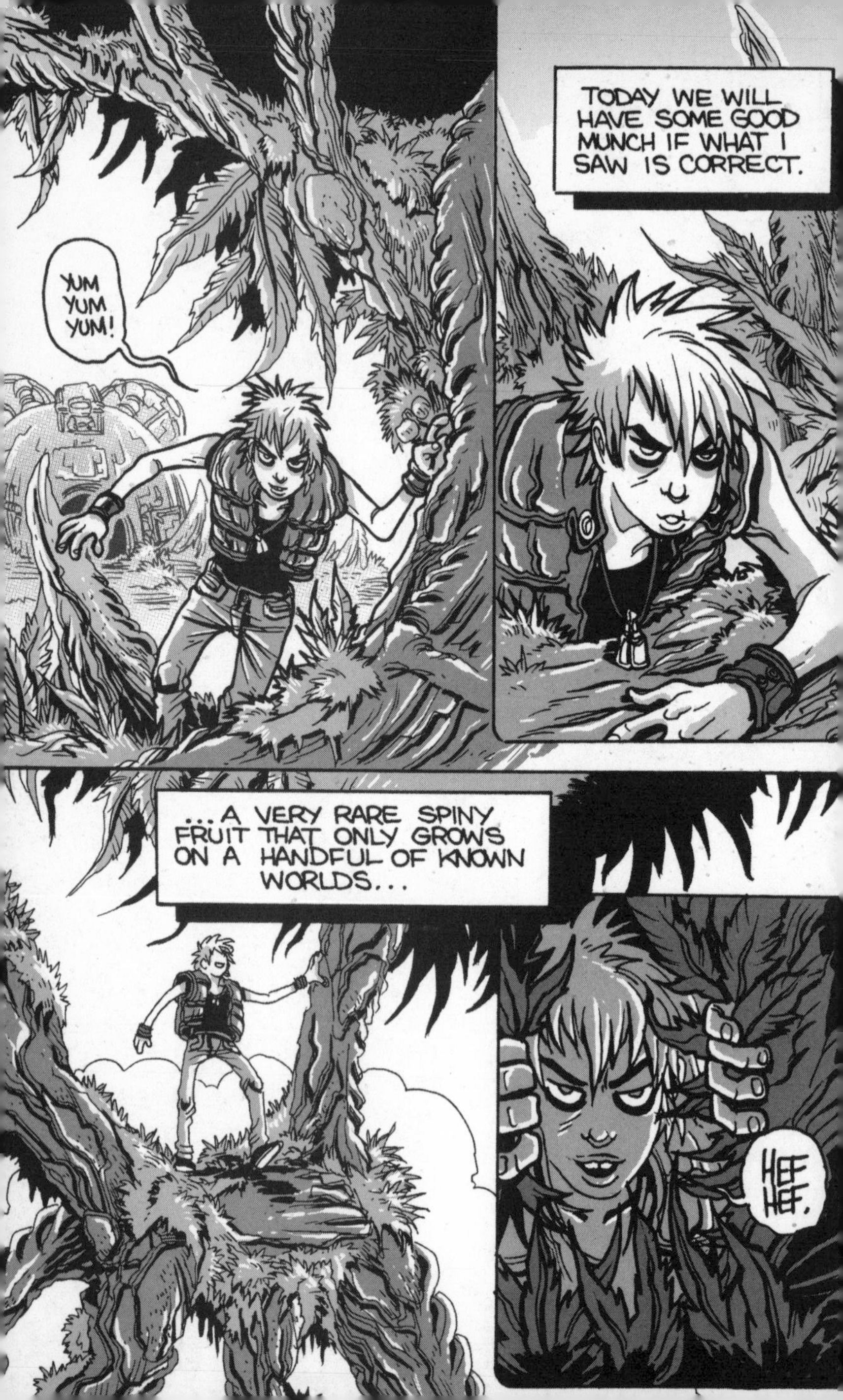
YUM
YUM
YUM!
TODAY WE WILL HAVE SOME GOOD MUNCH IF WHAT I SAW IS CORRECT.
...A VERY RARE SPINY FRUIT THAT ONLY GROWS ON A HANDFUL OF KNOWN WORLDS...
HEF HEF.

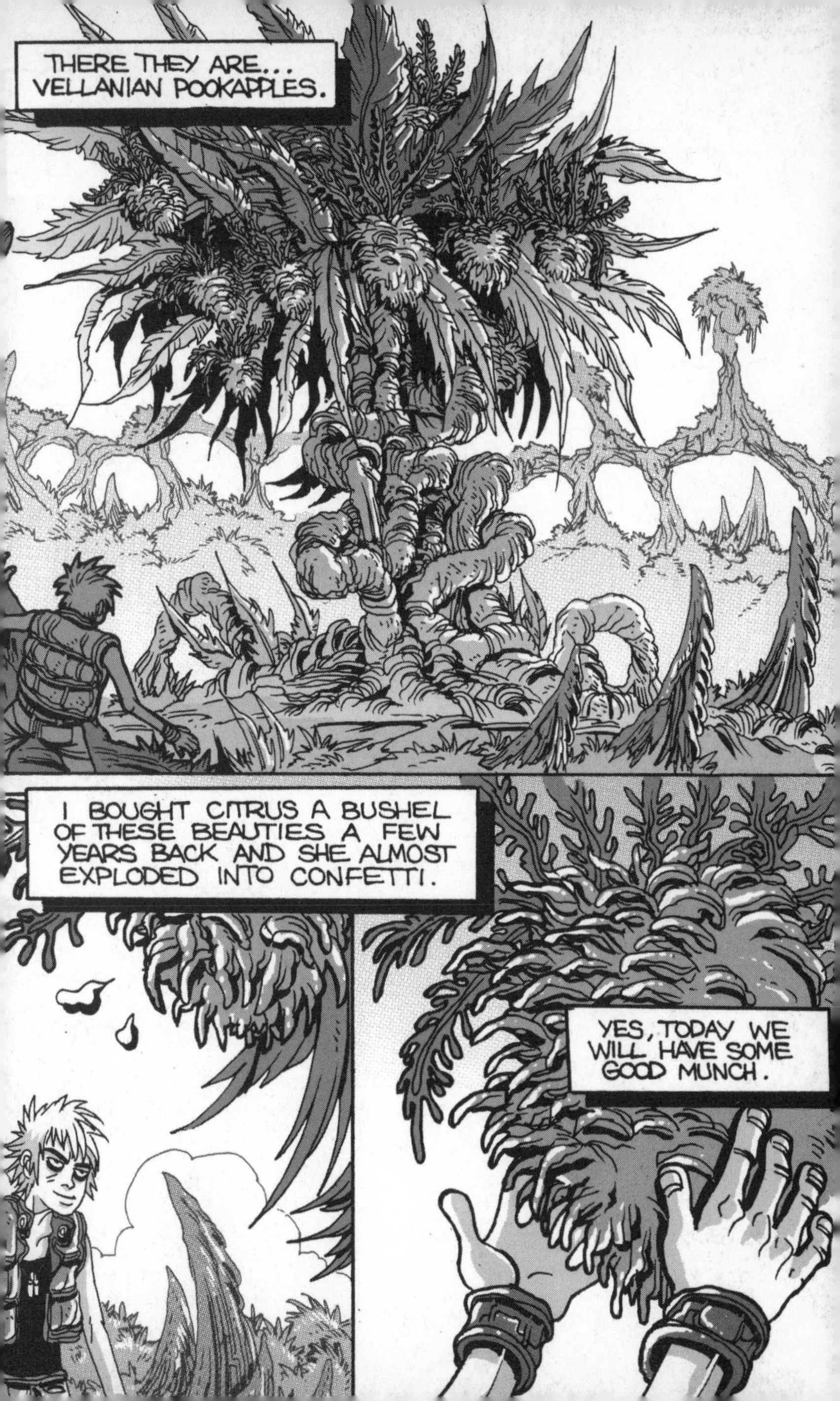
THERE THEY ARE... VELLANIAN POOKAPPLES.
I BOUGHT CITRUS A BUSHEL OF THESE BEAUTIES A FEW YEARS BACK AND SHE ALMOST EXPLODED INTO CONFETTI.
YES, TODAY WE WILL HAVE SOME GOOD MUNCH.

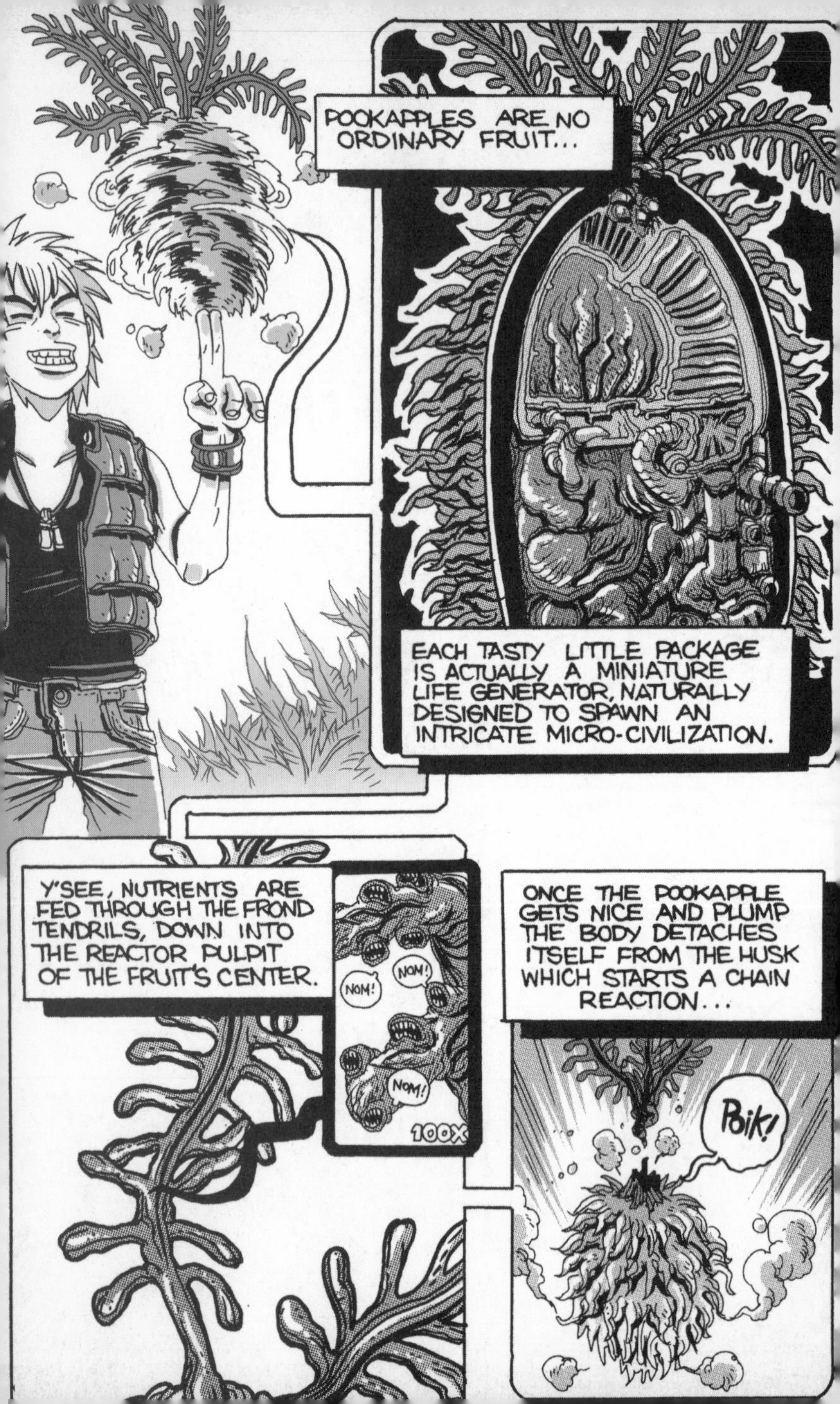

POOKAPPLES ARE NO ORDINARY FRUIT...
EACH TASTY LITTLE PACKAGE IS ACTUALLY A MINIATURE LIFE GENERATOR, NATURALLY DESIGNED TO SPAWN AN INTRICATE MICRO-CIVILIZATION.
Y'SEE, NUTRIENTS ARE FED THROUGH THE FROND TENDRILS, DOWN INTO THE REACTOR PULPIT OF THE FRUIT'S CENTER.
NOM!
NOM!
NOM!
100X
ONCE THE POOKAPPLE GETS NICE AND PLUMP THE BODY DETACHES ITSELF FROM THE HUSK WHICH STARTS A CHAIN REACTION...
POIK!

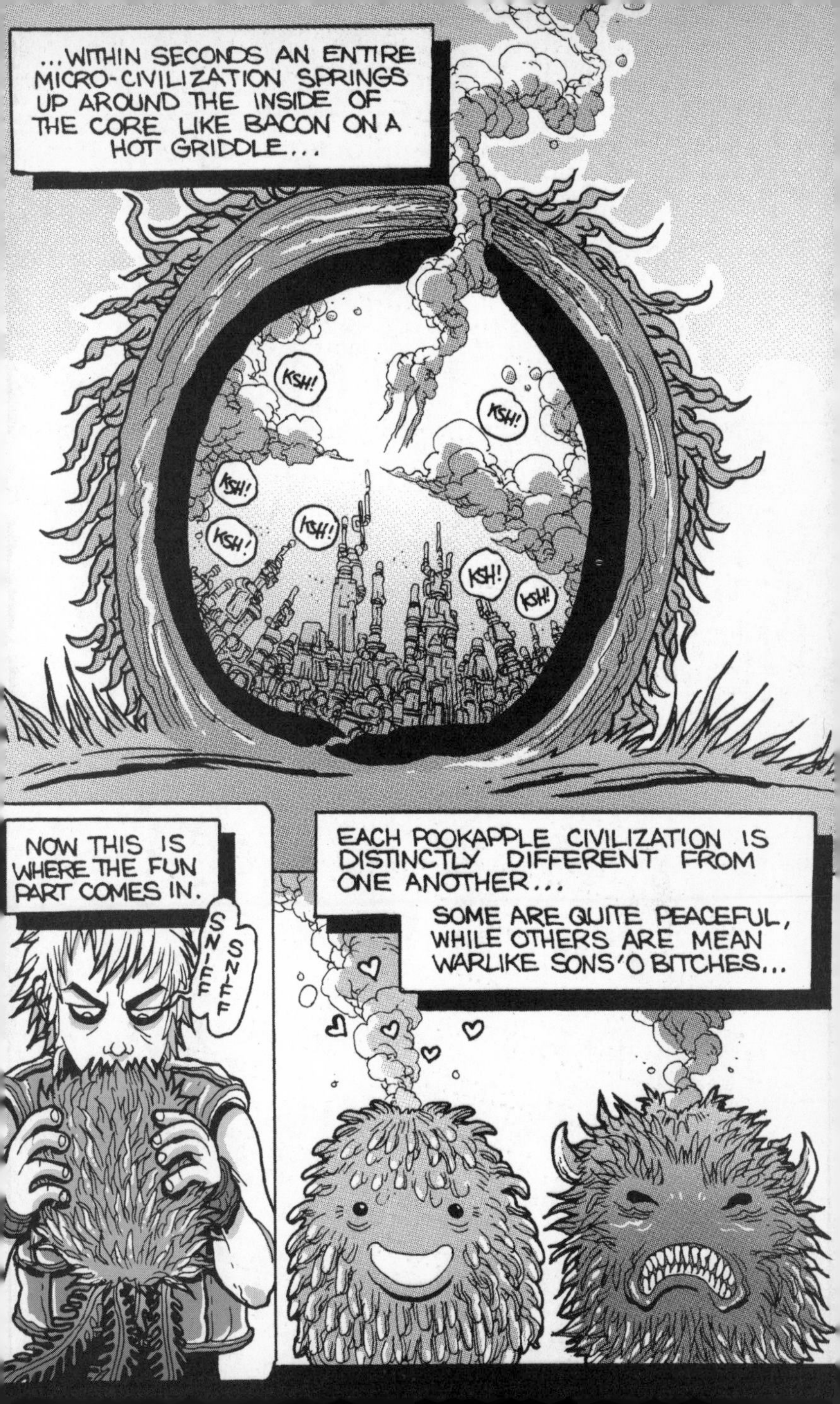
...WITHIN SECONDS AN ENTIRE MICRO-CIVILIZATION SPRINGS UP AROUND THE INSIDE OF THE CORE LIKE BACON ON A HOT GRIDDLE...
KSH!
KSH!
KSH!
KSH!
KSH!
KSH!
KSH!
NOW THIS IS WHERE THE FUN PART COMES IN.
SNIFF SNIFF
EACH POOKAPPLE CIVILIZATION IS DISTINCTLY DIFFERENT FROM ONE ANOTHER...
SOME ARE QUITE PEACEFUL, WHILE OTHERS ARE MEAN WARLIKE SONS'O BITCHES...

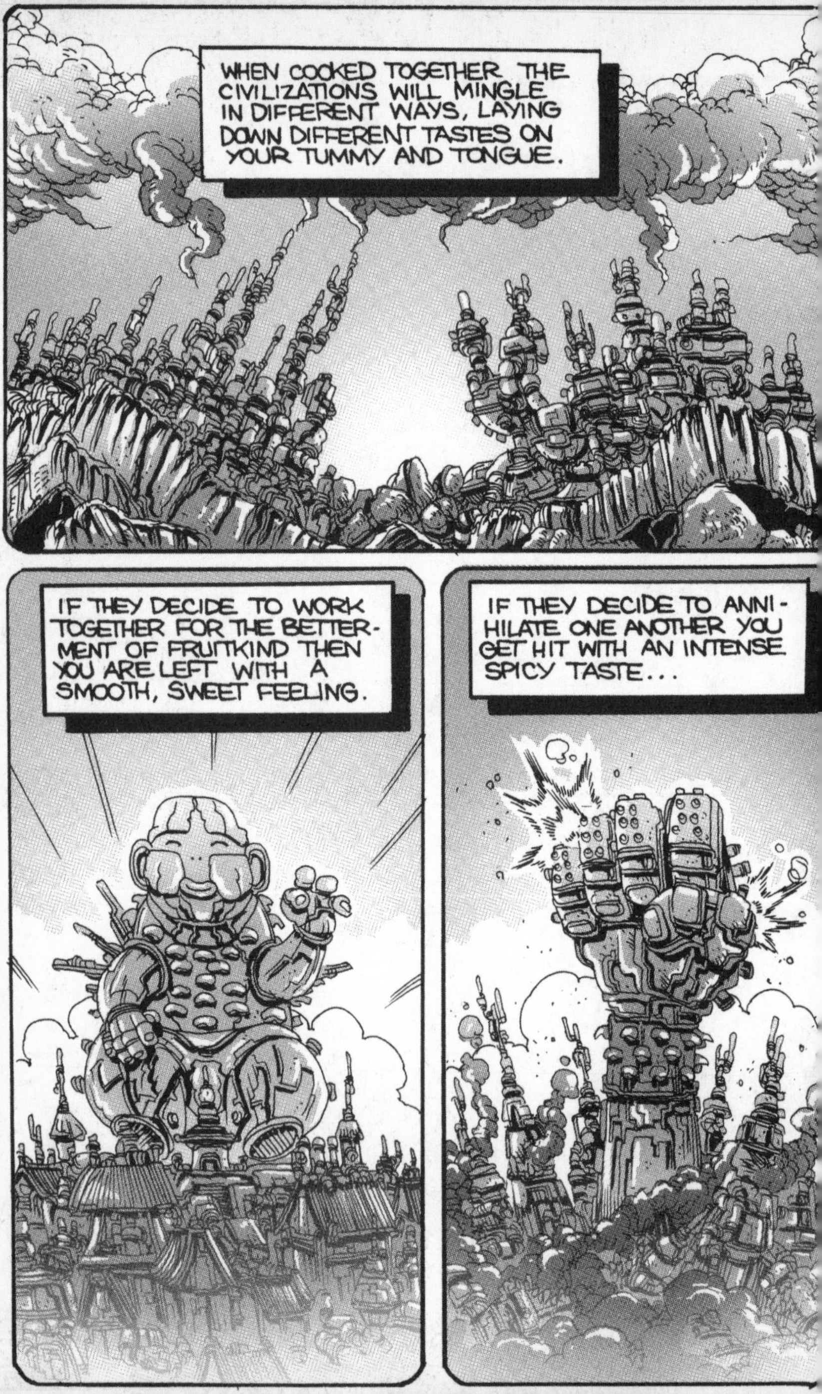
WHEN COOKED TOGETHER THE CIVILIZATIONS WILL MINGLE IN DIFFERENT WAYS, LAYING DOWN DIFFERENT TASTES ON YOUR TUMMY AND TONGUE.
IF THEY DECIDE TO WORK TOGETHER FOR THE BETTERMENT OF FRUITKIND THEN YOU ARE LEFT WITH A SMOOTH, SWEET FEELING.
IF THEY DECIDE TO ANNIHILATE ONE ANOTHER YOU GET HIT WITH AN INTENSE SPICY TASTE...

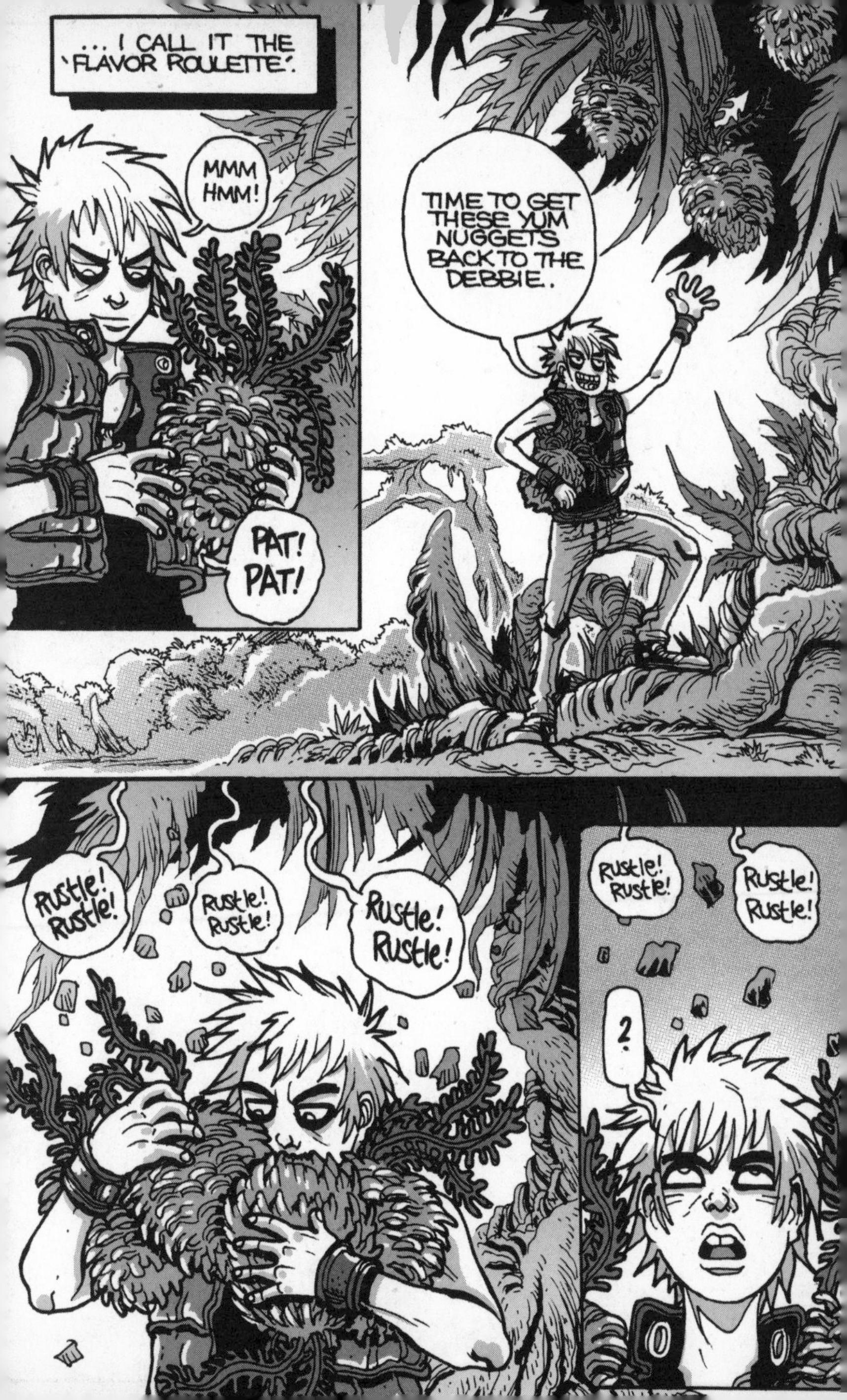

... I CALL IT THE 'FLAVOR ROULETTE'.
MMM HMM!
PAT! PAT!
TIME TO GET THESE YUM NUGGETS BACK TO THE DEBBIE.
Rustle! Rustle!
Rustle! Rustle!
Rustle! Rustle!
Rustle! Rustle!
Rustle! Rustle!
?

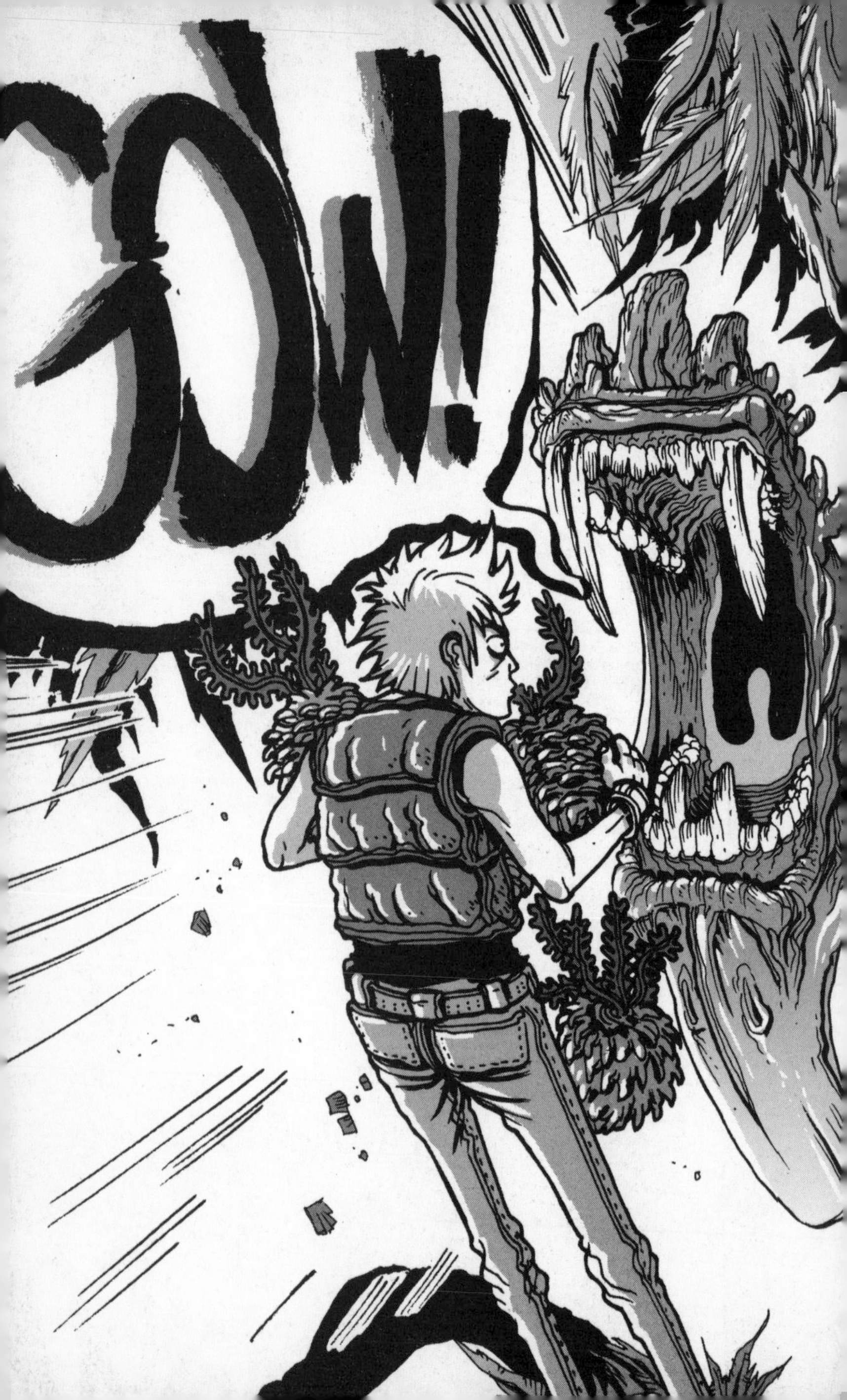
GOW!!

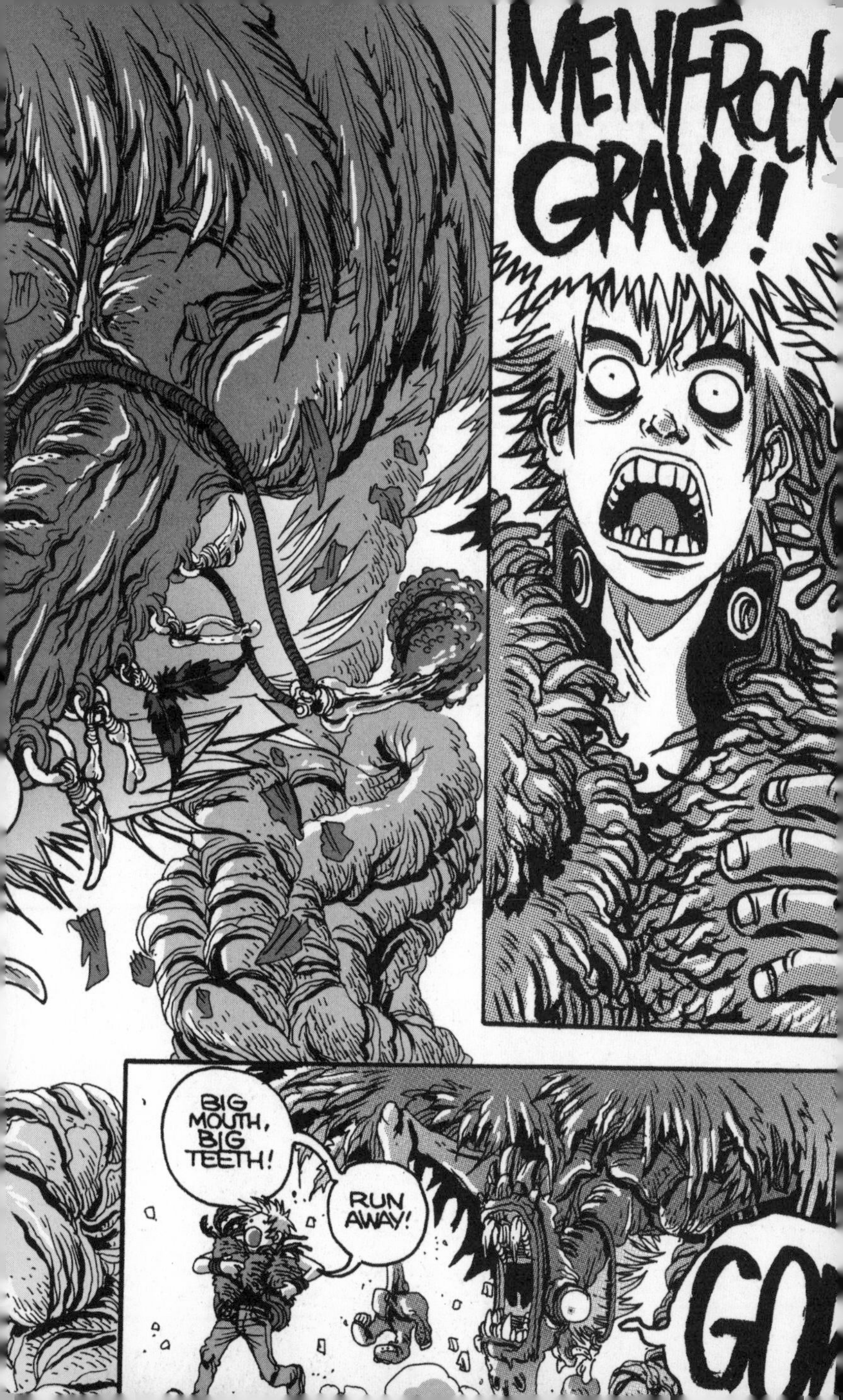
MENFROCK GRAVY!
BIG MOUTH, BIG TEETH!
RUN AWAY!

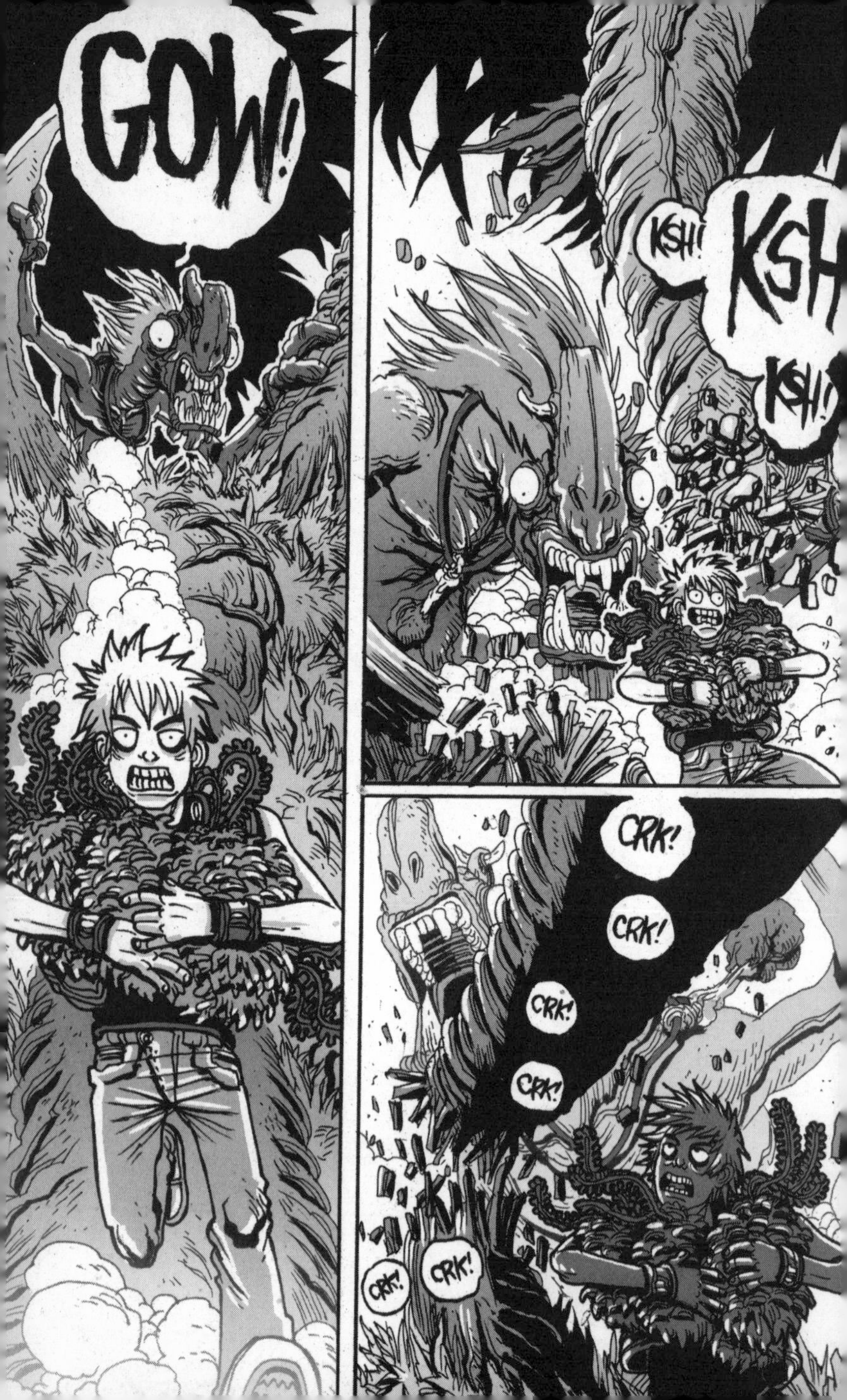
GOW!
KSH!
KSH
KSH!
CRK!
CRK!
CRK!
CRK!
CRK!
CRK!

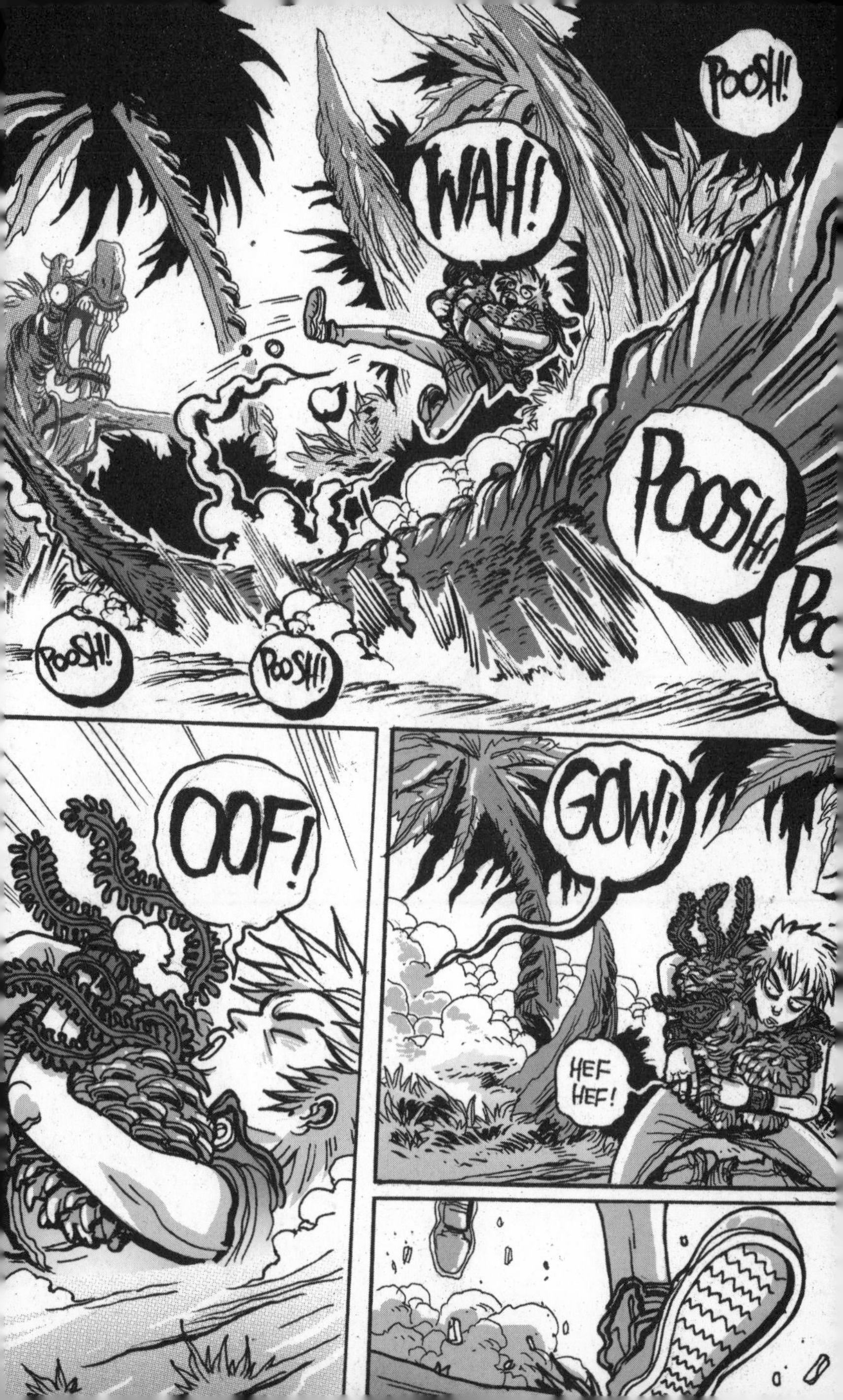
POOSH!
WAH!
POOSH!
Poo
POOSH!
POOSH!
OOF!
GOW!
HEF
HEF!

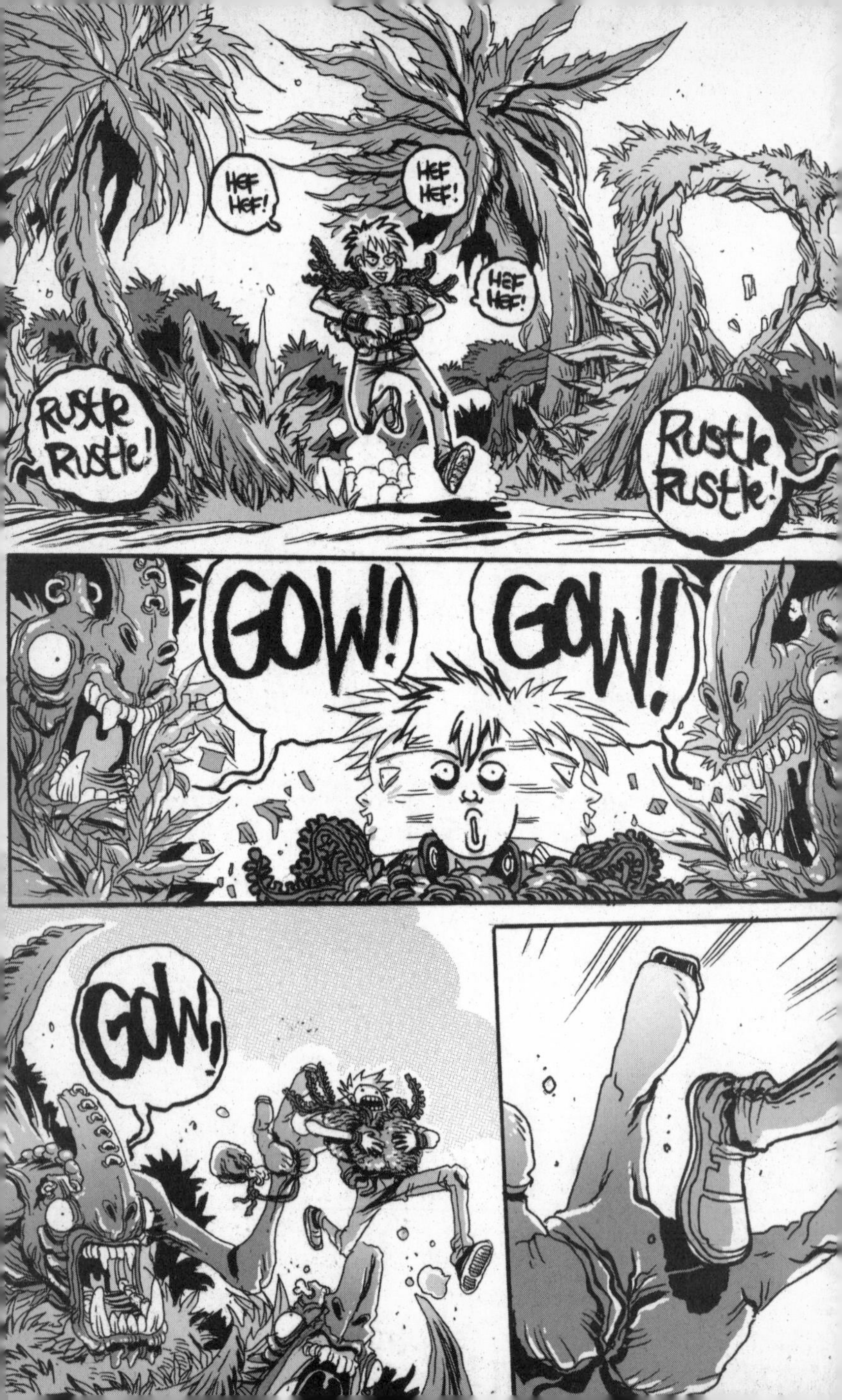
HEF HEF!
HEF HEF!
HEF HEF!
Rustle Rustle!
Rustle Rustle!
GOW!
GOW!
GOW!

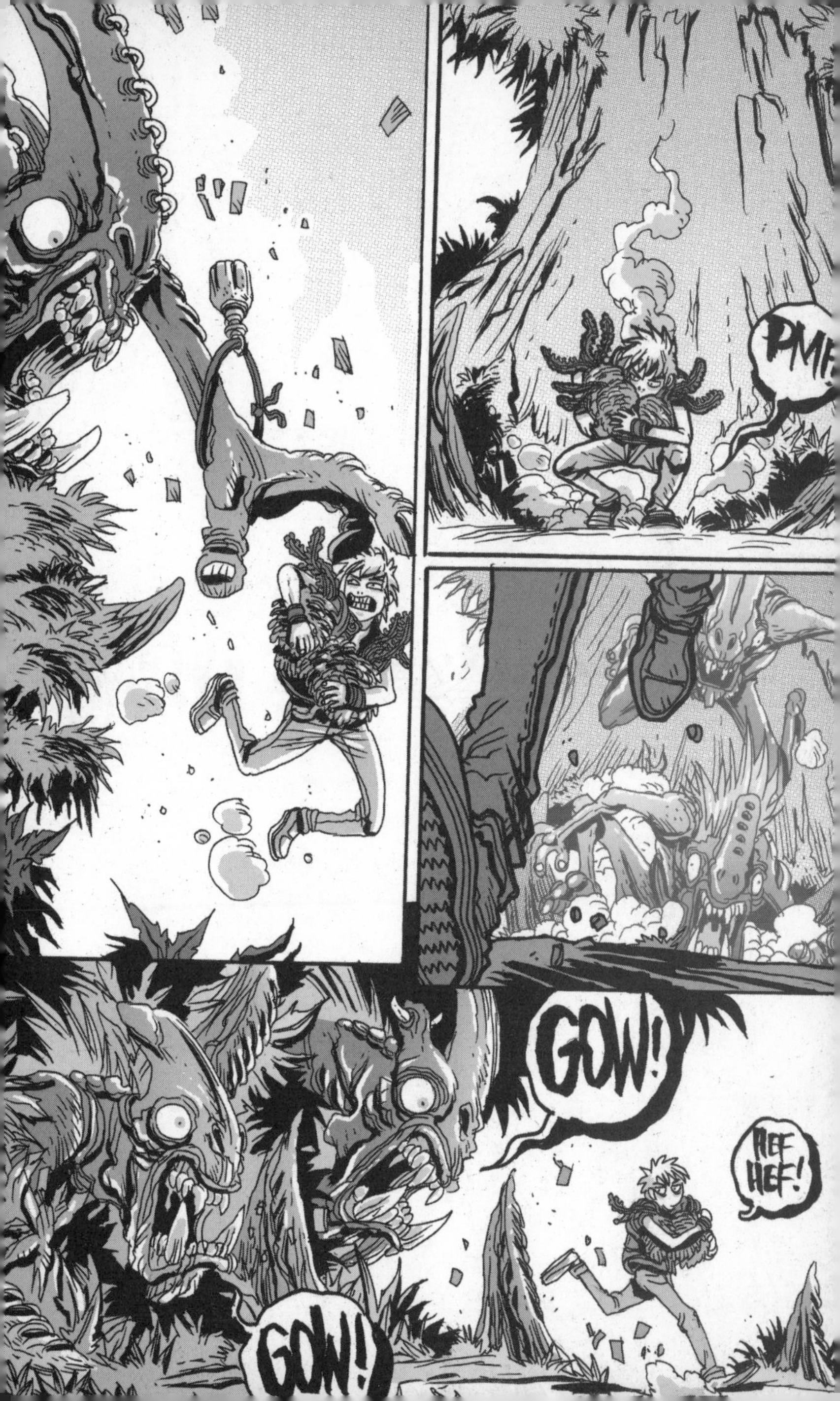
PMF!
GOW!
HEF HEF!
GOW!

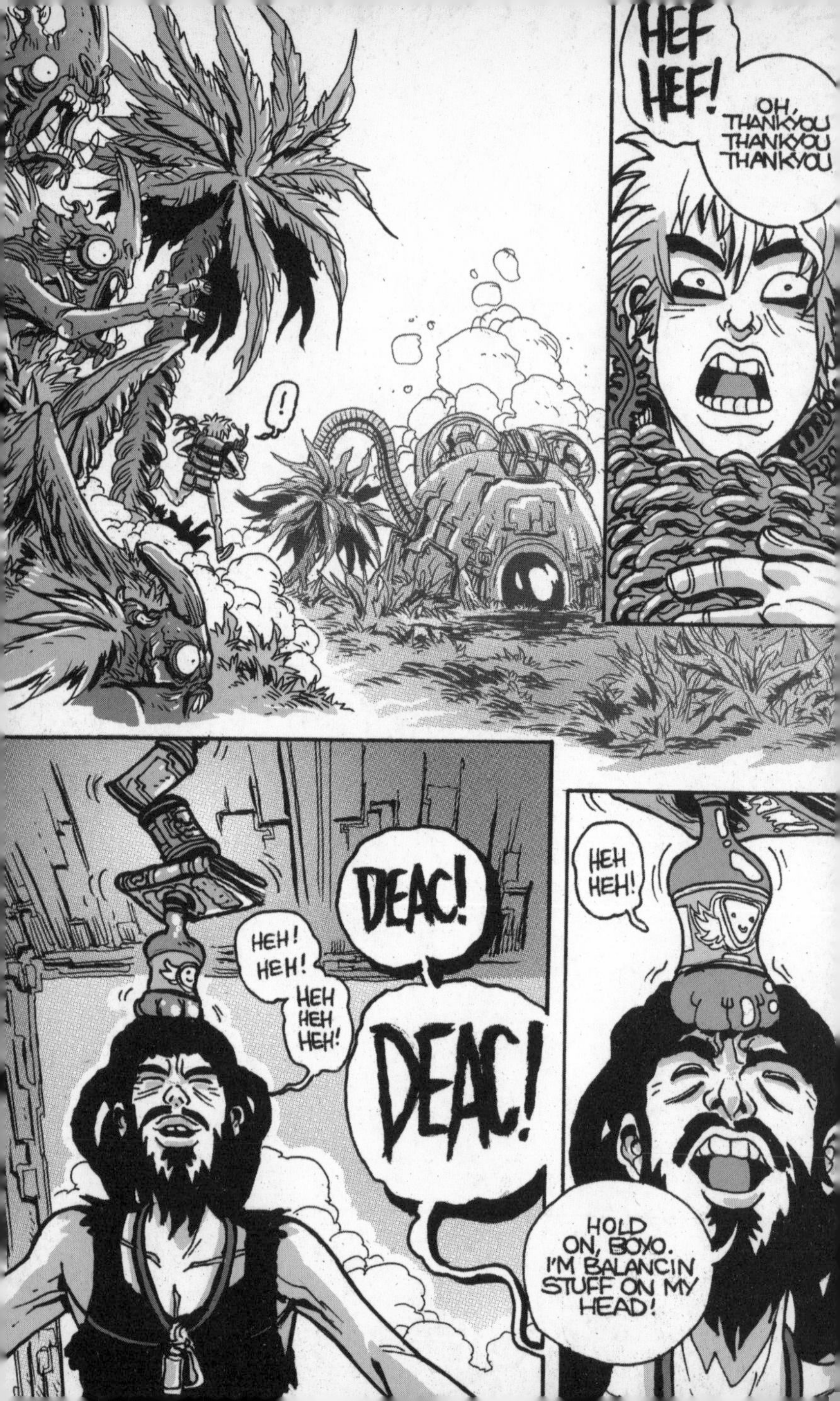
!
HEF HEF!
OH, THANKYOU THANKYOU THANKYOU
HEH! HEH!
HEH HEH HEH!
DEAC!
DEAC!
HEH HEH!
HOLD ON, BOYO. I'M BALANCIN STUFF ON MY HEAD!

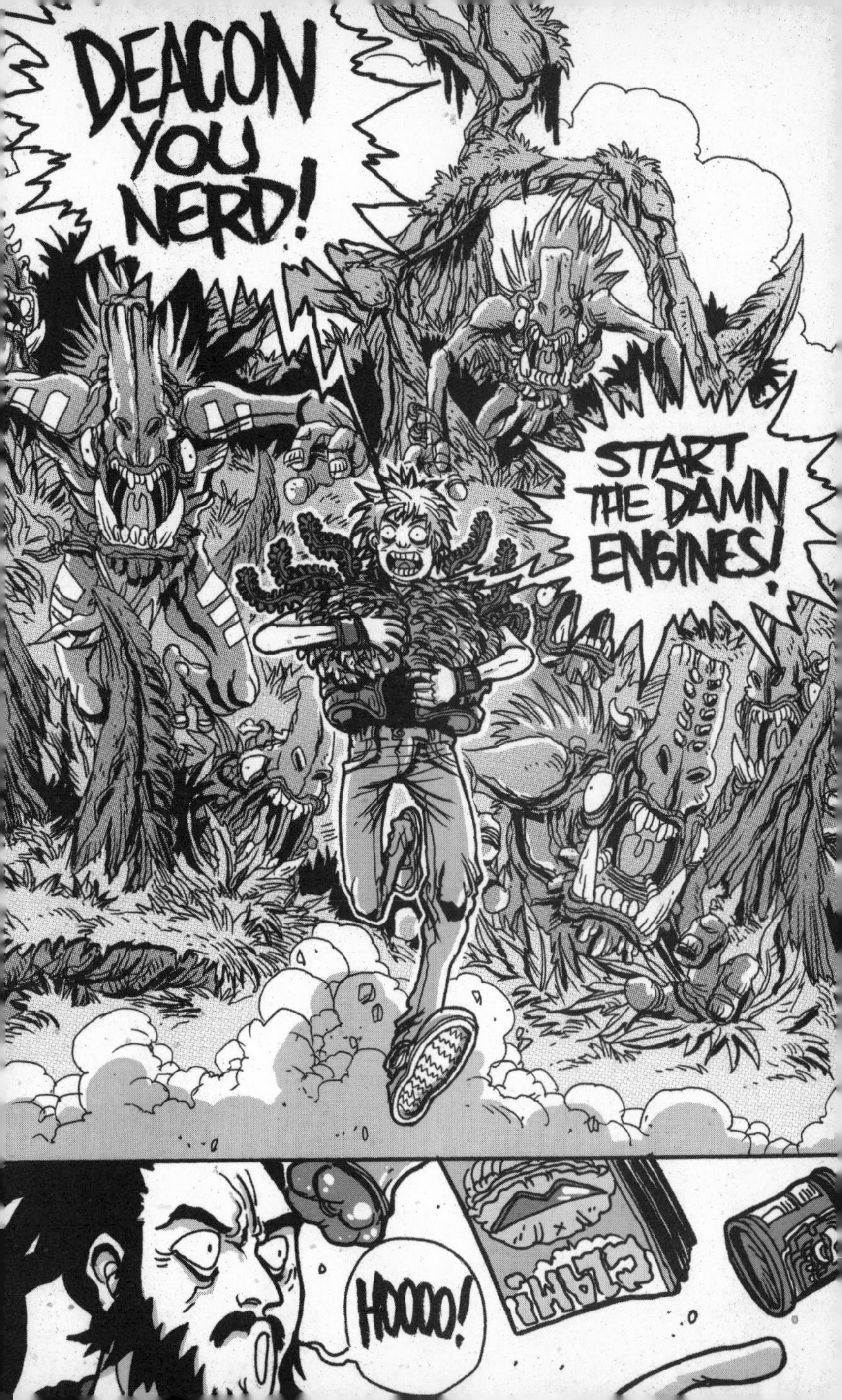
DEACON YOU NERD!
START THE DAMN ENGINES!
HOOOO!

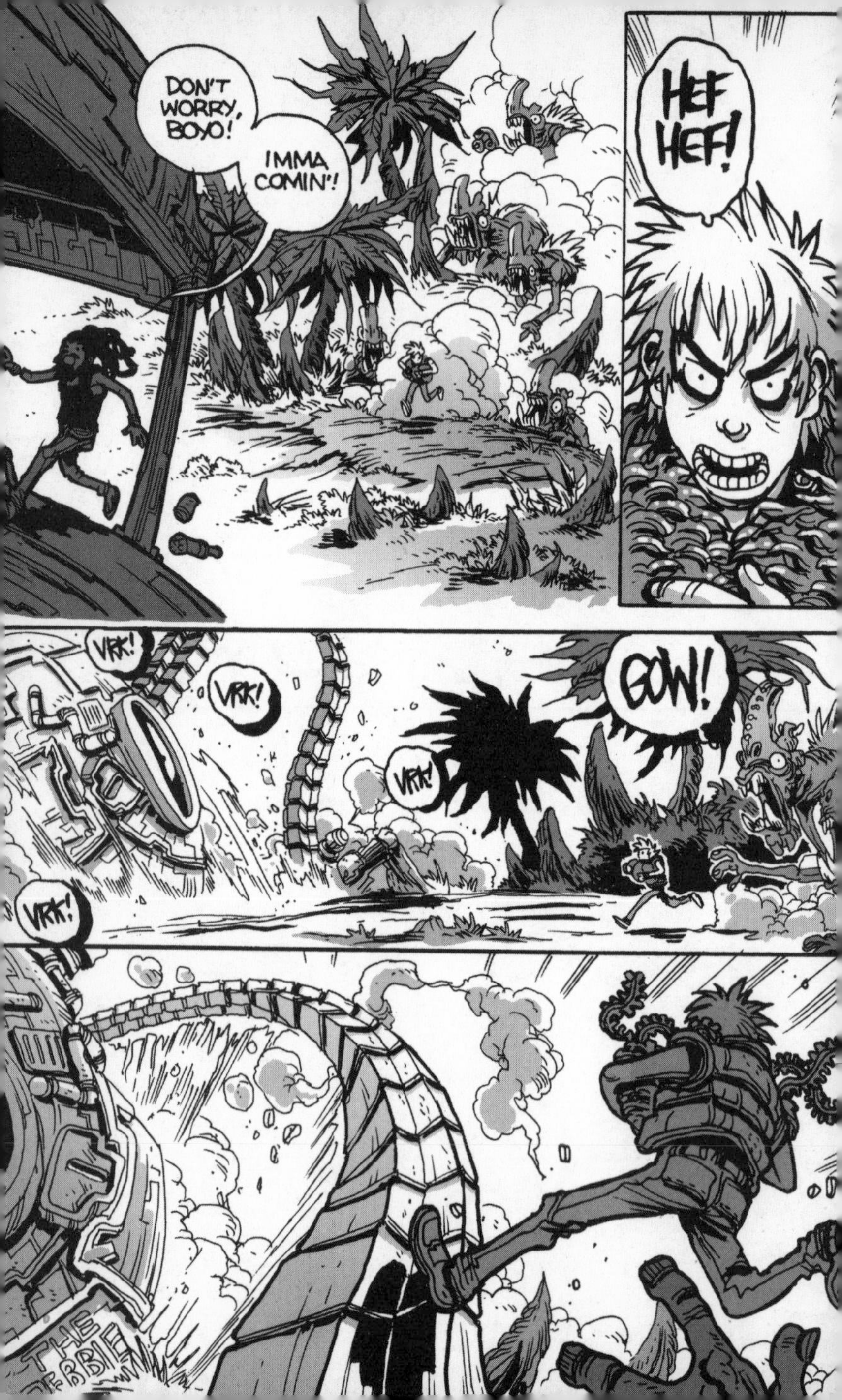
DON'T WORRY, BOYO!
IMMA COMIN'!
HEF HEF!
VRK!
VRK!
GOW!
VRK!
VRK!

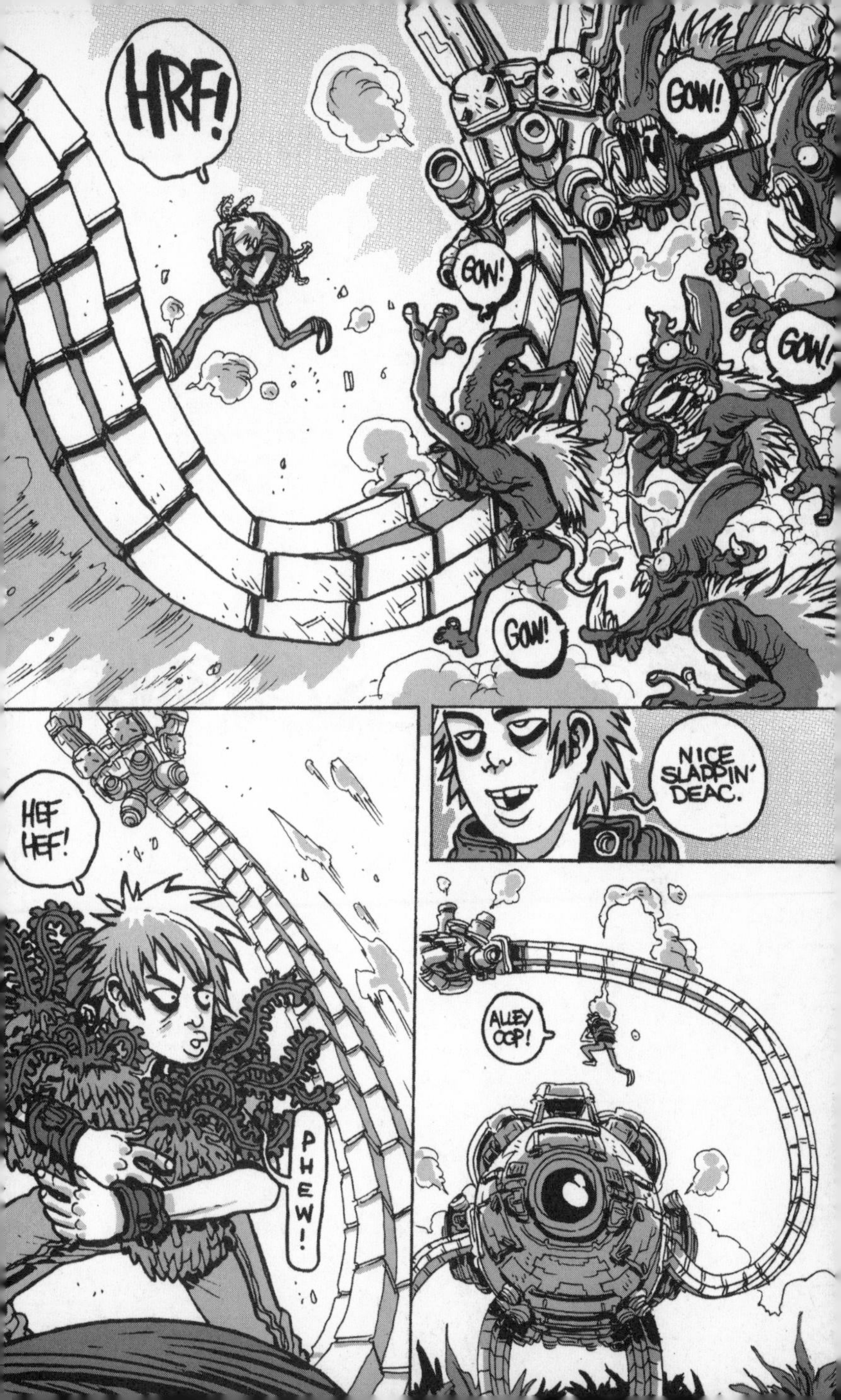
HRF!
GOW!
GOW!
GOW!
GOW!
NICE SLAPPIN' DEAC.
HEF HEF!
PHEW!
ALLEY OOP!

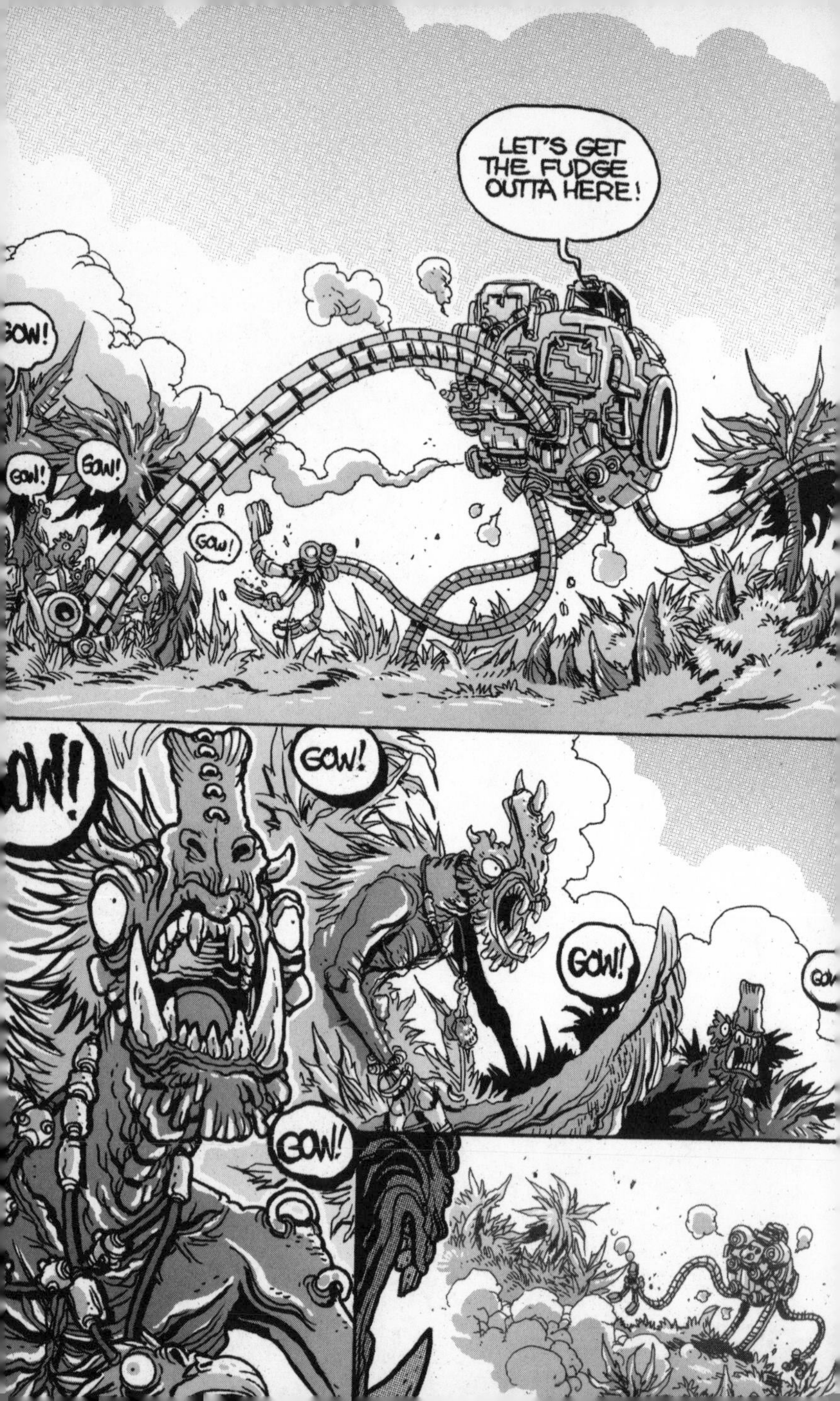
LET'S GET THE FUDGE OUTTA HERE!
GOW!
GOW!
GOW!
GOW!
GOW!
GOW!
GOW!
GOW!

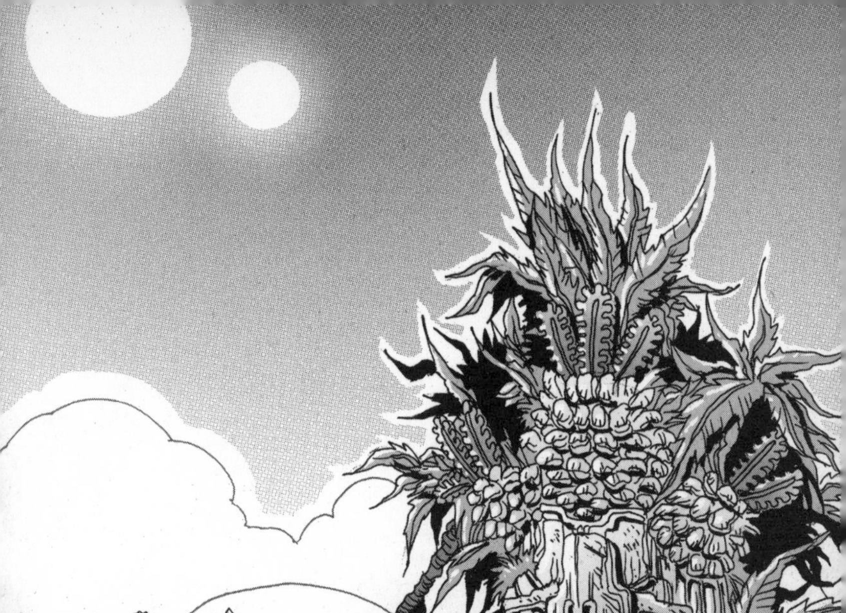

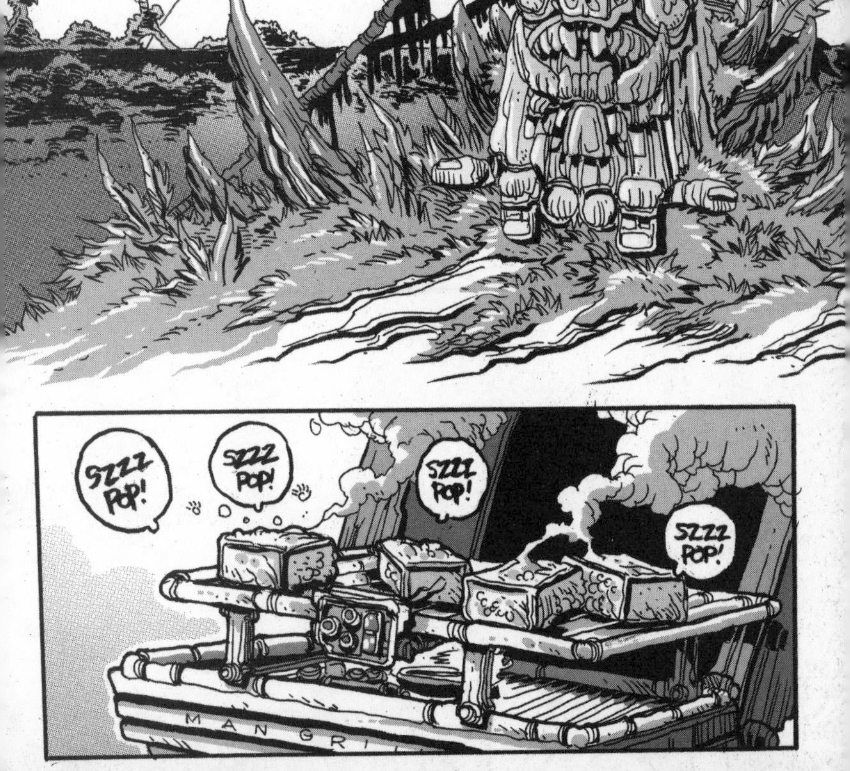

SZZZ POP!
SZZZ POP!
SZZZ POP!
SZZZ POP!
M A N G R I

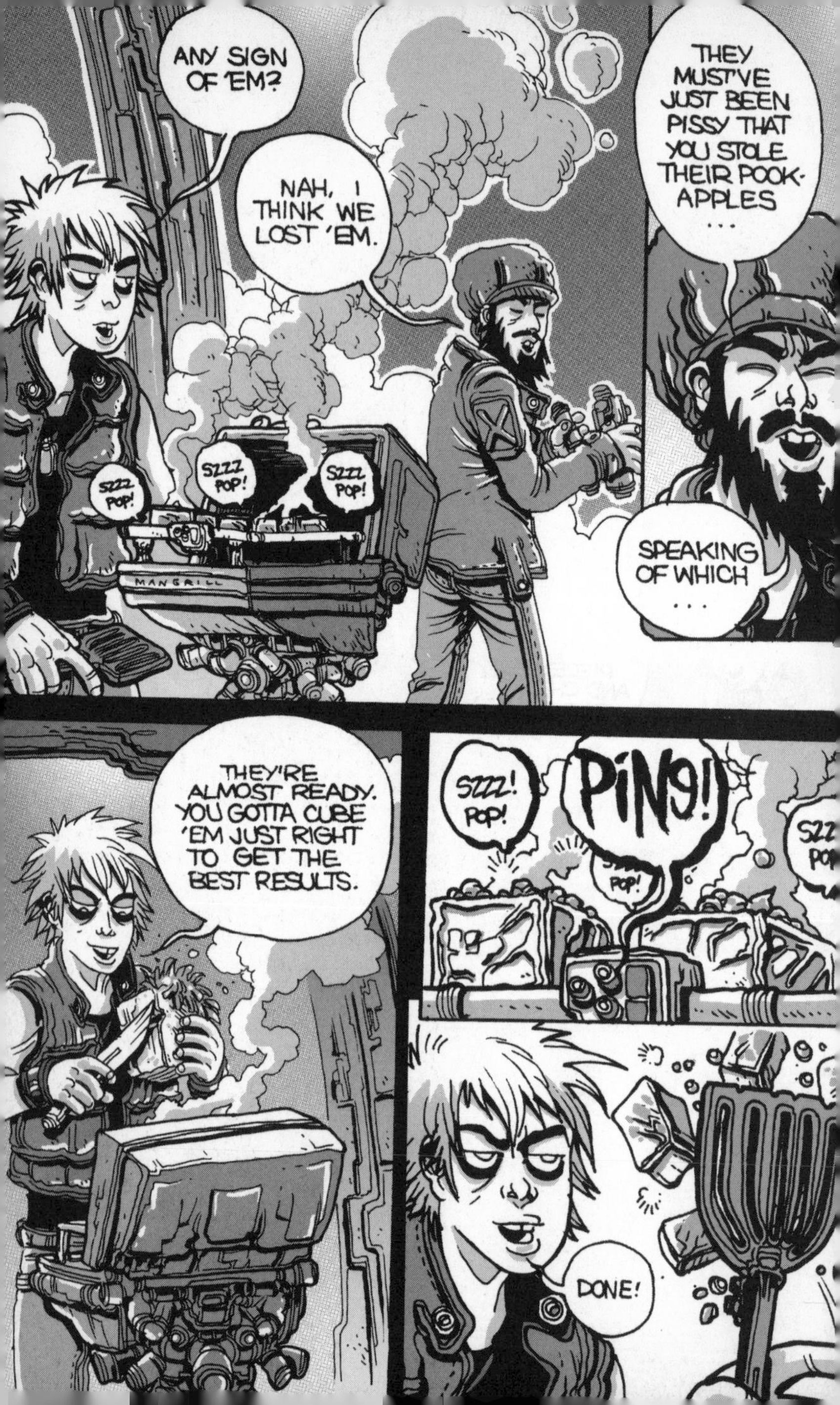
ANY SIGN OF 'EM?
NAH, I THINK WE LOST 'EM.
SZZZ POP!
SZZZ POP!
SZZZ POP!
MANGRILL
THEY MUST'VE JUST BEEN PISSY THAT YOU STOLE THEIR POOK-APPLES ...
SPEAKING OF WHICH ...
THEY'RE ALMOST READY. YOU GOTTA CUBE 'EM JUST RIGHT TO GET THE BEST RESULTS.
SZZZ! POP!
PING!
POP!
DONE!

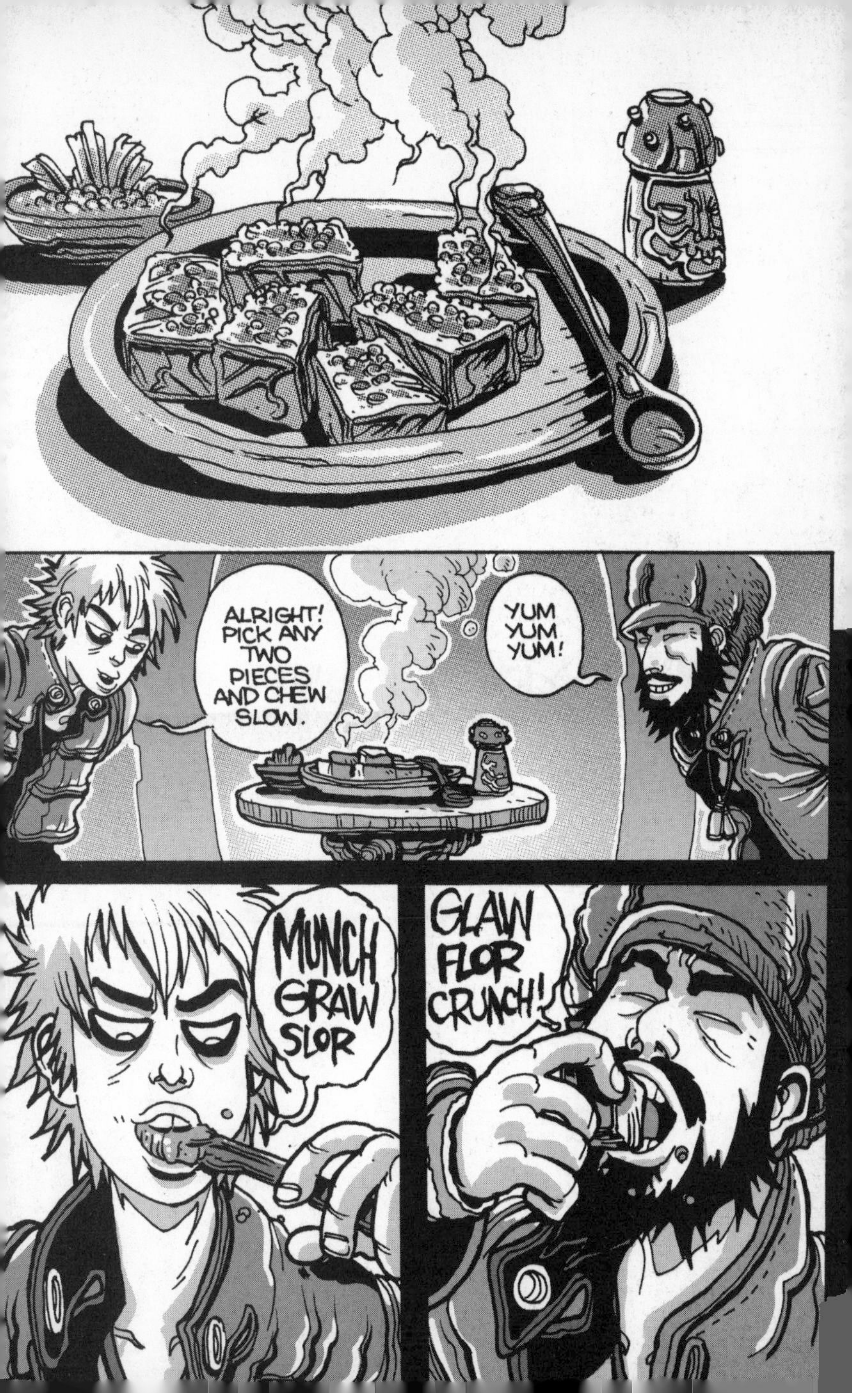
ALRIGHT! PICK ANY TWO PIECES AND CHEW SLOW.
YUM YUM YUM!
MUNCH GRAW SLOR
GLAW FLOR CRUNCH!

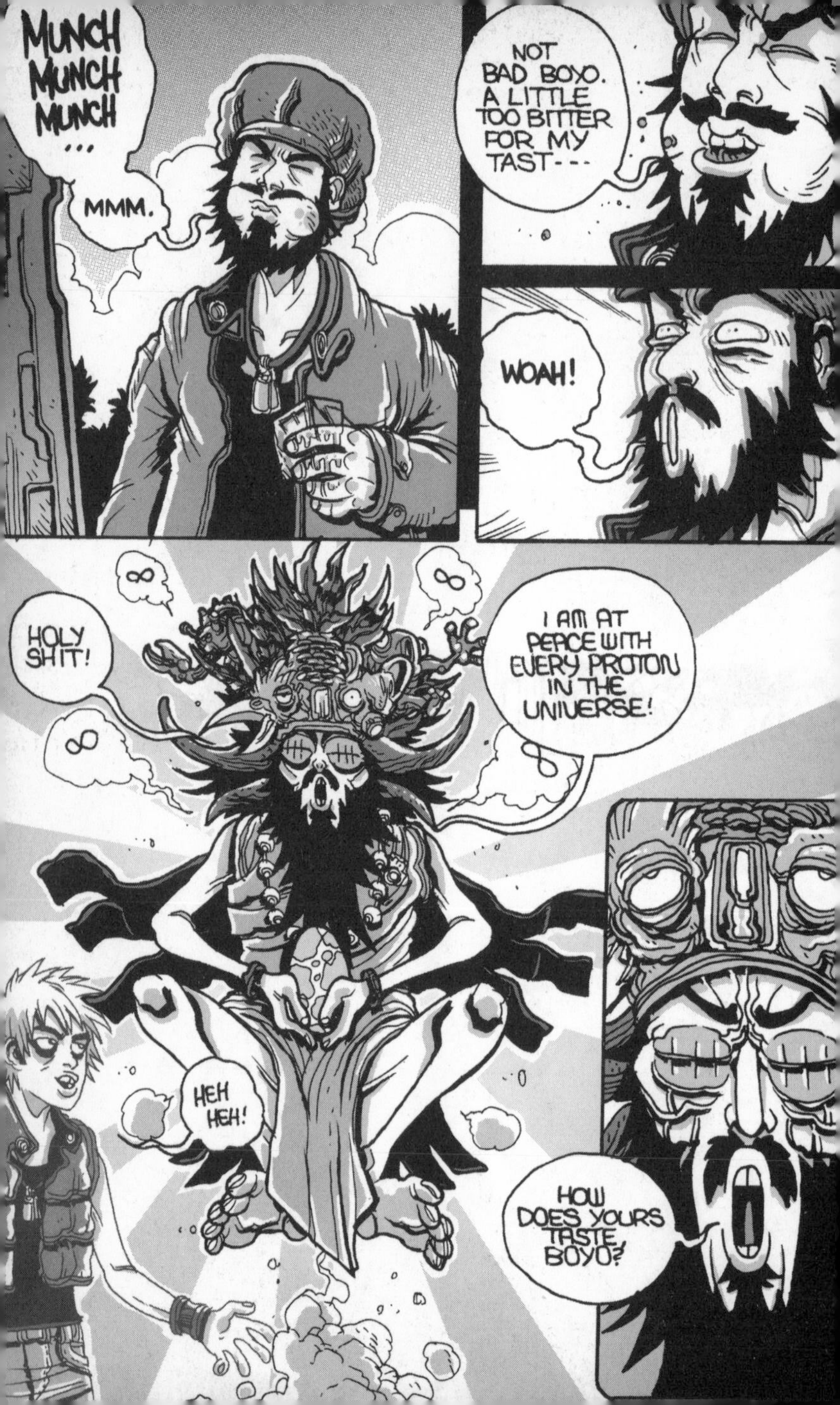
MUNCH MUNCH MUNCH ...
MMM.
NOT BAD BOYO. A LITTLE TOO BITTER FOR MY TAST---
WOAH!
HOLY SHIT!
∞
∞
∞
I AM AT PEACE WITH EVERY PROTON IN THE UNIVERSE!
∞
HEH HEH!
HOW DOES YOURS TASTE, BOYO?

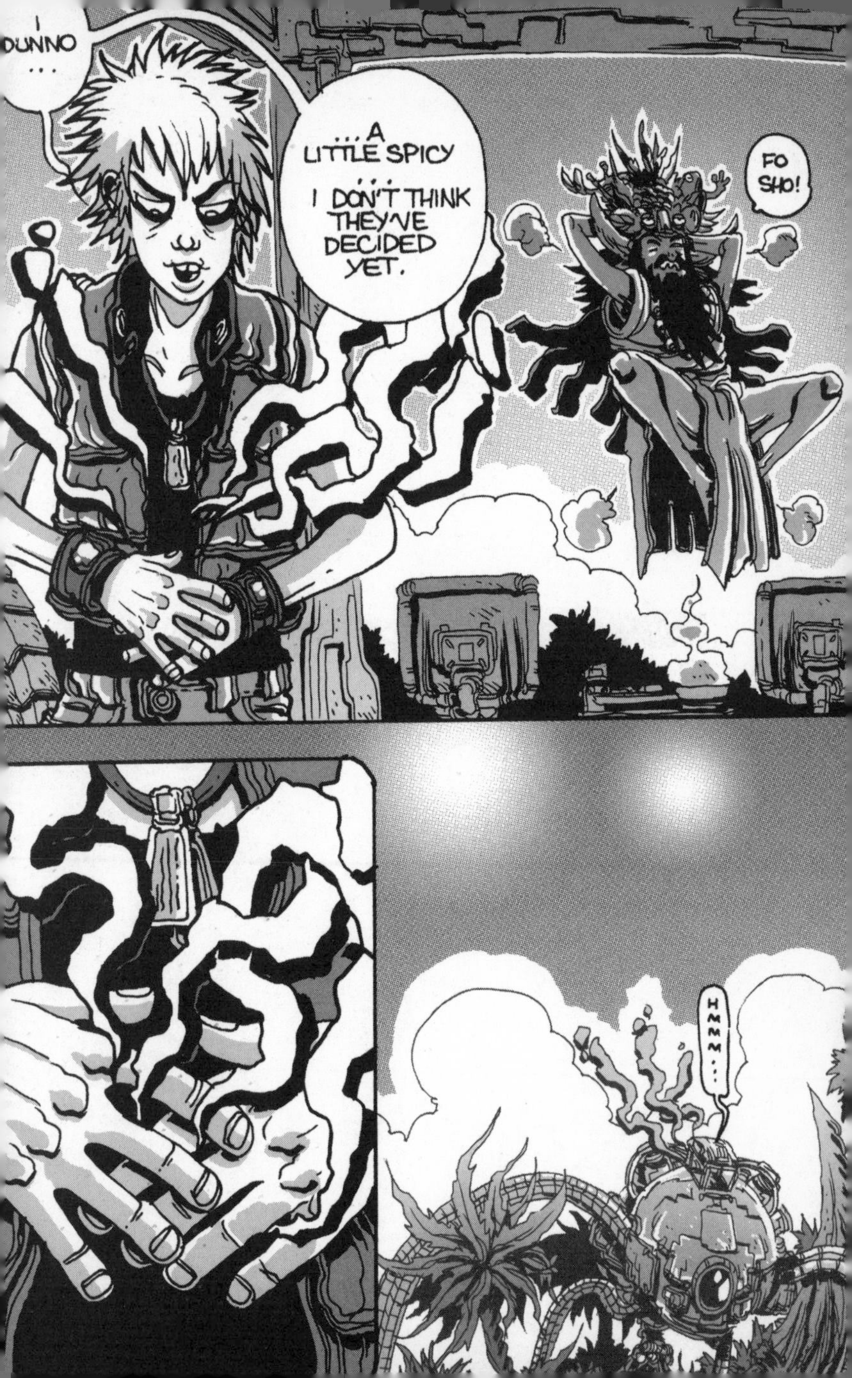
I DUNNO ...
... A LITTLE SPICY ... I DON'T THINK THEY'VE DECIDED YET.
FO SHO!
HMMM...

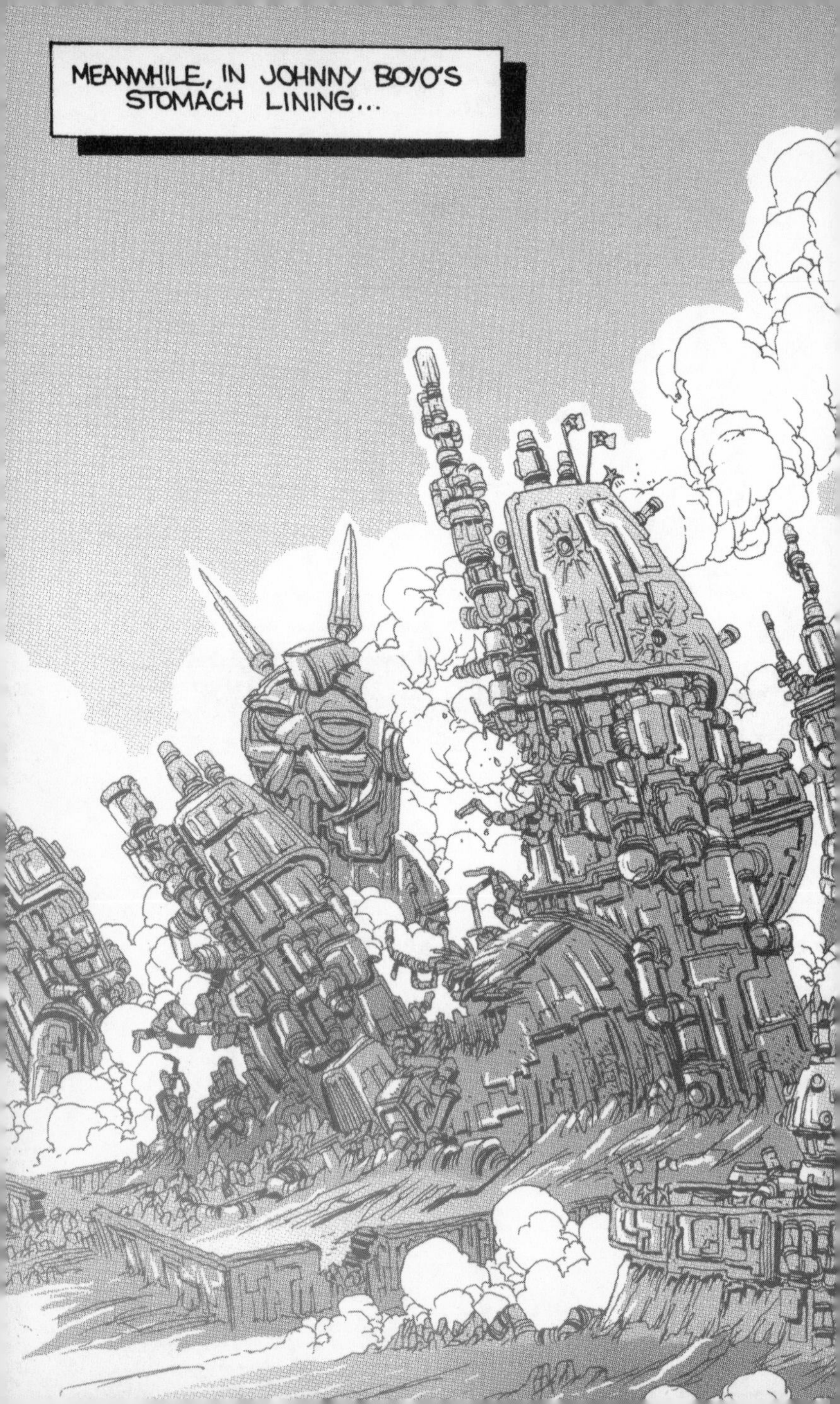
MEANWHILE, IN JOHNNY BOYO'S STOMACH LINING...

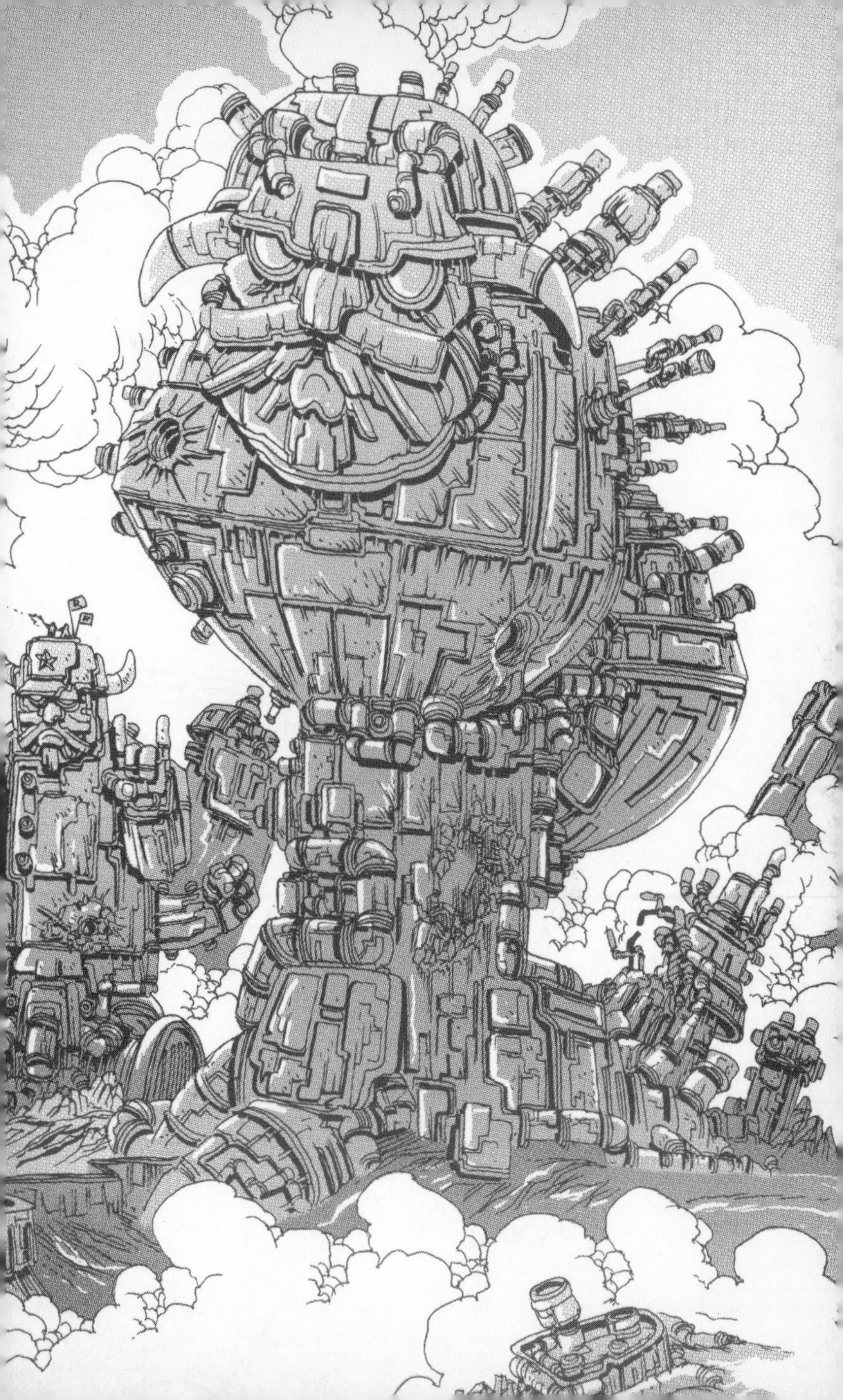

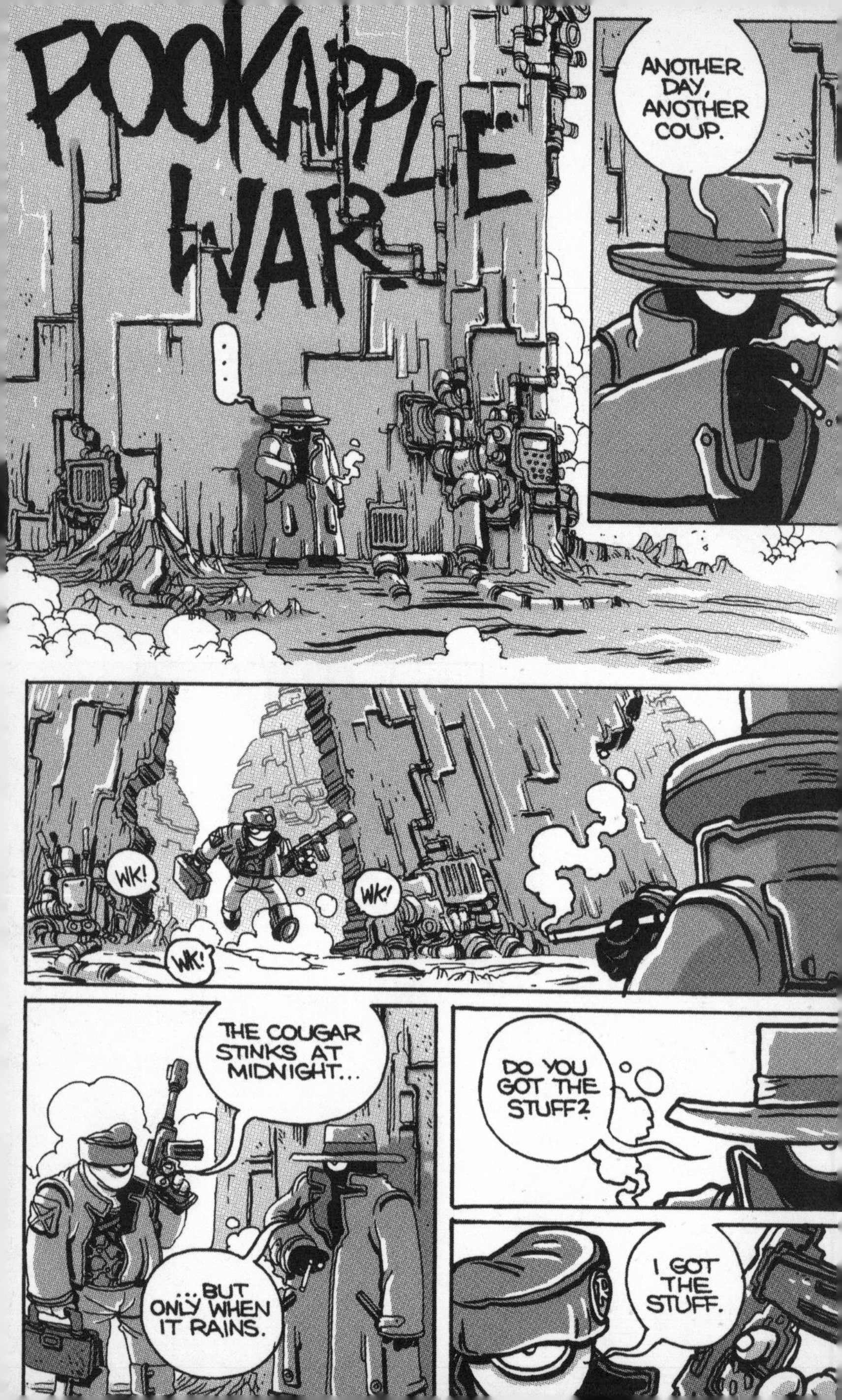
POOKAPPLE WAR-E
...
ANOTHER DAY, ANOTHER COUP.
WK!
WK!
WK!
THE COUGAR STINKS AT MIDNIGHT...
...BUT ONLY WHEN IT RAINS.
DO YOU GOT THE STUFF?
I GOT THE STUFF.

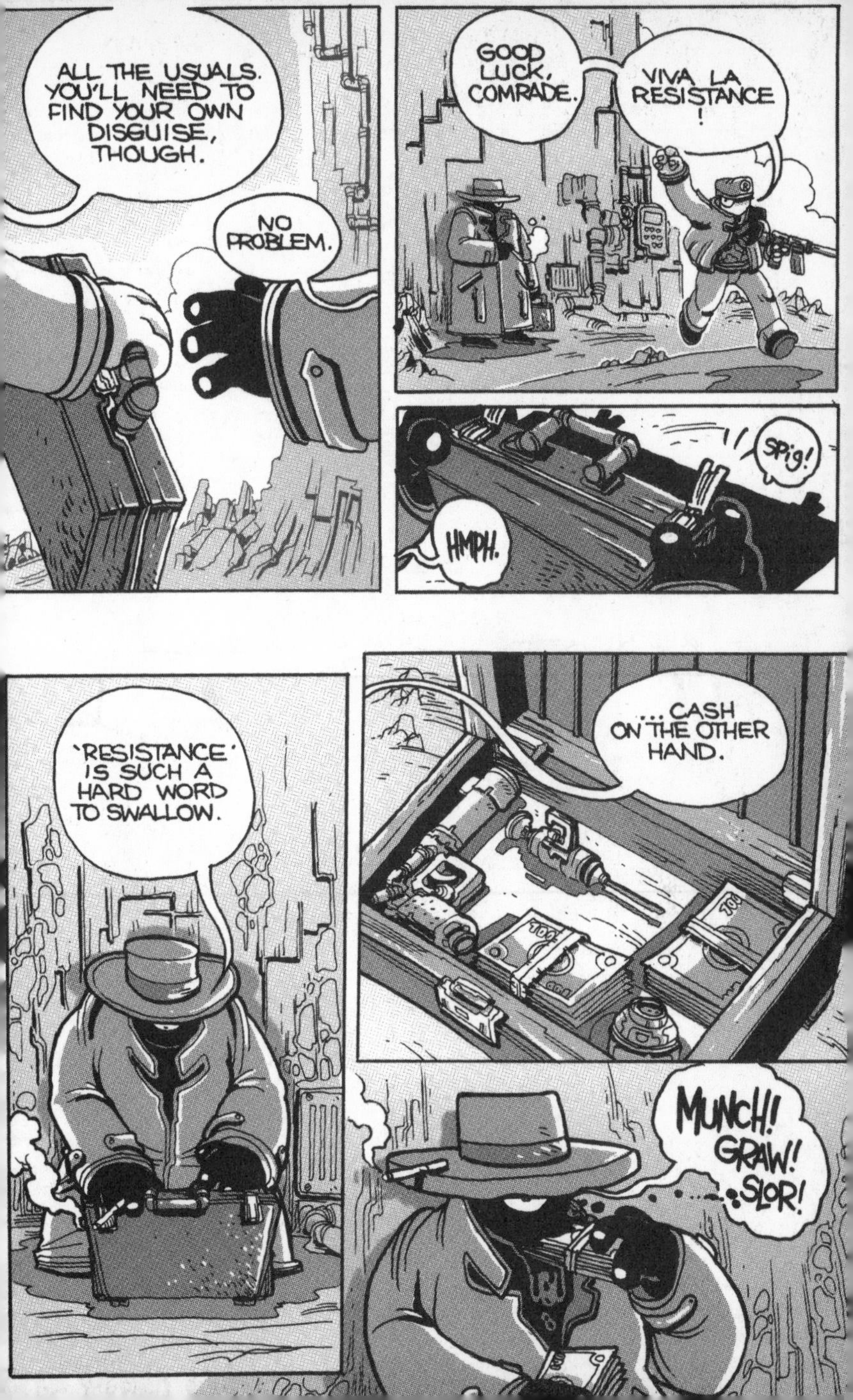
ALL THE USUALS. YOU'LL NEED TO FIND YOUR OWN DISGUISE, THOUGH.
NO PROBLEM.
GOOD LUCK, COMRADE.
VIVA LA RESISTANCE !
SPig!
HMPH.
'RESISTANCE' IS SUCH A HARD WORD TO SWALLOW.
...CASH ON THE OTHER HAND.
MUNCH! GRAW! ..SLOR!

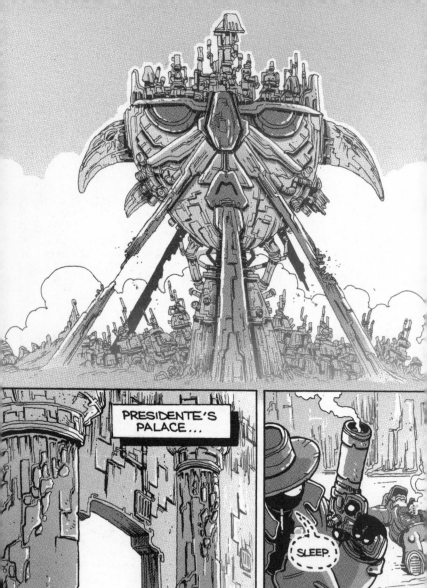

PRESIDENTE'S PALACE...

SLEEP.

SLEEP.

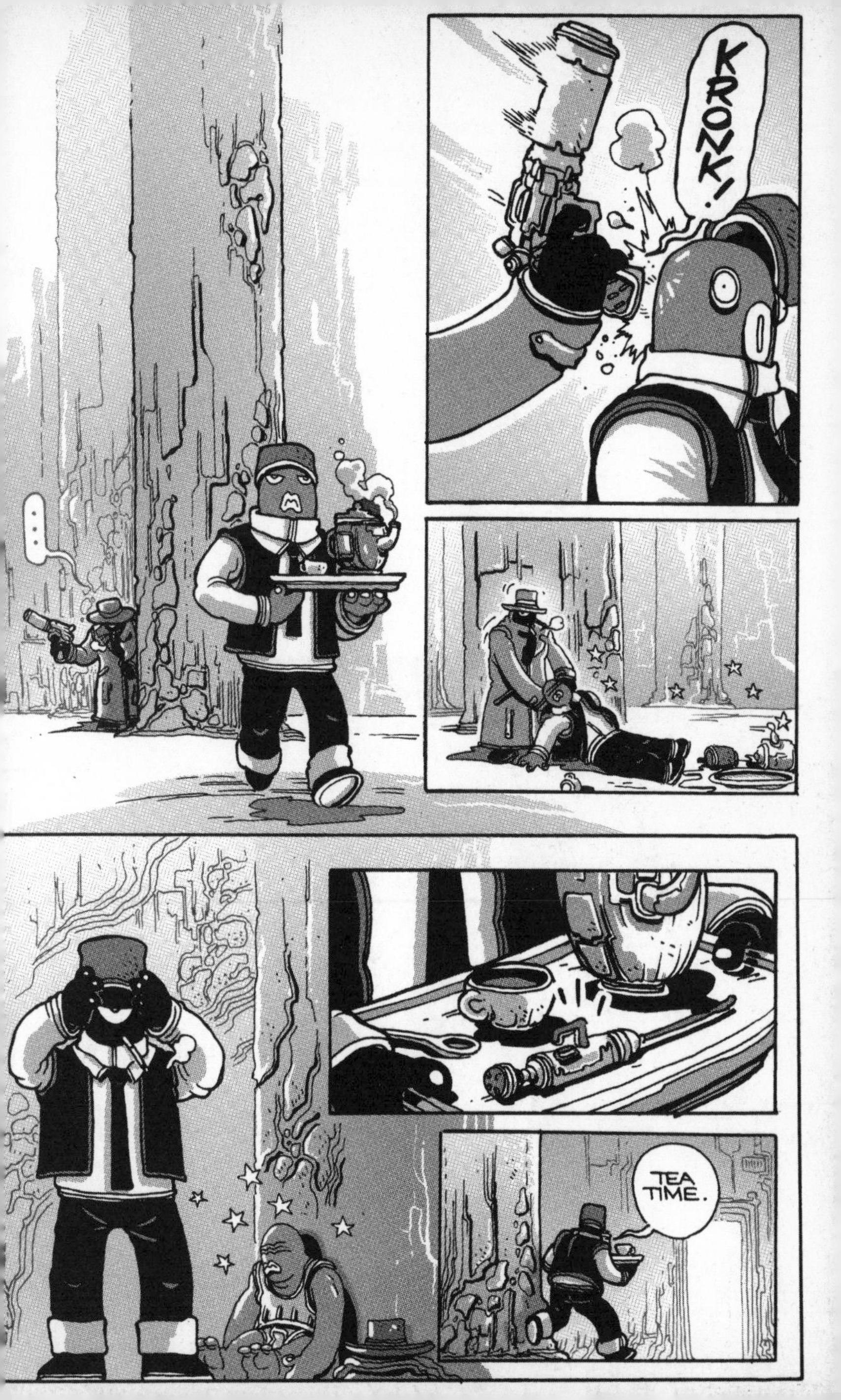
...
KRONK!
TEA TIME.

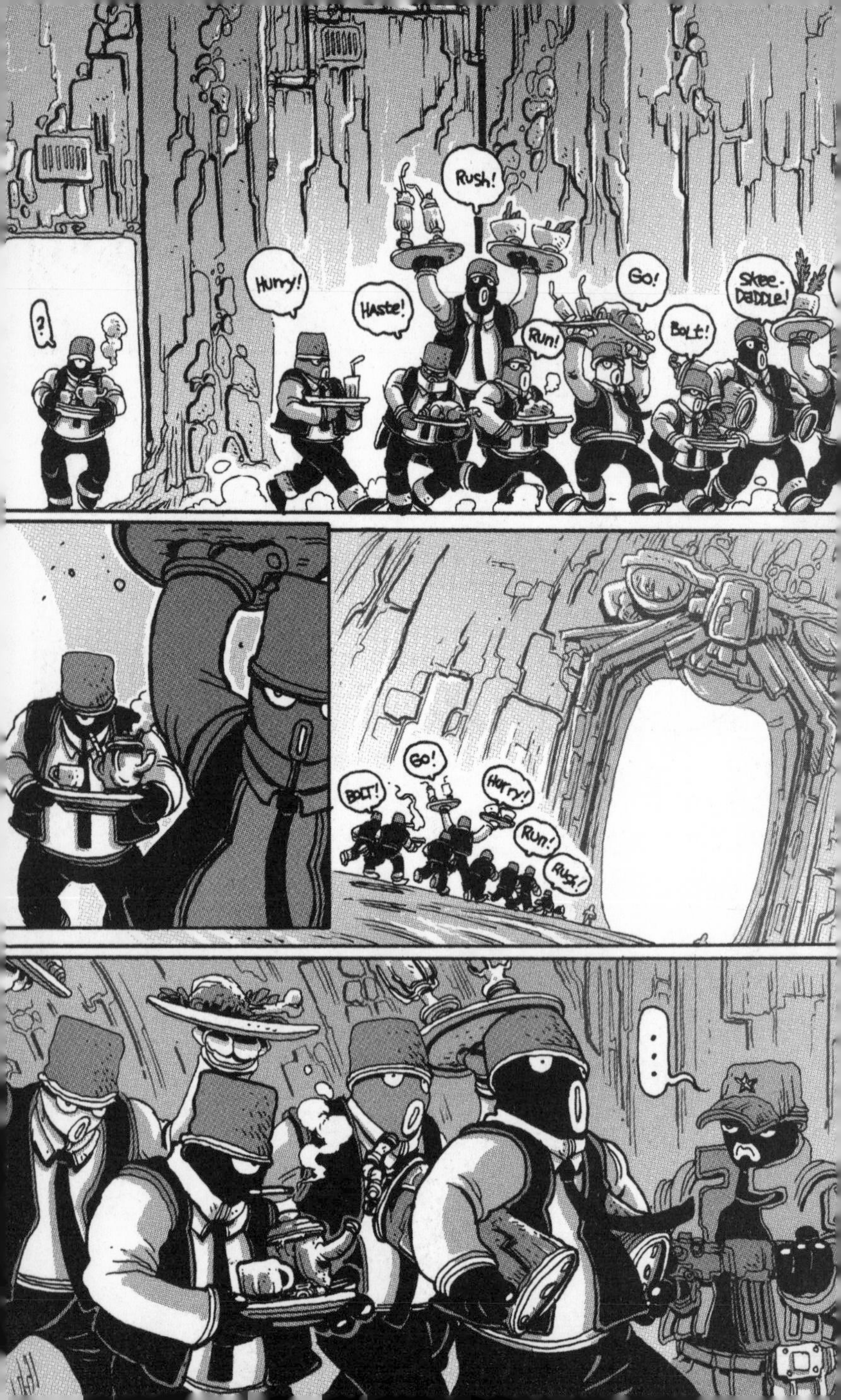
?
Hurry!
Haste!
Rush!
Run!
Go!
Bolt!
Skee-Daddle!
Bolt!
Go!
Hurry!
Run!
Rush!
...

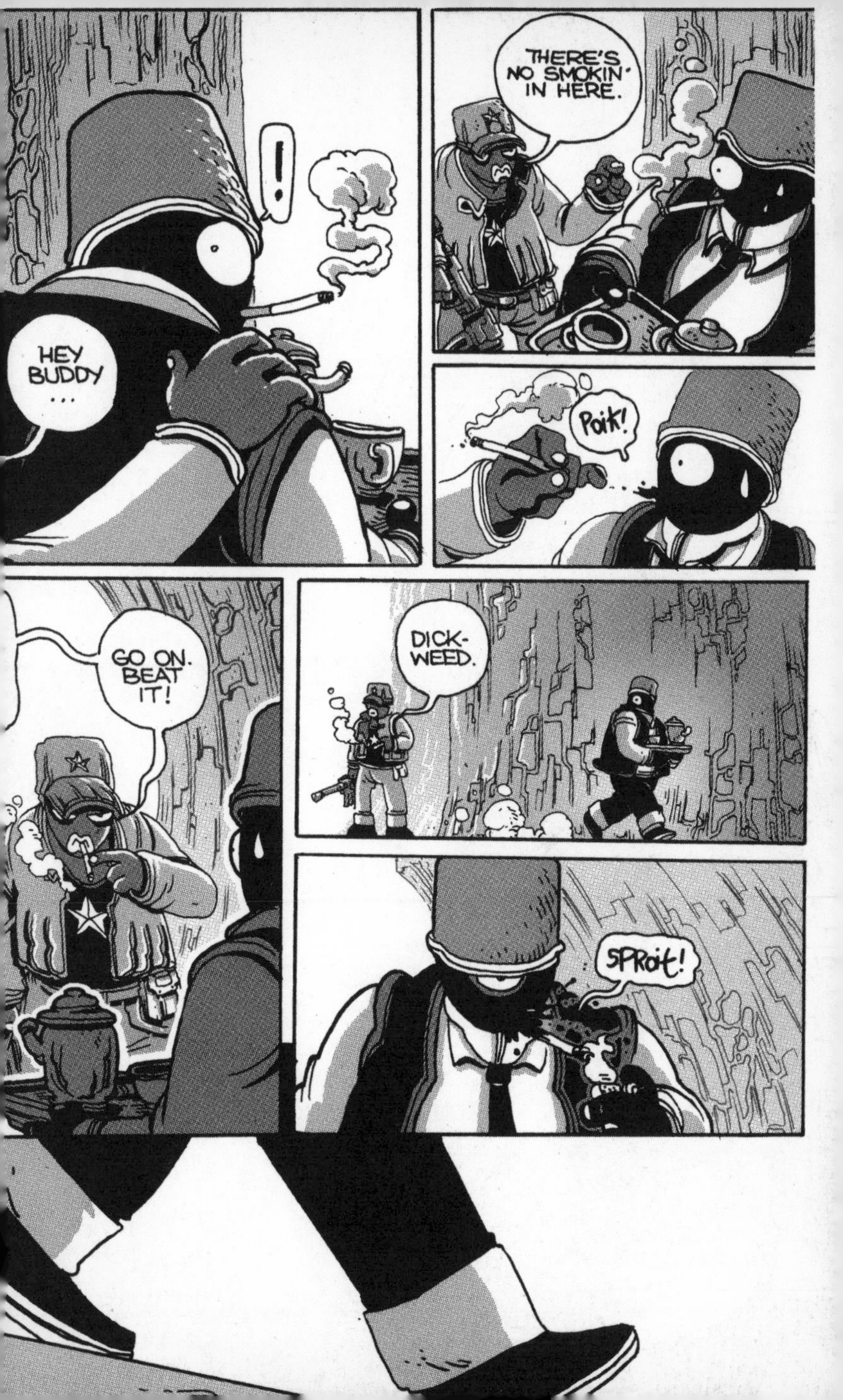
!
HEY BUDDY ...
THERE'S NO SMOKIN' IN HERE.
POIK!
GO ON. BEAT IT!
DICK-WEED.
SPROIT!

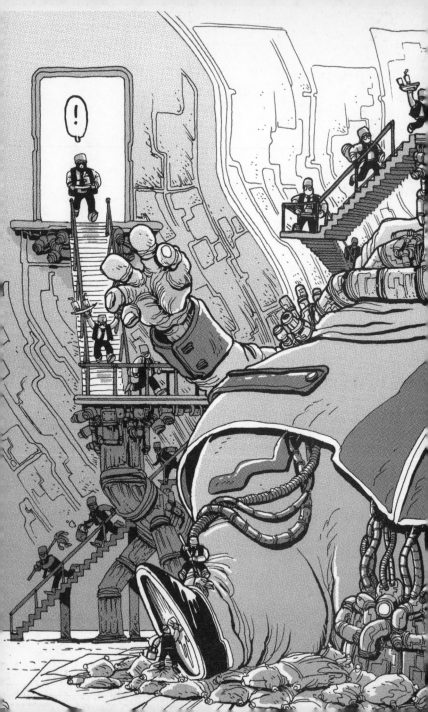

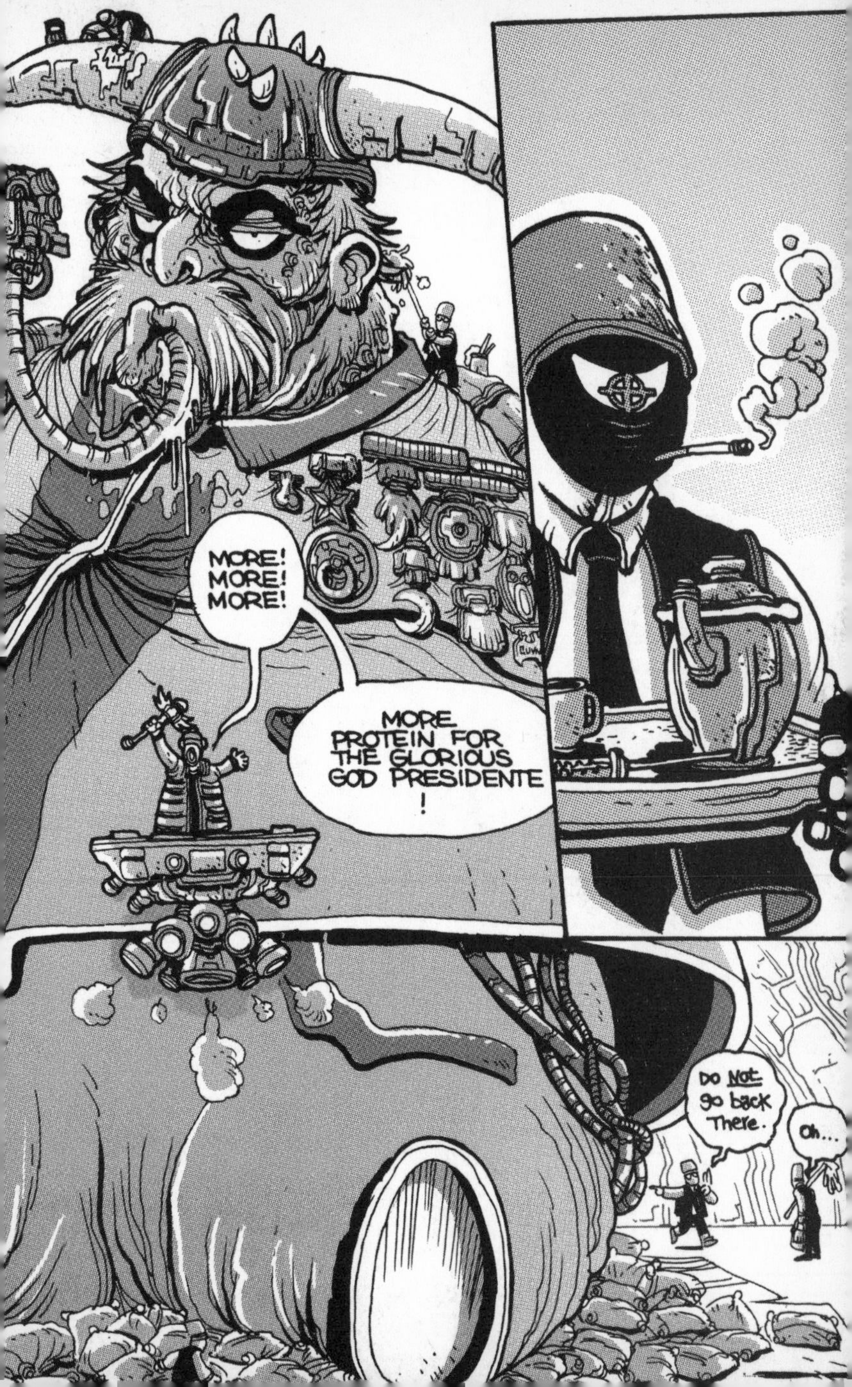
MORE! MORE! MORE!
MORE PROTEIN FOR THE GLORIOUS GOD PRESIDENTE !
Do Not go back There.
Oh...

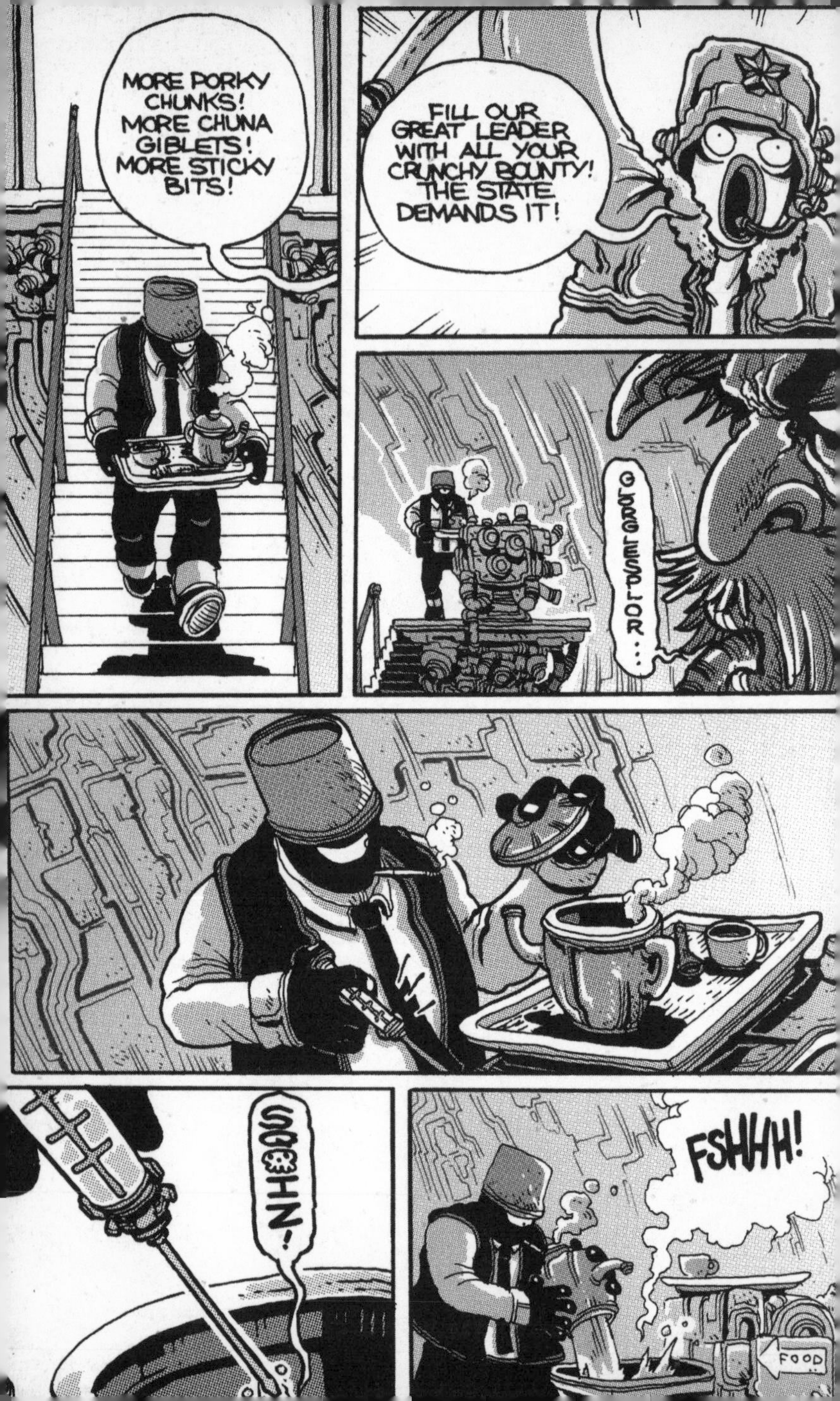
MORE PORKY CHUNKS! MORE CHUNA GIBLETS! MORE STICKY BITS!
FILL OUR GREAT LEADER WITH ALL YOUR CRUNCHY BOUNTY! THE STATE DEMANDS IT!
GLOGGLESPLOR...
SQ☠HZ!
FSHHH!
FOOD

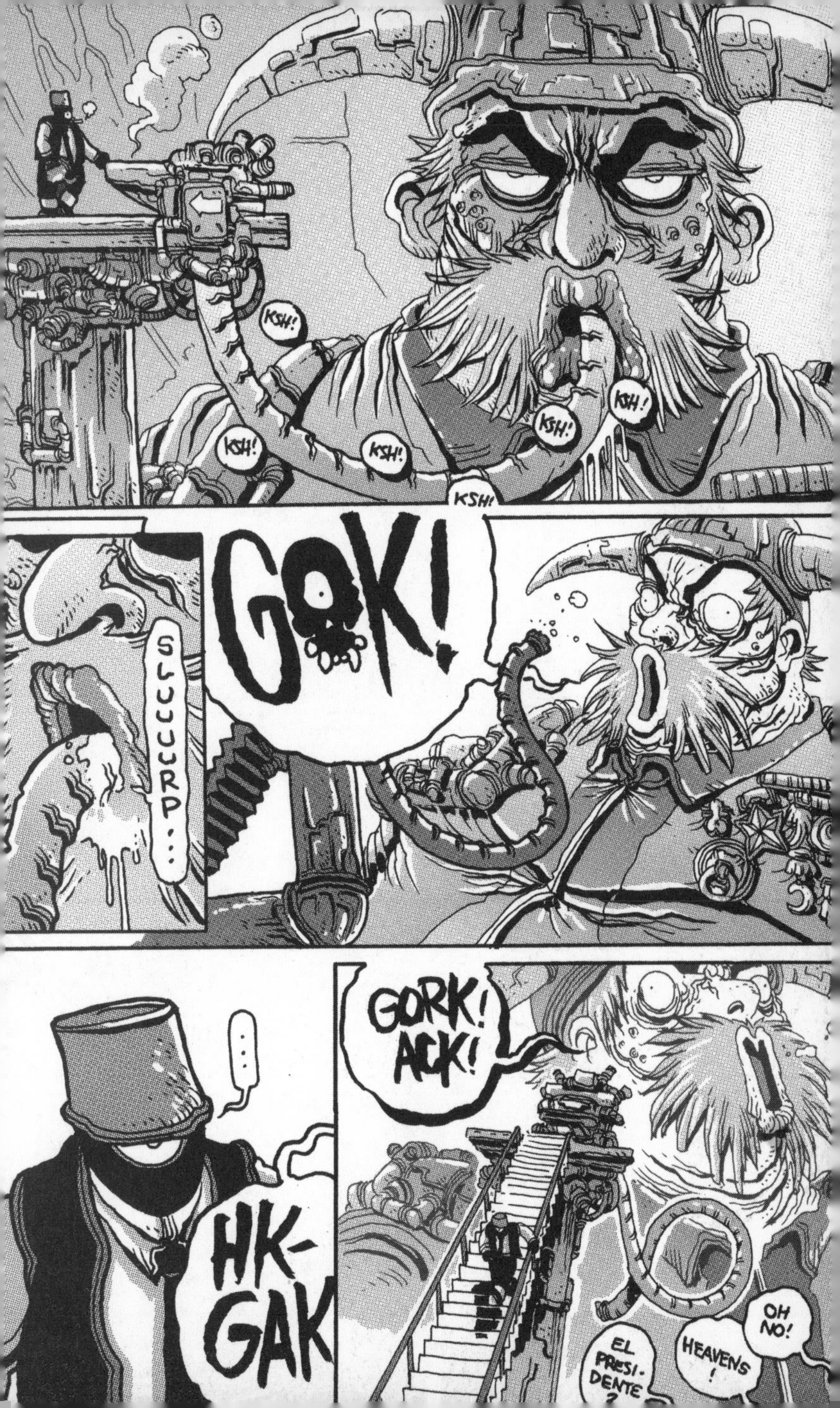
KSH!
KSH!
KSH!
KSH!
KSH!
KSH!
KSH!
SLUUUURP...
GOK!
...
HK-GAK
GORK! ACK!
EL PRESIDENTE?
HEAVENS!
OH NO!

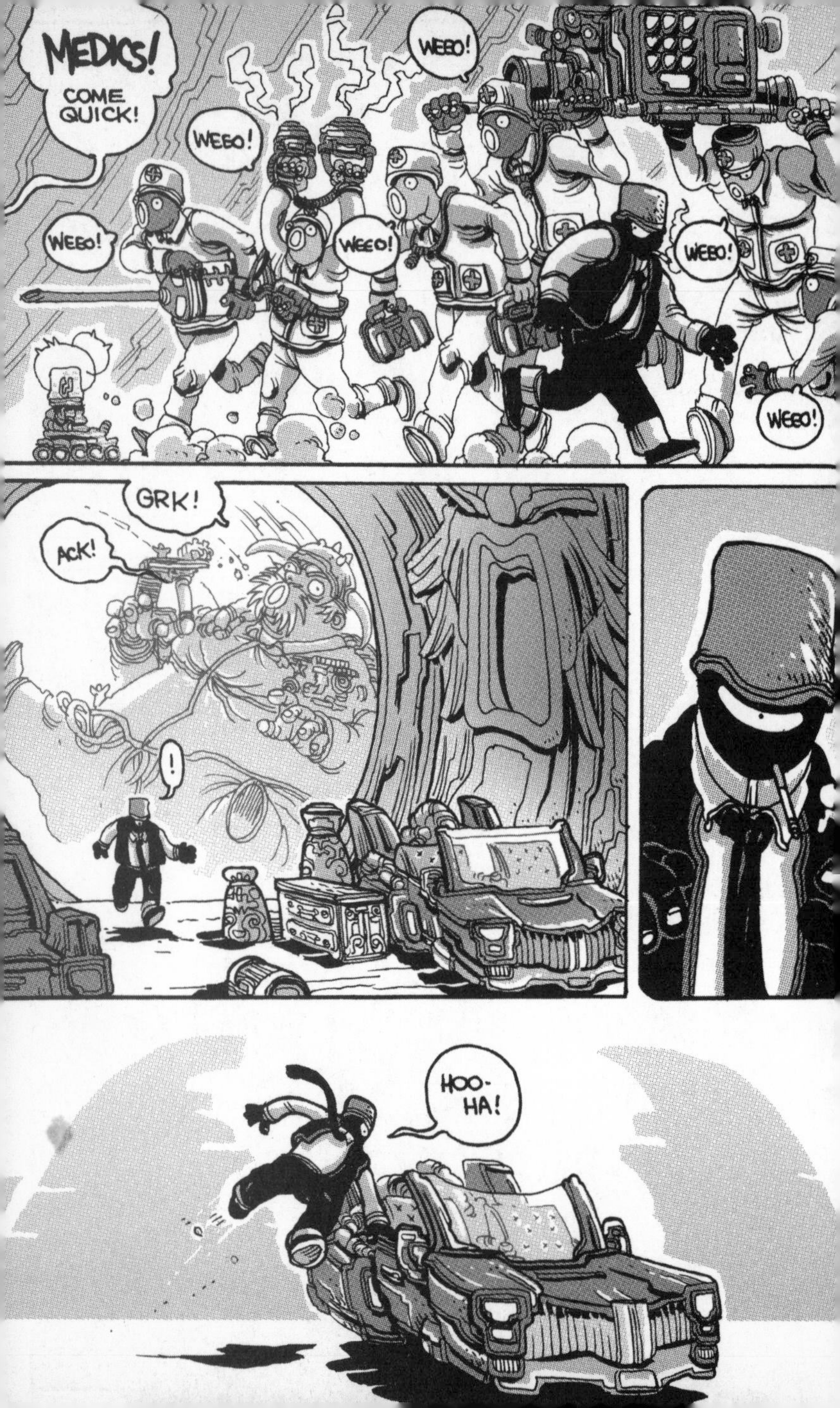

MEDICS! COME QUICK!
WEEO!
WEEO!
WEEO!
WEEO!
WEEO!
WEEO!
GRK!
ACK!
!
HOO-HA!

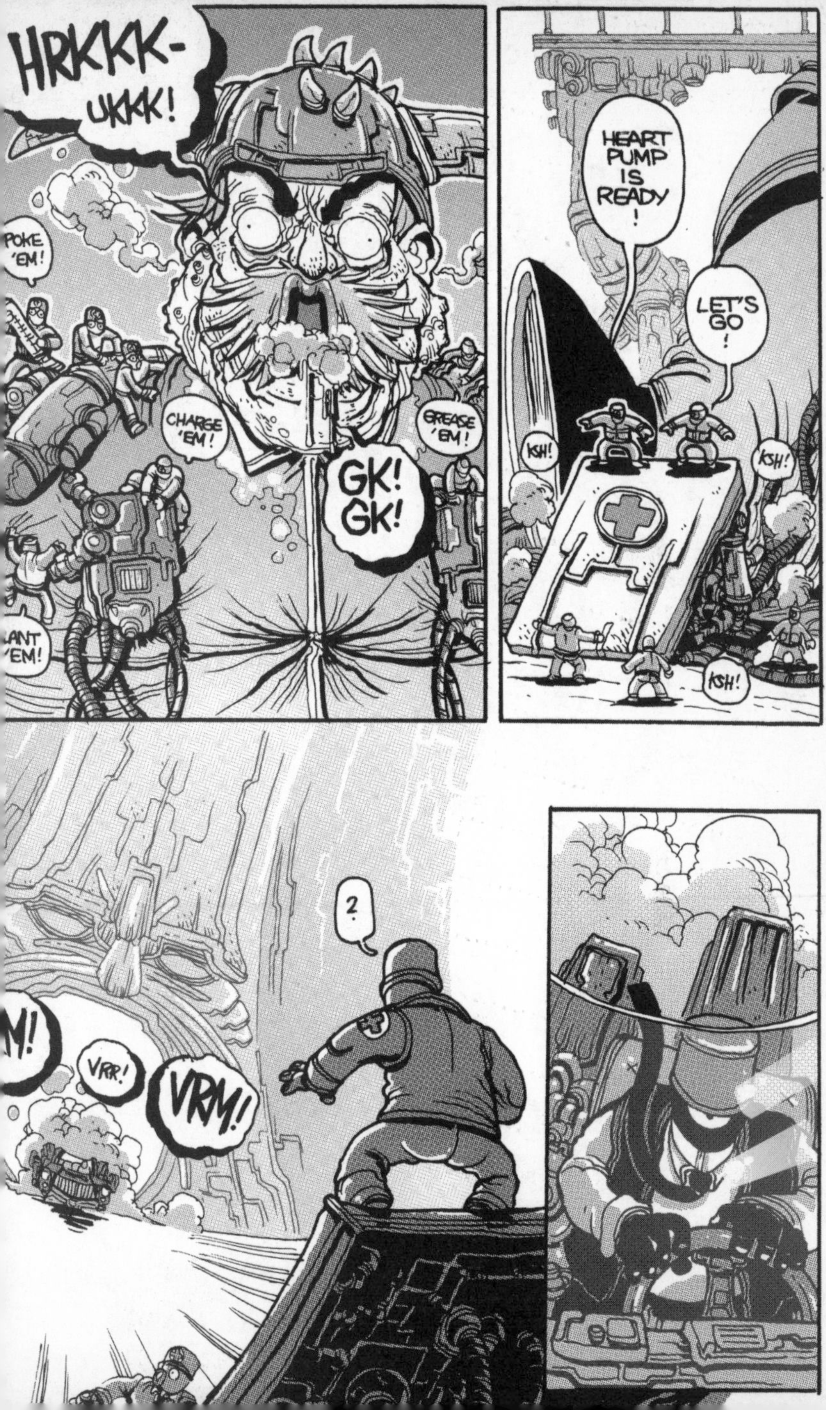
HRKKK-UKKK!
POKE 'EM!
CHARGE 'EM!
GREASE 'EM!
GK! GK!
LANT 'EM!
HEART PUMP IS READY!
LET'S GO!
KSH!
KSH!
KSH!
?
M!
VRR!
VRM!

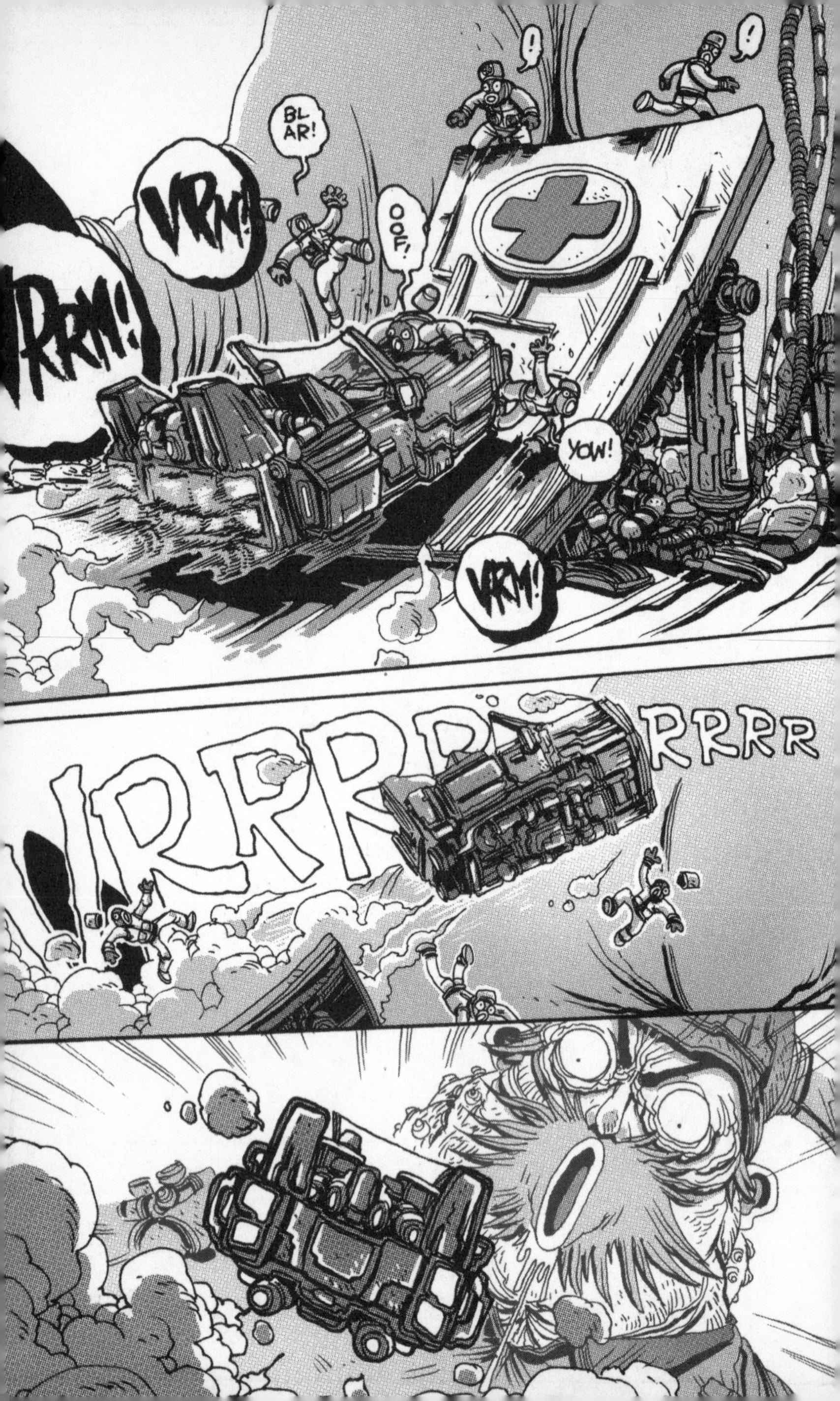

!
!
BL AR!
VRM!
RRM!
OOF!
YOW!
VRM!
RRRR

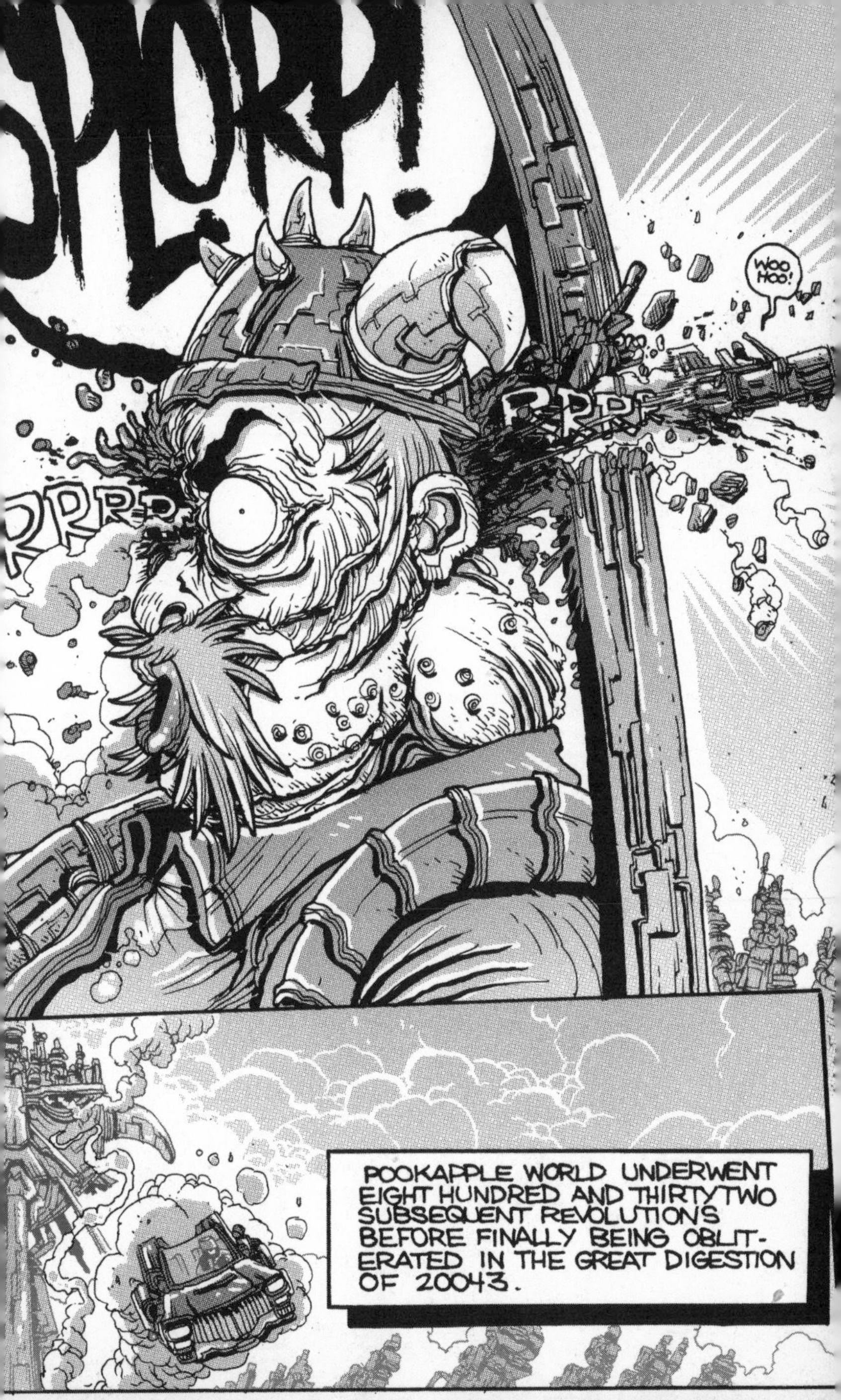
SPLORP!
WOO HOO!
RRRR
RRRR
POOKAPPLE WORLD UNDERWENT EIGHT HUNDRED AND THIRTYTWO SUBSEQUENT REVOLUTIONS BEFORE FINALLY BEING OBLIT-ERATED IN THE GREAT DIGESTION OF 20043.

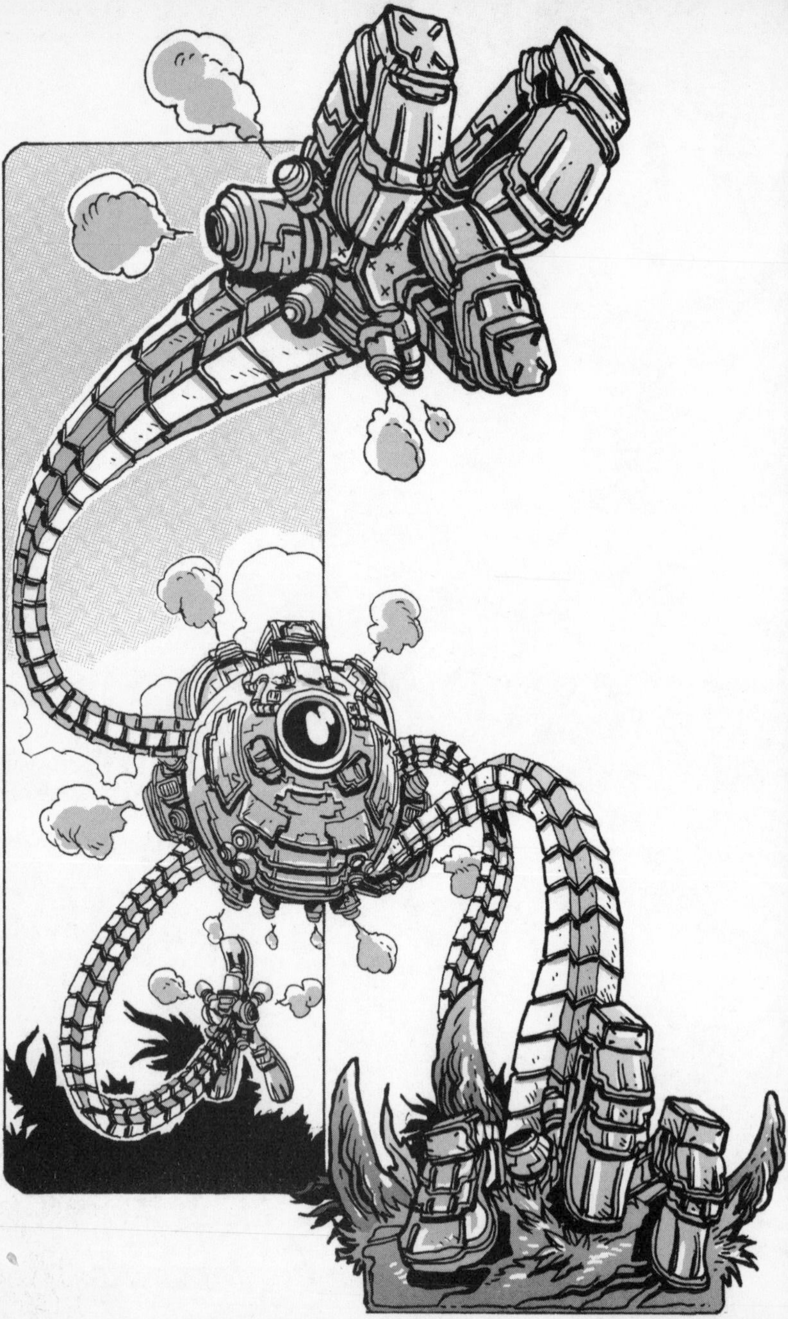

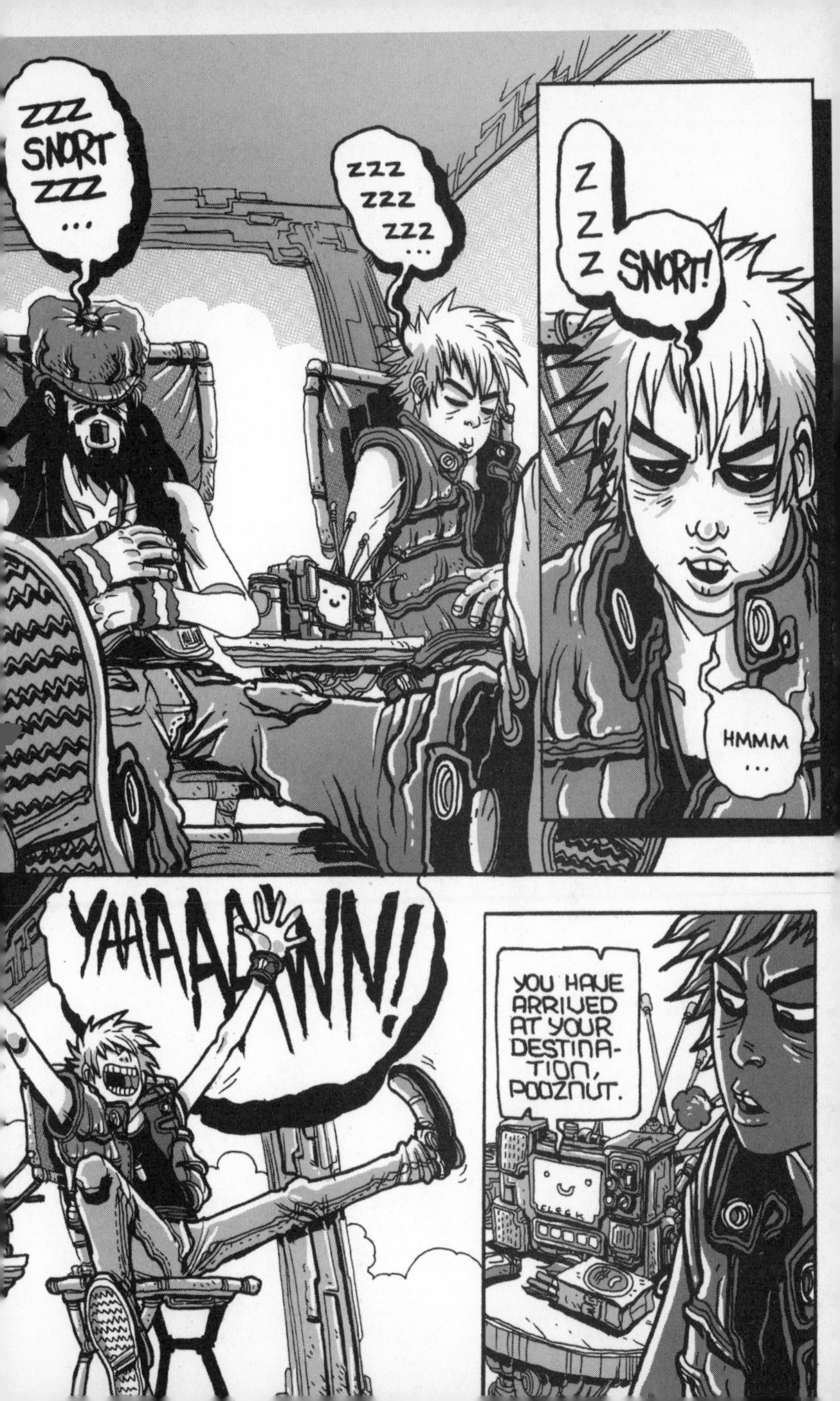
ZZZ SNORT ZZZ ...
ZZZ ZZZ ZZZ ...
Z Z Z SNORT!
HMMM ...
YAAAAAWN!
YOU HAVE ARRIVED AT YOUR DESTINATION, POOZNUT.

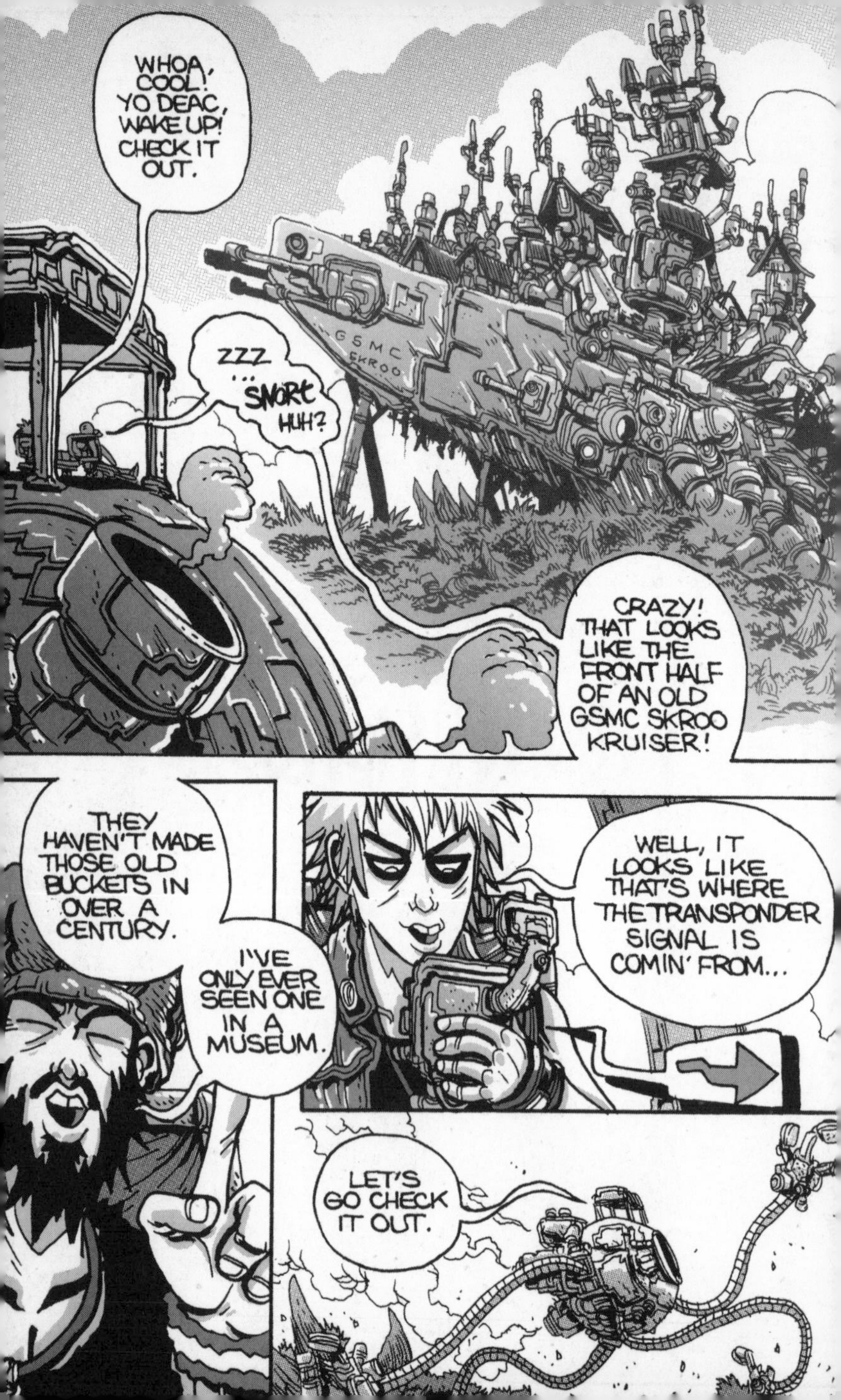
WHOA, COOL! YO DEAC, WAKE UP! CHECK IT OUT.
ZZZ ... SNORT HUH?
GSMC SKROO
CRAZY! THAT LOOKS LIKE THE FRONT HALF OF AN OLD GSMC SKROO KRUISER!
THEY HAVEN'T MADE THOSE OLD BUCKETS IN OVER A CENTURY.
I'VE ONLY EVER SEEN ONE IN A MUSEUM.
WELL, IT LOOKS LIKE THAT'S WHERE THE TRANSPONDER SIGNAL IS COMIN' FROM...
LET'S GO CHECK IT OUT.

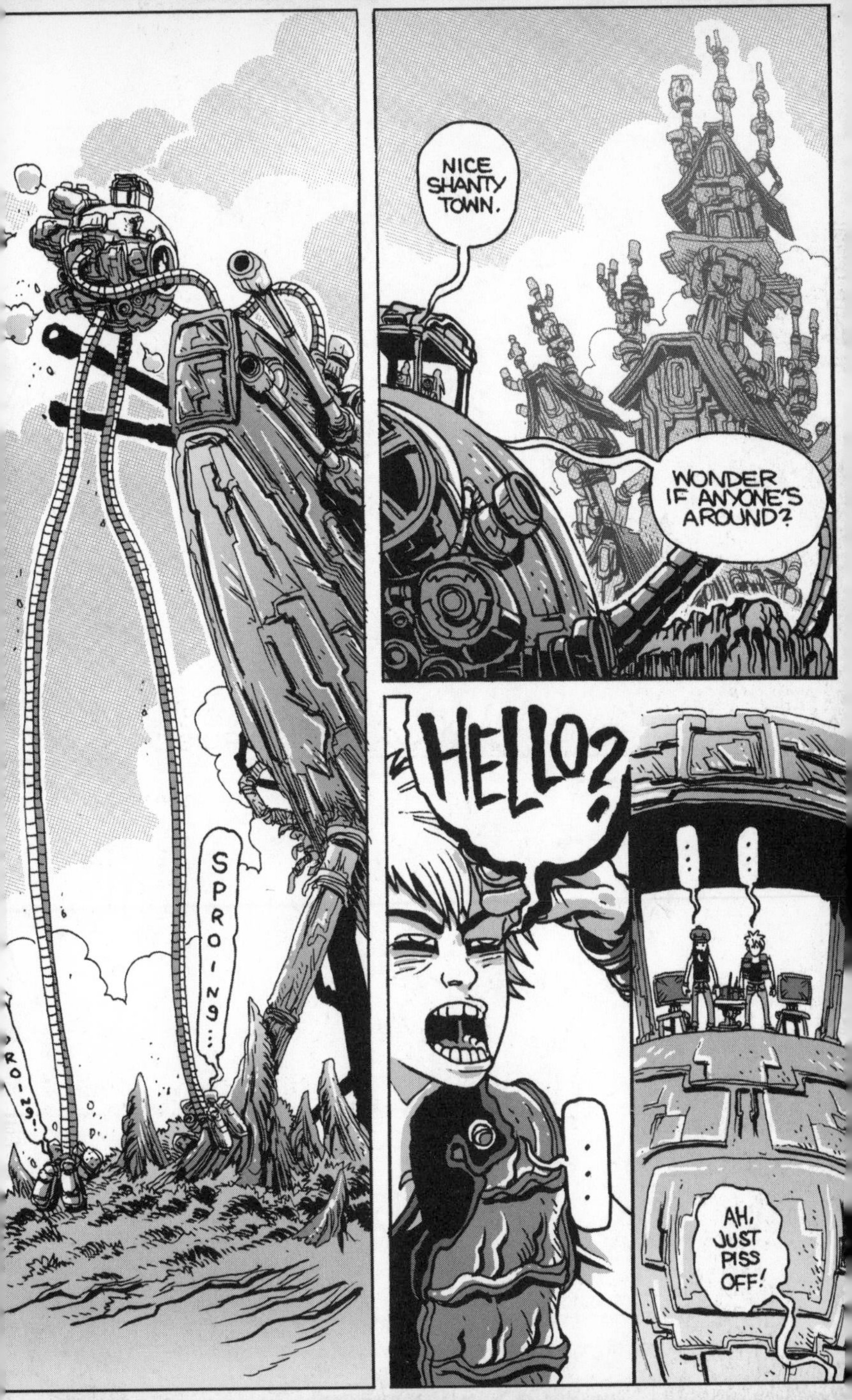
SPROING...
SPROING!
NICE SHANTY TOWN.
WONDER IF ANYONE'S AROUND?
HELLO?
...
...
...
AH, JUST PISS OFF!

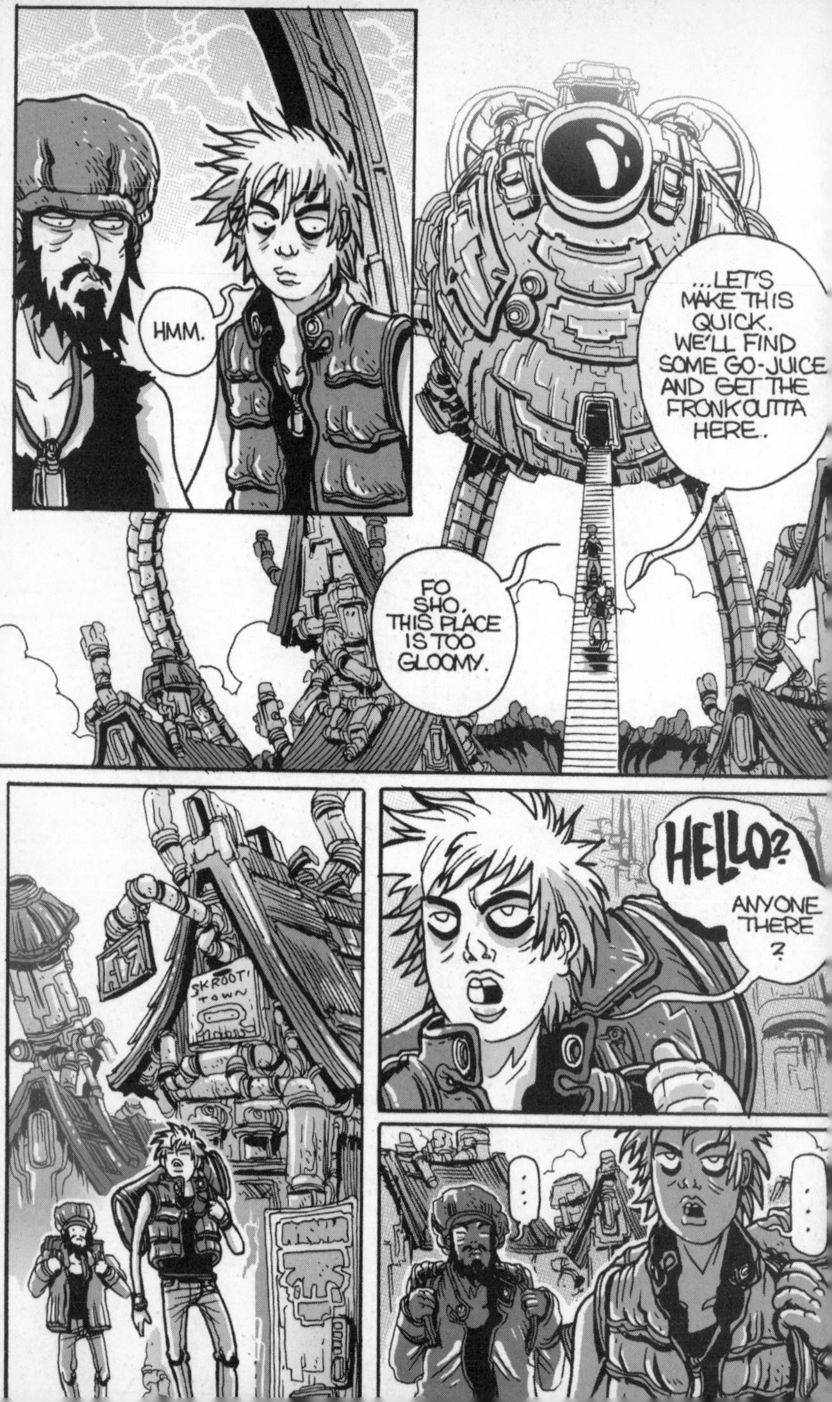
HMM.
...LET'S MAKE THIS QUICK. WE'LL FIND SOME GO-JUICE AND GET THE FRONK OUTTA HERE.
FO SHO. THIS PLACE IS TOO GLOOMY.
SKROOT TOWN
HELLO?
ANYONE THERE?
...
...

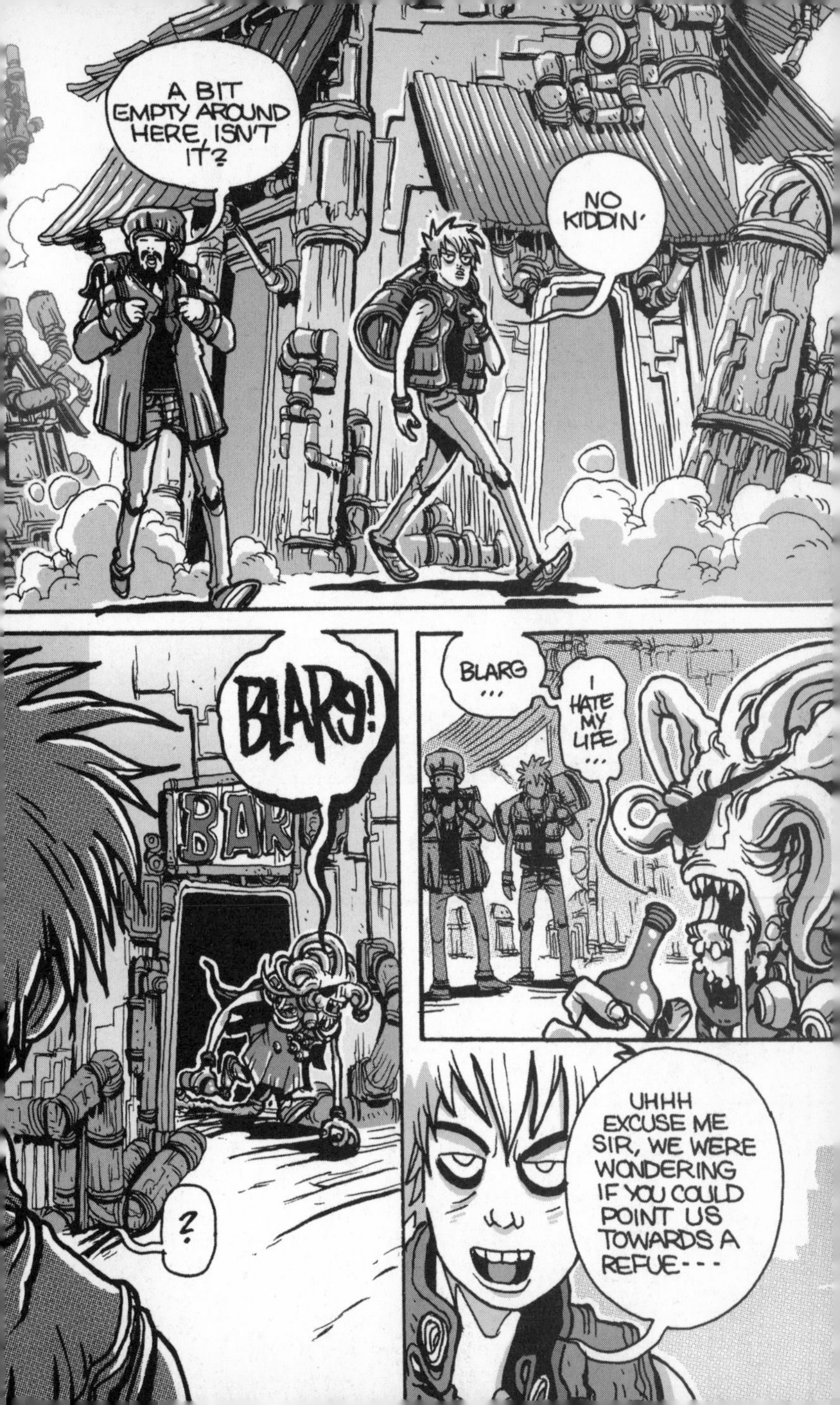
A BIT EMPTY AROUND HERE, ISN'T IT?
NO KIDDIN'
BLARG!
BAR
BLARG ...
I HATE MY LIFE ...
?
UHHH EXCUSE ME SIR, WE WERE WONDERING IF YOU COULD POINT US TOWARDS A REFUE---

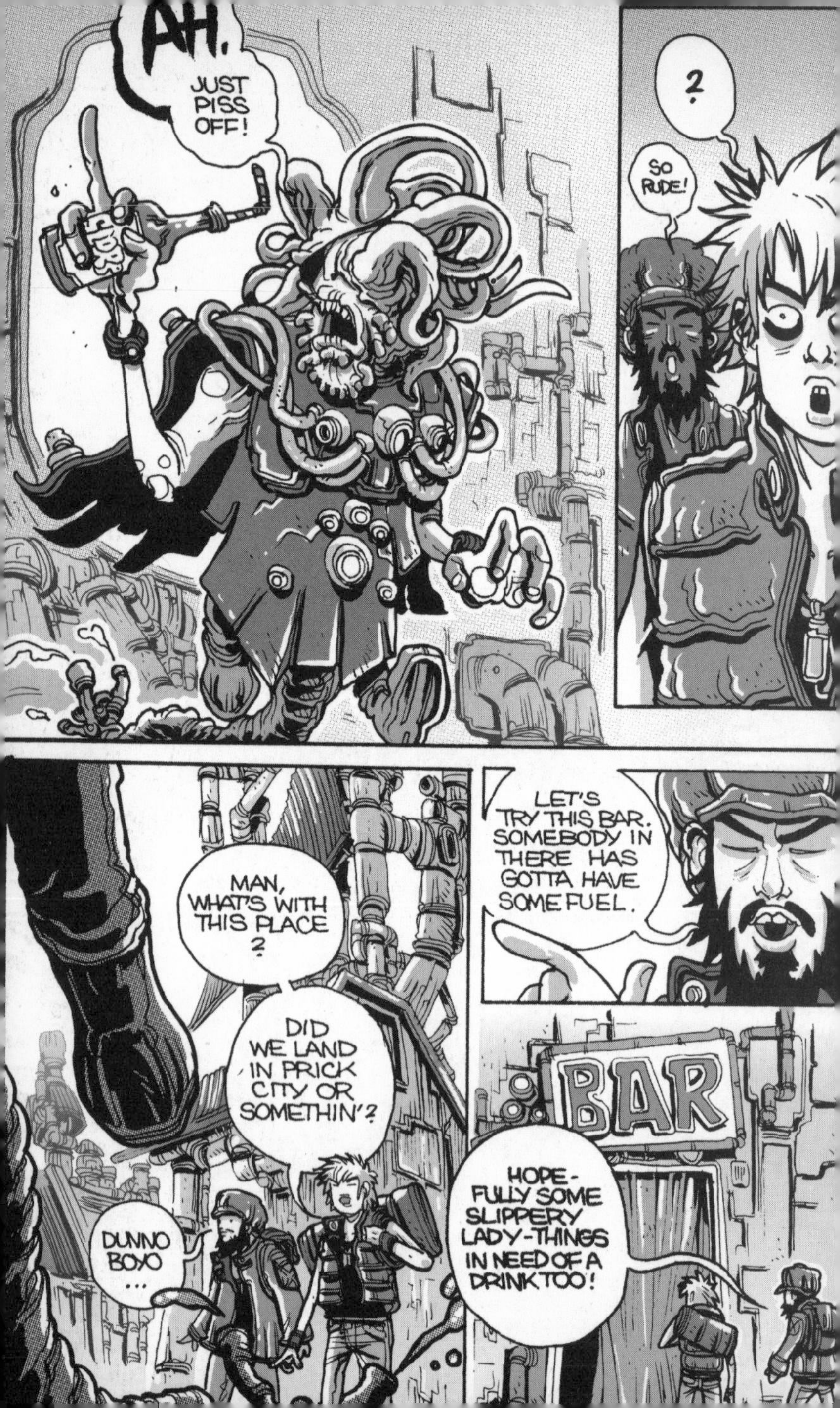
AH.
JUST PISS OFF!
?
SO RUDE!
MAN, WHAT'S WITH THIS PLACE ?
DID WE LAND IN PRICK CITY OR SOMETHIN'?
DUNNO BOYO ...
LET'S TRY THIS BAR. SOMEBODY IN THERE HAS GOTTA HAVE SOME FUEL.
BAR
HOPE-FULLY SOME SLIPPERY LADY-THINGS IN NEED OF A DRINK TOO!

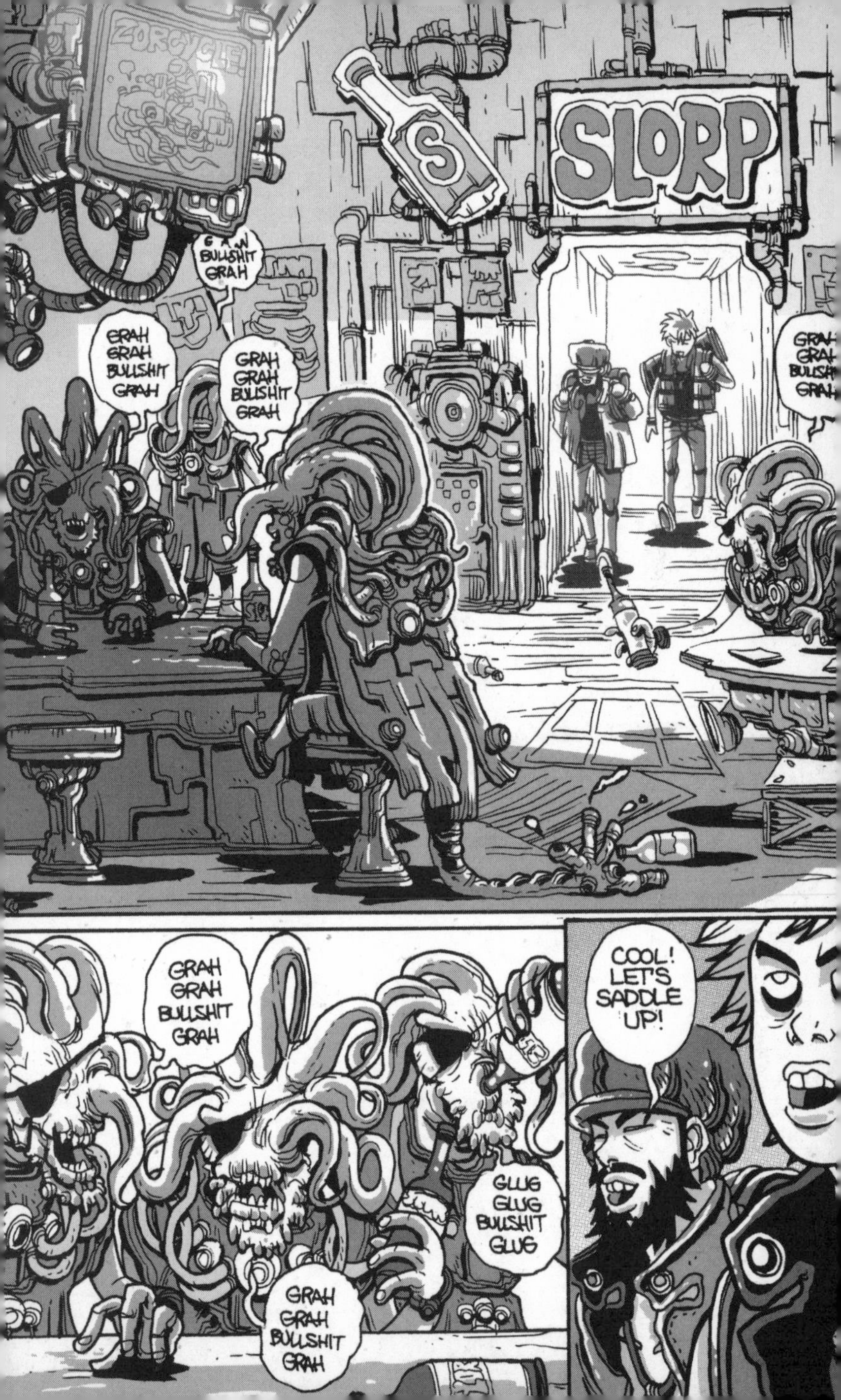
ZORCYCLE!
SLORP
BULLSHIT
GRAH
GRAH
GRAH
BULLSHIT
GRAH
GRAH
GRAH
BULLSHIT
GRAH
GRAH
GRAH
BULLSHIT
GRAH
COOL! LET'S SADDLE UP!
GLUG
GLUG
BULLSHIT
GLUG
GRAH
GRAH
BULLSHIT
GRAH

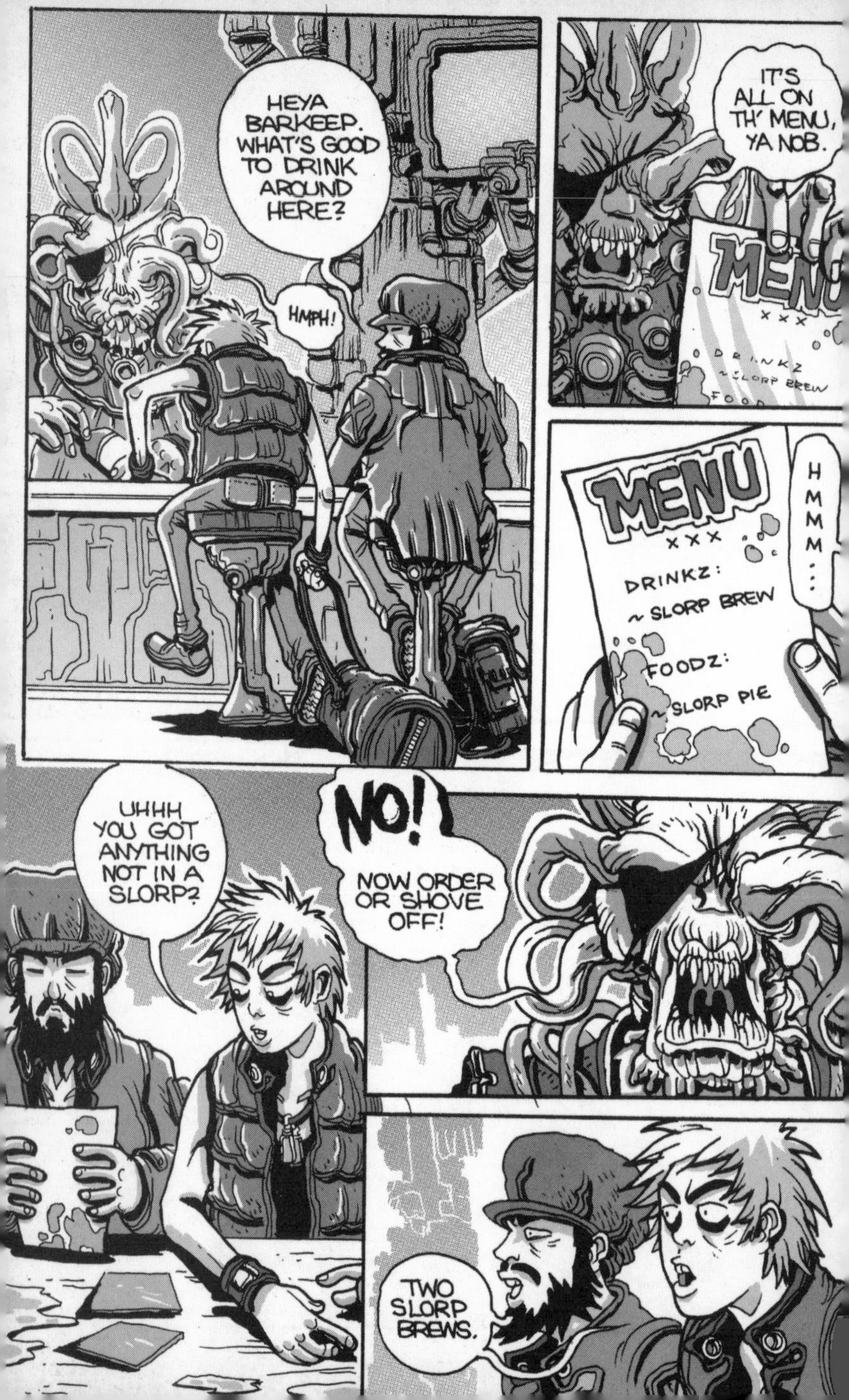
HEYA BARKEEP. WHAT'S GOOD TO DRINK AROUND HERE?
HMPH!
IT'S ALL ON TH' MENU, YA NOB.
MENU
XXX
DRINKZ:
~ SLORP BREW
FOODZ:
~ SLORP PIE
HMMM...
UHHH YOU GOT ANYTHING NOT IN A SLORP?
NO!
NOW ORDER OR SHOVE OFF!
TWO SLORP BREWS.

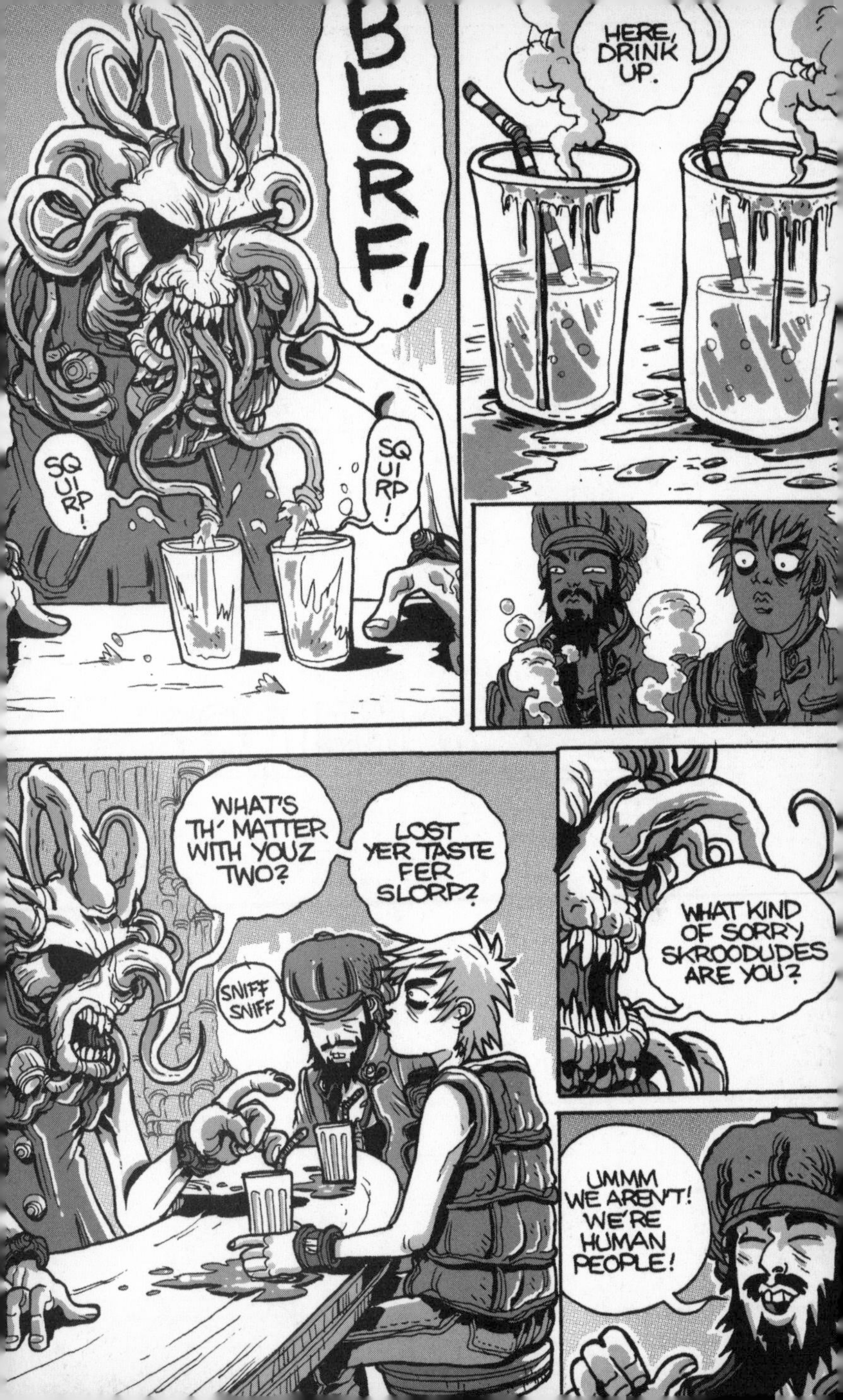
BLORF!
SQ UI RP!
SQ UI RP!
HERE, DRINK UP.
WHAT'S TH' MATTER WITH YOUZ TWO?
LOST YER TASTE FER SLORP?
SNIFF SNIFF
WHAT KIND OF SORRY SKROODUDES ARE YOU?
UMMM WE AREN'T! WE'RE HUMAN PEOPLE!

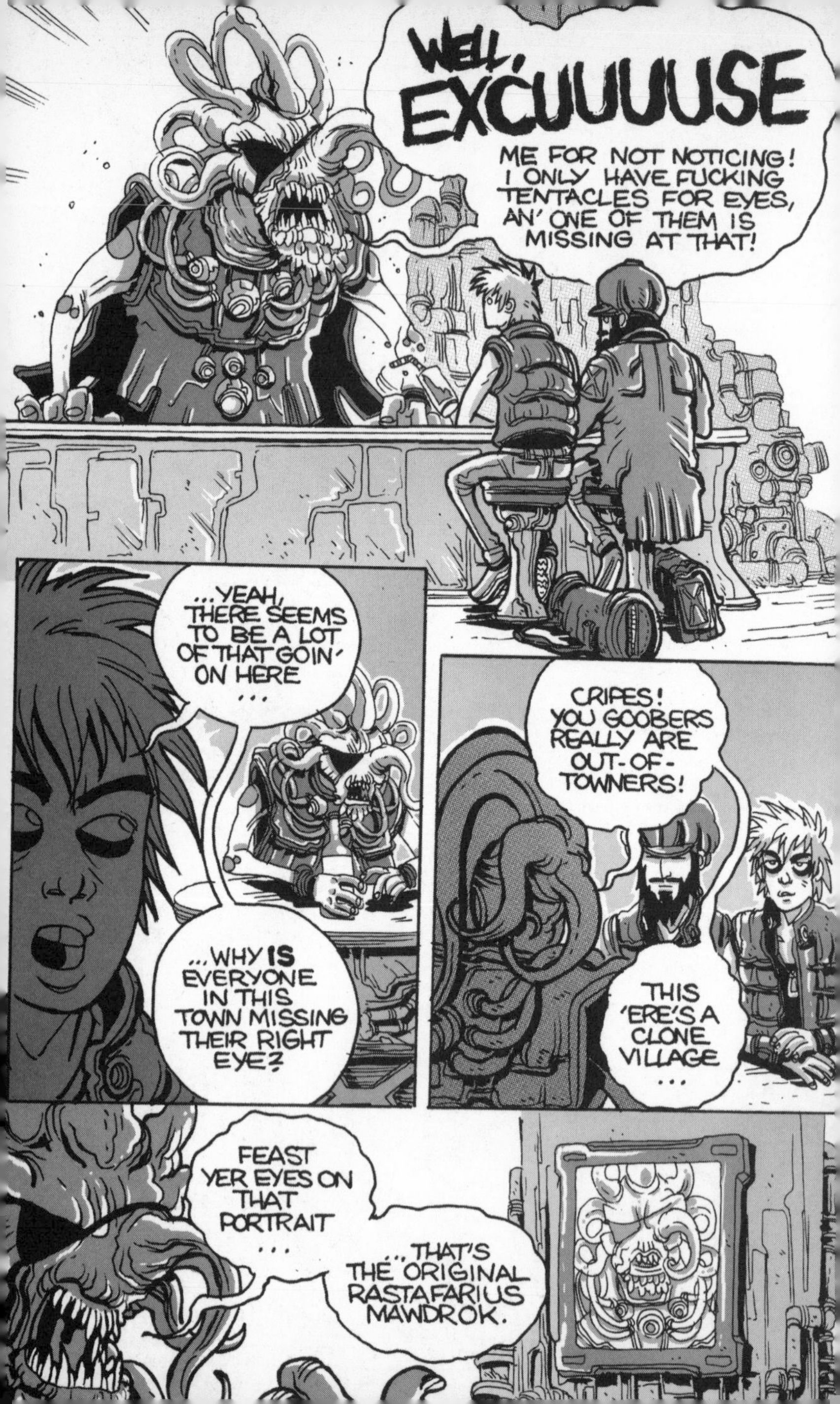
WELL, EXCUUUUSE
ME FOR NOT NOTICING! I ONLY HAVE FUCKING TENTACLES FOR EYES, AN' ONE OF THEM IS MISSING AT THAT!
...YEAH, THERE SEEMS TO BE A LOT OF THAT GOIN' ON HERE ...
...WHY IS EVERYONE IN THIS TOWN MISSING THEIR RIGHT EYE?
CRIPES! YOU GOOBERS REALLY ARE OUT-OF-TOWNERS!
THIS 'ERE'S A CLONE VILLAGE ...
FEAST YER EYES ON THAT PORTRAIT ...
...THAT'S THE ORIGINAL RASTAFARIUS MAWDROK.

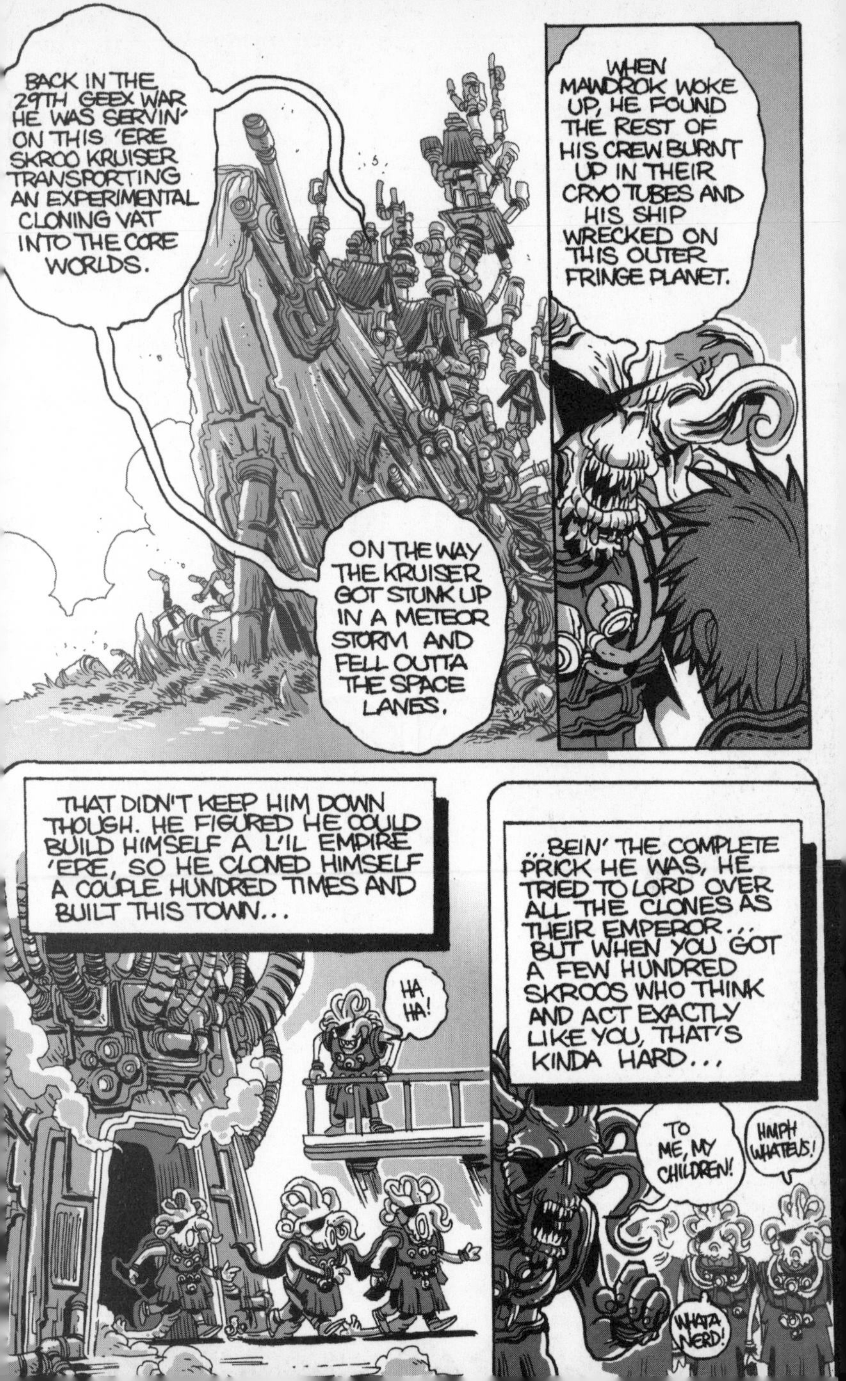
BACK IN THE 29TH GEEX WAR HE WAS SERVIN' ON THIS 'ERE SKROO KRUISER TRANSPORTING AN EXPERIMENTAL CLONING VAT INTO THE CORE WORLDS.
ON THE WAY THE KRUISER GOT STUNK UP IN A METEOR STORM AND FELL OUTTA THE SPACE LANES.
WHEN MAWDROK WOKE UP, HE FOUND THE REST OF HIS CREW BURNT UP IN THEIR CRYO TUBES AND HIS SHIP WRECKED ON THIS OUTER FRINGE PLANET.
THAT DIDN'T KEEP HIM DOWN THOUGH. HE FIGURED HE COULD BUILD HIMSELF A L'IL EMPIRE 'ERE, SO HE CLONED HIMSELF A COUPLE HUNDRED TIMES AND BUILT THIS TOWN...
HA HA!
...BEIN' THE COMPLETE PRICK HE WAS, HE TRIED TO LORD OVER ALL THE CLONES AS THEIR EMPEROR... BUT WHEN YOU GOT A FEW HUNDRED SKROOS WHO THINK AND ACT EXACTLY LIKE YOU, THAT'S KINDA HARD...
TO ME, MY CHILDREN!
HMPH WHATEVS!
WHATA NERD!

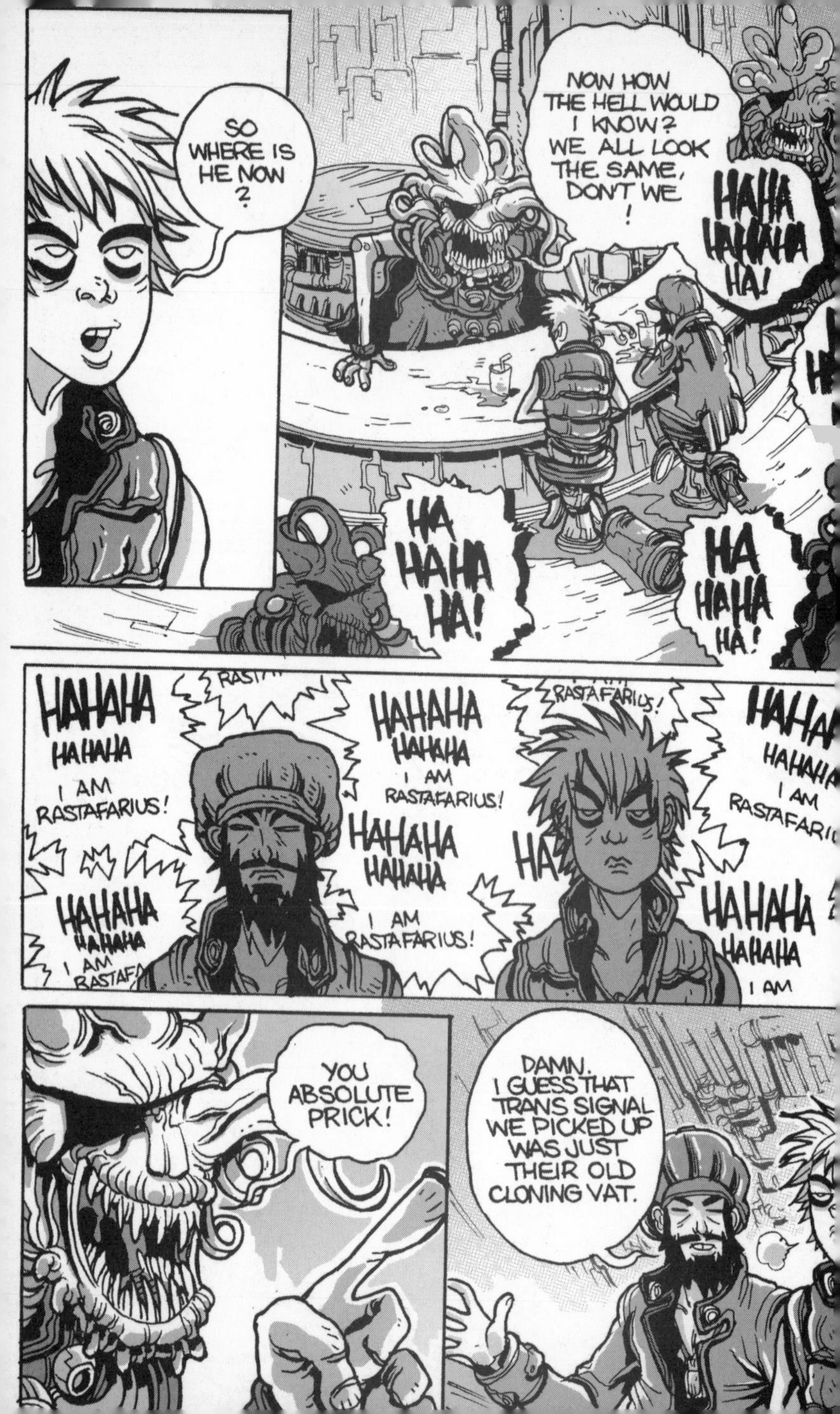
SO WHERE IS HE NOW ?
NOW HOW THE HELL WOULD I KNOW? WE ALL LOOK THE SAME, DON'T WE !
HAHA HAHAHA HA!
HA HAHA HA!
HA HAHA HA!
HAHAHA HAHAHA I AM RASTAFARIUS!
HAHAHA HAHAHA I AM RASTAFARIUS!
HAHAHA HAHAHA
I AM RASTAFARIUS!
HAHAHA HAHAHA I AM
HA
I AM RASTAFARIUS!
HAHAHA HAHAHA I AM
YOU ABSOLUTE PRICK!
DAMN. I GUESS THAT TRANS SIGNAL WE PICKED UP WAS JUST THEIR OLD CLONING VAT.

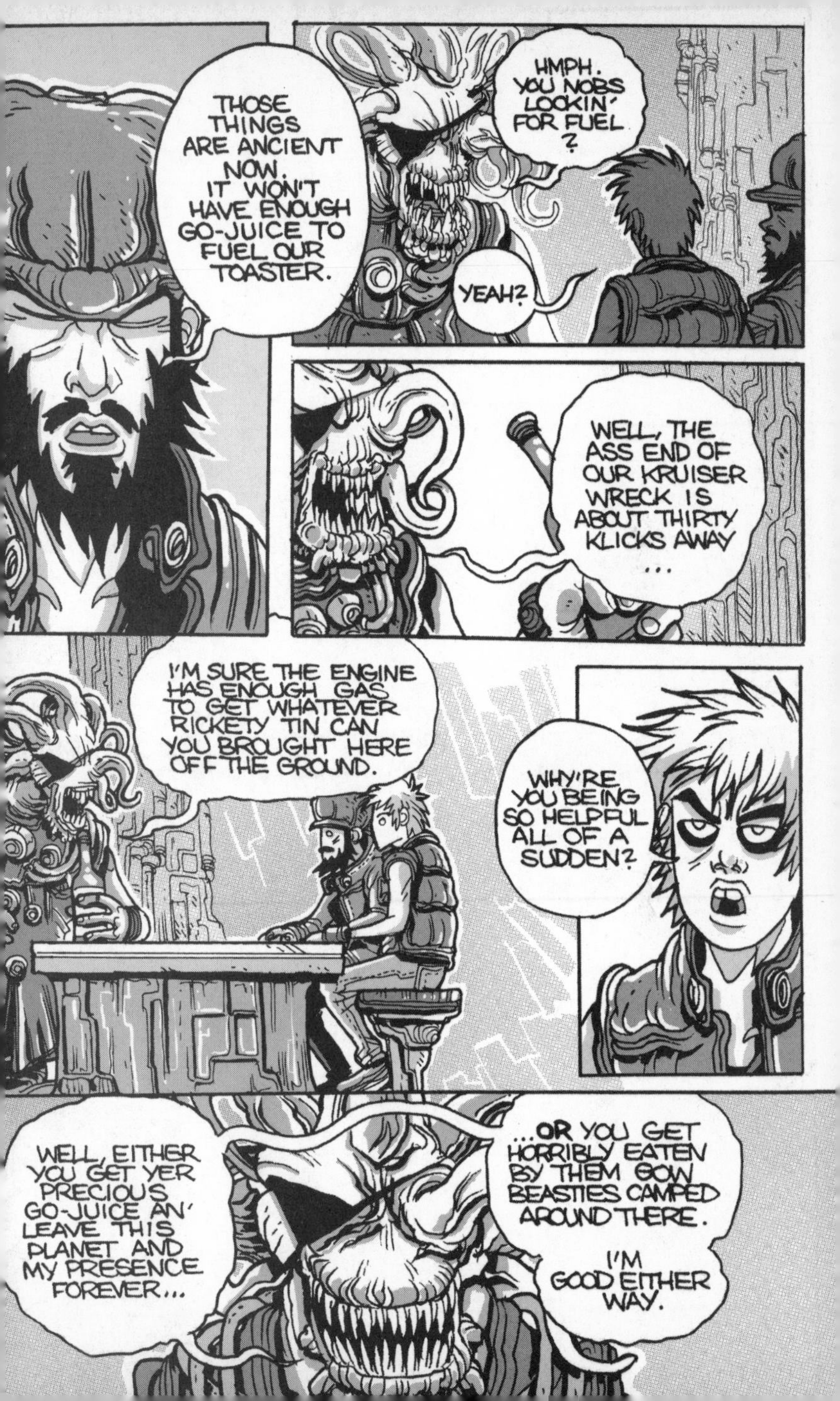
THOSE THINGS ARE ANCIENT NOW. IT WON'T HAVE ENOUGH GO-JUICE TO FUEL OUR TOASTER.
HMPH. YOU NOBS LOOKIN' FOR FUEL ?
YEAH?
WELL, THE ASS END OF OUR KRUISER WRECK IS ABOUT THIRTY KLICKS AWAY ...
I'M SURE THE ENGINE HAS ENOUGH GAS TO GET WHATEVER RICKETY TIN CAN YOU BROUGHT HERE OFF THE GROUND.
WHY'RE YOU BEING SO HELPFUL ALL OF A SUDDEN?
WELL, EITHER YOU GET YER PRECIOUS GO-JUICE AN' LEAVE THIS PLANET AND MY PRESENCE FOREVER...
...**OR** YOU GET HORRIBLY EATEN BY THEM GOW BEASTIES CAMPED AROUND THERE.
I'M GOOD EITHER WAY.

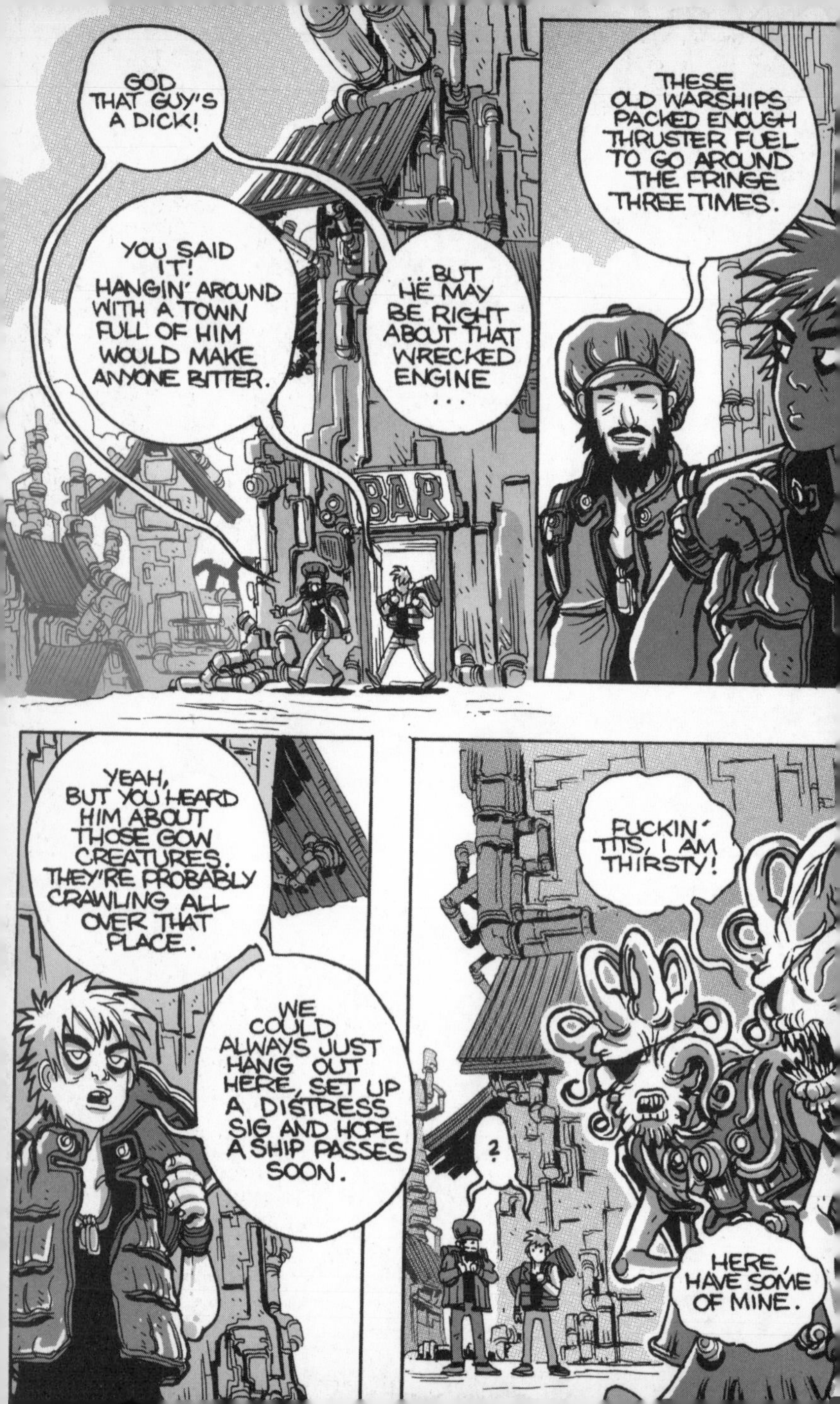
GOD THAT GUY'S A DICK!
YOU SAID IT! HANGIN' AROUND WITH A TOWN FULL OF HIM WOULD MAKE ANYONE BITTER.
...BUT HE MAY BE RIGHT ABOUT THAT WRECKED ENGINE ...
BAR
THESE OLD WARSHIPS PACKED ENOUGH THRUSTER FUEL TO GO AROUND THE FRINGE THREE TIMES.
YEAH, BUT YOU HEARD HIM ABOUT THOSE GOW CREATURES. THEY'RE PROBABLY CRAWLING ALL OVER THAT PLACE.
WE COULD ALWAYS JUST HANG OUT HERE, SET UP A DISTRESS SIG AND HOPE A SHIP PASSES SOON.
FUCKIN' TITS, I AM THIRSTY!
?
HERE, HAVE SOME OF MINE.

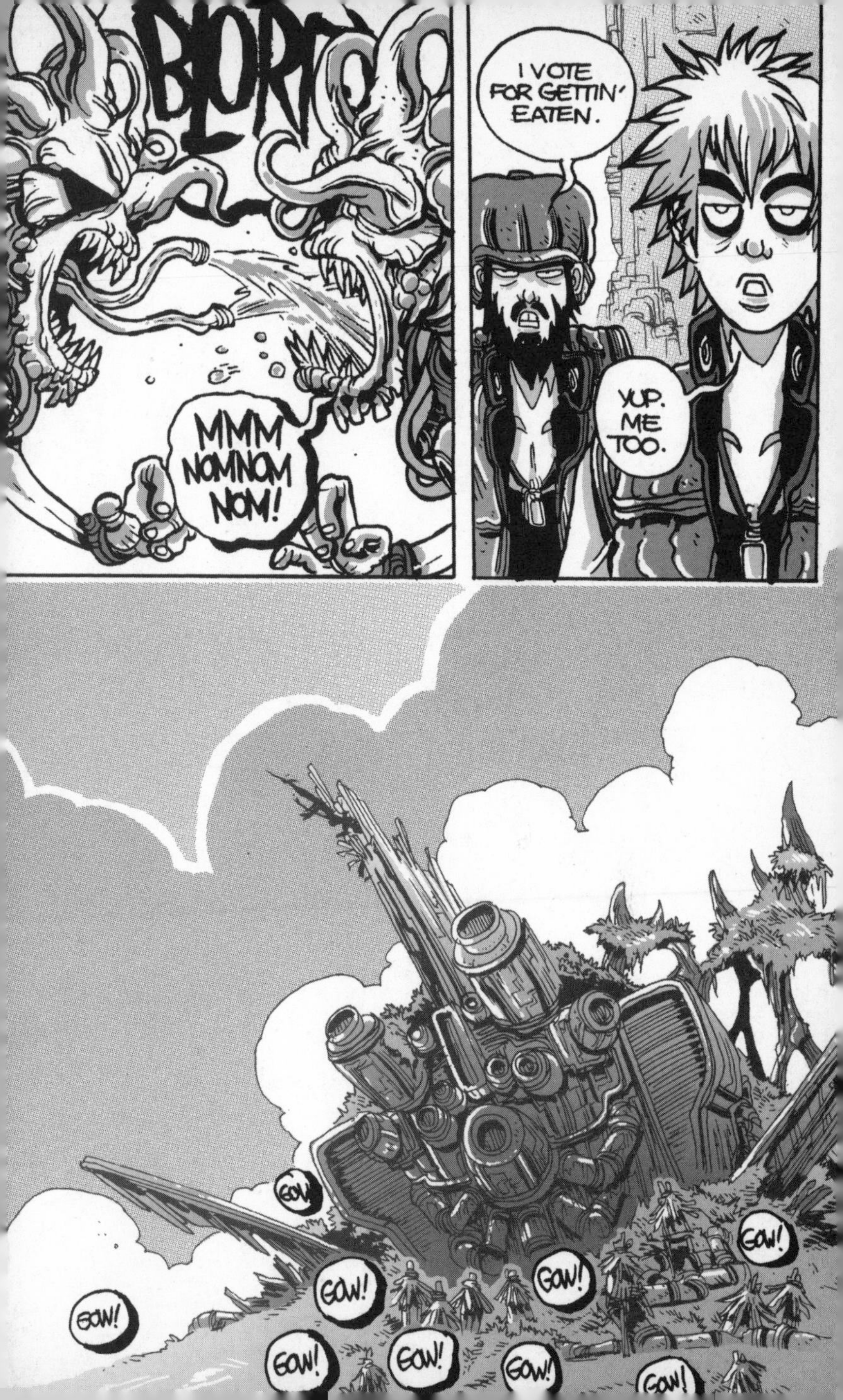
BLORT
MMM NOMNOM NOM!
I VOTE FOR GETTIN' EATEN.
YUP. ME TOO.
GOW!
GOW!
GOW!
GOW!
GOW!
GOW!
GOW!
GOW!
GOW!
GOW!

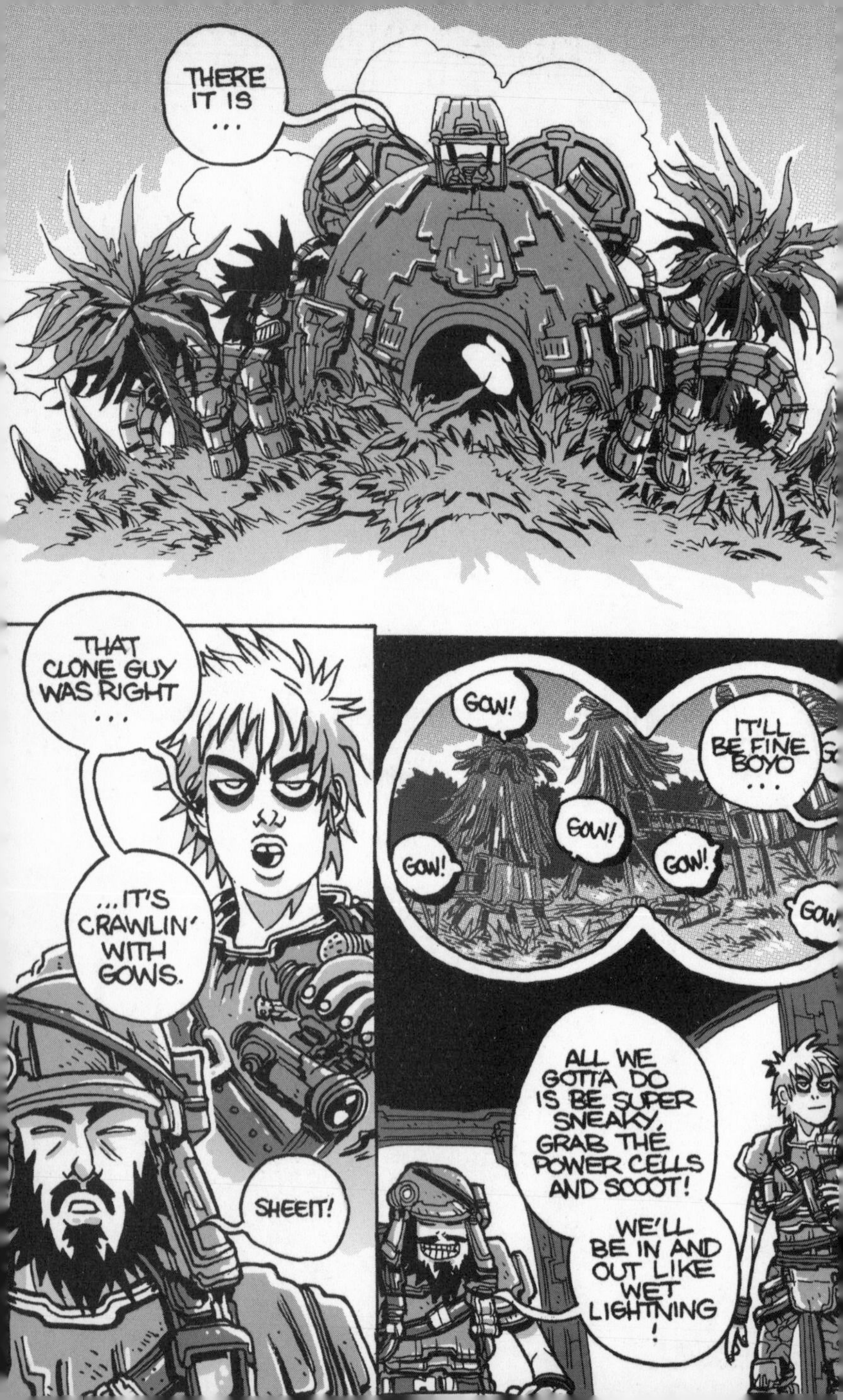
THERE IT IS ...
THAT CLONE GUY WAS RIGHT ...
...IT'S CRAWLIN' WITH GOWS.
SHEEIT!
GOW!
IT'LL BE FINE BOYO ...
GOW!
GOW!
GOW!
ALL WE GOTTA DO IS BE SUPER SNEAKY, GRAB THE POWER CELLS AND SCOOT!
WE'LL BE IN AND OUT LIKE WET LIGHTNING !

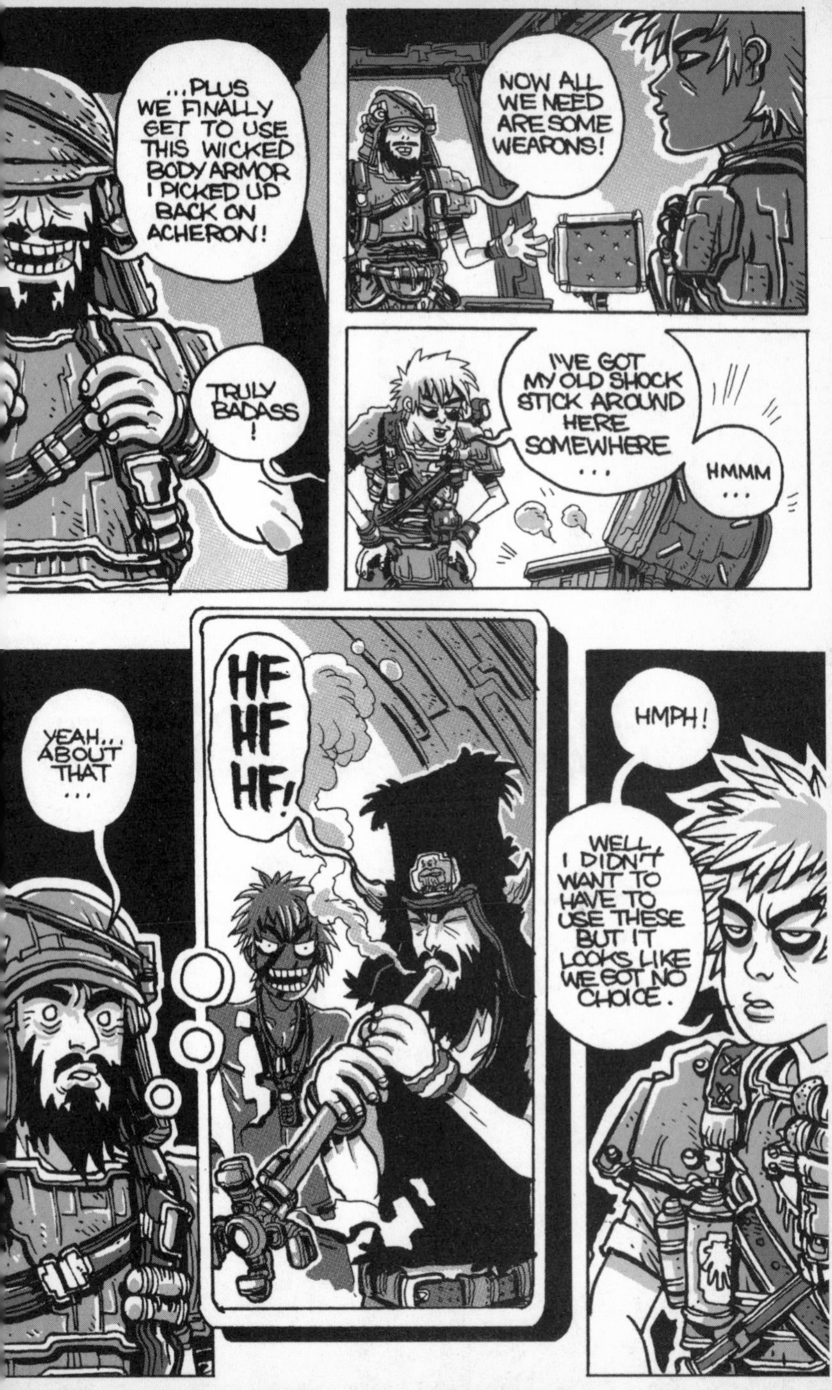
...PLUS WE FINALLY GET TO USE THIS WICKED BODY ARMOR I PICKED UP BACK ON ACHERON!
TRULY BADASS!
NOW ALL WE NEED ARE SOME WEAPONS!
I'VE GOT MY OLD SHOCK STICK AROUND HERE SOMEWHERE...
HMMM...
YEAH... ABOUT THAT...
HF HF HF!
HMPH!
WELL, I DIDN'T WANT TO HAVE TO USE THESE BUT IT LOOKS LIKE WE GOT NO CHOICE.

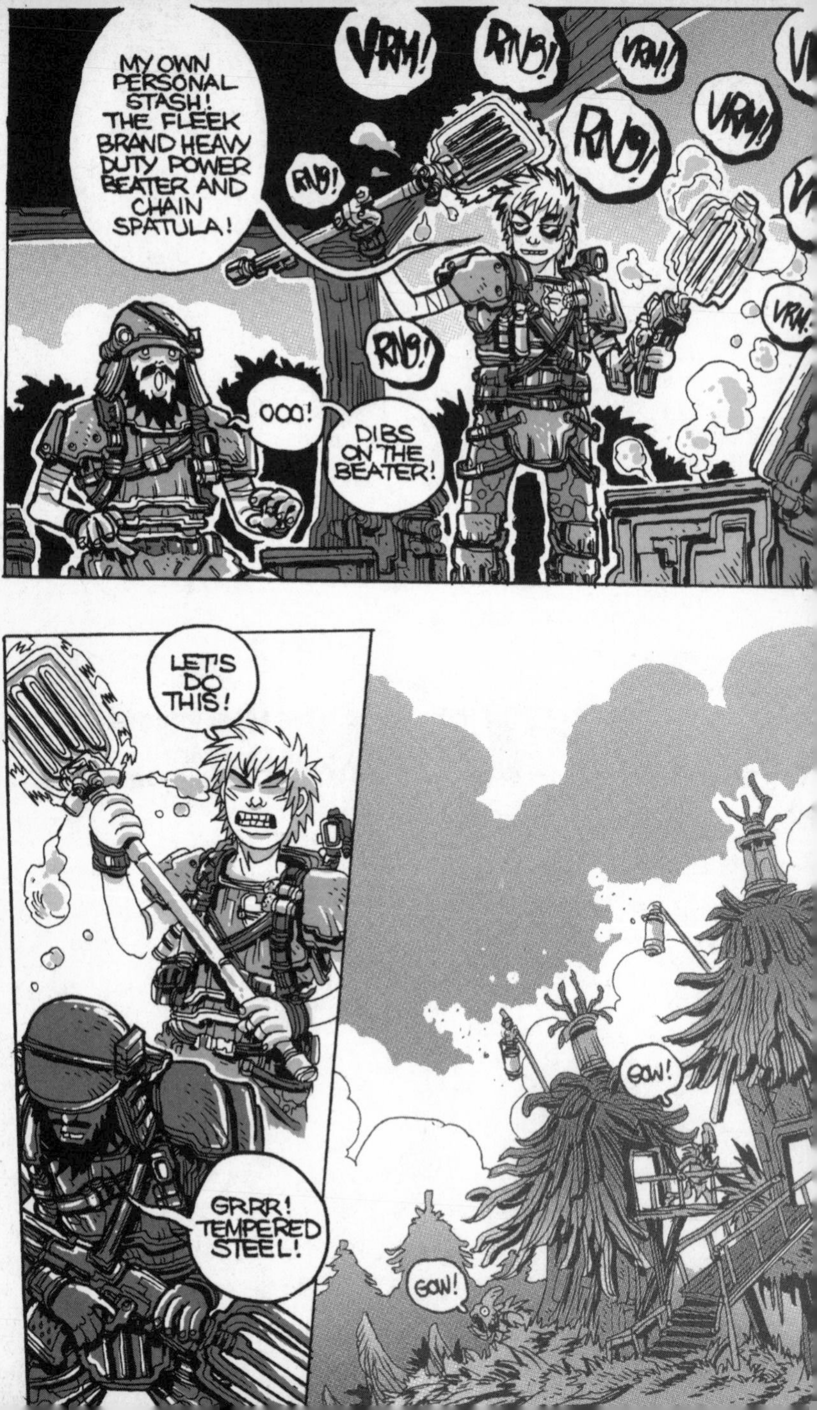
MY OWN PERSONAL STASH! THE FLEEK BRAND HEAVY DUTY POWER BEATER AND CHAIN SPATULA!
VRM!
RNG!
VRM!
RNG!
VRM!
RNG!
VRM!
RNG!
OOO!
DIBS ON THE BEATER!
LET'S DO THIS!
GOW!
GRRR! TEMPERED STEEL!
GOW!

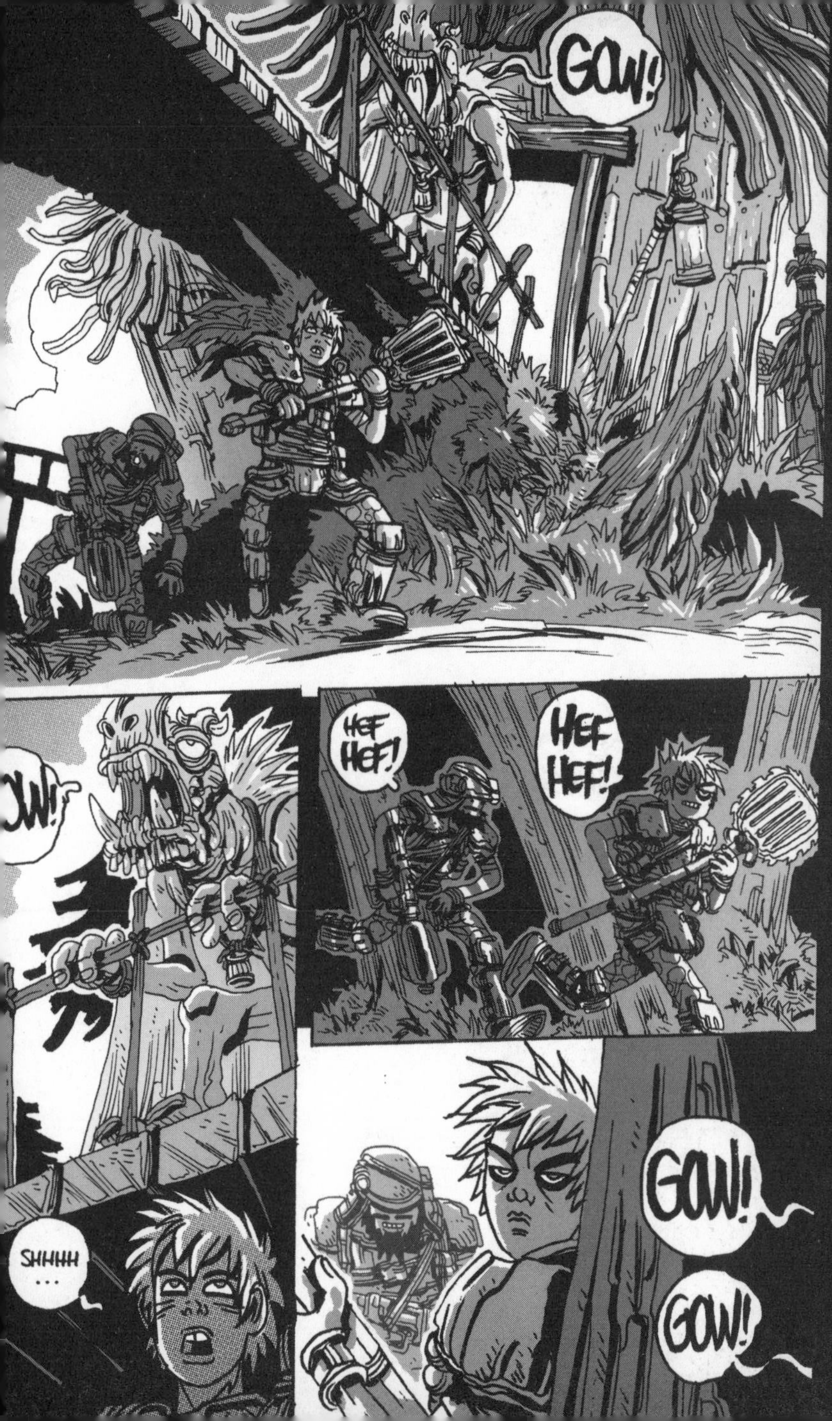

GOW!
OW!
HEF HEF!
HEF HEF!
SHHHH ...
GOW!
GOW!

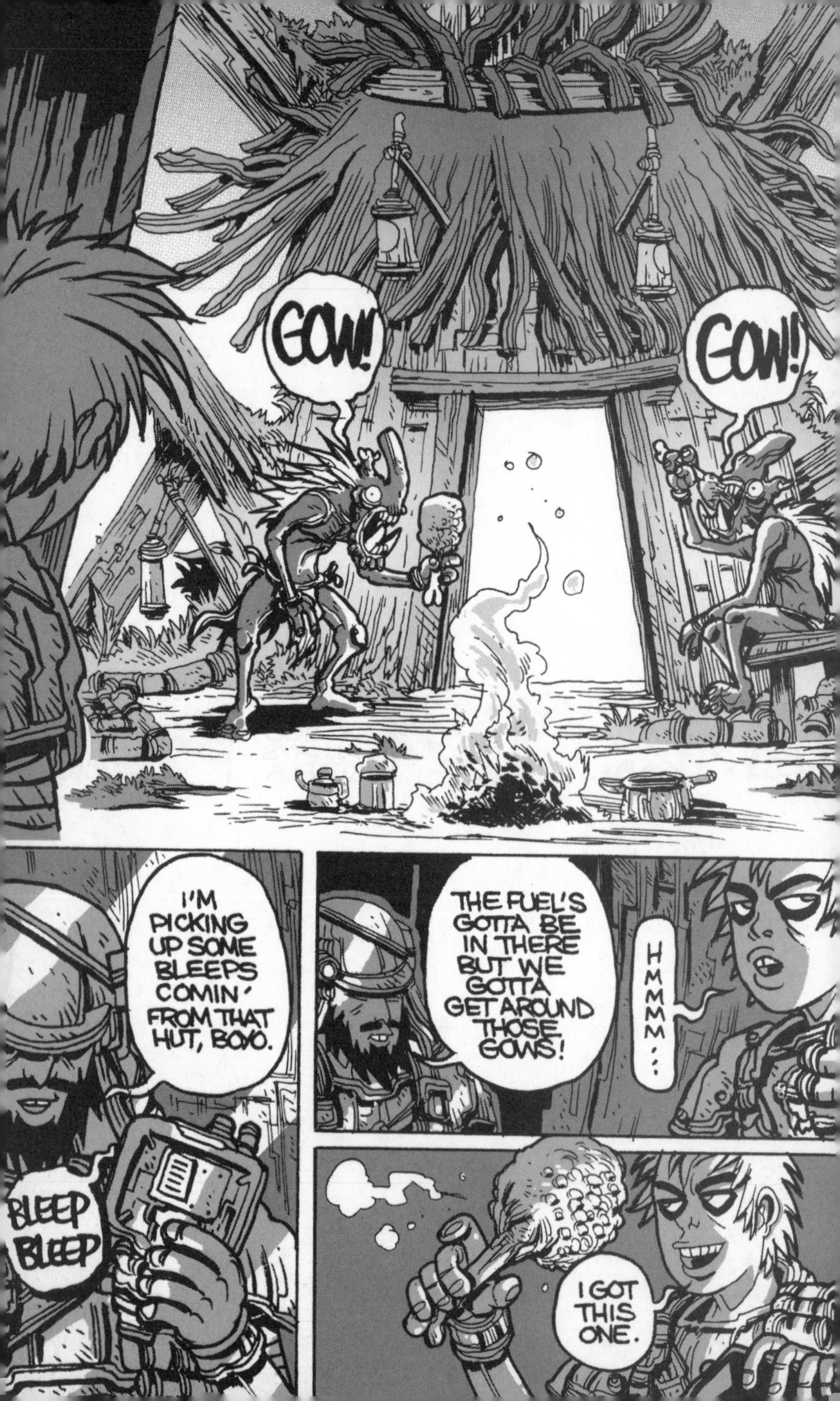
GOW!
GOW!
I'M PICKING UP SOME BLEEPS COMIN' FROM THAT HUT, BOYO.
BLEEP BLEEP
THE FUEL'S GOTTA BE IN THERE BUT WE GOTTA GET AROUND THOSE GOWS!
HMMMM...
I GOT THIS ONE.

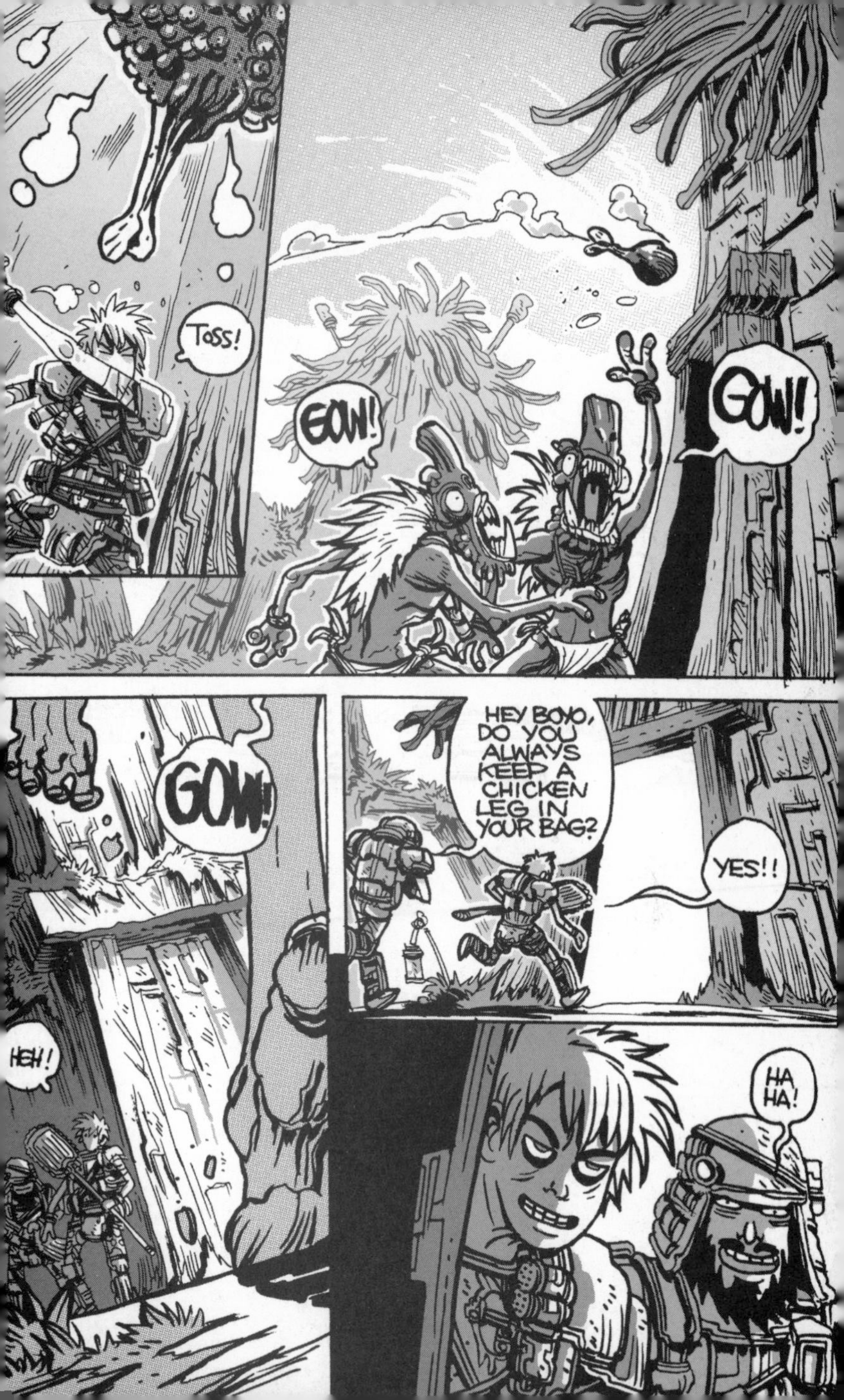
TOSS!
GOW!
GOW!
GOW!!
HEY BOYO, DO YOU ALWAYS KEEP A CHICKEN LEG IN YOUR BAG?
YES!!
HEH!
HA HA!

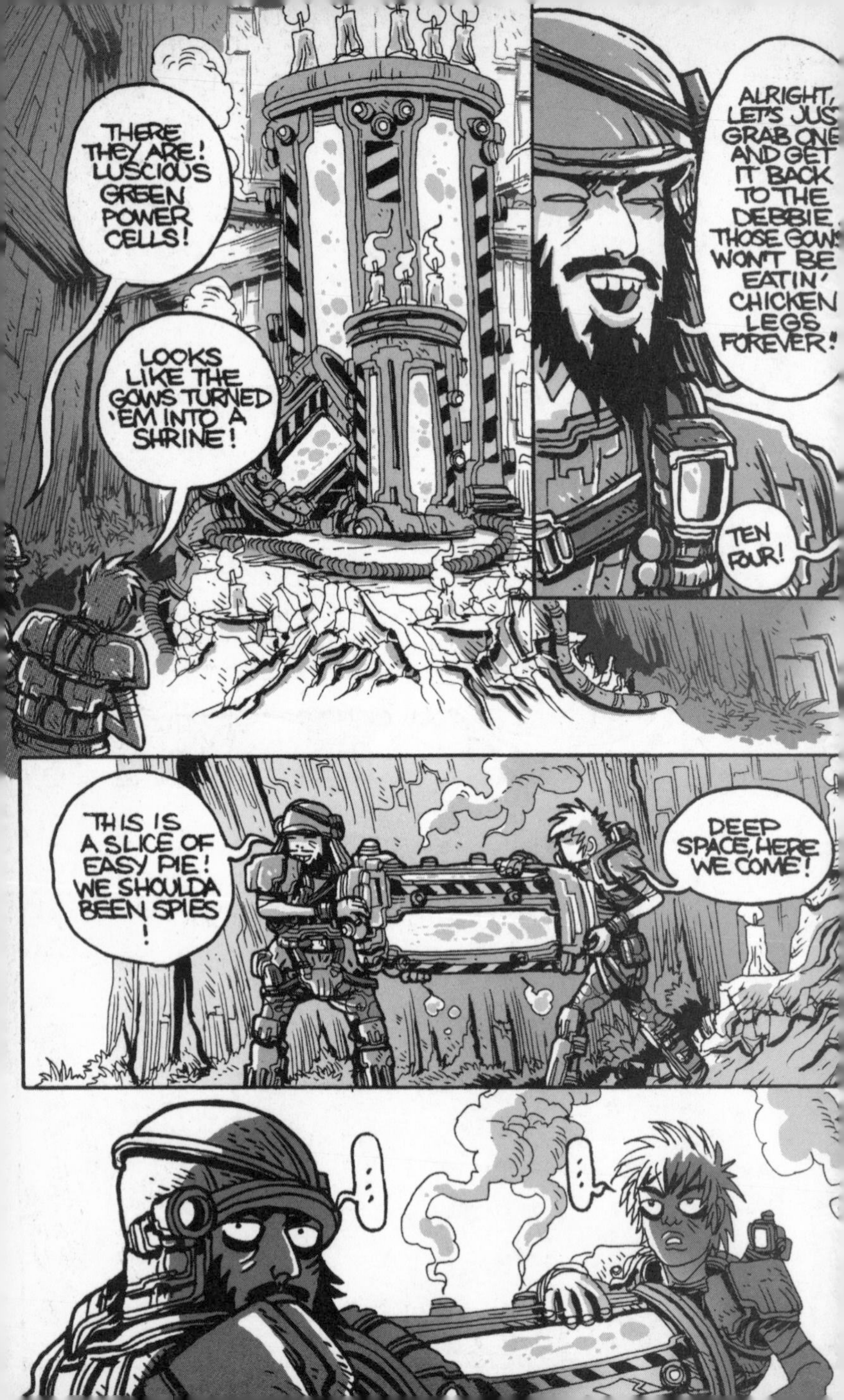
THERE THEY ARE! LUSCIOUS GREEN POWER CELLS!
LOOKS LIKE THE GOWS TURNED 'EM INTO A SHRINE!
ALRIGHT, LET'S JUS GRAB ONE AND GET IT BACK TO THE DEBBIE. THOSE GOWS WON'T BE EATIN' CHICKEN LEGS FOREVER!
TEN FOUR!
THIS IS A SLICE OF EASY PIE! WE SHOULDA BEEN SPIES!
DEEP SPACE, HERE WE COME!
...
...

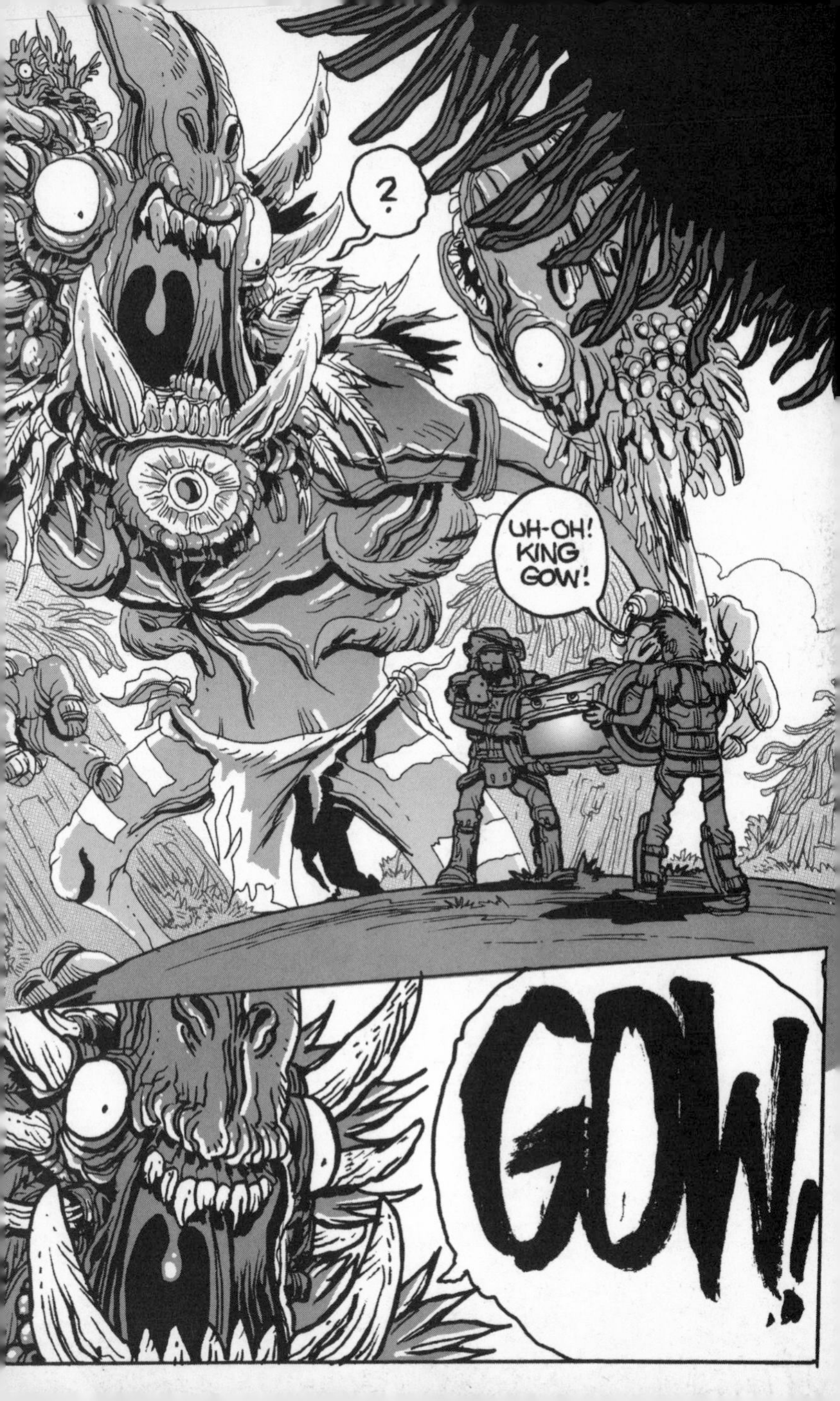
?
UH-OH! KING GOW!
GOW!!

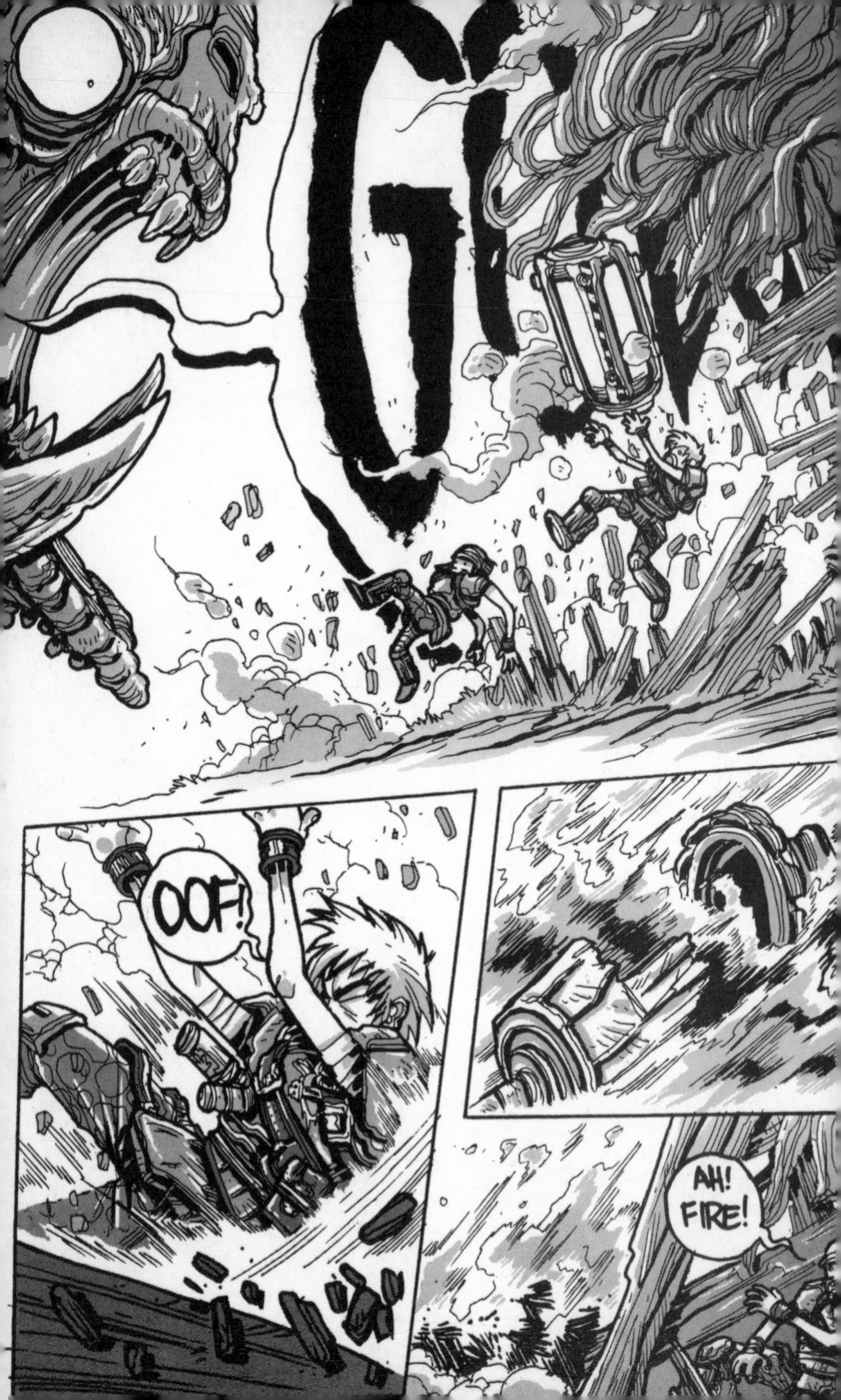
OOF!
AH! FIRE!

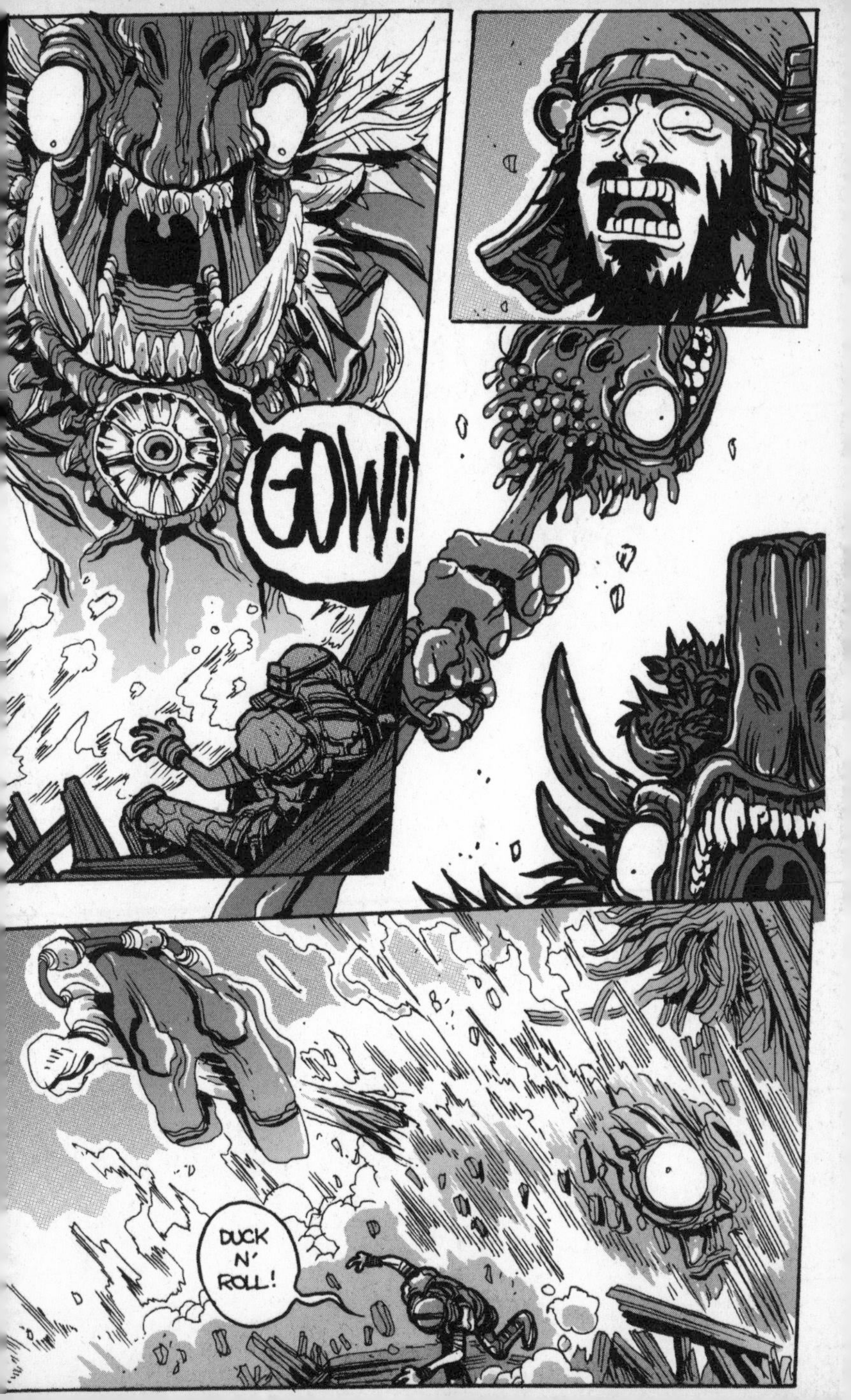
GOW!
DUCK N' ROLL!

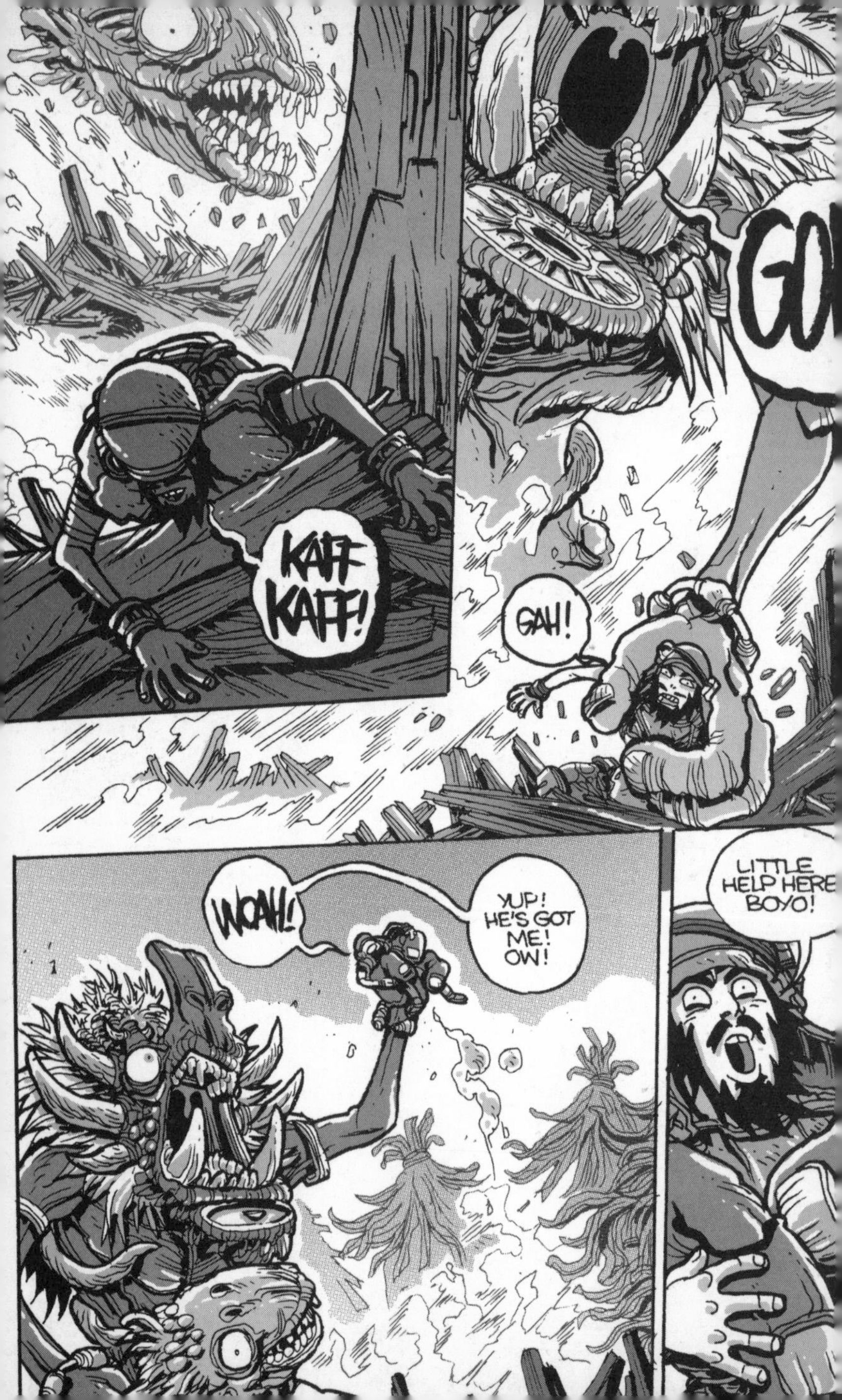

GO
KAFF KAFF!
GAH!
WOAH!
YUP! HE'S GOT ME! OW!
LITTLE HELP HERE BOYO!

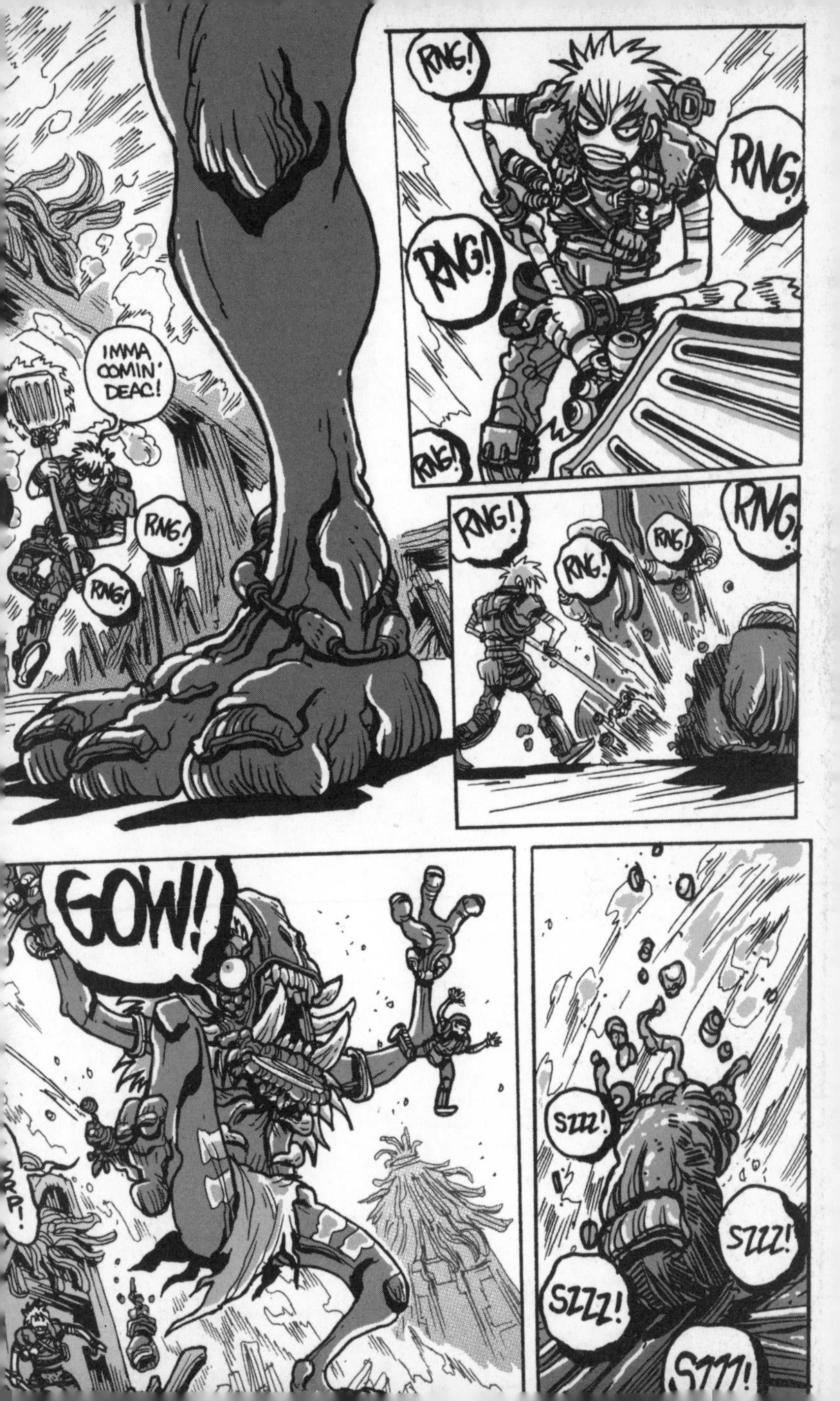
IMMA COMIN' DEAC!
RNG!
RNG!
RNG!
RNG!
RNG!
RNG!
RNG!
RNG!
RNG!
RNG!
GOW!
SRRP!
SZZZ!
SZZZ!
SZZZ!
SZZZ!

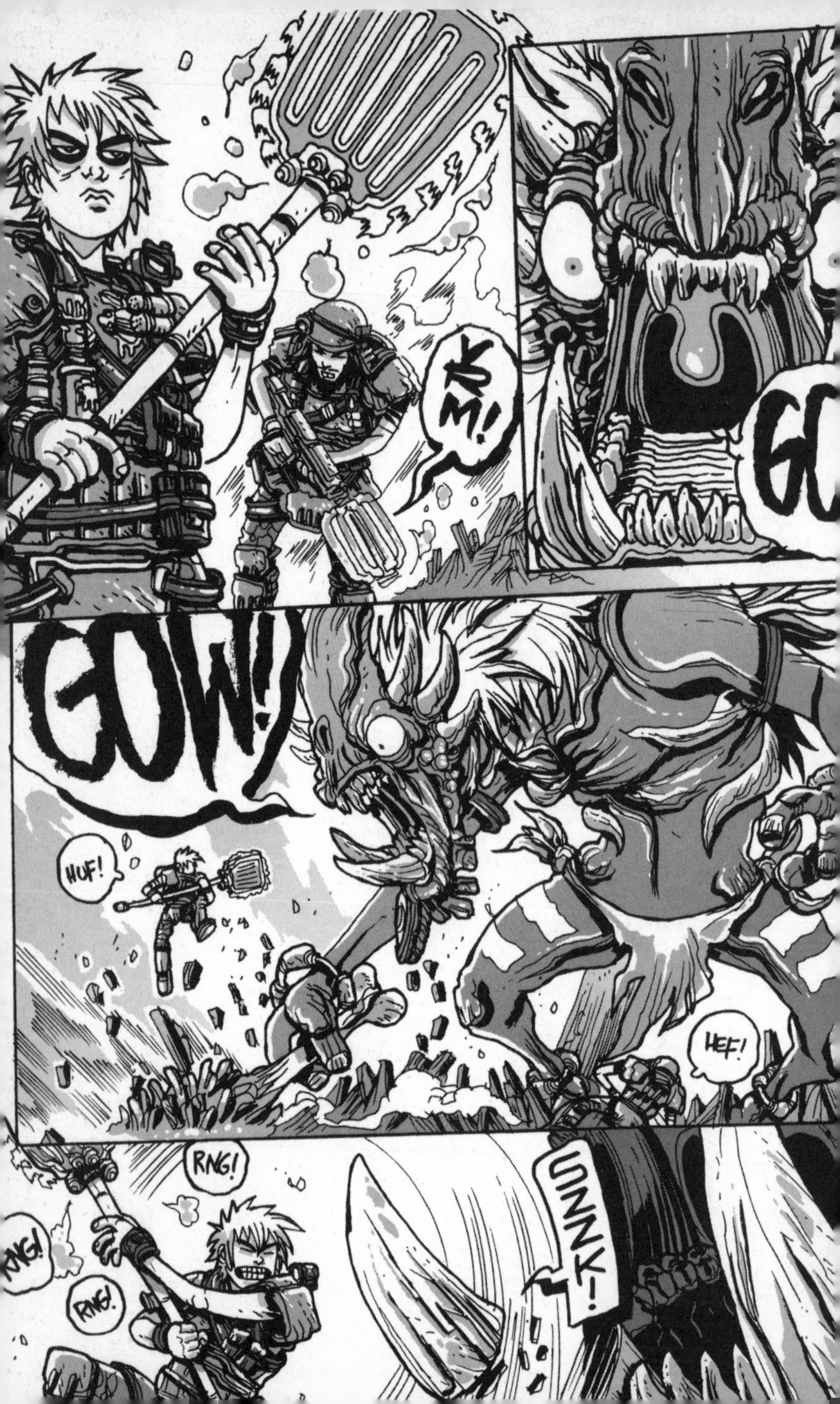

KRM!
GO
GOW!
HUF!
HEF!
RNG!
RNG!
RNG!
UNNNK!

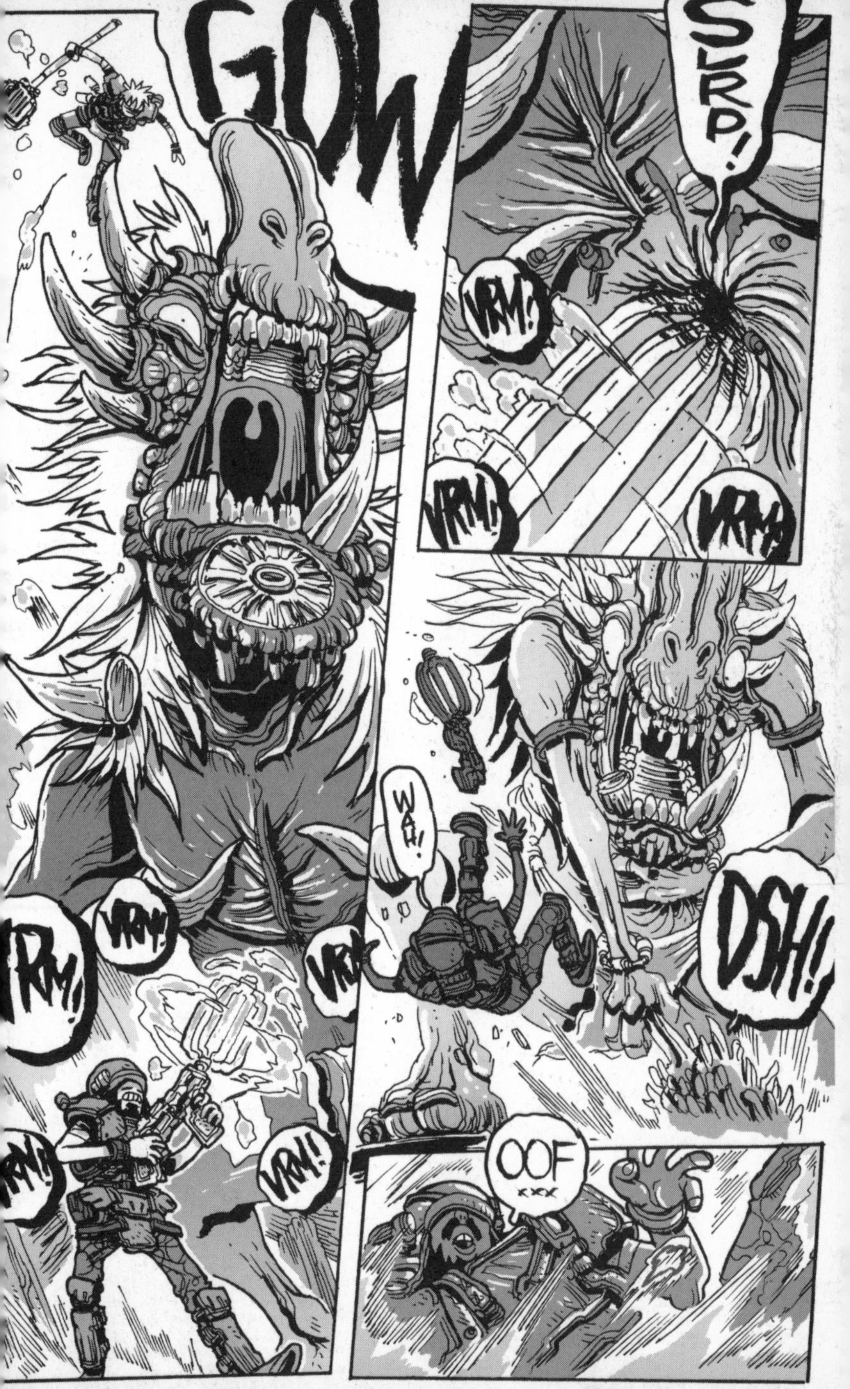
GOW
VRM!
VRM!
SLRP!
VRM!
VRM!
WAH!
DSH!
OOF

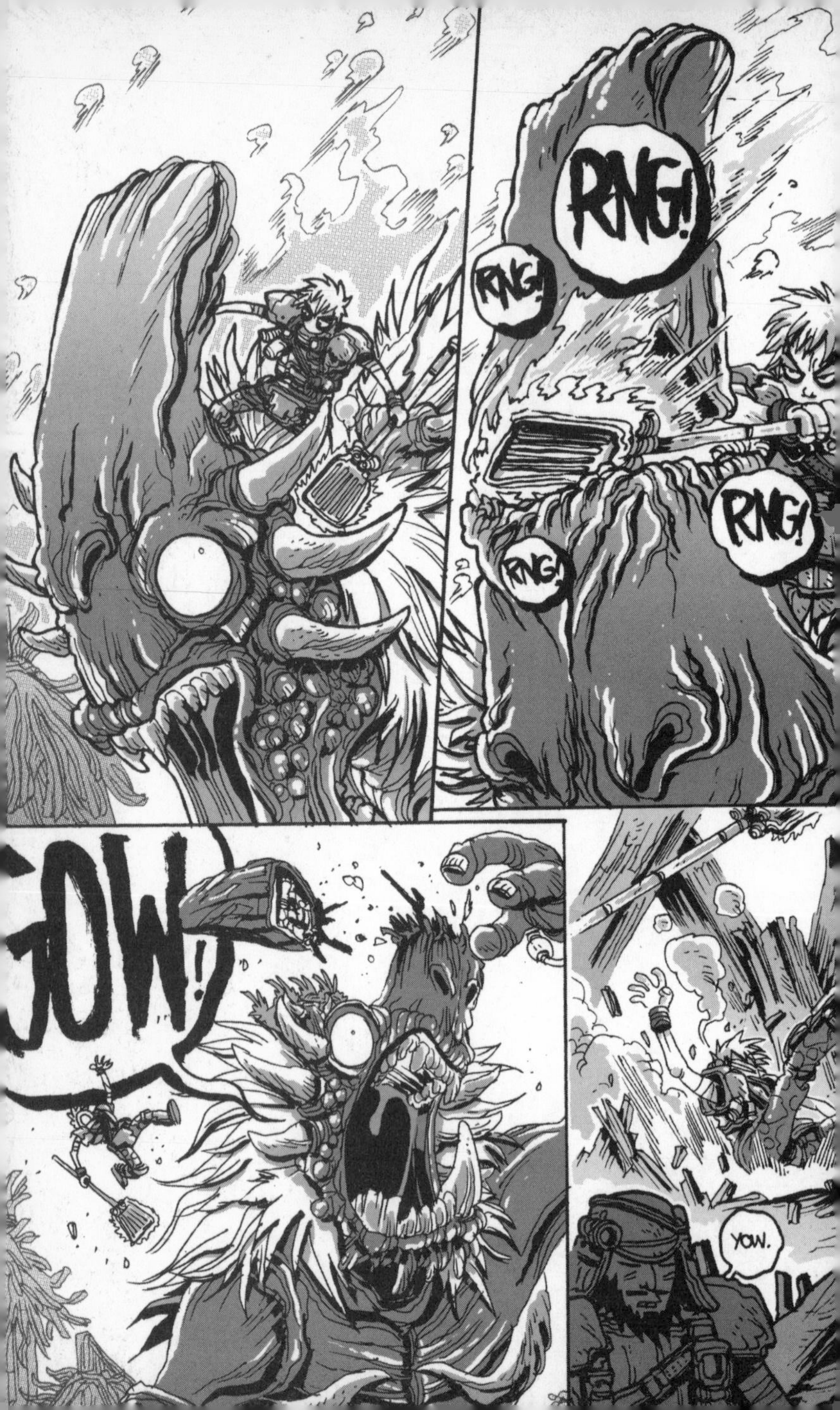
RNG!
RNG!
RNG!
RNG!
OW!
YOW.

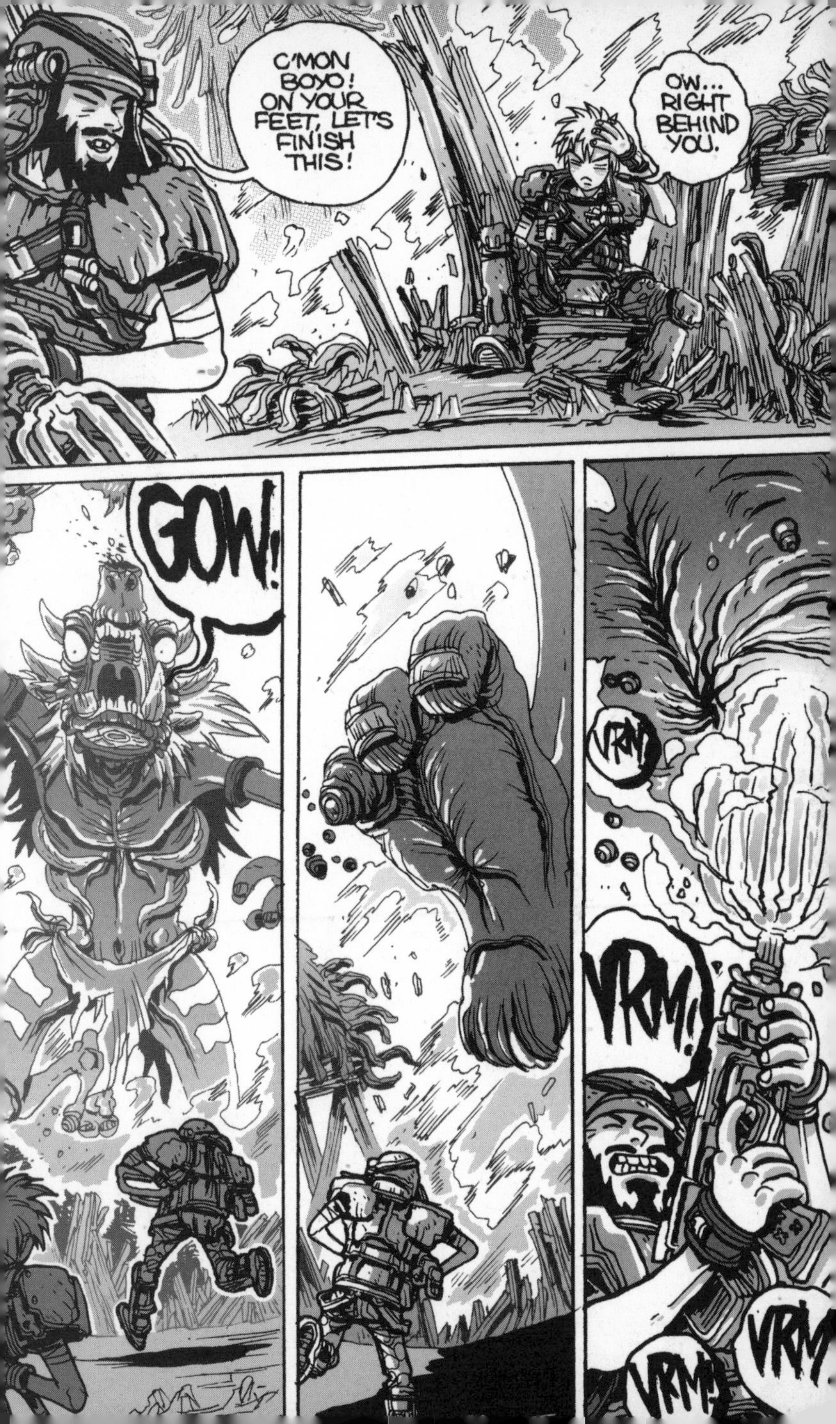
C'MON BOYO! ON YOUR FEET, LET'S FINISH THIS!
OW... RIGHT BEHIND YOU.
GOW!
VRM
VRM!
VRM
VRM!

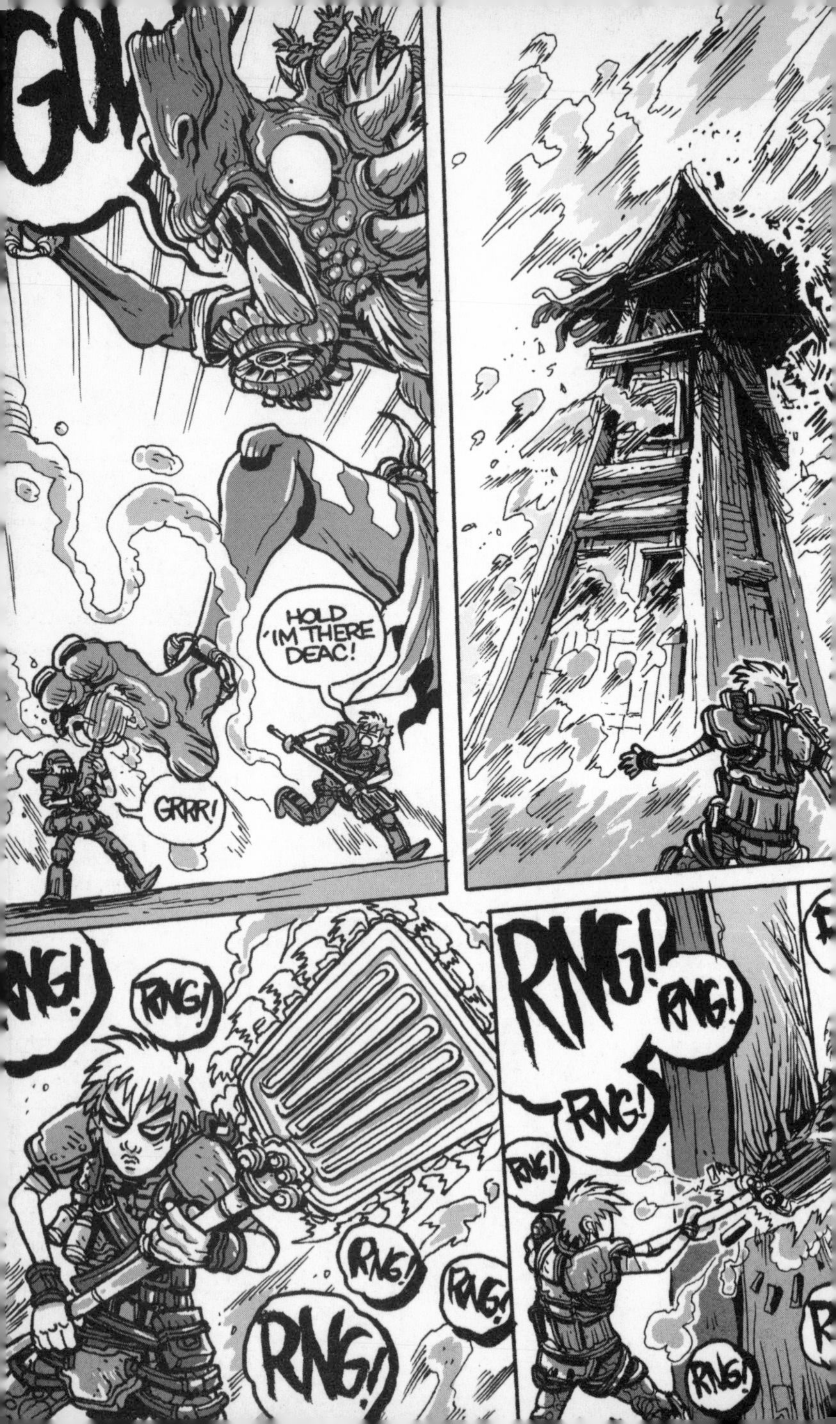
HOLD 'IM THERE DEAC!
GRRR!
RNG!
RNG!
RNG!
RNG!
RNG!
RNG!
RNG!
RNG!
RNG!
RNG!

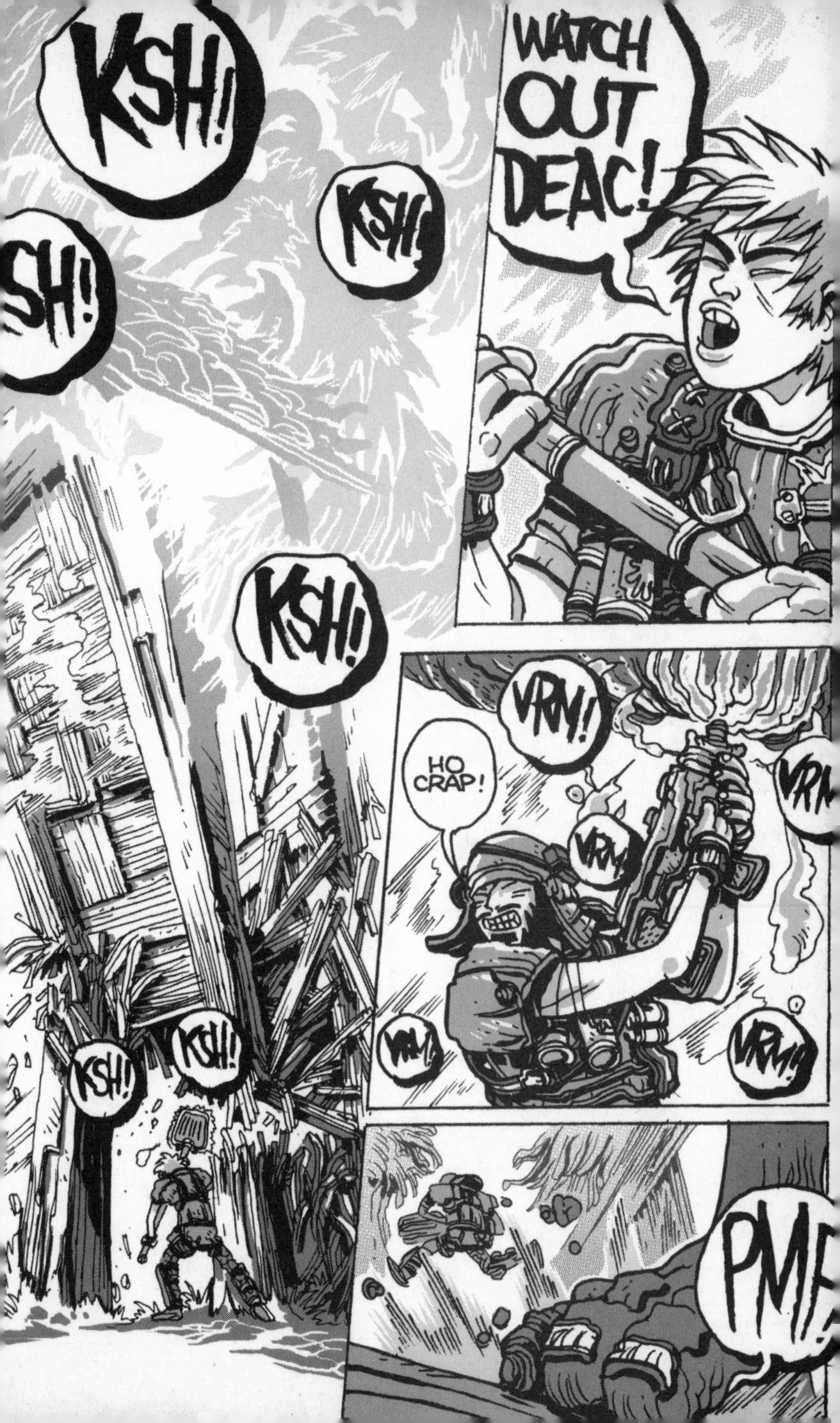
KSH!
KSH!
KSH!
WATCH OUT DEAC!
KSH!
KSH!
KSH!
VRM!
HO CRAP!
VRM
VRM
VRM
VRM
PMF

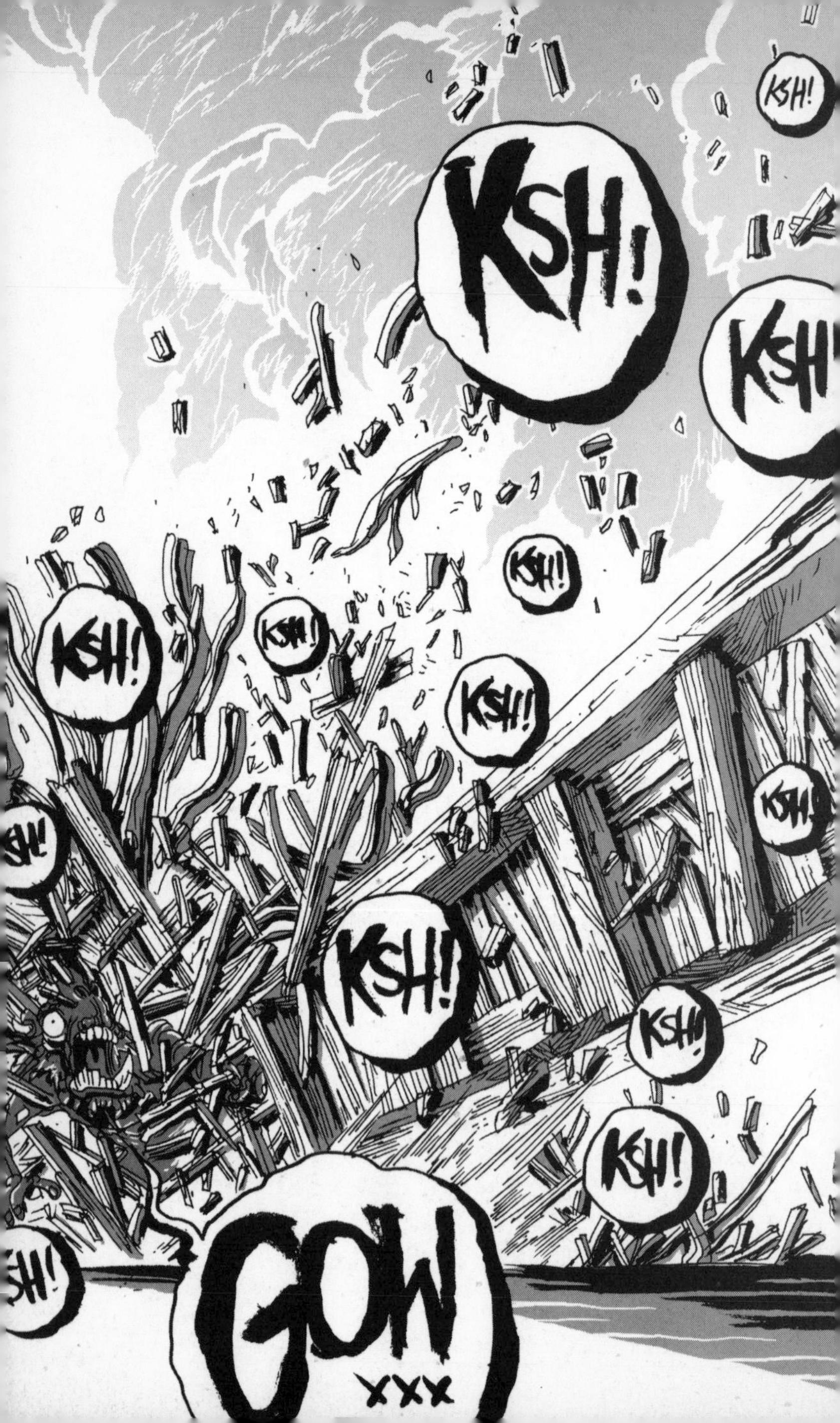
KSH!
KSH!
KSH!
KSH!
KSH!
KSH!
KSH!
KSH!
KSH!
KSH!
GOW

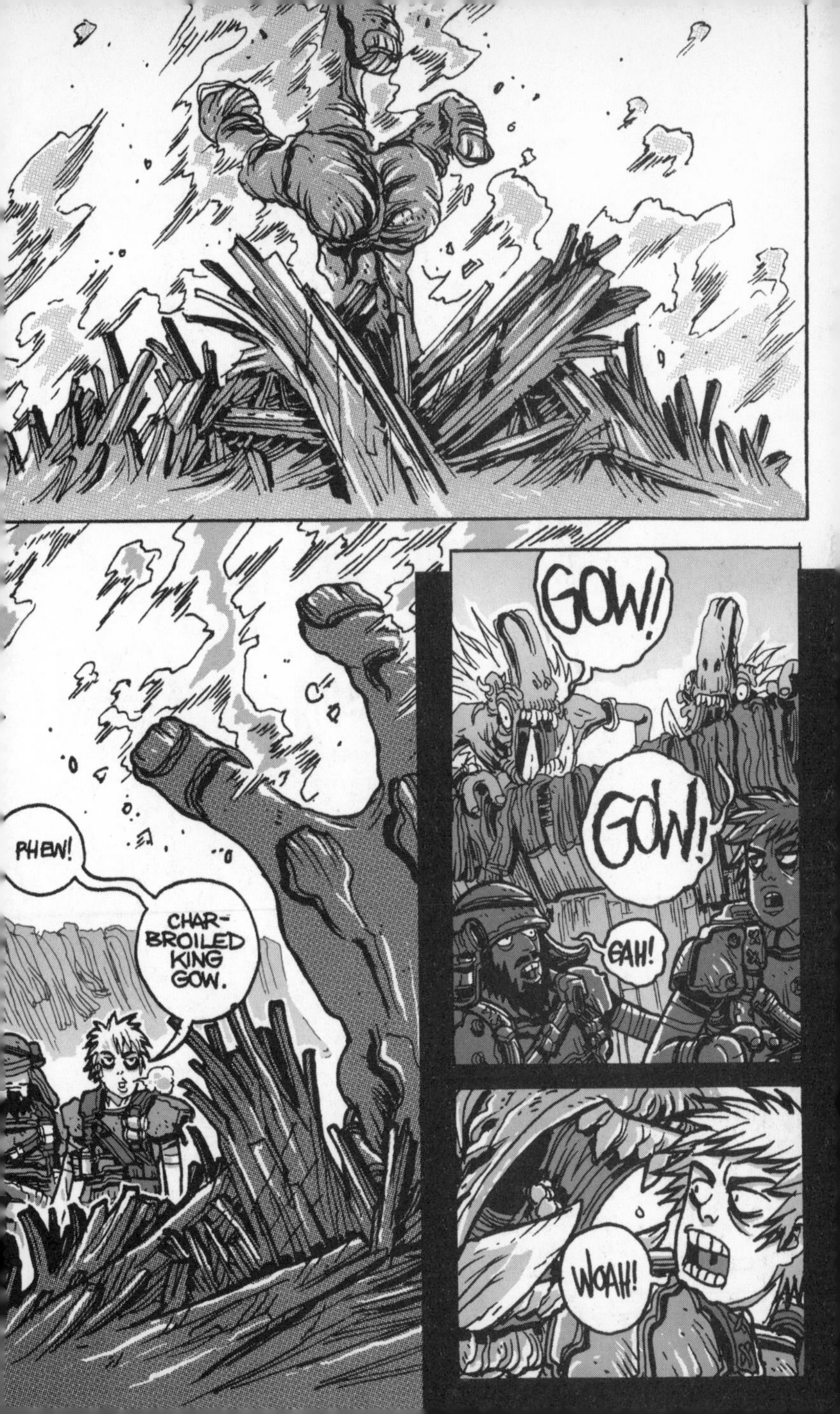
PHEW!
CHAR-BROILED KING GOW.
GOW!
GOW!
GAH!
WOAH!

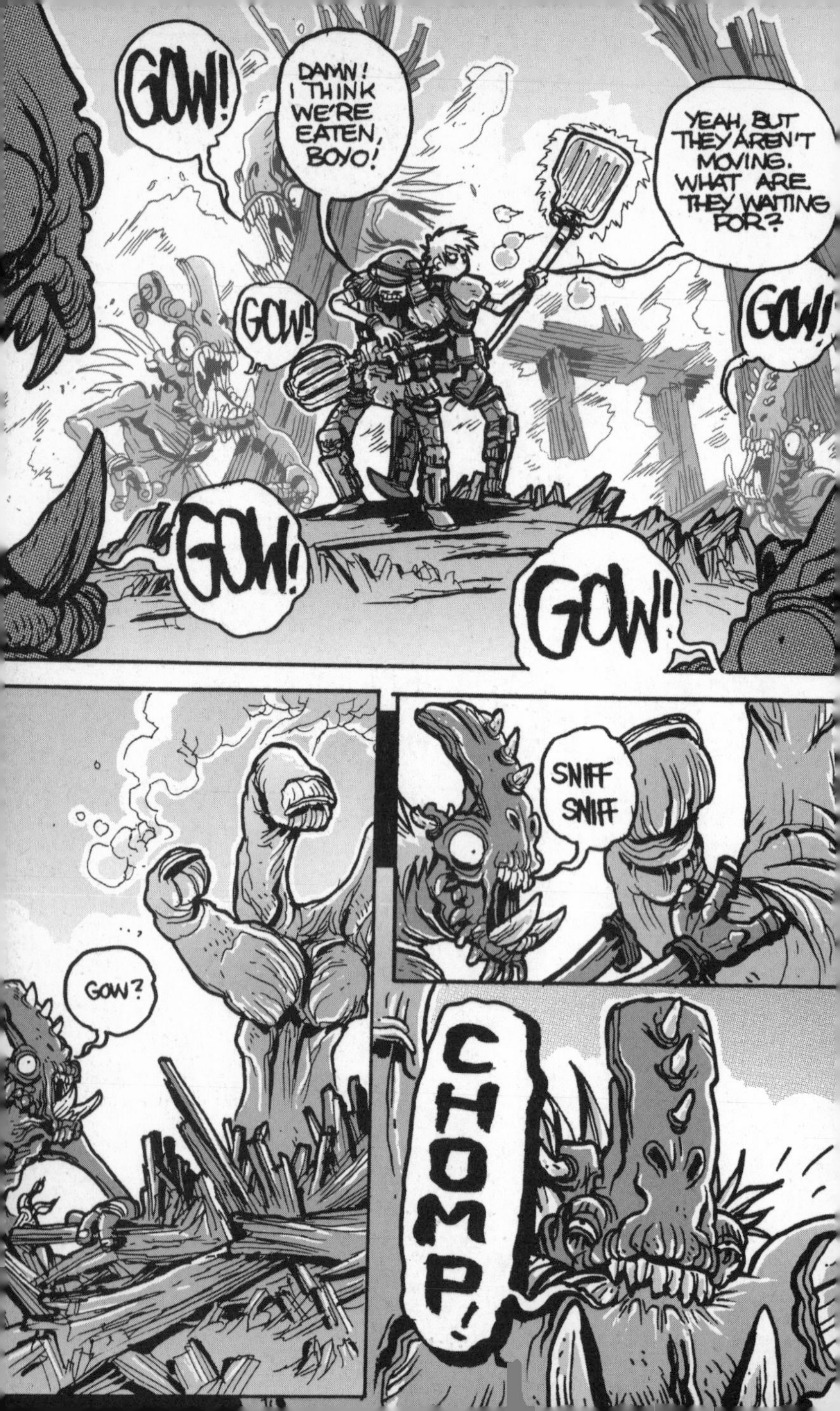
GOW!
DAMN! I THINK WE'RE EATEN, BOYO!
YEAH, BUT THEY AREN'T MOVING. WHAT ARE THEY WAITING FOR?
GOW!
GOW!
GOW!
GOW!
SNIFF SNIFF
GOW?
CHOMP!

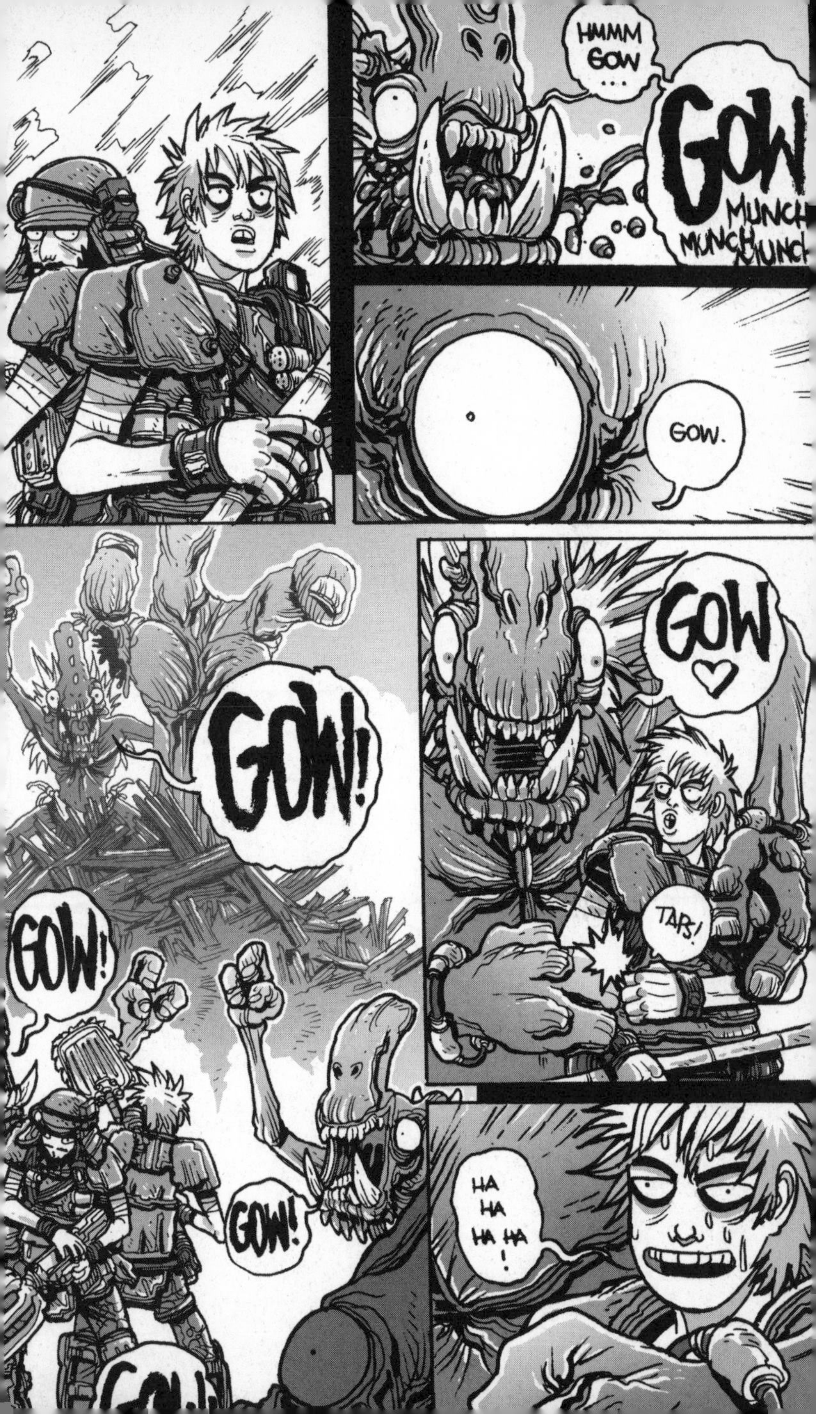
HMMM GOW ...
GOW
MUNCH MUNCH MUNCH
GOW.
GOW!
GOW ♥
TAP!
GOW!
GOW!
HA HA HA HA !

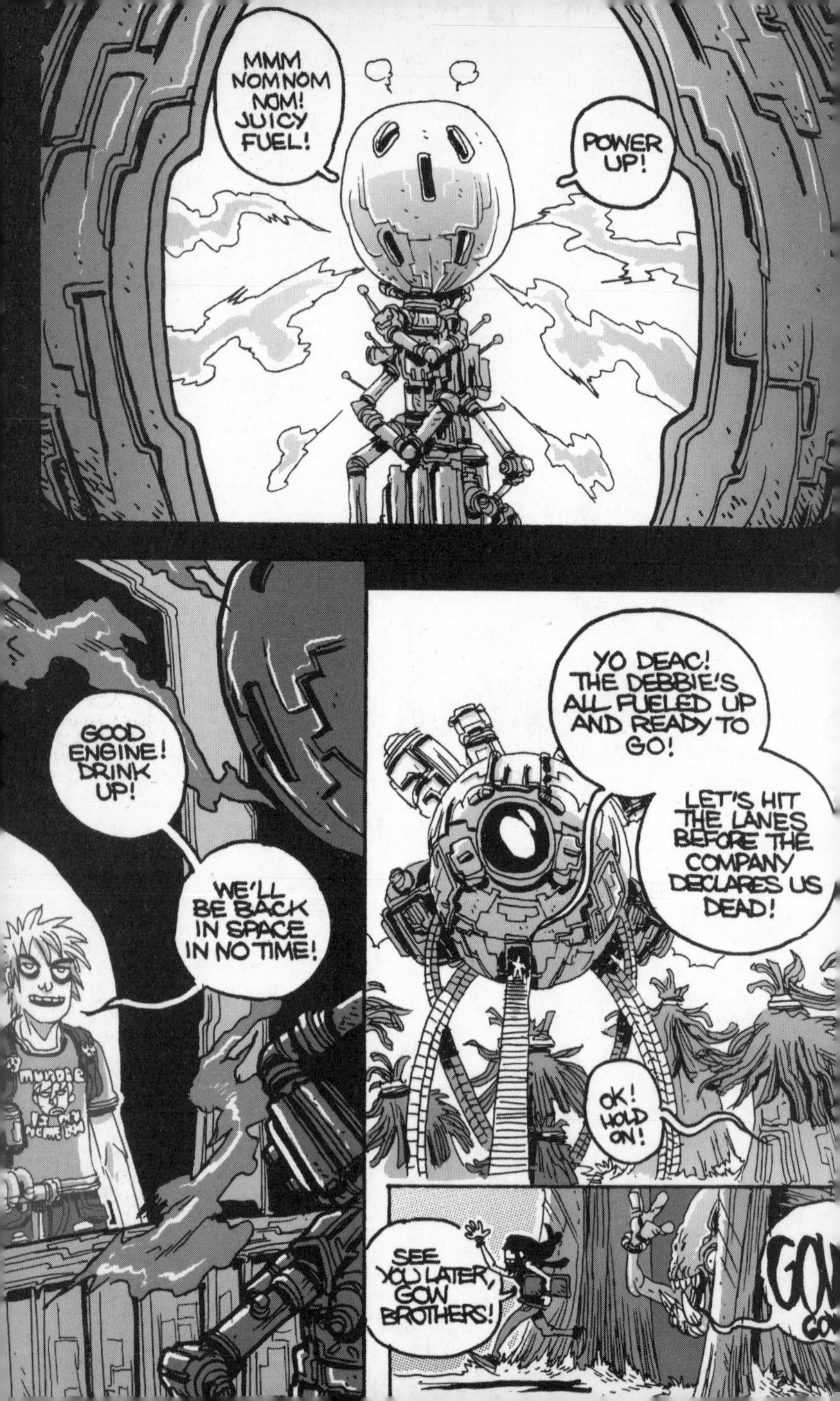
MMM NOMNOM NOM! JUICY FUEL!
POWER UP!
GOOD ENGINE! DRINK UP!
WE'LL BE BACK IN SPACE IN NO TIME!
YO DEAC! THE DEBBIE'S ALL FUELED UP AND READY TO GO!
LET'S HIT THE LANES BEFORE THE COMPANY DECLARES US DEAD!
OK! HOLD ON!
SEE YOU LATER, GOW BROTHERS!

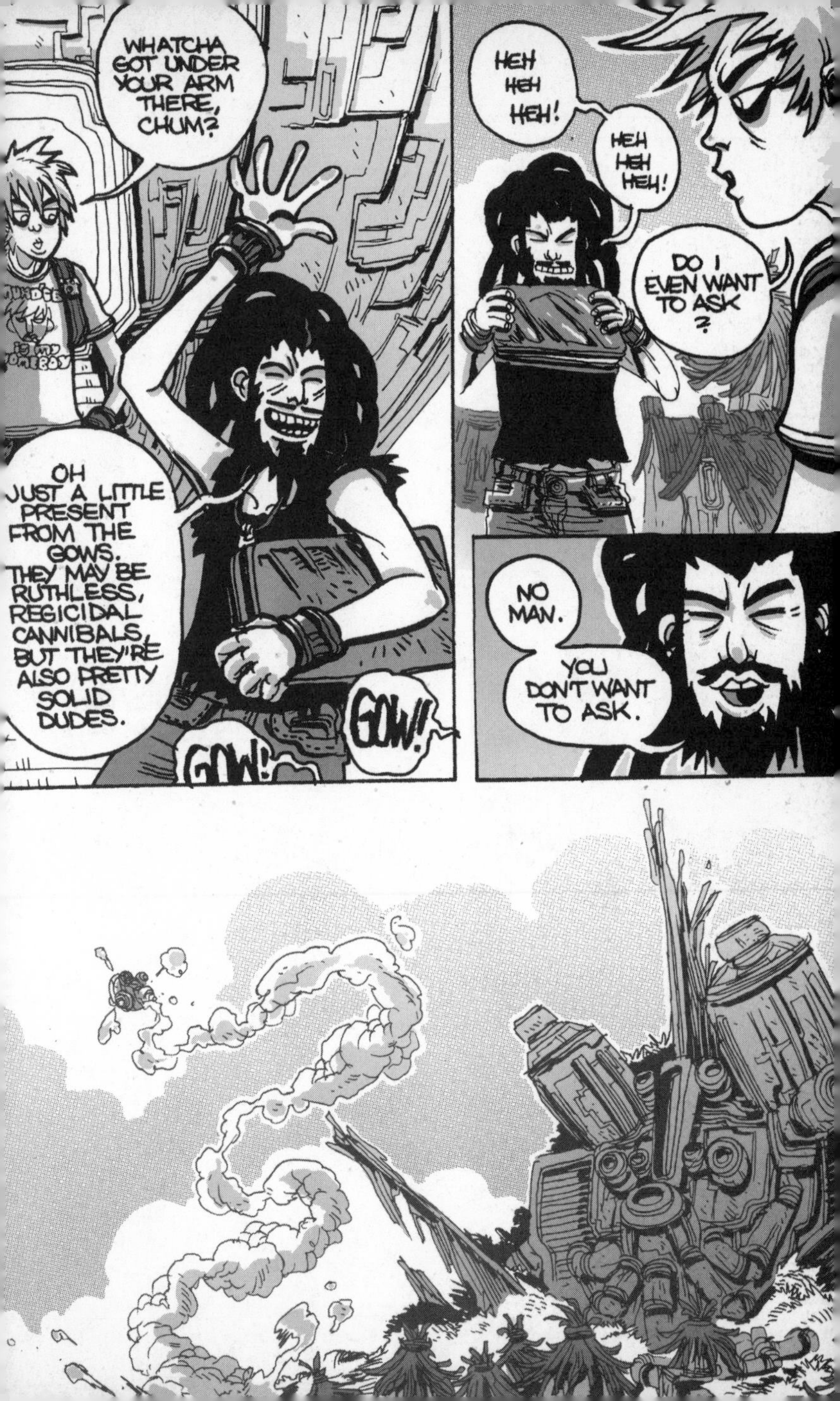
WHATCHA GOT UNDER YOUR ARM THERE, CHUM?
OH JUST A LITTLE PRESENT FROM THE GOWS. THEY MAY BE RUTHLESS, REGICIDAL CANNIBALS, BUT THEY'RE ALSO PRETTY SOLID DUDES.
GOW!
GOW!
HEH HEH HEH!
HEH HEH HEH!
DO I EVEN WANT TO ASK ?
NO MAN.
YOU DON'T WANT TO ASK.

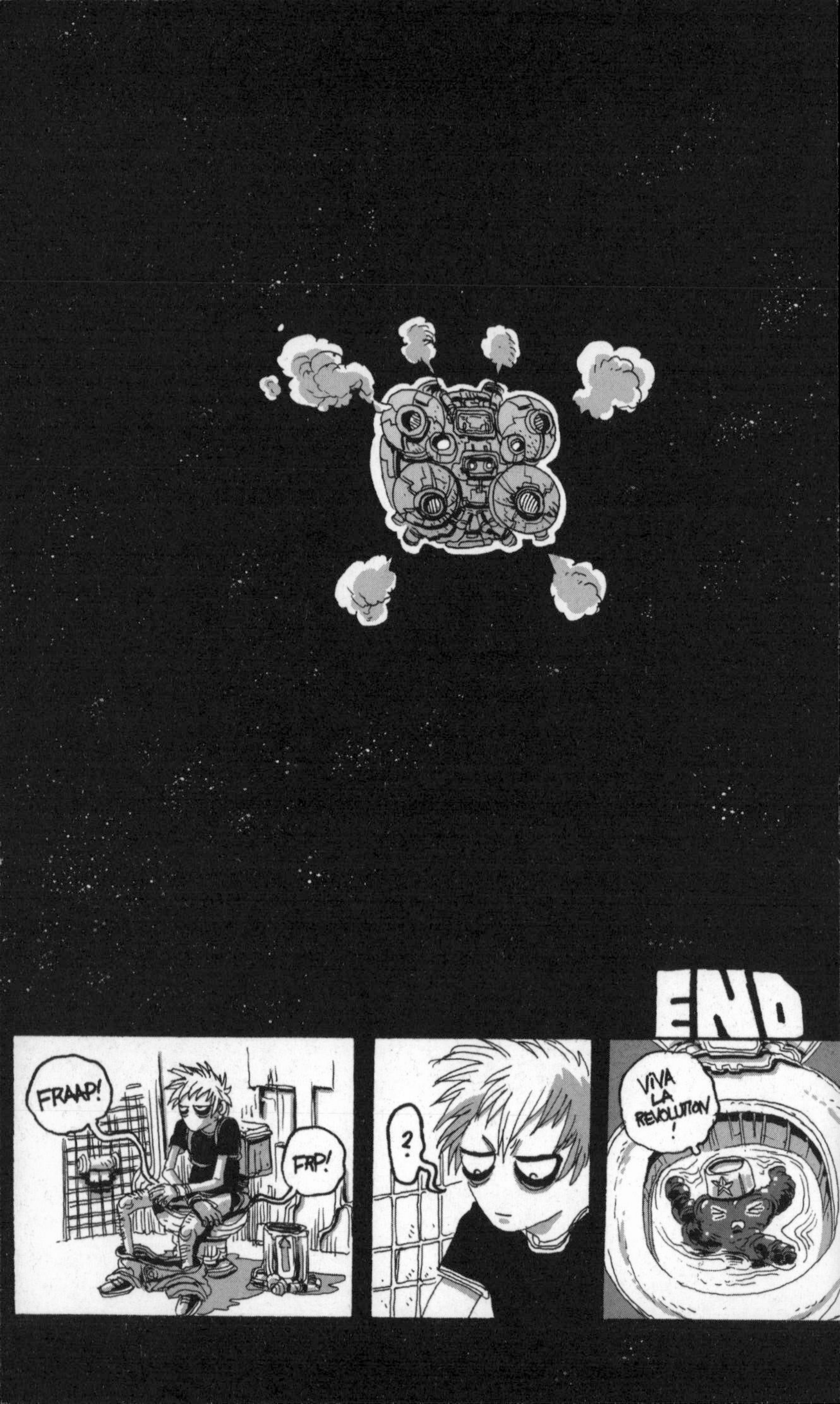
END
FRAAP!
FRP!
?
VIVA LA REVOLUTION !

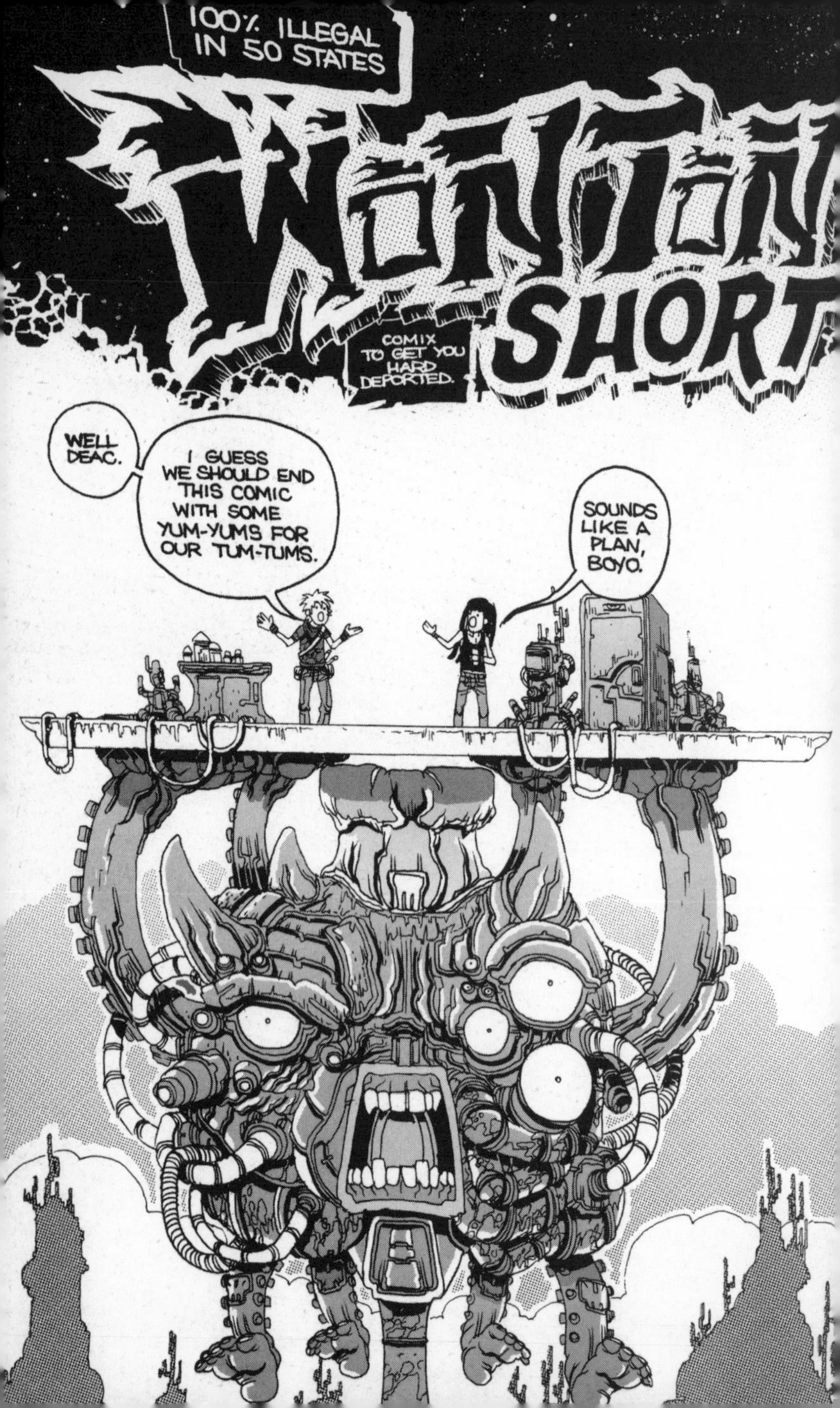

100% ILLEGAL IN 50 STATES
WONTON SHORT
COMIX TO GET YOU HARD DEPORTED.
WELL DEAC.
I GUESS WE SHOULD END THIS COMIC WITH SOME YUM-YUMS FOR OUR TUM-TUMS.
SOUNDS LIKE A PLAN, BOYO.

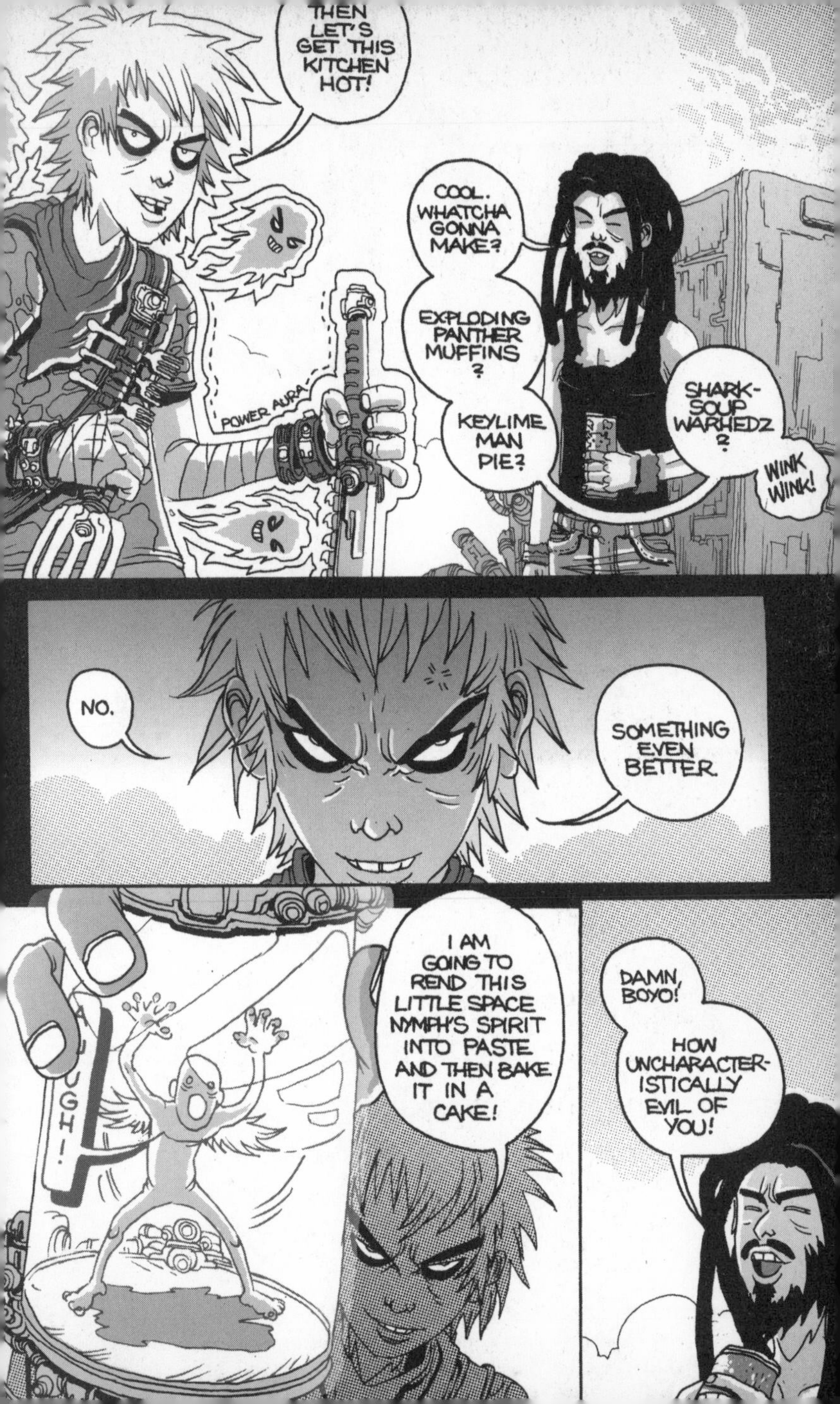

THEN LET'S GET THIS KITCHEN HOT!
POWER AURA
COOL. WHATCHA GONNA MAKE?
EXPLODING PANTHER MUFFINS?
KEYLIME MAN PIE?
SHARK-SOUP WARHEDZ?
WINK WINK!
NO.
SOMETHING EVEN BETTER.
UGH!
I AM GOING TO REND THIS LITTLE SPACE NYMPH'S SPIRIT INTO PASTE AND THEN BAKE IT IN A CAKE!
DAMN, BOYO!
HOW UNCHARACTER-ISTICALLY EVIL OF YOU!

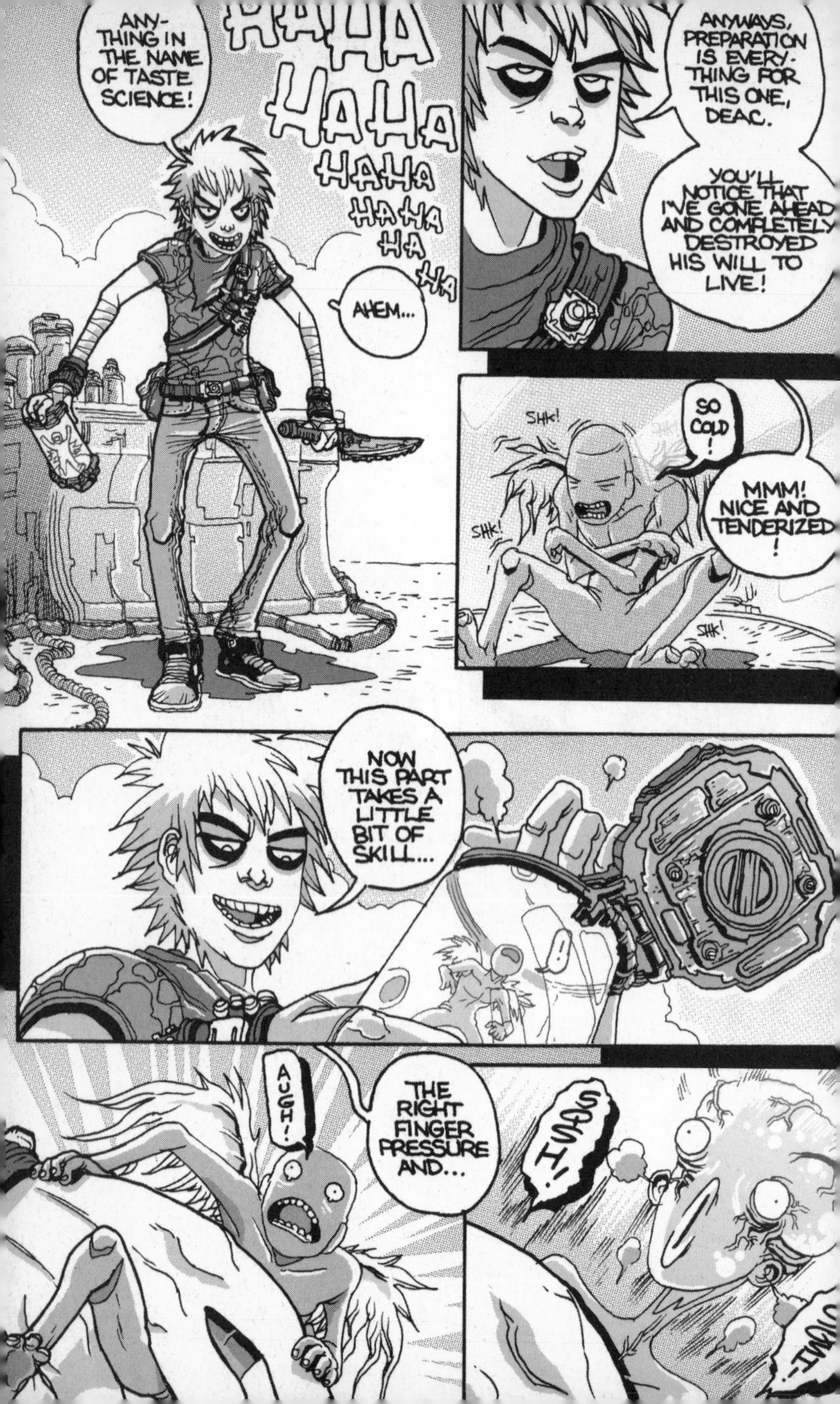
ANY-THING IN THE NAME OF TASTE SCIENCE!
HAHA HAHA HAHA HAHA HA HA
AHEM...
ANYWAYS, PREPARATION IS EVERY-THING FOR THIS ONE, DEAC.
YOU'LL NOTICE THAT I'VE GONE AHEAD AND COMPLETELY DESTROYED HIS WILL TO LIVE!
SHK!
SO COLD!
MMM! NICE AND TENDERIZED!
SHK!
SHK!
NOW THIS PART TAKES A LITTLE BIT OF SKILL...
AUGH!
THE RIGHT FINGER PRESSURE AND...
SQUISH!

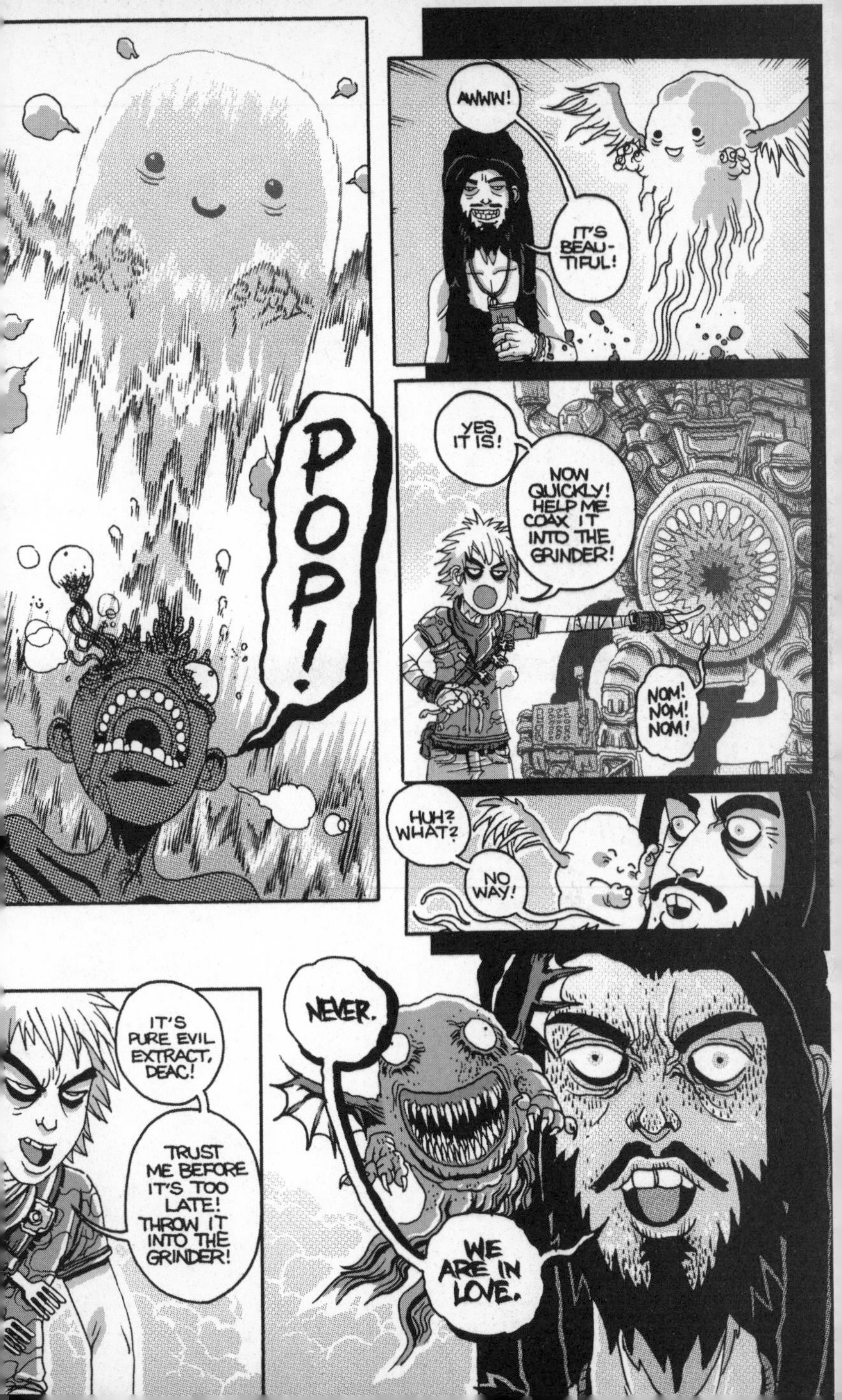
AWWW!
IT'S BEAU-TIFUL!
POP!
YES IT IS!
NOW QUICKLY! HELP ME COAX IT INTO THE GRINDER!
NOM! NOM! NOM!
HUH? WHAT?
NO WAY!
IT'S PURE EVIL EXTRACT, DEAC!
TRUST ME BEFORE IT'S TOO LATE! THROW IT INTO THE GRINDER!
NEVER.
WE ARE IN LOVE.

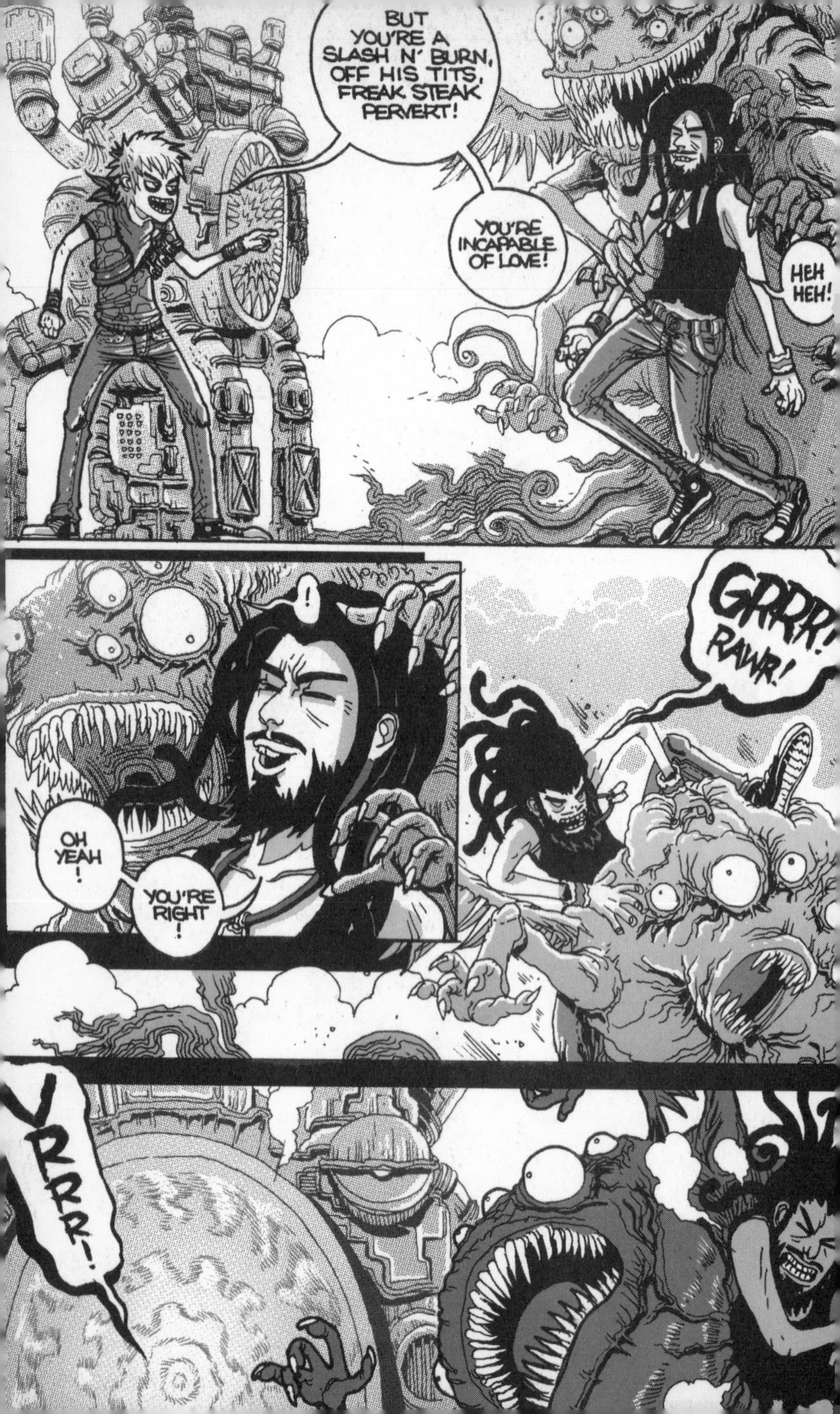
BUT YOU'RE A SLASH N' BURN, OFF HIS TITS, FREAK STEAK PERVERT!
YOU'RE INCAPABLE OF LOVE!
HEH HEH!
OH YEAH!
YOU'RE RIGHT!
GRRRR! RAWR!
YRRR!

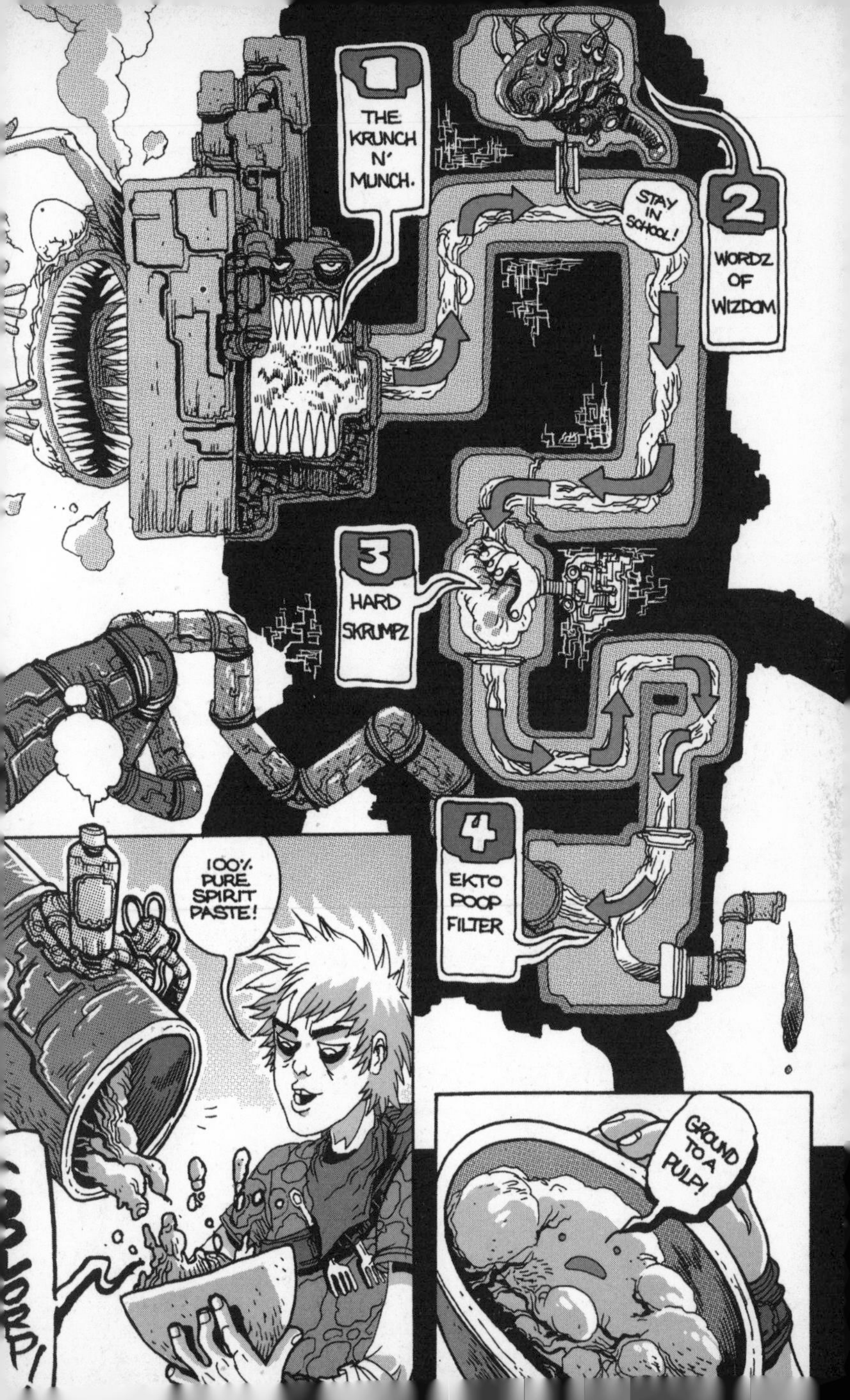
1
THE KRUNCH N' MUNCH.
STAY IN SCHOOL!
2
WORDZ OF WIZDOM
3
HARD SKRUMPZ
4
EKTO POOP FILTER
100% PURE SPIRIT PASTE!
GROUND TO A PULP!

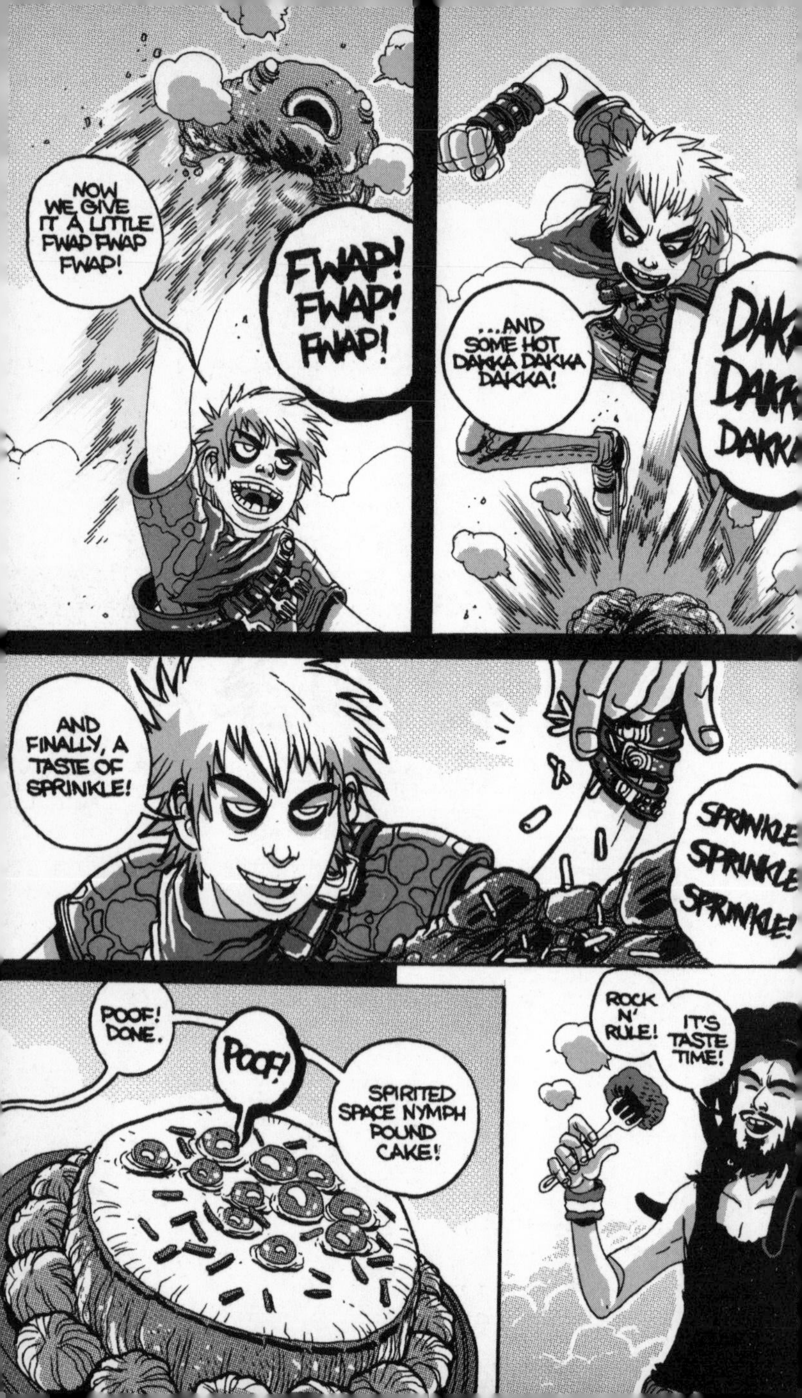
NOW WE GIVE IT A LITTLE FWAP FWAP FWAP!
FWAP! FWAP! FWAP!
...AND SOME HOT DAKKA DAKKA DAKKA!
AND FINALLY, A TASTE OF SPRINKLE!
SPRINKLE SPRINKLE SPRINKLE!
POOF! DONE.
POOF!
SPIRITED SPACE NYMPH POUND CAKE!
ROCK N' RULE!
IT'S TASTE TIME!

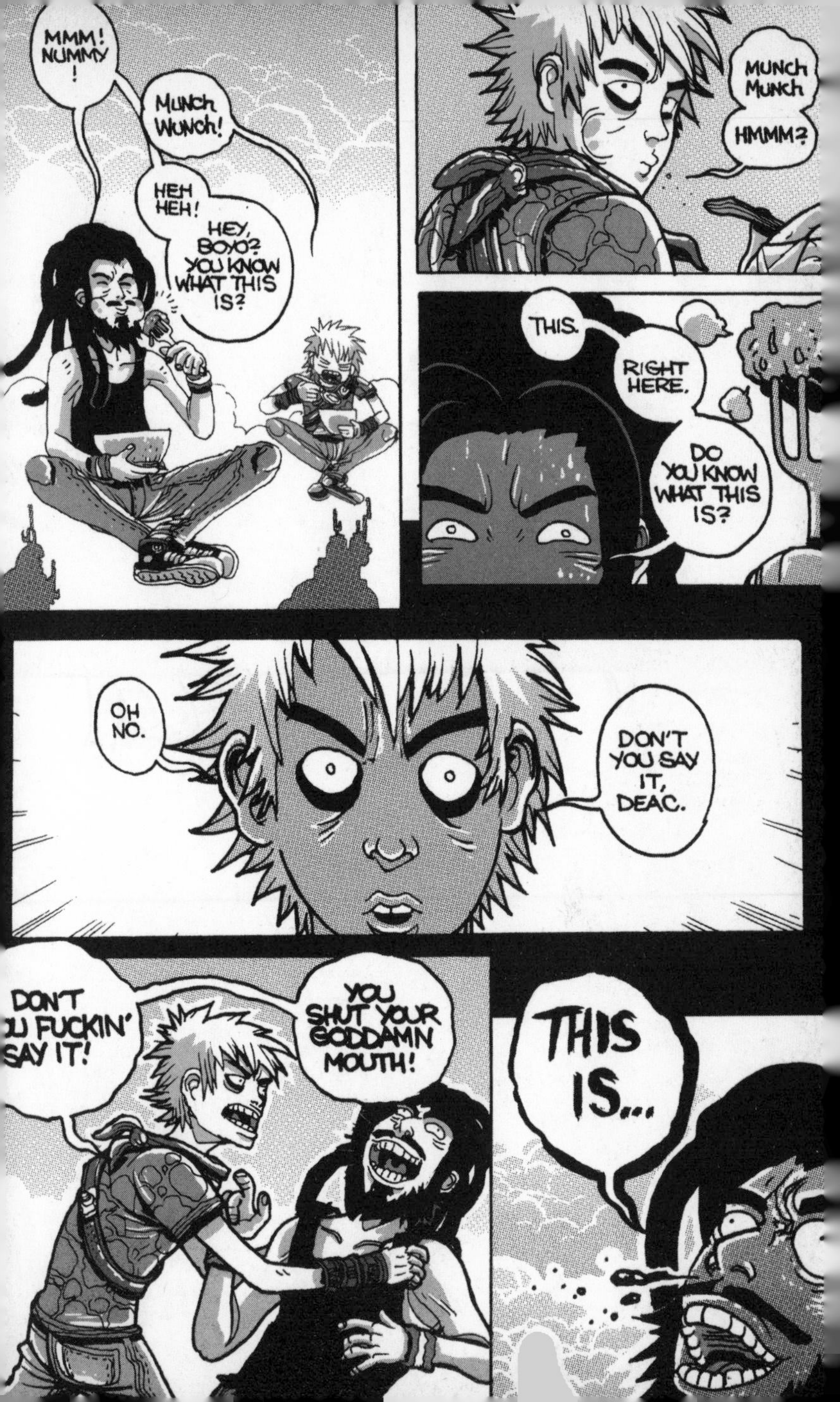
MMM! NUMMY!
Munch Wunch!
HEH HEH!
HEY, BOYO? YOU KNOW WHAT THIS IS?
MUNCH Munch
HMMM?
THIS.
RIGHT HERE.
DO YOU KNOW WHAT THIS IS?
OH NO.
DON'T YOU SAY IT, DEAC.
DON'T U FUCKIN' SAY IT!
YOU SHUT YOUR GODDAMN MOUTH!
THIS IS...

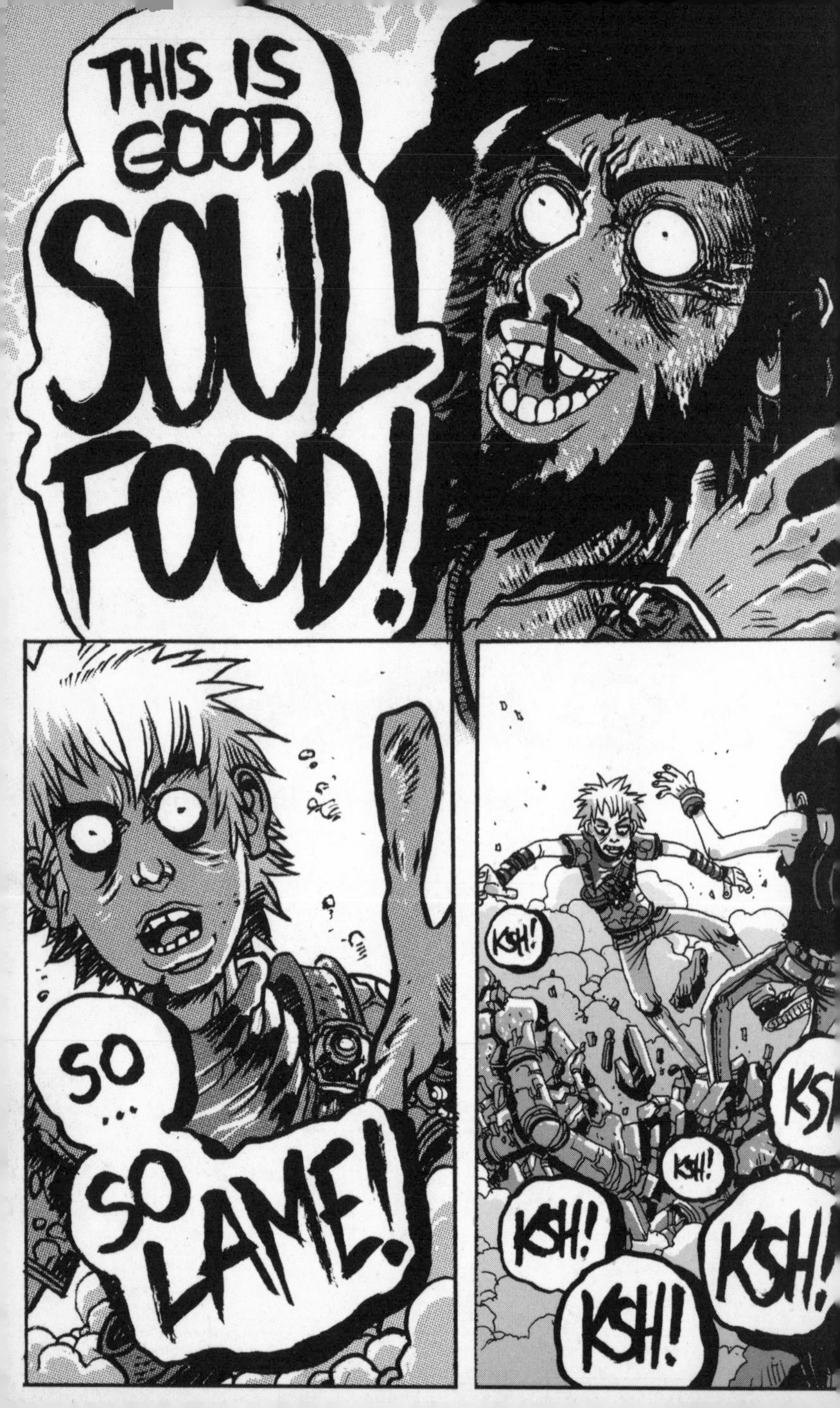
THIS IS GOOD SOUL FOOD!
SO... SO LAME!
KSH!
KSH!
KSH!
KSH!
KSH!

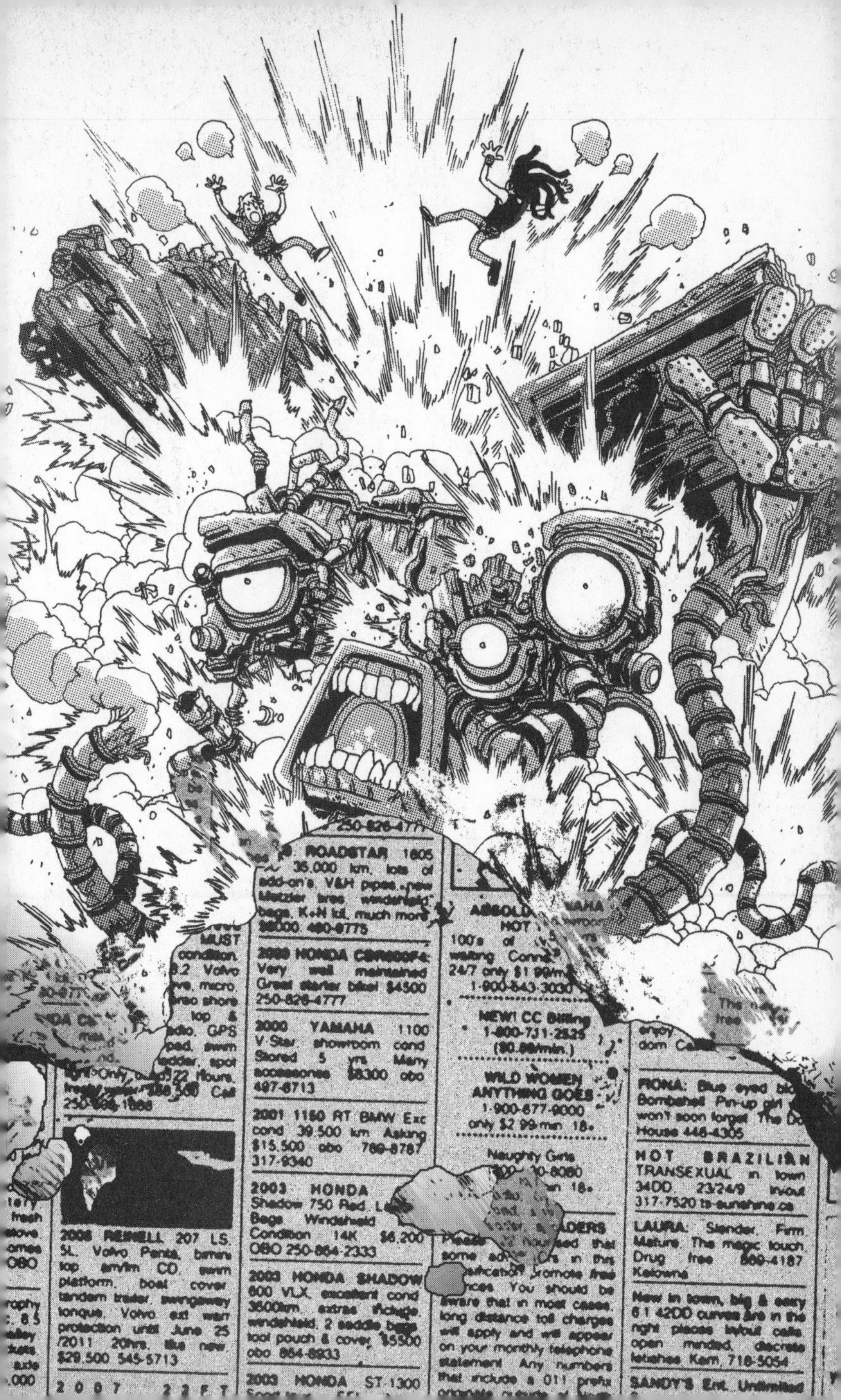
ROADSTAR 1605
35,000 km, lots of add-on's, V&H pipes, new Metzler tires, windshield, bags, K+N kit, much more
2000 HONDA
Very well maintained Great starter bike! $4500 250-826-4777
2000 YAMAHA 1100 V-Star, showroom cond Stored 5 yrs. Many accessories $8300 obo 497-6713
2001 1150 RT BMW Exc cond 39,500 km Asking $15,500 obo 317-9340
2003 HONDA Shadow 750 Red. Bags. Windshield Condition 14K $6,200 OBO 250-864-2333
2003 HONDA SHADOW 600 VLX, excellent cond 3600km. extras windshield, 2 saddle bags tool pouch & cover, $5500 obo 864-6933
2003 HONDA ST-1300
2006 REINELL 207 LS. SL. Volvo Penta, bimini top, swim platform, boat cover, tandem trailer, swingaway tongue. Volvo ext warr protection until June 25 /2011 20hrs. like new. $29,500 545-5713
2007 22 F T
MUST condition.
100's of
24/7 only $1.99/min
1-900-843-3030
NEW! CC Billing 1-800-731-2525 ($0.89/min.)
WILD WOMEN ANYTHING GOES 1-900-677-9000 only $2.99/min 18+
Naughty Girls
some advertisers in this publication promote free services. You should be aware that in most cases, long distance toll charges will apply and will appear on your monthly telephone statement. Any numbers that include a 011 prefix
FIONA: Blue eyed blonde Bombshell Pin-up girl you won't soon forget. The Doll House 448-4305
HOT BRAZILIAN TRANSEXUAL in town 3400. 23/24/9 in/out 317-7520 ts-sunshine.ca
LAURA: Slender. Firm. Mature. The magic touch. Drug free 869-4187 Kelowna
New in town, big & sexy 61 4200 curves are in the right places in/out calls open minded, discrete fetishes Kem 718-5054
SANDY'S Ent. Unlimited

ABOUT THE AUTHOR

James Stokoe is a xxxxxx xxxxxx who is no longer allowed to enter the United States of America. He loves Cholas, sandwiches and power loaders. He lurks 3Q miles off the coast of Canada waiting with his lovely lady, Marley Zarcone.